THE ECONOMICS OF AGRICULTURAL POLICIES

THE ECONOMICS OF AGRICULTURAL POLICIES

BRUCE L. GARDNER

Department of Agricultural and Resource Economics
University of Maryland

McGraw-Hill Publishing Company

New York   St. Louis   San Francisco   Auckland   Bogotá
Caracas   Hamburg   Lisbon   London   Madrid   Mexico
Milan   Montreal   New Delhi   Paris   San Juan
São Paulo   Singapore   Sydney
Tokyo   Toronto

1 2 3 4 5 6 7 8 9 0   HAL/HAL   8 9 5 4 3 2 1 0 9 8

ISBN 0-07-022857-4 PBK.

For more information about other McGraw-Hill materials, call
1-800-2-McGRAW *in the United States. In other countries, call*
your nearest McGraw-Hill office.

Library of Congress Cataloging-in-Publication Data

Gardner, Bruce L.
    The economics of agricultural policies.
    Bibliography: p.
    1. Agriculture—Economic aspects—United States.
2. Agriculture and state—United States.   I. Title.
HD1761.G245   1987   338.1'8   87–20367
ISBN 0-07-022857-4

To Matthew and Sarah

Contents

Preface

Beginning in 1977, I taught a graduate course in agricultural policy analysis at Texas A&M University, which I have continued to teach since 1981 at the University of Maryland. During the nine times the course was presented, it evolved ever further from material readily available in published texts, and culminated in this book. The underlying approaches are in the literature of welfare economics, public finance, and price theory—as cited in the References. However, systematic applications to agricultural commodity policies are scarce. This book is intended to remedy the lack.

Some of the models used and points made I had already published, and, accordingly, some paragraphs and in a few instances large chunks of previous papers of mine have been incorporated in this text. Chapter 3 uses material first developed in papers for the World Bank and for Resources for the Future, Washington, D.C. Chap. 6 contains extracts from "Public Policy and the Control of Agriculture," *American Journal of Agricultural Economics,* December 1978. Part of Chap. 7 is an elaboration of "Efficient Redistribution through Commodity Markets" from the May 1983 issue of this same journal. Chapter 10 reproduces most of "How Price Instability Complicates the Analysis of Price Supports," *Journal of the Northeastern Agricultural Economics Association,* October 1985, and "Is It Wrong to Fluctuate?," from the proceedings of a seminar sponsored by Southern Regional Project S-180, March 1985. A few pages in Chap. 11 are taken from "Public Stocks of Grain and the Market for Grain Storage," in G. Rausser, ed., *New Direction in Econometric Modeling and Forecasting in U.S. Agriculture,* North-Holland, New York, 1982. Finally, material from a lecture, "The Economics of Public Choice in U.S. Agriculture," presented at Macalester College, April 1983, is used in Chap. 12.

I thank the American Agricultural Economics Association, the American Enterprise Institute, and Elsevier Science Publishing Co., holders of copyrights on some of these publications, for permission to reprint. Thanks are also due to the Maryland students who in the past 3 years have been most helpful in spotting errors and infelicities in drafts of this material, and to Brian Wright of the University of California, Berkeley, for reviewing the complete manuscript.

Abbreviations

AAM	American Agriculture Movement
ASCS	Agricultural Stabilization and Conservation Service
c.i.f.	cost, insurance, and freight
CARA	constant absolute risk aversion
CBOT	Chicago Board of Trade
CCC	Commodity Credit Corporation
CGE	computable general equilibrium
EAR	expected average revenue
EEC	European Economic Community
f.o.b.	free on board
FAPRI	Food and Agricultural Policy Research Institute
FAPSIM	Food and Agricultural Policy Simulator
GATT	General Agreement on Tarriffs and Trade
GNP	gross national product
IPC	Integrated Program for Commodities
MST	marginal rate of surplus transformation
NPC	nominal protection coefficient
NPR	nominal protection rate
OECD	Organization for Economic Cooperation and Development
PIK	payment in kind
PPC	production possibilities curve
PSE	producer subsidy equivalent
SIC	social indifference curve
STC	surplus transformation curve
SWF	social welfare function
UNCTAD	United Nation Conference on Trade and Development
UPF	utility possibility frontier
USDA	U.S. Department of Agriculture
VMP	value of marginal product

Part One

Basic Economics of Commodity Policy

Chapter 1

Introduction

Agricultural policy is ubiquitous and contentious. An assessment by the World Bank finds that, of some 80 countries covered, only one (New Zealand) does not intervene in its commodity markets either to protect farmers from low prices or consumers from high ones. Contention is evident even among professionals who have the same information available to them. A survey of 245 U.S. agricultural economists asked for agreement or disagreement with the statement: "Current public policy regarding grain and cotton production is socially preferred to a laissez faire policy." Of those who offered an opinion, 50 percent agreed and 50 percent disagreed (Pope and Hallam, 1986, p. 577).

The sources of contention are apparent from newspaper accounts of these policies in almost every day's newspaper. The *New York Times* of December 10, 1986, carried stories with the leaders: "Famine-Stricken Sudan Says It Will Export Food," and "Food Riots in Zambia; Borders Are Closed," and the *Washington Post* on that same day carried a story, "King-Size Farm Subsidy for European Prince," about how the crown prince of Liechtenstein received $2.2 million for not growing rice in Texas. The *Times* wrapped up its editorial criticism of the U.S. Food Security Act of 1985 by stating: "We still want to believe that someday, America will face up to the scandal of farm programs shaped mostly by wealthy farmers.'' On a worldwide basis, the World Bank assessment of policies in both developing and industrial countries concludes that "they inhibit both economic and agricultural development and delay the alleviation of malnutrition and poverty in the developing world" (World Bank, 1986, p. 12).

The *Post* provided the following rationale for its opposition to the 1985 Act:

> Even the most die-hard supporter of farm subsidy programs would be hard-pressed to say they are working well. Despite record government outlays, farmers are plagued by big debts, high interest rates, weak prices, dwindling export markets and falling land prices. Thousands of farmers face foreclosure in the coming months, and bank failures in rural areas are already at post-Depression highs. While failing to support farm incomes, government programs have also built up costly surpluses and promoted over-intensive farming and soil erosion. Quite a record.[1]

Yet farm programs have vigorous supporters, and not just among their direct beneficiaries. Kenneth Boulding believes that efficiency is promoted by price supports because "the uncertainty involved in meaningless market fluctuations discourages innovation and investment and limits our getting richer. This is a point too much neglected by economists, as the remarkable history of American agriculture since price supports should have shown" (Boulding, 1983).

The historian Arthur Schlesinger provides an overview that seems quite widely held in his branch of scholarship:

> No sector of the economy has received more systematic government attention, more technical assistance, more subsidy for research and development, more public investment in education, in energy supply, and in infrastructure, more price stabilization, more export promotion, more credit and mortgage relief. National planning thus transformed a weak, disorganized and poverty prone sector of the economy into America's most spectacular productive success.[2]

Finally, Lester Thurow claims that U.S. agricultural policies should be emulated in other sectors of the U.S. economy on the grounds that "in agriculture what started as a desperate effort to prop up a very large, sick industry in the 1930s ended as an industry that is the world's most efficient. There is no reason that feat cannot be duplicated elsewhere."[3]

These extended quotations are meant to illustrate not only that agricultural policy discussion is contentious, but also that the evidence and analytical basis for the positions taken are not always clear. By analytical basis is meant the reasoning used to establish the connections between facts about agriculture, the policies of governments, and desired results for the economy. What is unclear in the quotations is how confident we can be in asserting that past programs have, for example, promoted overextensive farming, failed to support farm income, or made U.S. agriculture the most productive in the world. The problem is analytical in the sense that clearing things up involves taking the assertions apart and examining them piece by piece. How do we measure productivity? What is overextensive farming?

How can we establish that programs have failed to support farm income? Establishing this requires knowledge about the unobserved situation in which the programs did not exist. But which of the hundreds of counterfactual alternatives is appropriate for the purpose? And finally, how do we establish whether a program is "working well"? The quoted statements are characteristic also in that they are declared as matters of fact but nonetheless have a normative thrust—if we accept them we are impelled to favor certain policies over others.

The principal aim of this book is to present methods by which some assertions such as those quoted can be evaluated, and by which useful assessments of agricultural policies can be produced. One main ingredient of such evaluation and assessment is *positive* economic analysis, of the form: if policy A is undertaken, we can expect results B for observable economic variables. A second main ingredient is *normative* economics, judgments of the form: policy A is unwise. The book presents in detail approaches to modeling the agricultural economy that are helpful in applying both positive and normative economics. There is no attempt, however, actually to carry out the detailed empirical work necessary to resolve the controversies.

The book is divided into four parts, each containing three chapters. Part I introduces the issues and provides the basic supply–demand treatment of agricultural commodity policies. In Part II we go into more depth in developing models of the agricultural economy that can be used to analyze the effects of policies. Formal models are particularly helpful in assessing the likely effects of policies for one commodity on the markets for other commodities and on income distribution in agriculture. Only in Part III do we turn explicitly to evaluation of policies. From the evaluative point of view, the study of agricultural policy is a study in applied welfare economics. Part III outlines the necessary theory and develops in detail its application to farm commodity policies. Part IV explores both the positive and normative economics of three more specialized but important topics. Chapter 10 considers dynamics, uncertainty, and risk in agriculture. Chapter 11 carries further some implications of international trade in farm products. Chapter 12 explores the political economy of farm policy, seeking to understand why we observe the policies that we do.

EXTENT AND TYPES OF INTERVENTION

Table 1.1 shows the ratio of average producer price to the border (world market) price for selected commodities in industrial and in developed countries in

Table 1.1   Estimated Producer-to-Border Price Ratios, Selected, Commodities and Countries, 1980–1982

Products	Wheat	Coarse Grain	Rice	Dairy products	Sugar	Weighted average
Industrial-market economies:						
Australia	1.04	1.00	1.15	1.30	1.00	1.04
Canada	1.15	1.00	1.00	1.95	1.30	1.17
EC-10	1.25	1.40	1.40	1.75	1.50	1.54
EFTA-5	1.70	1.45	1.00	2.40	1.80	1.84
Japan	3.80	4.30	3.30	2.90	3.00	2.44
Spain and Portugal	1.20	1.30	1.00	1.80	1.70	1.33
Developing economies:						
Egypt	0.60	0.75	0.50	2.50	0.90	1.17
Nigeria	2.20	2.00	1.90	3.00	1.50	1.88
South Africa	1.50	1.10	1.00	2.30	0.90	1.19
Bangladesh	0.90	1.00	1.00	1.70	0.75	1.02
China	1.50	1.30	0.90	2.80	1.15	1.05
India	1.00	1.00	0.90	1.80	0.85	1.07
Indonesia	1.00	1.30	1.00	2.00	2.60	1.20
Korea, Rep.	2.30	2.35	2.55	3.00	1.00	2.74
Pakistan	0.90	1.00	0.70	2.00	0.75	1.12
Philippines	1.00	1.00	1.00	2.00	0.75	1.04
Taiwan	1.90	1.90	2.45	3.00	1.00	1.57
Thailand	1.00	1.00	0.90	1.80	0.90	0.89
Argentina	1.00	0.90	1.00	1.00	0.90	0.91
Brazil	1.30	0.90	0.80	1.60	0.80	0.96
Mexico	0.90	1.30	1.00	2.80	0.70	1.46

Source: Tyers and Anderson (1986).

1980–1982. The ratio, called the nominal protection coefficient (NPC), averages 1.4 for the industrial countries. Subtracting 1 from the NPC yields a nominal protection rate (NPR) of 0.4, meaning that producer prices are supported an average of 40 percent above world prices. The United States and the European Economic Community (EEC) have paid their producers as much as five times the world price for sugar, and Japan pays on average about 2½ times the world price for all the commodities surveyed.

The developing countries present a striking contrast, with NPCs less than 1 or (negative NPRs) not uncommon. Egypt, for example tends to hold producer prices below world prices. An NPC of 0.8 means that the commodity is taxed at a 20 percent rate. Estimates of NPCs for developing countries are particularly tricky because comparing the internal producer price to the world market price involves substantial and variable marketing margins and the conversion of domestic currency units to the currency in which world market prices are denominated (typically U.S. dollars). Because developing countries tend to overvalue their currencies, the official exchange rates used in these calculations tend to overstate the internal prices, so that the taxation of agriculture is even greater than the NPCs indicate. However, many developing countries also subsidize certain inputs, typically "modern" inputs like fertilizer, and this increases the effective rate of protection (or reduces the rate of taxation) from what the NPCs indicate.

NPCs are further misleading for a large country like the United States in grain or Brazil in coffee whose internal policies influence the world price. For example, the U.S. tobacco program supports the price of tobacco by restricting U.S. production. This drives up both the U.S. and world trading prices because U.S. exports are a non-negligible share of the world market. Yet the conventionally measured NPC for U.S. tobacco would be 1.0 because border distortions are absent.

More detail about U.S. farm programs is given in Table 1.2. Commodities are treated quite variously with different mechanisms of support, authorizing legislation, and extent of producer protection. Many commodities get no support at all, although some of these, like soybeans, are influenced by intervention in the markets for closely related commodities. It is thus misleading to speak of a "U.S. farm policy" in an aggregate sense, and most of our analysis will take place at the level of a single commodity market, and of interaction between related markets.

The analytical issues that arise in the positive economics of these programs include:

- How can the producer price effects (e.g., the NPRs of Table 1.2) as well as consumer price effects be estimated?
- How much do farmers, consumers, landowners, farm workers, agribusiness, and other interest groups gain or lose?
- What are the effects on further economic variables such as the productivity of agriculture, stability of prices, agricultural trade, and the growth of large-scale as opposed to small-scale farming?

To see how such issues arise in the policy arena and interact with political forces, let us consider a particular example in more detail.

POLICY OPTIONS: CASE STUDY OF DAIRY POLICY

U.S. dairy policy has evolved since the 1930s to include price supports for milk, restrictions on imports of dairy products, payments to farmers who agree to leave the business, and a system of marketing orders too complex to discuss here. In the 1980s, the level of the milk support price has been a prominent issue. Legislation periodically establishes a support price level. The Commodity

Table 1.2   Characteristics of U.S. Commodity Programs, 1985–1986

Commodity	Farm value, ($ billion)	Producers' price protection (NPR), %	Mechanisms of support
Beef cattle	30.6	2–3	Import tariff and voluntary restraint agreements
Milk	17.7	20–40	Government purchases, import quotas, price discrimination through marketing orders, payments to reduce output
Soybeans	12.1	0	Low-level CCC* loan support
Corn	11.6	15–20	Deficiency payments, CCC loan support, acreage controls, subsidized exports
Hogs	9.7	0	None
Wheat	8.4	15–25	Same as corn
Broilers and turkeys	7.7	0	None
Eggs	4.1	0	None
Cotton	3.4	20–35	Same as corn
Tobacco	2.8	20–30	Marketing quotas (but final product is taxed)
Hay	2.3	0	None
Potatoes	1.8	0	None
Sugar, beets and cane	1.5	300–500	Import quotas
Sorghum	1.3	15–25	Same as corn
Oranges	1.3	1–5	Regulation of seasonal flow to market (California and Arizona)
Rice	1.2	30–50	Same as corn
Tomatoes	1.2	0	None
Peanuts	1.1	25–40	Marketing quotas
Barley	1.1	15–25	Same as corn
Apples	0.9	0	None
Grapes	0.8	0	None

*CCC = Commodity Credit Corporation.
Source: U.S. Department of Agricultue; NPRs estimated by author.

Credit Corporation (CCC), owned and managed by the government, carries out the market interventions required to implement agricultural price support legislation. The CCC acquires stocks of dairy products. Since fluid milk is not readily storable, the CCC purchases powdered milk, butter, and cheese at wholesale prices designed to be equivalent to the farm-level support price for raw milk. During 1981–1986, the CCC purchased about $2 billion in dairy products each year, and has accumulated stocks amounting to about 20 billion pounds of milk equivalent. This surplus would not necessarily be a problem, particularly if shortage years were in prospect at which the CCC stocks could be sold. But U.S. production is showing a steady tendency to rise, and consumption to fall, without evidence of prospective random shocks that might create an economic use for stockpiled products. Consequently, the government has resorted to giving away butter and cheese: $2.5 billion of CCC stocks in fiscal year 1985; and in 1986 a program was instituted to pay some farmers, through assessments on others, for selling their herds and not producing milk.

In 1985, several important parts of U.S. farm commodity legislation expired. Several alternatives were considered for new dairy programs:

- The Reagan administration proposed cutting back the support-price levels.
- The House Agriculture Committee reported a bill maintaining price support levels but having an expanded production control program.
- Dairy producer interests opposed any substantial change.

A helpful way of organizing the analysis of the alternatives is an *option paper,* a list of the pros and cons of the policy alternatives, followed by discussion of them. For example, the pros and cons of cutting the support price can be outlined as follows:

Pros
   1. Government expenditures on CCC stocks are reduced, making taxpayers better off.
   2. Prices paid by consumers for dairy products fall, making consumers better off.
   3. Wastage of powdered milk, cheese, and butter which deteriorates while in storage is reduced.
   4. Reduced U.S. production eases pressure on land use for pasture and feed crops, reducing soil loss.
   5. Import constraints can be relaxed, making consumers better off and improving foreign relations.

Cons
   1. Lower price makes producers worse off and forces some out of business.
   2. Lower stocks means a reduction in domestic dairy distribution programs, making some poor consumers worse off.
   3. Lower farm income reduces demand for services provided to farmers, reducing incomes and perhaps increasing unemployment in rural areas.
   4. Farmers may respond to lower prices by attempting to maintain income by increasing production, actually worsening the surplus situation.
   5. Increased import competition and less milk manufacturing in the United States reduces profits and employment in this industry.

How can we evaluate such pros and cons? Two aspects of this activity should be sharply distinguished even though they may appear similar. First is evaluation of the economic argument embodied in each pro and con: is it a coherent argument, based on sound economic reasoning, and is there empirical evidence for quantitative conclusions? For example, should con number 4 (more output at lower prices) be given any credence? Economists typically find the argument implausible, but how confident can we be? Second, given evaluations of each pro and con, they must be added up to give an overall judgment on the policy option. The first set of evaluations implies primarily matters of fact, hypothesis, and judgment that do not require weighing of the interests of one group of people against another. The second step involves primarily this weighing. The scientific study of this second step constitutes the key element of welfare economics. Indeed, agricultural policy evaluation in the end reduces to a problem in applied welfare economics. Unfortunately, economists as professionals have less (although more than nothing) to contribute on the second point than on the first.

It might be thought that we could analyze the individual arguments without considering the adding up. But besides being uninteresting and even irrelevant by leaving out the bottom line of the whole exercise, the overall judgment must be considered in order to accomplish a good assessment of the individual arguments. The reason is that the choice of arguments—what counts as a pro or con worth considering—depends to some extent on how we see the overall issue. For example, the list of pros and cons of the dairy price-support cut did not mention the interests of foreign recipients of Public Law (P.L.) 480 (food aid) shipments of powdered milk who would be harmed by the production control approach. The list did not mention the interests of milk haulers, nor did it mention the consequences of the options for large as opposed to small farms, or for the upper Midwest as against the southern and far western dairy producers, or for the fate of "family farming" in dairying. In short, in putting forth a list of pros and cons we have already made a number of important judgments about the overall picture, namely giving many interests and consequences a zero weight. Moreover, we have excluded pros and cons of the form: This option would result in the loss of many votes for incumbents in milk-producing congressional districts. Such political consequences are of course crucially important in the practical context of policy.

The pros and cons as listed contain no numbers. This will not do. If the legislators and administrators were to accept the idea of cutting the support price, they could not proceed on a qualitative basis. They have to decide how much to cut the support price. Each possibility—from $11.60 to $11.50, or $11.00, or to $10.00, or to a moving average of past prices, or to an index of input costs—is a separate option requiring its own list of pros and cons. Moreover, the pros and cons must now be quantitative. Does the first 10-cent cut harm farmers less than the second 10-cent cut? Quantitative economics requires more investment in data, econometric evidence on how variables influence one another, and generally more technically demanding economics.

THE ROLE OF PRICE THEORY

The theory of price in competitive markets, or supply and demand analysis, is the basic analytical tool throughout this book. It is useful because it aids in sorting out the gainers and losers, and quantifying their gains and losses systematically. At the same time, reliance on supply and demand analysis involves important presuppositions about the agricultural economy and predisposes the assessment toward negative evaluations of policies that override market prices. It is important to keep in mind the limitations imposed by this approach. But while the limitations are real, there exists no serious competitor to supply–demand analysis as a tool in evaluation of agricultural policy.

Consider the elementary economics of the dairy program options. The pros and cons of option 1 are summarized with reference to supply and demand curves in Fig. 1.1. Cutting the support price reduces CCC expenditures on surplus dairy products because the CCC will pay a lower price for milk it buys and it will have to buy less milk. At the support price of $11.60, which effectively provides a perfectly elastic demand for milk at $\hat{D}$, the CCC acquires dairy products made from the difference between the 135 billion pounds produced at that price and the 120 billion pounds consumed through commercial channels. This 15 billion pounds costs $1.74 billion. If the milk support price were reduced to $10.50, this would allow the market price to fall, and we should see greater consumption of milk products and less production of milk. Suppose that the elasticity of demand is -0.6 and the elasticity of supply is 0.2. Then milk consumption, in response to the 10 percent price decline, will rise to 127 billion pounds, and milk production will fall by 2 percent to 132 billion pounds. Thus, CCC acquisitions are reduced to 5 billion pounds at a cost of $525 million, and the $10.50 support price option reduces budget costs by $1.2 billion.

Similarly, we can value the loss to milk producers as $1.10 per hundredweight of production and the gain to consumers as $1.10 per hundredweight consumed. There is an ambiguity here about the quantity to multiply by $1.10. If we count the gains only on the initial 120 billion pounds, we will ignore any net benefits to consumers from the additional 7 billion pounds. But counting the gains on the full 127 billion pounds would measure consumers' benefits only if they had purchased that much at $11.60. So neither the 120 nor the 127 quantity is correct, the 120 figure giving a measure of benefits that is too low, and 127, too high. A natural compromise is to multiply the price change times the average quantity of 123.5, giving a consumer benefit of $1.36 billion.[4] Similarly, we can measure the losses to producers as 133.5 billion pounds times $1.10, or $1.47 billion.

The other pros and cons point to considerations left out of our supply–demand calculations. Some should be incorporated and some require further analysis outside the supply–demand framework. Con 2 shows an omission in the analysis. We have treated CCC stock acquisition as a cost but have given

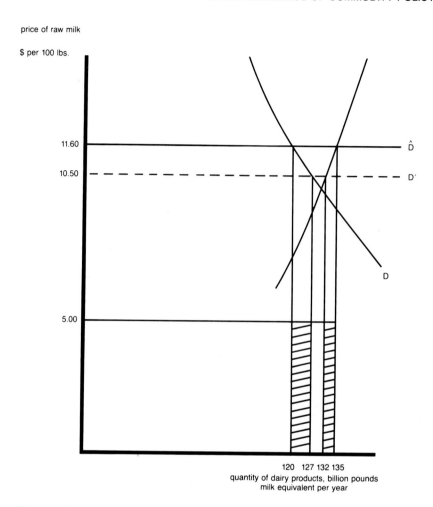

Figure 1.1 Price support for milk.

no value to the goods acquired. The commodities do have some value, however. In a buffer stock they would be resold on the market at a later time. More relevant for current dairy policy is that some of these commodities are donated to poor people, for example, $1.2 billion in cheese in fiscal 1985. If, subtracting out handling costs, these donations have a net value to recipients of $5.00 per hundredweight, then we should adjust the CCC budget savings downward on the 10 billion pound stock reduction by $500 million (the hatched area in Fig. 1.1). Such assessments are quite difficult to take into account, as treated in more depth in Chap. 10.

  Pro 3 brings in a set of costs that arise in every regulatory program, which will be called administrative costs. Having labeled them, we will not be doing anything with these costs analytically. But they are important for some policy decisions. Sometimes it pays also to consider the opposite side of administrative costs—that they generate income and jobs for administrators (and economic analysts).

Pros 4 and 5 and cons 3 and 5 involve consequences extended to the land market, the environment, the economic health of rural communities, effects on related product markets, effects up and down the marketing chain, even foreign affairs. These may or may not be important but have to be looked at by supplementing the simple supply–demand model. Attention to marketing channels can be particularly important in a case like dairy policy where the commodity supported is actually a wholesale processed product. The discussion of Fig. 1.1 is oversimplified in that the CCC operates indirectly to achieve the congressionally mandated milk price, as mentioned earlier. For example, in 1984 when the support price was $12.60 per hundredweight of milk, the CCC purchased cheese for $1.3475 per pound. The cheese price is calculated using an allowance of $1.37 for each hundredweight of milk converted into cheese and minus 36 cents for the value of whey as a joint product. This complicates the analysis of a change in the support price because a change in the CCC purchases of cheese might change the price of cheese manufacturing services or the price of whey along with the price of cheese. Such marketing-chain and joint product issues are taken up in Chap. 5.

The most vexing issues are the type raised by con 4, the idea that farmers would respond to a lower price by producing more. Numerous reasons have been given for such negatively sloped supply curves.[5] If they are right, the depiction in Fig. 1.1 is crucially flawed from the start; indeed if the negative slope of S were great enough, the CCC would have to purchase more the lower the support price. Even more radical ideas involve the randomness or perversity of farmers' behavior, making it impossible to predict in what direction output will move in response to any policy change. In what follows we will ignore these nihilistic possibilities and assume not only that people behave consistently and rationally within their constraints, but also and more simply that demand curves slope downward and supply curves upward.

It is a point well taken, however, that there is much conjecture and uncertainty in any attempt at quantitative policy analysis as sketched out with reference to Fig. 1.1. Our knowledge of the relevant supply elasticities is surprisingly weak given the number research studies devoted to estimating them. It is difficult also to pin down the location of supply and demand schedules so as to forecast surpluses or shortages for a future time when proposed policies will be in place, or to estimate the effects of policies in causing the prices and quantities observed in the past.

It is also difficult to assess the importance of spillover effects. For example, the Dairy Production Equalization Act of 1983 set out to reduce the number of dairy cows by 5 percent by paying farmers to cut back production. This chilled the hearts of beef cattle producers. The effect on beef cattle prices of dairy cow herd reduction might be thought minor since a 5-percent reduction in dairy cows would increase the quantities of beef marketed by less than 1 percent, and only temporarily (the dairy cows would be culled at some point anyway). Yet the beef cattle producers took the threat they saw in the 1983 act seriously, so much so that the American Meat Institute and livestock producers' organizations were at pains to argue strongly against the revival of this approach to dairy policy in the 1985 farm bill debate. (In the compromise bill that was finally enacted in 1985, a dairy herd buy-out plan prevailed, but it contained a requirement that the U.S. Department of Agriculture (USDA) purchase an extra 400 million pounds of beef to help use up the slaughtered dairy cows.)

Issues peripheral to supply–demand analysis of policy options that nonetheless play a large role in policy determination involve conservation of land and "structural" issues (larger versus smaller farms). In the 1985 farm bill debate, most participants seemed opposed to acreage controls, yet all the key policy-makers supported the idea of paying farmers to retire 20 to 30 million acres of "fragile" cropland. On the large-farm issue, it was politically damaging to the large 1983 acreage-control program to discover that a single large farm had received several million dollars for not planting a crop, and moreover, for not planting land that was flooded in the planting season, with federally subsidized irrigation water. These perceived absurdities are sometimes politically more potent than billions in a benefit–cost analysis.

A further suggestion of policy tying itself in knots is the following article, quoted by the *New Yorker* under the heading, "Clear Days on the Dairy Scene":

> Alta-Dena Certified Dairy has agreed to accept the money under an Agriculture Department program to reduce milk production surpluses. There are four other dairies in the nation slated to receive more than $1 million under the program. Alta-Dena comptroller Ray L'Heureux said that although the firm has not made a final decision on what to do with the money, "it may go toward planned expansion."[6]

In addition to the complicating factors that have been discussed, we often need to analyze the pros and cons in finer detail. The dairy policy discussion treats producers as a single interest group. Already we have seen reasons to distinguish small and large farms. One of the more troublesome issues in 1985 dairy legislation was a proposed change in regional differences in price supports which benefited southern and western producers at the expense of upper Midwestern producers.

Another important level of detail involves benefits to owners of different factors of production. It is alleged, for example, that price supports benefit mainly the owners of land. Investigation of this issue requires analysis of the relationship between commodity prices and factor prices. Then we can estimate income distribution effects by consideration of the distribution of factor ownership. This general topic is the subject of Chaps. 4 and 6.

NORMATIVE ECONOMICS

Generating the relevant gain or loss figures for each of the pros and cons and laying them out with all due humility is the first step in policy analysis. The second step is adding them up. This seems innocuous, but is often the most controversial part of policy analysis. In the analysis of option 1, neglecting the external issues, we had the following gains from reducing the support price:

CCC (taxpayers)	$ 1.2 billion
Recipients of CCC food aid	− 0.5 billion
Milk producers	− 1.5 billion
Milk buyers	1.4 billion

It is quite natural to add up these figures and conclude that the policy reform yields net benefits of $600 million and, therefore, should be undertaken. The normative rule is: add up the benefits and costs, and if the benefits exceed the costs, undertake the policy.

Theoretical welfare economics provides a systematic basis for exploring the legitimacy of such aggregation, and makes clear what we are implicitly assuming if we insist on simply adding up gains and losses. Welfare economics also is helpful in suggesting how to quantify an individual's gains and losses and the problems in aggregating within a group, for example of dairy product consumers. It is not capable of telling us "objectively" or "scientifically" what ought to be done, but it provides the best available framework for organizing our information on policy issues. This book, however, does not develop theoretical or applied methods of welfare economics in any systematic way. Some key issues are discussed in detail in Chap. 7, but only at an applied level. On the justification of the approaches used, and derivation of welfare measures, we will simply use results from (or refer the reader to) existing texts such as Boadway and Bruce (1984), Ng (1983), and Just et al. (1982).

Let us consider how the calculations of gains and losses fit in with ideas of social efficiency. Referring back to Fig. 1.1, consider the decision about how much milk to produce as being made by a social planner. The use of the demand function in this context is to provide information about how much consumers are willing to pay for various quantities of milk. Willingness to pay is our criterion for the social value of milk.[7] Thus, when 120 billion pounds per year are available, the social value of milk at the margin is 11.6 cents per pound. (The total value is much larger—and unmeasurable from the information given—because people would be willing to pay more per pound for smaller quantities.) Reducing the support price results in 7 billion pounds more milk consumed.

The social value of additional milk is given by the amount consumers are willing to pay for each additional pound. The fact that D declines as consumption increases means that each successive pound has a smaller social value, until at 127 billion pounds, the value is 10.5 cents per pound. Adding up the social value of all the additional milk, we have the area under D between 120 and 127 billion pounds. This is $770 million.

Similarly, the social cost of milk is the opportunity cost of the resources used in producing it—the returns they could receive in the best alternative use. The supply curve measures these costs, since it shows how much must be paid to get resources allocated to milk production rather than other activities. S rises as output increases because we have to use more resources (and perhaps more per unit output) to increase output, and will have to draw them from activities preferred to milk production at the original milk price. By reasoning similar to that for demand, the social cost of expanding milk production from 132 to 135 billion pounds, or in this case the social value of resources reallocated to other uses when the support price is cut, is the area under S between 132 to 135. This is $330 million.

The fall in CCC stock acquisition and donation is the sum of the consumption increase and production decrease, or 10 billion pounds. This was formerly donated at a net value to recipients of 5.0 cents per pound, so the net social saving from the policy reform must subtract out this $500 million. Thus, the net social gain from the policy reform is calculated as

Increased value of milk sold commercially	$ 330 million
Saved resources from less production	770 million
Lost value of milk donated	− 500 million
Net value of reform	$ 600 million

This is the same net figure as obtained earlier by adding up gains and losses. The identity is not accidental. Graphically, the $600 million is the sum of two shaded areas in Fig. 1.1. The earlier calculation proceeded by adding up horizontal slices of gains and losses, while the calculation here adds up vertical slices of marginal social value. Both necessarily add up to the same sum.

PITFALLS AND PROSPECTS

This chapter has introduced issues in agricultural policy, emphasizing the use of price theory in assessing the pros and cons of policy alternatives and the role of welfare economics to provide an overall assessment. This emphasis continues throughout the book, with more concentration on price theory in Chaps. 2

through 6 and more concentration on welfare economics in Chaps. 7 through 12. The content of every chapter involves primarily the application of economic models.

Some agricultural economists, and more so policymakers, distrust models and conclusions derived through their use. Models make assumptions about the world that are false. We want to deal with the world as it is. So why use models? Because the world is too complicated to take everything into account. We will end up making simplifications without realizing it. The man quoted in endnote 5 may believe he is making a statement based on observed fact, but he is not. It is a generalization based on a particular assumed motivation and behavior of producers. If spelled out, it would constitute a model but not a plausible one. A big benefit of models is that they make our assumptions and the steps of valid deduction from them explicit. Models also provide a framework for organizing hypotheses, so that we can see how to incorporate a new idea or fact with our old ones; or if a new fact does not fit we can judge what corrections to make and how to make them.

Contentious issues concerning the models of markets and welfare used in this book are the following:

- Are gains and losses measured appropriately? Much debate has occurred about the use and limitations of areas measured from supply and demand curves as in Fig. 1.1. Some technical issues alluded to in this chapter will be treated in detail later, but many will not. The ones that will be emphasized are income distributional elaboration, such as decomposing producers' surplus into factor rents.
- An objection to the social-cost accounting in Fig. 1.1 is that it compares situations with intervention to a competitive equilibrium that is assumed to exist in the absence of program. We will give considerable attention at several points to "second-best" arguments that intervention can generate a net social gain by counteracting market failures that exist in the non-program situation.
- It was clear in the list of pros and cons of dairy policy alternatives that many issues cannot be addressed satisfactorily in a simple supply–demand model. What are we assuming about the processing and food retailing industries? On a point related to programs themselves, the cost of raising the taxes that are used to make the payments should be incorporated. It has been estimated that at the margin in the United States, a dollar of taxes induces 20 to 50 cents in social (deadweight) losses by distorting labor–leisure choices, pushing funds into low-return tax shelters, and so forth (Browning, 1986). Moreover, payments involve costs of administering and enforcing eligibility for payments. Similar and perhaps more costly administrative costs are required for production controls. These should be added to the social costs of programs.
- One could go a step further and count the cost of lobbying for (and against) programs, or organizing producers to stake out a common position, as an element of costs. On the other hand, it can be argued that some programs

have social benefits over and above the immediate economic gains of producers, such as more secure food supply, more stable prices, and promotion of a system of family-operated farms. This requires taking a broader view of why farm programs are enacted and maintained in countries where farmers are a small minority of the population.

The main thrust of the following chapters elaborates the simple supply–demand model for policy analysis in two ways: (1) its conceptual elaboration to deal with, for example, international trade, joint products, and middlemen, and (2) the quantification of the model. For example, to obtain a useful analysis of the dairy program, we want to estimate the size of the hatched areas in Fig. 1.1. This requires estimating P_e and Q_e, a tricky task because we only observe $\hat{P}$ and $\hat{Q}$. This book does not discuss how to estimate the properties of S and D, but does spend a lot of effort on how, say, the elasticity of D determines the effects of market intervention as compared to a no-program situation.

We cannot hope to approach comprehensiveness in either depth or breadth. For example, we start with a market supply curve, and do not provide any of the theory of production economics that underlies it. This would require a whole book just for the case of a single competitive firm, and the aggregation of nonhomogeneous firms to obtain a rigorous foundation for a market supply curve isn't even a possibility (for this author). Instead, the market supply curve is taken as a behavioral function to be worked with as needs be. The foundations of welfare economics are similarly glossed over. This leaves us plenty to do, so much so that we will not even mention some policies and models of them that have been prominent in recent years. Instead, the focus is on a few key types of policies and methods of modeling their effects in ways that can be translated to practical quantitative policy assessments.

ENDNOTES

1. Editorial, *The Washington Post,* January 24, 1985.
2. Arthur Schlesinger, Jr., The political Galbraith, *Journal of Post-Keynesian Economics* 7; 8, Fall 1984.
3. Lester C. Thurow, Farms: A policy success, *Newsweek,* May 16, 1983.
4. Simple geometric representation of the values calculated will show that price change times average quantity is identical to ordinary consumers' surplus with a linear demand function. Some recent literature in welfare economics suggests essentially that in multiple-product contexts either the 120 or 127 quantity is preferable to the 123.5. Nonetheless, we will use average (Marshallian consumers' surplus) measures in the first part of this book.
5. "The point about price reductions is that they lead to every farmer doing his best to increase his own output so as to reduce his unit costs." John Cherrington, *Financial-Times* of London, July 1985, p. 30. The point about this claim is that

every farmer who can reduce unit costs by increasing output should do so whether there is a price reduction or not. More plausible reasons for negatively sloped supply curves have been given, but not confirmed empirically in aggregate data.

6. *The New Yorker,* February 1984.

7. The demand function is sensitive to *ability* to pay, i.e., income, not just willingness, and this is a fundamental complicating factor. But this is no hindrance to policy analysis so long as the policy change we are considering has a small effect on consumers' incomes. In cutting the milk price by $1.10 per hundredweight, a family that consumed half a gallon a day would save about $25 per year, or less than ¼ of 1 percent of even poverty-level family income. The shift in demand caused by an income change this small will usually have negligible effects on areas behind or under demand curves.

Chapter 2

Commodity Market Intervention

Policies that aim to increase farm incomes must either increase farmers' receipts or reduce their costs. Intervention in the commodity markets can increase receipts and in the factor markets can reduce costs. Our primary attention is given to increasing receipts by raising farm prices. Although many mechanisms for accomplishing this end have been tried, they boil down to two approaches: reducing supply or increasing demand.

Production controls can be used to reduce supply, while government commodity acquisitions can increase demand. Other ways to reduce supply include acreage controls and taxes on output. Other ways to increase demand include activities like government-subsidized school lunch programs and subsidized promotion of products through advertising.

In order to analyze policies systematically, we need a way to state the terms of a policy so that it can be interpreted in a supply–demand model. The statement typically reduces a policy to a single variable, a "policy instrument," such as the CCC support price of milk. The policy instrument is a variable that can be incorporated in a supply–demand model, and policy alternatives consist of different values being set for this variable. More fundamental alternatives consist of the introduction of a new instrument or combinations of instruments. Although choice of types of policy are the predominant topic of long-run (i.e., academic) debate, the crux of political debate on farm policy often turns on the level of a policy instrument: shall the target price for 1987 cotton be frozen at the 1986 level or cut 5 percent?

Incorporation of the operational procedures of a policy instrument into a supply–demand model can be tricky. For example, the U.S. Food Security Act of 1985 changed the way in which acreage and yield bases for direct payments were calculated, without changing the price guarantee. It is often harder to assess the likely consequences of such a procedural change than of a change in the price support level. Other complications arise when policy instruments are interrelated. For example, U.S. corn producers in 1985 were eligible for payments only if they agreed to idle 10 percent of their corn land.

Before getting into these complexities, crucial as they are, the simple analytics of policy instruments must first be studied. The analysis will be outlined first diagramatically and then in a mathematical model. The economics of intervention is more transparent in a diagrammatical treatment, but mathematical models are necessary for quantitative estimates of policy effects.

PRODUCTION CONTROLS

A production control program regulates the quantity of a commodity marketed. Such regulation is difficult administratively for commodities with dispersed marketing outlets, and perhaps impossible for crops fed to animals on the farm where they are grown. But the United States has marketing controls for tobacco and peanuts, and they exist in Canada for dairy, hogs, broilers, and eggs, under provincial authorities.

The quantity supplied is regulated by issuing rights to sell ("quota") in a limited amount to each farmer. The resulting supply curve to the market has an upper limit, which fits in with the no-program supply function as shown in Fig. 2.1. Output is restricted to $\hat{Q}$, less than the no-program output Q_e, even though producers would like to sell more at the higher price $\hat{P}$.

The gains and losses are easier to identify in Fig. 2.1 than in the dairy program as depicted in Fig. 1.1. Producers receive $\hat{P}$ instead of P_e on the quantity $\hat{Q}$ which they would sell even with no program. This gain is the hatched rectangle labeled A. However, producers would have sold more in the absence of the program. Since the supply curve measures industry marginal cost, the sum of costs saved by reducing output (the area under S between $\hat{Q}$ and Q_e) is less than the receipts lost by not being able to sell Q_e. The difference is the triangular area C. Therefore, the net gain to producers (more precisely resource suppliers)[1] is $A - C$.

Buyers of the commodity lose area A because they have to pay the higher

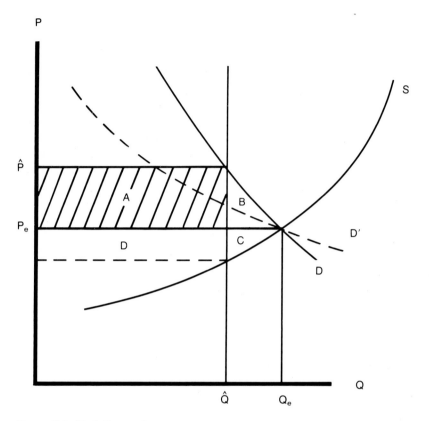

Figure 2.1 Marketing quota.

price for quantity $\hat{Q}$, and they also lose because they no longer have access to quantity $Q_e - \hat{Q}$. The value of this lost quantity to buyers is the area under the demand curve between $\hat{Q}$, and Q_e, but they only had to pay P_e when there was no program. Therefore, buyers lose area $A + B$.[2] Adding up the gains, we obtain $A - C - A - B = -(B + C)$. The triangular area $B + C$ thus measures the net loss analogous to that calculated earlier in Fig. 1.1.

Considering this program from the social planner's viewpoint, the production cutback saves resources whose value in alternative uses is given by the area under the supply curve between $\hat{Q}$ and Q_e. But the value to buyers of the product, as given by willingness to pay, is the area under the demand curve. So we end up by a more direct route at area $B + C$ as the social loss.

PAYMENTS TO PRODUCERS

Payments to producers are a common element in U.S. farm programs, but they are almost always tied to other policy measures, notably acreage controls. One

instance of a pure payment program is the National Wool Act. It establishes a
formula which each year determines a guaranteed price to producers of wool.
The difference between this price and the market price determines a payment
to be made to producers. For example, in 1984 the guaranteed price was $1.65
per pound. Early in 1985, the USDA estimated that the average price received
for wool during 1984 was 79.5 cents per pound. Since $1.65/0.795 = 2.075$, a
payment of 107.5 percent of a farmer's wool receipts would bring them up to
the guaranteed price level.[3] This payment rate is applied to each producer's
sales of wool as established by presenting receipts at the county Agricultural
Stabilization and Conservation Service (ASCS) office. There are no restrictions
on production or entry.

A supply–demand depiction of this program is shown in Fig. 2.2. The producers know approximately what the guaranteed price will be each year. They
aim to produce whatever amount they wish to supply at this price, i.e., the
quantity corresponding to $\hat{P}$ on the supply curve. (In 1984, wool production
was 93 million pounds.) The fact that this quantity clears the market at a lower
price, P_c, implies that excess supply exists at the guaranteed price, as in the

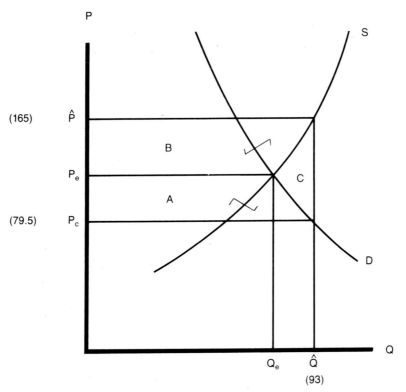

Figure 2.2 Payment program.

milk program. But here we do not support the market price, instead letting price fall as far as necesssary to get the product consumed.

The gains to producers are, first, receipt of a higher price than with no program for quantity Q_e and, second, the net gains on the additional quantity they choose to produce at the higher price. These gains sum to area B. Consumers gain because they pay a lower price on Q_e and can obtain additional wool that they value at more than the price P_c. Their gains sum to area A.

The payments add an element that was not present in the production control program: a cost to the taxpayers. The government must raise the rectangular area that measures the difference between $\hat{P}$ and P_c times $\hat{Q}$ ($80 million).[4] Since the payments are equal to $A + B + C$, subtracting the producer and consumer gains $A + B$ leaves area C as the net loss.

Area C can also be seen as the social cost from the social planner's viewpoint. The program results in expansion of output from Q_e to $\hat{Q}$. This generates output whose value in use is the area under the demand curve at a cost of drawing in resources whose value in other uses is the area under the supply curve. The difference between these areas is again the triangle C.

The supply–demand depiction is helpful because it aids in seeing how different market circumstances influence the consequences of payments. Suppose, for example, that output was unresponsive to price. This would make S a vertical line segment through Q_e. Then P_c would remain at P_e, guaranteeing $\hat{P}$ would cost the government much less, and the area of social loss, C, would disappear.

PAID DIVERSION

In 1984, the U.S. Dairy Production Stabilization Act paid farmers 10 cents per pound for milk they agreed *not* to produce. This program differs from production controls in not issuing marketing quotas within which all producers are required to stay. Diagrammatically, it combines features of Figs. 2.1 and 2.2. From the viewpoint of consumers, the situation is as depicted in Fig. 2.1: less output drives up the consumer price and consumers loss area A. From the viewpoint of producers the situation is more as shown in Fig. 2.2. The producers' gains are the same or greater than those in Fig. 2.2. The reason is that producers all have the option of producing all they like at price $\hat{P}$. No producers would participate in voluntary diversion if they could have earned more by producing all they desired at price $\hat{P}$, which generated gains B in Fig. 2.2. Therefore, the payments to cut production back to $\hat{Q}$ must be sufficient to yield total producer benefits of B or more. The amount of the minimum necesssary payments is the difference between Q_s on the supply curve at $\hat{P}$ and $\hat{Q}$ in Fig. 2.1, times $\hat{P}$ minus the variable costs saved by not producing $Q_s - \hat{Q}$. This would be the area under the supply curve between $\hat{Q}$ and Q_s, since the supply curve measures opportunity costs (which are variable costs in the relevant sense of the term).

As the preceding discussion indicates, it can be a tricky business to depict program provisions in a supply–demand diagram. It is easy to specify $\hat{Q}$ in a program description, but the economics of getting that $\hat{Q}$ as the market's output are not straightforward. In the case of paid diversion, there is the problem of who is eligible to be paid not to produce. It is, after all, an attractive enterprise. Entry into it must be limited. In the case of the 1984 dairy diversion program, a person could be paid only for reductions of between 5 and 30 percent of a base level of production, as contracted for each farm individually. The base level was the amount of milk sold in 1982 or the 1981–1982 average at the producer's discretion. This was a feasible procedure because milk in federally regulated areas is marketed through cooperatives and sold to dairy plants which had records of 1981 and 1982 shipments by each producer. But for most other commodities, there would be no good way to prevent overstatement of base production, or to monitor compliance with contracted output reductions.

This problem leads to acreage as the base for paid diversion programs in the grains. But then the government is not really controlling output, because yield per acre can be increased through more intensive use of fertilizer and other production practices. Moreover, a farmer's payment per acre is the same regardless of which particular acres are idled, so the farmer will idle the least productive cropland. Lack of precise knowledge about these factors makes the link between the policy instrument and the resulting output $\hat{Q}$ not at all straightforward to analyze.

POLICY INSTRUMENTS FOR INTERNATIONALLY TRADED COMMODITIES

For most agricultural commodities in most countries, there exists an international market on which goods can be purchased or sold at given prices. The trading prices are given not in the sense of being constant, but in the sense that the country cannot do anything that will change them significantly—they are exogenous variables confronting the country. For traded goods, domestic supply and demand are not typically equal. If the country produces more than it consumes at the world price, then it exports the excess. If it consumes more than it produces at the world price, then it imports. If the country wants to increase the price its farmers receive, it must isolate its domestic market. Policy instruments for accomplishing this include import tariffs, import quotas, and export subsidies.

Import Tariffs

If a country is an importer at the world price, it can increase its domestic producer price by levying a tax (i.e., tariff) on each unit of the commodity imported. This means that no one will sell in the country from foreign countries unless the price is high enough to cover the tariff. In Fig. 2.3, the horizontal line at the world price[5] P_e can be thought of as the supply function of imported goods, so that the total supply to the country with no intervention is the hatched curve SS_M. Domestic consumption is Q_e and production X_e. The tariff of amount t shifts the supply curve to SS'_M. This reduces consumption, increases production, and raises the domestic farm price to $\hat{P}$. Thus the tariff is itself a price support program, and no other is needed. This is in one sense a painless price support because it does not cost the government money but, indeed, raises revenue, equal to t times the quantity imported. But for consumers, the program is analogous to a production control program. They lose the area behind D between P_e and $\hat{P}$. For producers the program is analogous to a price support with no production controls. It generates increased economic rents equal to the hatched area. Adding up the gains to producers, consumers, and the government (i.e., taxpayers) we are left with the two shaded triangles as the social loss of the tariff.

Import Quotas

Instead of taxing imports, the country could simply limit their quantity to q. This imposed scarcity drives up the market price to the point that $D - S$ equals

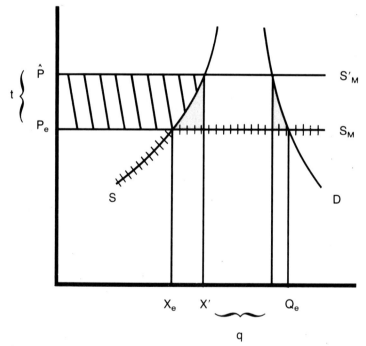

Figure 2.3 Import tariff or quota.

q. (Compare the extreme case in which imports are completely shut off. This raises price to the point, not shown in Fig. 2.3, where domestic S and D meet.) A quota of size q has the same consequences for producers and consumers as the tariff of size t. The difference is that there is no government tariff revenue. The rectangle between the shaded triangles accrues to whoever is given the right to buy the quantity q at the world price and sell at the domestic price. In the case of the most prominent agricultural import quotas in the 1980s, those of the United States, and the European Community (EEC) for sugar, import quotas are allocated free of charge to certain politically favored countries, as a foreign-aid benefit. But the importing country could sell import rights to the highest bidder, thus capturing the gains for its treasury as it would with a tariff.

Quotas work differently from tariffs under uncertainty, for example, when the world price varies. World agricultural commodity prices are notoriously unstable, so these considerations are important. Countries typically try to insulate their domestic markets, not permitting whatever $\hat{P}$ they have chosen to vary as much as P_e. The most important policies of this type are the variable levies on grains imposed by the EEC as a key element of its Common Agricultural Policy (CAP). The variable levy is a tariff that is changed on a weekly basis to reflect movements in P_e. If the world price of wheat at Rotterdam goes down \$10 per ton, the levy goes up by \$10 per ton. This maintains the EEC's $\hat{P}$ for wheat at a predetermined level.

The presence of a world market not only introduces new possibilities for policy instruments, it also places constraints on the use of domestic instruments. For example, suppose the importing country in Fig. 2.3 did not restrict imports but attempted to raise its farm price by means of production controls. This would be a futile exercise. S could be shifted to the left but this would simply increase imports and leave the price unchanged. Similarly, if the country tried to support the price of $\hat{P}$ by means of government purchases, it would be thwarted by a flood of imports. Graphically, a perfectly elastic government demand at $\hat{P}$ and a perfectly elastic supply of S_M never intersect. Thus, the United States has to supplement its dairy price support program by import quotas for dairy products.

On the other hand, a direct payment approach is still feasible for an importer. Guaranteeing price $\hat{P}$ requires payments equal to $(P - P_e)$ times X'. Consumers still pay price P_e for quantity Q_e, although additional domestic production $(X' - X_e)$ replaces imports. The social loss from this program consists only of the left-hand triangle, indicating that other things equal to direct payments are preferable to import restraints.

Export Subsidies

The situation of a country that exports at the world price, like Australia in wheat, is shown in Fig. 2.4. The horizontal line at P_e can be thought of as a

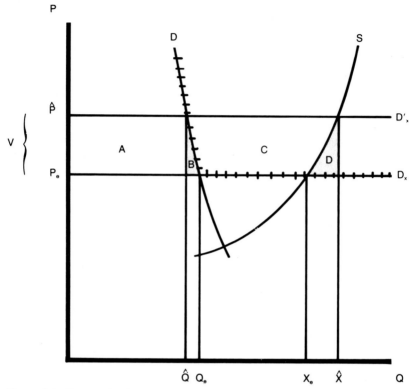

Figure 2.4 Export subsidy.

perfectly elastic demand function for the country's exported commodities,[6] so that total demand for Australia's wheat is the hatched curve DD_X. The producer price can be raised to $\hat{P}$ by paying the amount v for every ton of wheat exported. If the subsidy is paid directly to farmers, they will divert their commodities to the export market until the domestic price has risen to the world price level plus v. Only then will farmers be satisfied with the allocation of their wheat to the domestic and foreign markets. If the subsidy were paid to exporting firms, they would be able to make pure profits by buying and selling at P_e and pocketing v, except that competing exporters will bid away these profits. They will do this by offering higher prices for domestic wheat, competitive equilibrium being established when the domestic price exceeds the world price by exactly v. No matter how the subsidy is paid out, we end with the effective domestic price for exported wheat shifting by amount v to D_x'. Consequently output increases to $\hat{X}$ and exports increase to $(\hat{X} - \hat{Q})$ at a cost to the government of subsidy payments equal to area $B + C + D$. Producers' gains are area $A + B + C$. Consumers are worse off because the diversion of wheat to the export market drives up the price they pay—similar to what happens with production controls or import tariffs—and they lose area $A + B$. The net gain is $(A + B + C) - (A + B) - (B + C + D) = -(B + D)$. That is, for all the groups together there is a net loss equal to the sum of triangular areas B and D.

The domestic policy implications are similar to those of the import case. A production control program leaves the producer price unchanged and so accomplishes nothing and loses part of the export market. If a production control program was so drastic that it cut output below Q_e, it would raise the domestic price. But if the price were raised much, the country would become an importer. The most that price could rise would be the difference between the country's f.o.b. (free on board) and c.i.f. (cost, insurance, and freight) border .prices.

Similarly, a price support program in which the government bought wheat at a price above P_e would have first to buy up all the wheat that would have been exported at P_e before it could raise the domestic price. And if the support price were raised above the c.i.f. border price, the program would be swamped with imports. Despite its being a traditional exporter, this threat to the U.S. wheat price support program (from Canadian imports primarily) was deemed serious enough in the 1950s that the United States pressed in the GATT negotiations for a waiver to permit import quotas to defend domestic price support programs. In the mid-1950s (1954–1956), internal market prices in the United States were 45 percent above Canadian internal prices, as compared to normal margin of no more than 15 percent.[7]

The direct payment approach is still feasible, as in the importer's case. Guaranteeing price $\hat{P}$ requires payments of $A + B + C + D$. Consumers pay P_e (not $\hat{P}$), which is the difference from the export subsidy case. The net loss is area $D = (A + B + C) - (A + B + C + D)$. Thus, the payment approach has an efficiency advantage over the export subsidy.

Antifarmer Policies

Table 1.1 indicated that many countries tax rather than subsidize farmers. All the policy instruments discussed to this point subsidize them. What are the taxing policies and policy instruments?

In the case of an exporting country, exports can be taxed rather than subsidized. Argentina for many years has taxed its wheat exports. Alternatively, a quantitative restriction—export quota or embargo—can be placed on exports, as the United States did with soybeans in 1973. This reduces $\hat{P}$ below P_e in Fig. 2.4 and results in losses of economic rents by producers, gains to consumers, gains to the government (if the export tax is used rather than an embargo) and social losses analogous to those shown for import restrictions in Fig. 2.4.

In the case of an importer, an import subsidy would make consumers better off at the expense of taxpayers and farmers.

A domestic-based policy instrument that can be used to exploit farmers is a tax on all production, the converse of the payments approach. The supply–demand depiction of this policy is the standard analysis of an excise tax.

The converse of a price support is a price ceiling, or legal maximum price, placing $\hat{P}$ below P_e. As with price supports, this type of policy instrument is ineffective with unrestricted trade. The producers simply export all they produce at price P_e (even if the country was originally an importer). If all producers must sell to a government marketing board, which is feasible for an export crop like cocoa or tea in some countries, the board can tax farmers simply by setting its buying price at a reduced level. The issue of feasibility then is a matter of preventing exports outside the marketing board's control.

POLICY INSTRUMENTS IN A MATHEMATICAL MODEL

The formal basis for supply–demand analysis begins with a model that in its simplest version states that the quantity produced of a commodity increases as its price increases, and that this relationship can be specified as a supply function,

$$Q_s = S(P_s), \ S' > 0 \tag{2.1}$$

where S' is the derivative of the supply function S, Q_s is quantity produced, and P_s is supply price, that is, the price received by producers for each unit of output. The function S, as well as the behavioral functions to follow, is assumed continuously differentiable over positive values of P and Q. It measures the marginal social cost of producing Q. In economic terms, it is the opportunity cost of the quantity Q; it reveals what price must be paid to attract the necesssary resources to produce Q instead of the best alternative uses available for the resources at the margin.

Consumption of the commodity is represented by the demand function

$$Q_d = D(P_d), \ D' < 0 \tag{2.2}$$

The demand function measures the marginal social value of the quantity Q_d, which is determined by the amount that consumers are willing to pay for that quantity. The model is closed by the existence of equilibrium $Q_s = Q_d$, and the corresponding price P_e, where $P_s = P_d$ is the market-clearing or equilibrium price.

The supply–demand model is a partial equilibrium model, partial because all prices other than the commodity's own price, and all nonprice variables other than the quantity of the commodity, are omitted. This would be appropriate if these variables were really unimportant (or important but unchanging constants); but they are not. Nonetheless, they are omitted for the present.

Many agricultural policies do not regulate market price or quantity directly. They regulate subsidy payments, tariffs, acreage, and other related variables. For purposes of policy analysis, these policy instruments need to be included in the supply–demand model.

Producer Subsidy

Consider a policy of paying producers a subsidy of V per unit produced, for example, 20 cents per bushel of corn. The producer now receives not the market price only, but the market price plus V. The equilibrium price received by producers, including the subsidy, is now different from the equilibrium price paid by consumers, while the equilibrium is still characterized by $Q_s = Q_d$. This is one reason why policy analysis is more straightforward when expressed in terms of price-dependent supply and demand. Thus, Eqs. (2.1) and (2.2) become

$$P = S^{-1}(Q) - V \qquad\qquad (2.3)$$
$$P = D^{-1}(Q) \qquad\qquad (2.4)$$

where S^{-1} and D^{-1} are the inverses of the functions S and D, obtained by solving Eqs. (2.1) and (2.2) for P. It is assumed that S and D generally are functions for which inverses exist, and that the functions are such that equilibrium exists at positive P and Q for positive values of V. For simplicity of notation the -1 notation will be dropped, and inverse supply and demand functions wil! be written as $S(Q)$ and $D(Q)$, the Q being written as a reminder of what is on the right-hand sides.

It is important to see that the left-hand side of Eq. (2.3) is *not* P_s, but $P_s - V$. This expression is equal to P_d. Substituting Eq. (2.4) in Eq. (2.3) and solving for V shows that V is the difference between the supply price, which is $S(Q)$, and demand price, $D(Q)$. Since V is positive, this means we must be in the region where the supply curve is above the demand curve, i.e., output is greater than the competitive output when a subsidy exists.

We want to investigate what happens to P and Q as V changes, beginning at market equilibrium, where $P = P_d = P_s$ and $Q = Q_s = Q_d$, and writing out the differentials of Eqs. (2.3) and (2.4):

$$dP = S'(Q)dQ - dV \qquad\qquad (2.5)$$
$$dP = D'(Q)dQ \qquad\qquad (2.6)$$

Using the definitions of elasticity of supply ϵ and demand η, we can write

$$S'(Q) = \frac{1}{\epsilon}\frac{P}{Q} \qquad D'(Q) = \frac{1}{\eta}\frac{P}{Q}$$

Substituting these expressions in Eqs. (2.5) and (2.6) and equating them,

$$\frac{1}{\epsilon}\frac{P}{Q}dQ - dV = \frac{1}{\eta}\frac{P}{Q}dQ$$

Dividing by dV and solving for dQ/dV,

$$\left[\frac{1}{\epsilon} - \frac{1}{\eta}\right]\frac{P}{Q}\frac{dQ}{dV} = 1 \qquad (2.7)$$

$$\frac{dQ/Q}{dV/P} = \frac{1}{1/\epsilon - 1/\eta}$$

where dQ/Q is the percentage change in Q and dV/P is the change in the subsidy as a percentage of price.

To find the change in market price (which, since V enters the supply equation, is P_d, the demand price), solve Eq. (2.6) for dQ and substitute into Eq. (2.5):

$$dP = \frac{1}{\epsilon}\frac{P}{Q}\left[\frac{\eta Q}{P}\right]dP - dV$$

$$dP = \frac{\eta}{\epsilon}dP - dV \qquad (2.8)$$

$$dP\left[1 - \frac{\eta}{\epsilon}\right] = -dV$$

$$\frac{dP}{dV} = \frac{-1}{1 - \eta/\epsilon}$$

The percentage change in price is the change in price divided by price; here it is dP/P. Since $dP/P \div dV/P = dP/dV$, Eq. (2.8) shows how a change in a subsidy, expressed as a percentage of the commodity price, changes the commodity price in percentage terms. This is convenient because we can ignore the units in which prices are measured. Thus a "10-percent subsidy" refers to $V/P = 0.10$, and increasing it to 0.11 gives a value of dV/P of 0.01.

Equations (2.7) and (2.8) are typical comparative-statics results in policy analysis. They tell us how equilibrium price and quantity change when the policy control variable V changes.

In particular, Eq. (2.8) shows how the result of a subsidy paid to producers depends on the relative size of supply and demand elasticities. In general, it says that so long as supply and demand elasticities have their normal signs ($\epsilon > 0$, $\eta < 0$), then $dP/dV < 0$. That is, when the subsidy increases, price decreases. On the question of the magnitude of the price effect, consider first the limiting cases. If $\eta = 0$ or $\epsilon = \infty$, we have $dP/dV = -1$. Thus, using finite changes rather than infinitesimals (a practice with which one must be cautious), if the subsidy goes up 10 cents, price goes down 10 cents. Consumers get the full benefit of the subsidy even though it was paid to producers, while producers are made no better off. At the other extreme, if $\epsilon = 0$ or $\eta = -\infty$, $dP/dV = 0$, that is, price is unchanged. Another special case occurs if $\epsilon = -\eta$, e.g., the supply elasticity is 0.8 and demand elasticity is -0.8. In this case $dP/dV = -\frac{1}{2}$. The incidence of the subsidy is that producers and consumers divide the gains equally.

Equation (2.8) constitutes a subsidy simulation model. Suppose you were asked to analyze a proposed policy of paying cotton producers 20 cents per pound of cotton they sold. You could build an econometric model of industry incorporating past subsidies and then use the regression coefficients to derive a price effect of a 20-cent subsidy. But alternatively, you could find evidence, perhaps from existing studies on ϵ and η for cotton, and plug the values in Eq. (2.8). You could also assess the potential error caused by error in your estimate of ϵ or η. You could even present the results concisely to a mathematically illiterate client by means of Table 2.1.

Consumer Subsidy

Many countries have consumer subsidies. The government acquires commodities at market prices, perhaps but not necessarily through price support programs, and resells them at lower prices. In some cases the commodities are even given away. A cash subsidy paid to consumers of the same size, V, that we have already analyzed when paid to producers, is modeled by adding V to Eq. (2.3) rather than subtracting V from Eq. (2.4). This change means that the market price is now price on the supply curve P_s, rather than P_d as it was in the producer-subsidy model.

Table 2.1 Percentage of Each 1-Percent Subsidy that Accrues to Consumers*

	Elasticity of supply (ϵ)						
	0.1	0.2	0.3	0.4	0.5	1.0	5.0
-0.1	0.50	0.67	0.75	0.80	0.83	0.91	0.98
-0.3	0.25	0.40	0.50	0.57	0.63	0.77	0.94
-0.5	0.17	0.29	0.38	0.44	0.50	0.67	0.91
-0.7	0.13	0.22	0.30	0.36	0.42	0.59	0.88
-1.0	0.09	0.17	0.23	0.29	0.36	0.50	0.83
-2.0	0.05	0.09	0.13	0.17	0.20	0.33	0.71
-5.0	0.02	0.04	0.06	0.07	0.09	0.17	0.50

Elasticities of demand (η)

*From Eq. (2.5), negative values are positive here because a price decline is a gain to consumers. The price gain to producers is obtained by subtracting each entry from 1.0.

To do the comparative statics of this subsidy, consider a simpler but equivalent specification of supply and demand to that underlying Eq. (2.7). Expressing comparative statics results in terms of elasticities implies that elasticities are parameters—they remain unchanged when the policy instrument changes. This is only strictly true for constant-elasticity equations. Therefore, we were implicitly assuming that Eq. (2.3) and (2.4) had the constant-elasticity functional forms

$$P_s = BQ_s^{1/\epsilon} \qquad P_d = AQ_s^{1/\eta} \tag{2.9}$$

where B and A are constants. Note further that (1) these functions are linear in the logarithms of Q and P, and (2) the differential of a natural logarithm is a measure of percentage change. Let V now be a multiplicative factor of demand, equal to $1 + v$, where v is the subsidy as a percentage of P, for example, if $v = 10$ percent then v is 1.1. Differentiating the natural logs of Eqs. (2.9), initializing at zero subsidy where $V = 1$ and $P_s = P_d = P$,

$$EP = \frac{1}{\epsilon} EQ \tag{2.10}$$

$$EP = \frac{1}{\eta} EQ + EV \tag{2.11}$$

where EP and EQ are $d \ln P$ and $d \ln Q$, that is, dP/P and dQ/Q or percentage change in P and Q. EV is $d \ln (1 + v) = dv/P$, that is the change in the subsidy rate as a percentage of price. EV thus has the same economic meaning as dV in Eq. (2.7). Dividing by EV and equating Eqs. (2.10) and (2.11),

$$\frac{EQ}{EV} = \frac{1}{1/\epsilon - 1/\eta} \tag{2.12}$$

This result is identical to Eq. (2.7): the producer and consumer subsidies have identical effects.

The effect on price is obtained by dividing Eq. (2.10) by EV and substituting Eq. (2.12) into Eq. (2.10).

$$\frac{EP}{EV} = \frac{1/\epsilon}{1/\epsilon - 1/\eta} \tag{2.13}$$

Equation (2.13) differs from Eq. (2.8) only because the market price in Eq. (2.13) is P_s from the supply function while in Eq. (2.8) P is P_d from the demand function. To get the demand price effect we have

$$\frac{EP_d}{EV} = \frac{1}{\epsilon}\frac{EQ}{EV} = \frac{1/\eta}{1/\epsilon - 1/\eta} = \frac{-1}{1 - \eta/\epsilon}$$

that is, the same result as Eq. (2.8).

A subsidy of given size has exactly the same effects on output, producer price, and consumer price whether the subsidy is paid to producers or consumers. This is an elementary point, but it seems elusive in policy discussions, where it is sometimes presumed that a consumer subsidy is not beneficial to producers in the way that a producer subsidy is.

Commodity Taxes

The real converse of a subsidy is a tax on sales of a commodity. A tax is just a negative subsidy. It is analyzed in the supply–demand model simply by changing the sign of V. What we find then is that Q always falls, P_d rises, and P_s falls—all moving in the opposite direction from the subsidy incidence. Again it doesn't matter who pays the tax; the consequences of a tax on groceries are the same whether the store pays the tax and includes it in the posted price the consumer pays (as with gasoline) or whether the store posts prices before tax and the consumer pays the tax as a separate item (as with state sales taxes). In the former case, we have the model where V is added to the supply price, and the market price is P_d. In the latter case, we have the model where V is subtracted from the demand price, and the market price is the grocer's supply price P_s.

It is possible to think of reasons why these two situations would not cause identical results. It might be that consumers in the latter case might forget about the tax they will have to pay at the cash register, looking only at the posted P_s prices on the grocery store shelves, and buy more than if the posted prices were P_d prices including the tax. Many people seem to believe that such irrational behavior occurs with more subtly assessed taxes, such as whether the employer pays social security taxes directly to the government without including them in workers' salaries (as is done with half of U.S. social security taxes) or the employer pays the employee a wage nominally including the tax and then deducts the social security tax (as is done with the other half of U.S. social security taxes). Do workers think they are better off in the former case where they don't see any deductions and believe that their employers are "paying the tax" in a sense that the employers are not in the second case? It is possible in any such case that nominal incidence does make a difference, but there is no room for this in the supply–demand model of subsidy or tax incidence.

Traded Goods

Consider a subsidy paid to domestic producers of an imported product, with supply and demand as depicted in Fig. 2.3. How does Eq. (2.8) apply? The situation was described as a perfectly elastic supply to the country, including the imported supplies. So Eq. (2.8) is -1, meaning that a 10-percent subsidy reduces P_d by 10 percent, and leaves P_s unchanged. But this is incorrect. Consumers have to pay the world price, which is unchanged. The analytical error is that the supply curve including imports should not be used. Suppliers of imports do not receive the subsidy. We move along the *domestic* supply curve. The given world price means that for this problem the demand curve is perfectly elastic for all quantities less than Q_e. Thus, Eq. (2.8) is evaluated with $\eta \to \infty$, that is, $dP/dV = 0$. The subsidy leaves the market price unchanged and producer receipts per bushel rise by the full amount of the subsidy.

For an exported good, as in Fig. 2.4, we have already depicted $\eta \to \infty$ and again we obtain the result that $dP/dV = 0$.

Related Instruments

The policy instruments in price-support programs are often not subsidies like V. Many farm programs are formulated with reference to support-price levels. Prices at the support level are *proximate* targets or objectives, "proximate" to distinguish them from ultimate goals to which farm policy is addressed, such as increasing farmers' incomes. The policy instruments used to achieve these objectives are represented by variables, such as subsidy payments, governmental purchases of commodities, or regulated acreage levels. Let us consider several options.

Legal Minimum Price.   The market price itself becomes a policy instrument in nonagricultural programs such as regulated utility rates or minimum wage legislation. A similar approach has been proposed for agriculture, a recent example being the program advocated by the American Agriculture Movement (AAM) in the late 1970s. The AAM asked for a law simply stating that it would be illegal to pay less than $5.00 (or, in some versions, 90 percent of parity) per bushel of wheat. The Minnesota legislature passed such a law in 1985 and had it not been vetoed by the governor we would have had nice experiment in state-level intervention in a commodity with a national market.

The minimum-price policy can be analyzed by making P_d in Eq. (2.2) a policy instrument $\hat{P}$. Then we simply solve for $\hat{Q}$ as the amount that consumers are willing to buy at the legislated price. This is the constrained equilibrium output, which is less than no-program output. Why would suppliers produce this amount? They must produce the amount that would be supplied at the price P_s where output is $\hat{Q}$, which is a price not only lower than P_d but lower price than the no-program price P_e. This seems an unlikely result. Why wouldn't producers expand output along Eq. (2.1), producing the profit-maximizing quantity for the legislated price?

What would happen if they did? They would not be able to sell output in excess of quantity demanded at $\hat{P}$. Rather than accept nothing for the excess output, they would presumably try to reach illegal "black market" agreements, mutually beneficial to seller and buyer, at a price below $\hat{P}$. Unhindered black market trading, i.e., a legal price requirement that is not enforced, would reestablish the no-program market equilibrium.

Suppose that the law is completely enforced. If producers cannot sell their output at $\hat{P}$, it rots unused. The resulting competitive equilibrium is one in which expected profits are bid away, i.e., the expected marginal cost of producing and selling a unit of output equals the legally established price. The form that competition would take for the limited market would depend on the characteristics of the product and its marketing, but in any case is likely to be wastefully costly. Presumably this is one reason why the AAM approach has not caught on.

Maximum Price. A way of exploiting producers is to permit no sales at prices above a legislated level. This is done for rental rates in housing by some U.S. local governments, but is rare in agriculture, the notable recent example being President Nixon's beef price ceiling of 1973. In developing countries and centrally planned countries this approach is more common. It is tempting especially when a government-run or licensed-monopoly marketing agency exists. The agency simply offers the farmers a price below P_e and makes it illegal to sell to another buyer. This approach encourages smuggling and black markets just as legal price minimums do. Assuming black markets are prevented, the maximum price results in output on the supply curve at the legislated maximum, as in $\hat{P}_{max}$ in Fig. 2.5. Note that there is a minimum price, $\hat{P}_{min}$, that causes the same output, $\hat{Q}$. The two policies have the same social cost triangle, but the price floor redistributes rents to producers from consumers, while the price ceiling redistributes from producers to consumers. The gains to consumers from the price ceiling, $\hat{P}_{max}$, are area $A - C$. Net losses accrue to consumers, if any, who formerly consumed the product but are unable to acquire it at the ceiling price. If $\hat{P}_{max}$ is brought low enough, area C will inevitably come to exceed A. When this occurs, the policy will be counterproductive from the viewpoint of consumers as a group.

We can represent the quantity corresponding to a price $\hat{P}$ fixed through regulation (rather than being a maximum or minimum), without specifying whether $\hat{P}$ is higher or lower than P_e, by writing

$$\hat{Q} = \min [S(\hat{P}), D(\hat{P})]$$

Production Control. For this policy, Q becomes itself a policy instrument. A production-control policy that restricts Q to $\hat{Q}$ is modeled by replacing Eq. (2.1) by $\hat{Q}$, and substituting into Eq. (2.2) to obtain the price effect. Differentiating yields

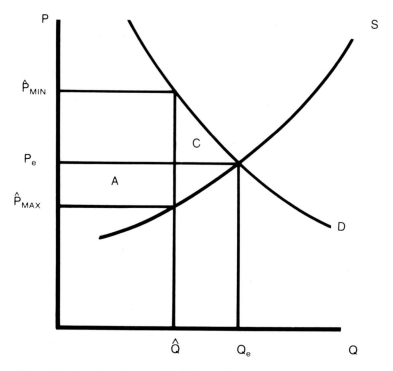

Figure 2.5 Legal maximum and minimum prices.

$$\frac{d \ln P}{d \ln \hat{Q}} = \frac{1}{\eta} \tag{2.14}$$

a simpler result even than Eq. (2.8).

Guaranteed Producer Price (Target Price). Under the U.S. Food Security Act of 1985, this is the main policy instrument for grains and cotton. In
the model, it is analyzed simply by replacing P_s in Eq. (2.1) by the target price
$\hat{P}$. The resulting output determines the market price from Eq. (2.2). Thus, we
no longer have a simultaneous supply–demand system but one-way causality
from $\hat{P}$ to Q to P_d. The quantitative effects are calculated using elasticities as
in Eq. (2.8).

Note that the constrained equilibrium is characterized by a value $(\hat{P} - P_d)$
equal to the value of a subsidy V that would generate that same equilibrium in
Eq. (2.3) and (2.4). Thus, given supply and demand curves, for any target
price level, we can find an equivalent subsidy level such that the constrained
equilibrium for the two policies is identical. Yet they are not equivalent police
regimes. They yield different results over a range of supply–demand conditions. For example, if demand shifts to the right, a policy regime characterized

by a target price $\hat{P}$ will result in smaller payments, and the net production incentive (i.e., comparing program to no-program equilibrium) is less. But a policy characterized by a given subsidy level V will maintain the production incentive and generate higher producer returns when demand shifts to the right.

Market Price Support

This is the classic form of intervention, accomplished most directly as discussed in Chap. 1 for dairy products by a standing offer of the USDA to buy commodities at the support price. Price again becomes a policy instrument, but in this case is an exogenous variable in both Eq. (2.1) and (2.2). Consequently, Q_s from the supply function must exceed Q_d from the demand function for any support price above the no-program price, the difference between them being governmental purchases.

For given supply and demand curves, an alternative policy, equivalent to the market price support, is a program setting the quantity of governmental purchases Q_g as a policy instrument. This type of policy exists in the U.S. school lunch program, where governmental purchases are based in part upon a commodity being designated as "in surplus" and needing a stronger market. As with the comparison of a target price to a subsidy program, a policy regime defined by a choice of Q_g is not fully equivalent to a price-support regime defined by choice of $\hat{P}$. When demand increases, government purchases decline, but price is not affected (unless government purchases fall to zero) under the price-support program; but under a policy characterized by a level of Q_g, market price rises as demand increases.

Consider the constant-elasticity functions (2.9). Parallel to the treatment of price-dependent supply and demand functions in Eqs. (2.10) and (2.11), we can express percentage changes in Eqs. (2.1) and (2.2) as

$$EQ = \epsilon EP \tag{2.15}$$

$$EQ = \eta EP + EQ_g \tag{2.16}$$

where EQ_g is the change in government purchases as a percentage of Q. Equating (2.15) and (2.16), and dividing by EQ_g,

$$\frac{EP}{EQ_g} = \frac{1}{\epsilon - \eta} \tag{2.17}$$

Equation (2.17) is always positive, and P rises more the less elastic is either supply or demand. In the subsidy case, $Q_s = Q_d$ but $P_s > P_d$. In the government purchase case, $P_s = P_d$ but $Q_s > Q_d$. From Eq. (2.15), Q is Q_s. To get Q_d we must subtract Q_g from Q_s.

Q_g is conceptually the same as the CCC stocks in Fig. 1.1. That is, for any equilibrium characterized by a price-support level $\hat{P}$, we can specify a government purchase that will achieve the same results for P_s, P_d, Q_s, and Q_d.

THE GLOBAL VIEW AND "LARGE" COUNTRIES IN TRADE

If a country exports or imports a large enough share of world supplies of a commodity, its policies will influence world prices. In such cases the given value P_e in Figs. 2.3 and 2.4 does not exist. Instead we have situations such as those depicted in Fig. 2.6. The left-hand diagram of each panel represents a country introducing a policy (the "instigator" country). In panel A, the instigator is an importing country: demand exceeds domestic supply at every price. The difference between quantity demanded and quantity supplied at each price, the coun-

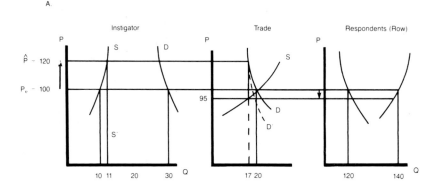

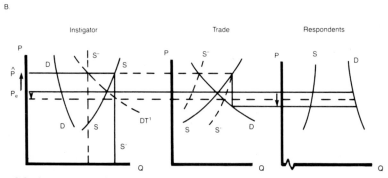

Figure 2.6 Large-country border policies. *(A)* Large-country importer; tariff or deficiency payment. *(B)* Large-country exporter; export subsidy or deficiency payment. *DT* = *D* (instigator) + excess *D* (respondent) at each price.

try's "excess" demand, is the demand for imports. This excess demand function is plotted as D in the middle diagram, representing the international trading sector. The right-hand diagram aggregates all the rest of the world supply and demand for the commodity. These countries are called "respondents." They may have their own policies, but for the present, we assume they maintain the same S and D functions, generating the excess supply which the instigator faces as its supply of imports. The change from Fig. 2.3 is that this supply of imports is no longer perfectly elastic. In this example, the instigator consumes 20 percent (30/150) of world production, and it imports one-seventh (20/140) of the respondents' output. This means that the instigator's import quantities influence the world price.

Now when the instigator attempts to achieve domestic price $\hat{P}$ by means of a tariff, it finds not only that less of the commodity is imported, but that as imports fall from 20 to 17, the world trading price falls to 95. This means that the tariff will have to be set higher to drive price up to $\hat{P}$, in this case $25 as compared to $20, if the world price had been given at 100 as it was in Fig. 2.3. The term "world price" has lost its meaning as an exogenous fulcrum against which the instigator policies may operate. This is a potential boon to the instigator who now has monopsony power in the market. The consequence of this for policy choice is discussed later.

The large-country case is also different for the instigator of domestic intervention. Consider a deficiency payment to guarantee producers $\hat{P}$ of 120. What happens to the consumers' (market) price and the world price? We get output of 11, as shown in panel A, the same as with the tariff. But here we cannot simply observe where the vertical line at 11 cuts the domestic demand curve to find the market price. It is necessary to bring in the world market. To analyze the world market effects graphically, the excess demand curve is drawn for the instigator, defined as domestic demand minus a supply curve that becomes vertical at $Q = 11$ (because even if the market price falls below 120, producers know they will receive 120). This generates the excess demand curve D' in world trade, with the market price, and the border price in the respondent countries, being determined where D' intersects S. Thus, the world price falls less if a given domestic producer price, $\hat{P}$, is attained by means of deficiency payments than if it is attained by means of a tariff.

Figure 2.6 B analyzes analogous policies for an instigator that is an exporter large enough to influence world price. Here it is the demand curve for the instigator's exports that was perfectly elastic in the small-country case. The less elastic curve implies monopoly power for the exporter, the consequences of which are explored in Chap. 11.

A deficiency payment program guaranteeing instigator producers price $\hat{P}$ can be represented in panel B by the new domestic supply curve S' and shifted excess supply curve in trade, S', following reasoning parallel to that outlined for the importer in panel A. The new excess supply curve S' intersects D at a lower world price. An export subsidy could also achieve price $\hat{P}$ in the instigating country by paying a subsidy to exporters equal to the distance between $\hat{P}$ on the supply of exports S and the demand price vertically beneath it. The export subsidy increases the instigator's export supply even more than the deficiency payment. Thus, the world price is not depressed as much by a deficiency payment scheme as by an export subsidy that achieves the same domestic producer price. The economic reason is that the deficiency payment scheme reduces the market price in both the instigator and respondent countries, while the export subsidy reduces the price only in the respondent. Therefore, in order to sell the commodities necessary to get to price $\hat{P}$ on the instigator domestic S curve, a lower respondent country price is needed in the export subsidy case.

The comparison of these policies is a contentious issue in U.S.–EEC policy debates because the EEC asserts that U.S. deficiency payments are a de facto export subsidy. Our analysis shows that while the two policies both drive down world trading prices and increase the instigator's exports, they aren't identical in effect. In particular, the instigator's consumer prices move in opposite directions in the two cases. Thus, it is natural for the United States to see its target-price program for grains as essentially different from an export subsidy, but it is natural for the EEC to see the two policies as essentially the same.

A production control policy that shifted domestic supply and excess supply corresponding to S'' can also achieve the domestic producer price $\hat{P}$ for the instigator. This policy is very different in the world market, driving the world price up to $\hat{P}$ instead of depressing it. Thus, if the EEC were displeased with deficiency payments they ought to be pleased with production controls. And, indeed, it was said of U.S. grain production cutbacks in its 1983 paid diversion (payment in kind, PIK) program that it provided a price umbrella under which the EEC, and other competing exporters, could expand output and reduce U.S. world market shares. However, consumers in the respondent countries have the opposite preference—they are better off with instigator deficiency payments than with production controls. And since respondents as a whole import more than they export, the EEC objections are the opposite of what one might expect.

Because of their ability to exploit consumers worldwide, production controls are a natural policy for an exporter with monopoly power to consider. So are export restrictions such as export quotas. We will return in Chap. 11 to the pros and cons of these policy options, our purpose here being only to introduce the supply-demand depiction of their market price effects in the large- as compared to small-country case.

COST-REDUCING INTERVENTION

Attempts by governments to reduce farmers' costs are just as widespread and more varied in type than commodity price supports. Many countries provide subsidized fertilizer, or credit. This is true in some of the countries shown in

Table 1.1 as having NPCs less than 1, that is, as taxing farmers. Consequently the NPC may be misleading, and "effective" rates of protection have been developed to provide as an indication of the overall consequence of governmental intervention by subtracting input subsidies from output taxes. This subject cannot be adequately analyzed in a simple supply–demand model when an input subsidy only applies to one or several but not all inputs. As in the case of output controls that use policy instruments related to one input, notably acreage controls, a model is required that identifies at least two categories of inputs (those subsidized and those not). This is the topic of Chap. 4.

We can, however, consider now policies that simply reduce costs and, hence, shift the supply function, for example, by subsidizing all inputs equally or by promoting technical change.[8] These policies, too, are widespread in both the developing world and in the industrial countries. In the United States, the federal government was engaged in measures to help farmers reduce costs for 70 years before farm commodity programs became important, dating the beginning of the activity formally to the Morrill Act of 1862 which set the stage for public funding of agricultural research, technical education, and extension.

We introduce cost-reducing policies in a supply–demand diagram by shifting the supply curve down. This seems straightforward, but sometimes it seems more natural to think of technical change as shifting the supply curve to the right. We think of technical change as giving us more output from the same quantity of inputs, so we want to shift supply to the right. This is generally misleading, however, and can lead to analytical problems. The quantities of inputs are not given, even at the individual farm level, much less the market level. In P, Q space we must stick to output and price concepts to avoid problems, and this means thinking of technical progress as lower costs to produce a given quantity rather than more output for given inputs.[9]

To represent cost-reducing policies as a downward shift in supply, we subtract the reduction, ΔC, from the inverse supply curve (the industry marginal cost) to get the new, lower supply curve. After the change, we will have price lower than the old marginal cost (for any given output) by ΔC. Algebraically, we rewrite Eq. (2.3) as

$$P = S(Q) - \Delta C \qquad (2.18)$$

But now, if we do our comparative statics on changes in ΔC (an increased investment in research, say), we get exactly the same results as Eqs. (2.7) and (2.8), except ΔC replaces V. That is, a cost-reducing policy is exactly equivalent to a production subsidy.

The social-cost calculations are different, however, because we do not know if the government had to pay ΔC times $\hat{Q}$ (the postpolicy output). The argument for governmental subsidy of research is that a dollar spent on research yields more than a dollar of cost reduction (because it does not pay for private firms to undertake sufficient investment in research), so the sum of producers' and consumers' gains outweighs the government costs. Instead of a triangular deadweight loss, we get a net social gain. (This discussion ignores most of the real issues in governmental support for agricultural research, such as its capital-good aspect and the role of private versus public institutions. Our goal here is simply to show the consequences in a one-period supply–demand model.)

From the viewpoint of producers and consumers, the consequences of technical progress that reduces costs by 10 percent are identical to the consequences of a 10-percent, producer-subsidy payment. How is it then that while it seems well accepted that subsidies make producers better off, many have believed that technical progress makes farmers worse off? A standard text asserts that "The result [of output-increasing technology] is depressed prices and incomes for farmers as output expands at a greater rate than demand." (Tweeten, 1971, pp. 169–170). While it is true that output expands more than demand (which does not shift at all in these comparative statics), the relevant point from Eq. (2.8) is that market price falls less than ΔC reduces cost (except in the limiting cases of perfectly elastic supply when $\Delta C = \Delta P$).

However, complications exist that can justify the pessimistic view about technical progress making farmers worse off. One set of complications involves dynamics and a distinction between farmers who vary in capability to adopt and profit from technical change. These require going beyond static models and are discussed in Chaps. 6 and 9.

Heterogeneous producers cause complications in a static model when they require a distinction between marginal and intramarginal output. Equations (2.7) and (2.8) analyze marginal changes. At the margin producers are made better off when P rises or costs fall. What about intramarginal producers? While they are clearly better off in the case of a producer price rise, the problem is more complicated for the supply shift because the shift may not be equal in magnitude at all points on S. In Eq. (2.3) we know by specification of the policy that V is the same for all units of output. But we do not know this about ΔC. If it is true that ΔC is the same for all output, then the technical change is additive in cost, and the old and new supply curves are vertically parallel. This guarantees that producers as a group will gain from technical progress just as much as from an equivalent subsidy (i.e., $V = \Delta C$). The possibilities for shifts in S that are not vertically parallel, and the economic meaning and consequences of such shifts, are treated in Chap. 6.

An issue causing concern in the United States is the consequence of technical progress given the existence of surpluses caused by support prices. The imminent commercial use of bovine growth hormone (bgH) in dairy production has caused trepidation even though it may reduce the cost of producing milk by 20 percent. As reported in the *Washington Post* (April 2, 1986),

> Economists at Cornell have predicted that FDA approval of bgH could have a dramatic adverse effect on the dairy industry, which is grappling with massive over-

production and a government program to reduce purchases of surplus milk, butter and cheese that have cost more than $6 billion in the last three years.

In terms of the models of this chapter, there is no reason for this concern from producers' viewpoint. The program just means that demand is made perfectly elastic at the support price, and farmers can sell even more at lower cost without any price decline. But the government's costs and stocks would rise substantially. However, the government's costs could be kept the same by reducing the support price as much as costs decline. Then consumers would gain because they buy more milk at a lower market price, and farmers would gain because price would still bear the same relation to costs as it did before bgH, and the market would be larger (how much depending on the elasticity of demand).

Still, in addition to the complications already outlined for technical change, we have the added problem of adjusting policies appropriately. More systematic treatment of simultaneous existence of several policy instruments is deferred to Chaps. 8 and 9.

Cost-Reducing Policies and Trade

In a small-country exporter, the producers gain most from a cost reduction since demand for output is perfectly elastic at the world price; whereas, consumers gain nothing since they still have to pay the world price. Thus it would not occur to agricultural economists in Canada, Australia, or New Zealand that technical progress in their export products might make their farmers worse off. Rather, the big threat would be other countries experiencing technical progress while the exporter did not. Similarly, these countries as respondents are especially vulnerable to input or output subsidies by large-country instigators.

A small-country importer is in the same position with respect to its producers. But the overall picture for an importing country is different because it consumes more than it produces. It is still true that the country's producers lose when events in other countries reduce world prices. But consumers gain even more than producers lose.

Further discussion of these and related issues is contained in Chap. 11, the point here being to outline how differently the situation looks given the supply–demand situation of a small country in trade as compared to the closed economy view typically taken in U.S. treatments of technical change (such as in Brandow, 1977, or Cochrane and Ryan, 1976).

SYNTHESIS

This chapter has considered two aspects of economic models for purposes of policy analysis. The first is the conceptual supply-demand depiction of market intervention, epitomized by the diagrams. The second is the quantitative comparative statics of these models. Disparate examples of both topics have been considered. This section pulls things together.

Many of the qualitative results discussed in this chapter are summarized in Table 2.2, which shows effects of policies of different types on prices and quantities. One of the ways in which formal modeling of a policy can be useful is in discovering policies that may be superficially different but have fundamentally the same effects. In Table 2.2, two policies are equivalent if they have the same set of + and − effects on prices and quantities. We can also see which policies fall into broader categories and the limits of such classification.

For example, whenever P rises (falls) in the trade sector, P also rises (falls) in the respondent countries and Q_s and Q_d change accordingly. Therefore, once we have specified the directional change of P in the trade sector, we already know the directional effects of the respondents' variables. Within the trade sector, P and Q always move in opposite directions when the instigator is an exporting country; but P and Q move in same direction when the instigator is an importing country. The reason is that the exporter drives down (up) the world price by placing more (less) on the world market, but the importer drives down (up) the world price by taking less (more) off of the world market. A

Table 2.2 Effects of Market Interventions by a Large Country

Policy	Instigating country				Trade sector		Rest-of-the-world respondents		
	Q_s	Q_d	P_s	P_d	Q	P	Q_s	Q_d	P
Instigating country an exporter									
Production control	−	−	+	+	−	+	+	−	+
Production subsidy	+	+	+	−	+	--	−	+	−
Export control	−	+	?	−	−	+	+	−	+
Export subsidy	+	−	+	+	+	−	−	+	−
Government purchase	+	−	+	+	−	+	+	−	+
Minimum price	−	−	+	+	?	?	?	?	?
Maximum price	−	−	−	−	?	?	?	?	?
Production tax	−	−	−	+	−	+	+	−	+
Cost-reducing program	+	+	+	−	+	−	−	+	−
Instigating country an importer									
Production control	−	−	+	+	+	+	+	−	+
Production subsidy	+	+	+	−	−	−	−	+	−
Import quota	+	−	+	?	−	−	−	+	−
Import subsidy	−	+	−	−	+	+	+	−	+
Government purchase	−	−	+	+	+	+	+	−	+
Minimum price	−	−	+	+	+	+	+	−	+
Maximum price	−	−	−	−	+	+	+	−	+
Production tax	−	−	−	+	+	+	+	−	+
Cost-reducing program	+	+	+	−	−	−	−	+	−

corollary of the preceding generalization is that a large country's intervention can never have desirable results for both consumers and producers in other countries.

Could we categorize policies completely by whether they are world-price increasing or world-price decreasing? No, because the domestic effects are quite different. For example, the production control and the production tax are world-price increasing, but the former increases domestic producer returns while the latter decreases them. So we need to know also whether policies are protective for producers or exploitative of producers.

This two-way classification (world price increasing/depressing, domestic producer protective/exploitative) is still insufficient to categorize all the policies. For example, government purchases and production controls are both world-price increasing and producer protective, but the former induces increased output (as in U.S. dairy) and the other reduced output (as in U.S. peanuts). This is perhaps a less fundamental distinction but can be important for environmental concerns about intensity of land use, and it makes a difference in the economic rents producers gain from a given $\hat{P}$. So a third criterion for classification is whether a program is output-increasing or output-decreasing.

The three-way classification, as we might expect by now, is insufficient too. For example, production subsidies and export subsidies are both world-price depressing (which is why the EEC sees them as equivalent), both are producer protective, and both are output increasing. But they differ in that production subsidies drive down domestic consumer prices and export subsidies increase them. So a fourth criterion is whether a program is consumer protective or consumer exploitive.

These four criteria—based on four effects: (1) world price, (2) instigator producer price, (3) instigator output, and (4) instigator consumer price—seem sufficient to categorize all the interventions in Table 2.1. With 4 two-way possibilities, we have $2^4 = 16$ possible types of policies, which is not much of a simplification.

Equivalencies

It is, nonetheless, useful to have a feel for equivalencies among policies, to know that a cost-reducing program is equivalent to a production subsidy program, at least as far as the qualitative P and Q effects go. From the discussion in this chapter, we have the following equivalencies, which can be classified according to the degree of isomorphism (shorthand for "having the same form"): complete, limited, partial, and reverse isomorphism.

Complete Isomorphism. Complete isomorphism comprises programs so similar that they are not shown as separate interventions in Table 2.2. The example discussed earlier was that a consumer subsidy is equivalent to a producer subsidy. The test of complete isomorphism is that from time series data on prices, quantities, and the amount of the subsidy, you could never infer which of these policy regimes you were observing. Other examples are: (1) import quotas allocated to foreign exporters (as in U.S. and EEC sugar quotas) or import licenses allocated to domestic importing companies; (2) export subsidies paid to importing countries (as in U.S. P.L. 480, Title II), or export subsidies paid to exporting companies (as in some U.S. grain-export programs).

Limited Isomorphism.   Limited isomorphism means that for any given static equilibrium established by one policy, the other can be set up to generate exactly the same values of all nine price and quantity variables listed in Table 2.2. This means that two such policies fit into one of the 16 categories under the four criteria that we worked through. But under conditions of change in the underlying market conditions, the intervention's results would change differently, so an observer could deduce which policy was in effect.

Examples discussed in this chapter:

1.   *Production subsidy and deficiency payment.* For any value of V established, a target price at the P_s level resulting from V would have generated the same static equilibrium. However, if demand, say, should shift, maintaining the target price and maintaining V would yield different results. The producer price would rise under the given production subsidy but not with a given target price, so output and other variables would change differently, too.

2.   *Government purchases and market support prices.* Instead of the government buying quantity Q_g, thus boosting the market price to $\hat{P}$, the government could announce that it stands ready to purchase commodities at price $\hat{P}$ (as in the dairy price-support program). Then the private market will absorb Q_d at $\hat{P}$ and the government will get the rest. But this must be the same Q_g as under the quantity-specified policy, because $\hat{P}$ is by construction the same. In terms of an example, the existence of an announced support price of $1.35 per pound of cheese in 1983–1984 resulted in delivery of 571 million pounds of cheese to the government; the same results could have been achieved by having the government buy 571 million pounds of cheese without announcing a support price.

Again, this limited isomorphism is a static result and would not carry through if market condition changed. And we can think of reasons why the results would be different for the two policies even for given supply–demand conditions if people were uncertain about those conditions, or about the government's policy. It could very likely make a difference whether the government bought Q_g without announcement or as part of a preannounced policy. It would also make a difference what the government intended to do with the cheese, and what was announced about this. These complications notwithstanding, a fundamental similarity exists between the price-support and quantity-purchase programs that it is analytically helpful to be aware of (and foolish to be ignorant of). This similarity is what the notion of limited isomorphism signals.

3. *Import quota and import tariff.* Again, a country using an import quota can achieve the same results for all *P*'s and *Q*'s by appropriate choice of a tariff and use of its revenues. But maintaining the two policies would yield different results if world market price fell. With a given tariff level, domestic price would also fall. With a given import quota, domestic price would not fall and the instigating country has insulated its price from the world market.

3a. *Import quotas and variable tariffs (levies).* These are sometimes said to be equivalent in a sense in which import quotas and fixed tariffs are not. The variable levy system of the EEC is used to insulate EEC internal prices by adjusting the import duty at any time the world price changes so as to keep the level of internal prices constant. In this sense the import quota and variable levy have complete and not just limited isomorphism. But this would not be true for the response to internal market shocks within the EEC. The adjusting of the variable levy to keep internal prices constant would involve varying the level of imports, so the isomorphism with an import quota breaks down.

4. *Production subsidy and cost-reducing program.* These are the same in Table 2.2. A discussion of the limits of the isomorphism requires a fuller treatment of input markets and costs, in Chap. 4.

5. *Production control and minimum price.* There is some ambiguity with respect to the international consequences of a minimum price. An exporting country could require foreign buyers to pay the minimum price. If so, this equivalence results, since foreigners would only buy the smaller amount for which they are willing to pay this higher price. But this price could also have been achieved using production controls. On the other hand, if foreigners do not have to pay the minimum price, this policy is equivalent to a special production control program that the United States uses in peanuts. Domestically consumed output is sold at a higher regulated price, while exported output is sold at what it will bring on the world market. The control here has to involve limiting access to the domestic market, since producers would naturally prefer to sell all their output at the high domestic price.

For a minimum price policy in an importing country, the question is whether imports also must sell at the minimum price. If so, there would be quite a scramble to see who gets to sell the limited quantity that consumers would buy at the higher price. If domestic producers were given preferential access, their output could rise. But this would require some sort of import restraint, which places us in another policy category. If imports can be bought at less than the minimum price, they will replace domestic production until the world price is driven up to the minimum price. This is equivalent to the results of a production control. (Neither is likely to be a sensible policy, but that is not the point here.)

Partial Isomorphism. Partial Isomorphism means that two policies are isomorphic in *almost* all respects. For example, export subsidies and production subsidies have the same results in Table 2.2 except that the former is consumer exploitative and the latter is consumer protective. There are too many cases of partial isomorphism to be worth going through. Indeed, almost all policies are partially isomorphic if we take the term loosely enough. One example worth mentioning, though, is that each policy that either an importing or exporting country can carry out has the same directional effect on all variables whether the instigator is an importer or an exporter, *except* that the direction of Q in the trade sector is reversed.

Reverse Isomorphism. This leads to the more interesting case of reverse isomorphism, where two policies have opposite effects on all variables. A good example is a production subsidy and a production tax. They are structurally so similar—the same mathematical model describes both with the only difference being a change in sign on the policy instrument—that they are closer to complete isomorphism than are the limited and partial cases.

Two final interesting cases in Table 2.2. are the export control and import quota. They are the only interventions that have domestic price results that cannot be signed a priori. The export control could either increase or decrease the instigator's producer price. The increase would arise if the increased export revenues from a higher world price offset the lower domestic price. In this case, the policy is very attractive to the instigator since both producers and consumers gain. Similarly, for the import quota, it is possible that the consumer price could fall. This would occur if the higher prices paid for domestic output were offset by lower world prices caused by the instigator's reduced imports. The instigator's good results depend on its market power in world trade, monopoly power for the exporter and monopsony power for the importer.

These situations are analyzed further in Chap. 11, as is the set of complications for all policies when the "respondents" really do respond with counterpolicies of their own and are not just passive.

Small-Country Policies

A table like 2.2 could be constructed for small countries. It would be much simpler. All the effects in the trade sector and respondent countries would be zero since small countries by definition have negligible effects there. Moreover, many of the domestic price effects must be zero except for policies involving trade restraints. Only import or export tariffs, quotas, or subsidies can change both P_p and P_c in the instigating country. Production controls and government purchasing change neither P_c nor P_p. Production subsidies or taxes can influence the producers' return by making P_p equal to the world price plus the subsidy, or world price minus tax. The isomorphism between production and consumption subsidies holds when the consumption subsidy does not apply to imported commodities. If a subsidy were paid to consumers for all units consumed, whether domestically produced or imported, the consumer price would fall below the world price and P_p would remain unchanged at the world price.

An Alternative Approach to Synthesis

An attractive but questionable shortcut in measuring intervention is to characterize every policy in terms of its producer subsidy equivalent (PSE). For a deficiency payment program, this is the payment per unit output. For an import quota, it is the percentage rise in the domestic price over the world price caused by the quota. In terms of our diagrams, we would use $(\hat{P} - P_e)/P_e$ for each program for each commodity. For an input subsidy, we add the reduction in cost per unit of output. The USDA (1987) reports measurements of PSEs for a large collection of countries and commodities.

The appeal of the PSE approach is that it dispenses with diagrammatic areas and classifications for different types of intervention, and provides a single number to summarize the policy (or two numbers if the consumer price is different from the producer price, in which case there is also a consumer subsidy). Two serious difficulties face the approach.

First we need an estimate of P_e, price in the absence of the program. Except in the small-country case, where we can simply use the world price as P_e, it is often a substantial analytical task to estimate P_e. One really has to bring back all the details of supply and demand functions that the PSE looked attractive because it did without. If one attempts to take a shortcut in estimating a PSE for a large country like the United States, one ends up with either a shot in the dark or else an estimate known to be incorrect. For example, the USDA (1987) procedure on deficiency payments gives us $(\hat{P} - P_c)/P_c$ in terms of Fig. 2.2; but what we want is $(\hat{P} - P_e)/P_e$. With equal supply and demand elasticities, the short-cut procedure gives us a PSE roughly twice as large as its true value. If the supply and demand elasticities are known, the error in the short-cut procedure can be assessed. But, of course, if the elasticities are known, the correct PSE can be calculated in the first place. The USDA approach on large-country production controls, such as U.S. acreage set-asides, is to assign them a PSE of zero since no price distortion can be observed (USDA, 1987, p. 27). In terms of Fig. 2.1, the world market price is the same as the producer price $\hat{P}$. What we should have is $(\hat{P} - P_e)$, which may be hard to estimate but is certainly underestimated by assuming it is zero. This is particularly important in the USDA study because they report PSEs for 1982–1984, the period during which the United States had its largest acreage idling program ever (20 percent of cropland acreage in the PIK program of 1983).

Second, even a perfectly measured PSE does not tell the whole story of producer benefits. Comparing Figs. 2.1 and 2.2, it is apparent that a production control program generates less benefits to producers (absolutely and as a percentage gain in revenues) than a deficiency payments program without production controls that generated the same $\hat{P}$. One task undertaken in later chapters is to study more systematically the relative benefits to producers and consumers of these two program types. It is sweeping too much under the rug to say that if these two programs have the same price effects, hence the same PSEs, we should count them as equal from producers' viewpoint.

In short, we are not going to follow the grand synthesis of policies through PSEs, but will simplify only by using the policy isomorphisms identified here. This leaves us with several program types that have to be treated separately, all of which require at least some specific economic modeling and econometric information about the commodity market being studied. The role of the models developed in this chapter is to provide a conceptual framework for looking at the consequences of different types of intervention and combinations of these types. The role of the algebraic comparative statics is to translate the conceptual specification into quantitative simulation results for particular policy alternatives. To see how this works in practice, the next chapter turns to methods for the analysis of a particular set of agricultural policies.

ENDNOTES

1. Since S is an industry-level curve with factor prices variable, the move from Q_e to $\hat{Q}$ will reduce the prices of specific factors (i.e., those with upward sloping supply to the industry). If these are not all owned by producers, then the losses in C will not all accrue to producers.

2. The losses are attributed to buyers rather than consumers because it may occur that the rise in price of a raw material like tobacco will not be fully passed through to consumers. The circumstances under which this will occur, and the measurement of resulting gains and losses, is taken up in Chaps. 5 and 8.

3. On a U.S. average basis. A producer who had lower quality wool or worse luck in marketing receives the same percentage payment, therefore, a lower price guarantee, as better or luckier producers. This approach is employed "to encourage producers to improve the quality and marketing of their wool" (*USDA–ASCS Commodity Fact Sheet,* July 1985).

4. Actual payments were $91 million, higher because payments are also made for the wool on unshorn lambs which are sold for meat.

5. The world price is measured at the border, usually reported as a c.i.f. (cost, insurance, and freight) price for the country. This makes it roughly comparable to domestic prices. There still may be noncomparability because of internal transport and the stage of processing of imported as compared to farm-gate goods, however.

6. The appropriate border price for exports is f.o.b. ("free on board") meaning ready to be shipped abroad but not including any overseas shipping or other marketing costs.

7. In USDA, *Agricultural Statistics,* 1972, p. 18. The comparison is between a U.S. price at Minneapolis and Canadian price in Northern Manitoba.

8. Some tricky problems arise in specifying technical change that gives a simple parametric supply shift, that is, an additive or multiplicative constant, or in specifying what "subsidizing all inputs equally" means when there are fixed factors. The assumption here that we have cost-reducing policy instruments that shift S as postulated.

9. It is true that in the most common supply–demand models, in which the functions are linear or log-linear, there is a rightward shift in supply that is equivalent to any arbitrary downward shift. But what if supply looks like:

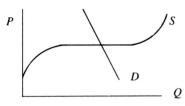

Then it is conceivable that a rightward shift would give us no change in price; but a downward shift always would. Or, in a simpler case, what if S were perfectly elastic throughout its range? It would be quite wrong to predict that technical change would leave price unchanged, but shifting S to the right gives this result. (It might be thought that similar problems for the downward shift view arise when S is perfectly inelastic—output fixed. In this case, however, the idea of technical change has no meaning. The commodity is costless anyway. Either it is just there, like water in a lake, or if it is a result of a production process the process must be costless, in the sense of using no inputs with alternative uses, say a freely flowing fountain of youth in the desert. In these cases the only sense we can give to technical progress is more water in the lake or a faster-flowing fountain. But this is really just an exogenous quantity increase; if you could get it by investment it would become a form of technical change but then supply would not be perfectly inelastic.)

Chapter 3

Supply–Demand Analysis of U.S. Policies

The study of actual policies is more complicated than the comparative statics of policy instruments in models using elasticities or single-market diagrams. First, policies often involve the use of several instruments simultaneously. For example, the mid-1980s, dairy policy includes a support price, production controls, import quotas, and subsidized distribution to consumers. Second, it is insufficient to analyze changes only. We have to provide information on the levels of prices and quantities caused by a policy, which requires not only percentage-change results but also an accurate depiction of the situation from which these changes start. Third, we often have to pay attention to the effects of policy for one commodity on the markets for other commodities. This is particularly important for closely related commodities in either demand or supply. For example, an important consequence of the U.S. sugar policy is the development of a high-fructose corn syrup (HFCS) industry, because the two products are good substitutes in consumption. In the Mississippi Delta, cotton and soybeans use similar land and so are substitutes in production. Corn and soybeans are substitutes on both the demand and supply sides.

U.S. policy for the grains provides a good case study of all three points, and is instructive of the scale of and trends in U.S. farm programs. This chapter develops a supply–demand analysis of these policies.

POLICY INSTRUMENTS

The federal programs for wheat and corn were introduced in the 1930s and have been modified over time as economic and political changes occurred. The history can be viewed as a series of policy experiments in which an idea is tried out and problems that arise from it lead to its being trimmed, modified, or (rarely) abandoned. Thus, an initial attempt to support prices by government acquisition under the Hoover administration's Federal Farm Board did nothing to stem continued excess supplies. So the keystone of the New Deal's Agricultural Adjustment Act of 1933 was payments to farmers in return for ploughing up or not planting crops. In the 1960s, when support prices were again too high to clear the markets, while serious acreage controls were not politically possible,[1] the support prices were lowered but direct government payments to producers were introduced to cushion the losses of farmers.

The principal policy instruments in the grain programs of the Food Security Act of 1985, governing the 1986–1990 crops, are: a market support price, acreage controls, and direct payments, all operating simultaneously. This set of instruments was established in essentially its present form in the Agricultural and Consumer Protection Act of 1973,[2] but the relative importance and details of implementation of each of the three has changed considerably over the past 12 years.

Loan Rate

Market prices for grains are supported by means of loans from the Commodity Credit Corporation (CCC). The CCC, as any lender might, makes loans to producers using the producers' stored commodities as collateral. The unique features of CCC loans are:

1. The CCC is required by law to accept grain from eligible producers in exchange for a loan equal to the number of bushels placed "under loan" times a price fixed in legislation and USDA administrative regulations, called the "loan rate," e.g., $3.30 per bushel for wheat in 1985.

2. If the producers choose not to repay the loan in cash, the CCC must accept the grain under loan as payment in full (including interest). This feature makes the loan "nonrecourse," in the sense that the CCC cannot insist upon full dollar repayment.

The result of these features is that farmers will turn grain over to the CCC if the market price falls below the loan rate plus accumulated interest. Consequently, the CCC ends up acquiring as much grain as is necesssary to maintain the market price at or near the loan rate. On the other hand, if price rises above the loan rate plus interest by the end of the loan period (usually 9 months), the producer will pay off the loan, redeem the grain, and either sell the grain at market price or store it at the producer's own risk.

The loan rate can be represented in supply–demand terms as a perfectly elastic segment of the demand curve that provides a market for unlimited quantities at the supported price level. A full analysis must consider what the CCC will do with its acquired grain. The most interesting possibilities involve the CCC selling the grain in subsequent high-price years (generated, for example, by a major drought or an unanticipated surge in export demand). The possibilities for stabilization policies along these lines will be treated in Chap. 10. For the present, we will consider CCC stock acquisition in a year in which yield and demand are at a normal (trend) level.

In Fig. 3.1 excess supply at the loan rate represents what is expected to happen under the program. A problem for the program is what to do with the stocks acquired. For U.S. grains, this has involved food-aid programs, subsidized exports, and most importantly acreage controls. Also, when stocks become burdensome despite these efforts, there is great pressure to cut loan rates. This happened in 1986 when the grain loan rates were cut 25 to 30 percent from their 1985 levels. Producers' returns did not fall correspondingly, however, because of increased deficiency payments.

Deficiency Payments

The payments equal the difference between a legislated "target" price and the higher of the loan rate or actual market price. Since the payments bring receipts per bushel up to the target price level, the target price can be thought of as a guaranteed producer price. As such it sets the incentive to p₁oduce the crop. By itself, the target price guarantee acts like a production subsidy as discussed earlier for wool. It encourages output and lowers the price paid by consumers while increasing the producer price, with the government's payments making up the difference. When the loan rate is above the market-clearing price, the target-price incentives cause increases in CCC stocks.

Figure 3.1 represents the situation for wheat in 1985. It fixes a total demand function for U.S. grain at point B by using USDA's domestic use and export estimates for 1985–1986 of 2.1 billion bushels at a U.S. average farm price of \$3.30 per bushel (the loan rate). The rest of the demand function is found by assuming a demand elasticity of -0.5, a typical estimate in recent empirical work. (In a full-fledged piece of policy analysis, a major part of the effort would be devoted to determining the appropriate estimate of this elasticity, but here we are interested mainly in the structure of the analytical model.) Since normal yield as of 1985–1986 implies an output of about 2.4 billion bush-

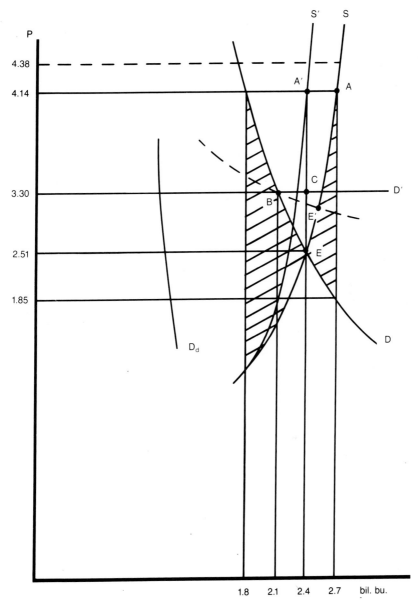

Figure 3.1 U.S. wheat program.

els, the program generates an expected excess supply at the support price of 300 million bushels. With prospective stocks at 1.8 billion bushels (current excess supply plus carryover stocks from the previous year), the social value of the stock accumulation is small, and the costs of storing and handling the surplus are in the hundreds of millions of dollars. These costs set the stage for production controls.

Acreage Reduction Programs

Production controls that directly regulate farmers' output or marketing do not exist for the grains. The approach has been tried, particularly with cotton, but proved unpopular with farmers and difficult to administer. Geographic production patterns have been shifting, yields increasing, and the many outlets for disposing of grain (including feeding one's own livestock) make it impractically costly to enforce a production limit on farmers. Instead, inducements are made to get farmers to divert land from the supported crop and hold this acreage idle or use it for certain permitted uses only.

Every acreage control program has to specify at least four elements: (1) the nature of the inducement to participate; (2) the amount paid to farmers per acre or per bushel, if any; (3) the eligible acres or bushels that each farmer has; and (4) what constitutes compliance with diversion requirements. For the grains the inducements are: first, a penalty for not participating in required acreage reductions, namely ineligibility for deficiency payments or CCC loans; second, a payment in cash or in kind for part of the required acreage diversion, or for additional voluntary diversion. The 1985 wheat program required a 30 percent diversion, with 10 of the 30 percent paid $2.70 per bushel that could have been grown on that 10 percent.

The acreage base used to calculate required diversion is established for each farm at the county office of the Agricultural Stabilization and Conservation Service (ASCS). The ASCS is the administrative agency within the USDA that has responsibility for carrying out the commodity programs. It has an office in each state plus some 3000 county offices. In addition to several thousand employees, a local committee of three persons, usually farmers, handles local appeals of decisions and other administrative matters. The county offices assign each local producer a "program yield" as well as an acreage base. They determine the amount of output, for example, bushels of wheat, on which deficiency payments are paid to farmers who qualify by idling the necessary acreage and using that acreage as required (in the 1985 wheat program, not growing any commercial crops, protecting from water or wind damage, not harvesting or grazing during the five main wheat-growing months).

An acreage-control program of this type can only be effective at controlling production if farmers choose to participate and if the participants comply with the acreage-idling requirements. The economics of participation turns on the benefits exceeding the costs. The main benefits of participation are: deficiency payments, eligibility for CCC loans, and eligibility for disaster payments (in counties where federal crop insurance is not available). The first of these is most important, by far, for most producers since the market price is typically not far from the loan rate, and in most counties federal crop insurance is available. The calculation of benefits from participation based on expected deficiency payments is

$$E(B) = (P_T - P^*)(1 - \alpha) A_0 Y_0 \qquad (3.1)$$

where P_t is the target price, P^* is higher of the loan rate or the average price received by farmers in June–October, α is the percentage of the wheat acreage based required to be idled, A_0 is the farmer's wheat acreage base, and Y_0 the program yield per acre. Consider a farmer with a 100-acre wheat base and a 36 bushel per acre yield. Since $\alpha = 0.3$ for 1985, the farmer receives payments on 70 acres or 2520 bushels. The price P^* could reasonably have been expected, and turned out to be the loan rate of $3.30. Therefore, the expected benefit from participation is ($4.38 − $3.30)(2520) = $2722.

The costs of participation can be reckoned in terms variable costs saved by not growing a crop on idled acres. For wheat, USDA estimates variable expenses (seed, fertilizer, chemicals, custom operations, fuel, repairs, and other purchased items) on a U.S. average basis as of 1984 at $55 per acre.[3] At a 36 bushel per acre normal yield for 3 years, this implies $1.53 per bushel. This figure excludes labor costs, which are estimated at $10.82 per acre. Hired labor and the owner's labor that is transferred to other activities when acreage is idled should also be counted as variable expenses. Assuming that all hired and owner's labor is a variable expense, we add $10.82 per acre or 30 cents per bushel to give total variable expenses saved by idling acreage at $1.83 per bushel not produced. Since $3.30 could by assumption have been earned had wheat been grown, the cost to the farmer of idling land is $1.47 per bushel that could have been grown. On the 30 acres diverted in our example, this is (30)(36)($1.47) = $1588, or $52.90 per acre. But this cost is reduced by the payment of $2.70 on the output of 10 acres, or 360 bushels: 360 × $2.70 = $972. The sum of costs of participation is

$$C = \alpha R A_0 - \alpha' P_d A_0 Y_0 \qquad (3.2)$$

where R is the returns to land and associated resources that the land could have earned if farmed, α' is the paid diversion percentage (0.10 in 1985), and P_d is the paid diversion per bushel that could have been produced.

Subtracting Eq. (3.2) from Eq. (3.1) to obtain up the expected net benefits of participating:

$$E(B) - C = (1.08)(0.7)(100)(36) - (0.3)(52.92)(100)$$
$$+ (0.1)(2.70)(100)(36) = \$2110$$

This amounts to $21 per base acre or 84 cents bushel actually produced.

Wheat yields vary from 10 to 20 bushels per acre in dry areas to 80 to 100 bushels per acre in the Corn Belt, so the calculations vary a lot by region. In dry areas, leaving land fallow increases its soil moisture and, hence, its productivity in the subsequent year, so the cost R is less than indicated here. This increases participation but means that output is not actually being reduced as much as the percentage of land diverted would suggest. In addition, if a farm contains fields which vary in productivity, as they often do, the farmer will rationally choose the lowest-yielding land. This further cuts the costs of participation but further reduces the program's effectiveness in controlling output.

These factors, plus the existence of nonparticipants and failure to comply (by not cutting the acreage by the required amount) mean that a 30-percent acreage-reduction program normally reduces output by a substantially smaller percentage. This phenomenon is called "slippage." The slippage coefficient is defined as:

$$1 - \frac{\% \text{ change in output}}{\% \text{ acreage reduction}} \tag{3.3}$$

This coefficient has been estimated as about 0.35 for wheat in recent years, meaning that a 30-percent acreage reduction cuts output by $30 \times 0.65 = 19$ percent. Moreover, one-third of wheat in 1985 was grown by nonparticipants, so the 30-percent program enrolled 20 percent of the land, implying a 13-percent output reduction.

In Fig. 3.1, this information is used to locate the supply curve that would be expected in the absence of the program. What we observe is acreage and yield with the program, yielding output of 2.4 billion bushels. From the earlier calculation we add 84 cents to the $3.30 loan rate to obtain a $4.14 incentive price for program participants. This gives us point A' on S', which is the industry-level marginal cost curve given the idled acreage.

While point A' is observable, the rest of the marginal cost curve is not, and it is conceptually distinct from a market supply curve. S' would be traced out experimentally by varying the target price, holding the market price constant. Three types of adjustment by producers are made as, say, the target price in Fig. 3.1 falls from its initial value. First, as the target price falls, the incentive of producers to participate declines. As fewer farmers participate, the shift in supply (horizontal difference between S' and S) declines. When P_T falls to some critical level in the neighborhood of—no lower than—the expected market price, no one participates and the curves S and S' coincide. Second, as the producer incentive price falls, it does not pay to use as much nonland inputs.

If the yields on which payments are made change with actual yield, as they have in the past, albeit not with immediate or perfect adjustment, there will be some positive response of output to increasing price even when acreage is fixed.[4] Third, as the target price falls, producers will have less incentive to keep acreage up in order to maintain a base for future years' payments, which again implies some positive supply response to price. Finally, output at point A' includes nonparticipants as well as participants. Nonparticipants would not change their behavior as the target price changes, except insofar as they plant more acreage as the target price rises in order to build a base for future payments should they decide to participate in the future.

Note that the behaviorally constrained supply curve is not the same as the constant-acreage marginal cost function. Indeed, if the first effect (declining participation) dominates, the supply response to a target price decline could be positive.

An alternative way of looking at the restricted supply function is to consider what would happen if, counter to the preceding exercise, the *market* price fell, while holding the target price constant. Nonparticipants would reduce output along their unconstrained marginal cost functions. Participants would leave output unchanged. Some nonparticipants would become participants, shifting S' to the left. All these effects imply a negative output response to a falling market price.

Which is the "correct" behavioral response curve under program constraints, the one varying the target price or the one varying the market price? Neither. Indeed, the simultaneous existence of participants and nonparticipants creates an insurmountable aggregation problem in that the former respond to the target price and the latter to the market price; supply is a function of different variables for the two groups, and even though both prices are measured on the vertical axis of Fig. 3.1, one cannot add the two supply functions horizontally. We might avoid this problem by specifying participants' supply as a function of market price. Then we get the result that, as market price rises toward the target price, participation drops to zero and S' and S coincide as before. But this time $S' = S$ at the target price level, which is clearly wrong for Fig. 3.1 (because the market price is well below the target price). This points up the problem that under a deficiency payment program with given target price, the "supply curve" shifts when the demand curve shifts! For example, if the export market strengthened and D cut S' at point A, this would cause S' to shift toward S as participation fell.

Fortunately, simulating the no-program situation involves only the elasticity of the no-program supply curve and the location of point A'. Using the estimate that at A' we have $S' = 0.87S$ generating S as shown in Fig. 3.1.

Summarizing the discussion, we locate demand and supply curves under the 1985 wheat program by observing price and quantity demanded at point B, and production under the program constraints at 2.4 billion bushels. Then estimating the producers' incentive price gives us point A' on the supply curve, and estimating the program-generated shift in supply gives the conjectural supply curve with no program at point A. To simulate the no-program price and output, we use estimates of supply and demand elasticities to extend S and D to their intersection at point E.

Algebraically, we can find the demand curve by writing the constant elasticity form with the price and quantity at point B:

$$Q_0 = K_1 P^{-0.5}$$
$$2.1 = K_1(3.30)^{-0.5} \qquad K_1 = 3.815 \qquad (3.4)$$

Similarly, for the supply curve we have:

$$2.8 = K_2(4.14)^{0.3} \qquad K_2 = 1.828 \qquad (3.5)$$

Equating supply and demand to find Q_e and P_e is done most easily by taking logs to get linear equations:

$$\log (3.815) - 0.5 \log P_e = \log (1.828) + 0.3 \log P_e$$
$$1.339 - 0.5 \log P_e = 0.603 + 0.3 \log P_e$$
$$0.736 = 0.8 \log P_e$$
$$0.920 = \log P_e$$
$$2.51 = P_e$$

This implies equilibrium output of 2.41 billion bushels. Thus, at point E, $P = 2.51$ and $Q = 2.41$.

Assuming the comparative statics of the program and no-program situation as depicted in Fig. 3.1 is correct, what are the gains, costs, and deadweight losses? Using the crude surplus measures, consumers lose from the program, paying $3.30 per bushel instead of $2.51, a cost to them of 79 cents on an average of 2.25 billion bushels, or $2.0 billion. Taxpayers pay $1.08 times 2.4 million bushels or $2.59 million.

The producers' gains and social (deadweight) losses from the program are trickier to analyze. Output under the program turns out to be just slightly less than without it: 2.40 compared to 2.41 billion bushels. Why? Because the acreage controls almost exactly offset the increased production incentive caused by the deficiency payments. From our discussion of a simple price-support program in Chap. 2, recall that deadweight losses were generated because the programs generated either too much or too little output. Indeed, if the program attempted to achieve a producer price of $4.14 by production controls alone, the deadweight loss would be the diagonally hatched area to the left of E ($950 million). Similarly, a pure price guarantee with no production controls would generate the diagonally hatched deadweight-loss area to the right of E ($510 million). Imposing both controls at once generates the "correct" output and eliminates both areas. This is a kind of second-best policy; given one distortion in a market, an additional distortion need not increase social losses but can be chosen to reduce them.

Still, it is not the case that social losses have been eliminated, for the whole story has not been told yet. There would be an almost zero deadweight loss if the producers' gains were the difference between the $4.38 target price and the $2.51 no-program price times the 2.4 billion bushel output. Then the producers' gains would be $4.49 billion. This falls short of the consumers' and taxpayers' losses, calculated above as $4.73 billion, by $240 million (the triangular area BCE). However, the accounting is not yet complete. Producers' gains have been overstated because the costs of leaving acreage idle have not been counted. The relevant calculations have already been done in estimating the net gain from participating, which turned out to be $4.14 per bushel. Thus the area between $4.38 and $4.14 and to the left of S', which adds up to $580 million, is also part of the deadweight loss; it measures the opportunity returns (rental value in best alternative use) of the idled land. Moreover, there is another possible cost to producers that the earlier calculations did not consider. It results from the incentive, assuming a farmer's program yield can be increased by boosting his actual yield, to use more fertilizer, pesticides and so forth, when the program exists. The extent to which this occurs determines the slope of the restricted supply curve S'. This means that the marginal cost of producing wheat is higher because of the program, and this increase is borne by producers, so must be subtracted from producers' gains. Graphically, it is the shaded area between S and S', which amounts to about $300 million as drawn.[5] Thus the producers' gains have been reduced from $4.49 billion to $4.49 − $0.58 − $0.30 = $3.61 billion.

There remains another complication in the calculation of social loss, caused by the loan program and CCC stocks. Suppose the government had not acquired these stocks, which could be accomplished by keeping the wheat program intact except for reducing the loan rate to $2.50 or less (indeed, that was what was done in the 1986 wheat program). Then consumers would have purchased more at the lower market price, and the area BCE would not have been lost. Moreover, when the CCC is acquiring stocks, we have to consider the cost to the government of buying and storing the surplus wheat, less the expected gains from selling the wheat later. This gets into complex issues of dynamics (events followed through time) that our comparative statics approach cannot handle. It is possible that stored grain could be sold in years of shortage to yield a net social gain, as mentioned earlier and treated in detail in Chap. 10. For the present let us suppose—as seems to be the case—that the 1985 wheat program parameters are set at levels that involve year-in, year-out buildup of stocks, so that the CCC acquisitions must be distributed as food aid or otherwise disposed of while the demand and supply picture remains as shown. The value of grain thus distributed can be taken as the market clearing price for that quantity, that is, about $2.50 per bushel, so that the economy gets back *BCE*, and the social losses are just the transaction costs of the government's buying, storing, and distributing the surplus. This is the optimistic scenario. The pessimistic scenario is that the surplus wheat's value is essentially exhausted by the transaction costs, wastage, and disruption of markets into which surpluses are sent. Then, the social loss might be the entire CCC outlay on its acquired wheat; graphically this is the rectangle between 2.1 and 2.4 billion bushels up to the $3.30 loan rate ($1.0 billion), and even more if storage costs are high enough.

That these costs are in fact thought to be high is apparent in government's sometimes desperate grasping for program mechanisms to dispose of CCC stocks. In fiscal 1985, CCC donations amounted to $2.5 billion (valued at CCC acquisition cost), mostly for dairy products distributed domestically to the needy. For the grains, an important mechanism in the 1980s has been PIK programs in which CCC stocks are used to pay producers instead of cash. PIK payments were used in 1983 as the main element of the largest U.S. acreage reduction program ever, in which 77 million acres (20 percent of U.S. cropland) was idled. The wheat program used PIK payments for acreage control in 1983, 1984, and 1986. This has come to be, probably, a relatively efficient surplus disposal mechanism, so that the distributed commodities are not stored for long, indeed may still be under loan, and can be valued at roughly the market price of grain. Note, however, that this approach cannot work while maintaining a loan rate as high as in Fig. 3.1 relative to the market-clearing price for annual production, else the distributed commodities would recirculate into CCC stocks again. Thus, in the 1985 program, with a high loan rate and no PIK, we should count at least area *BCE* as a part of the program's deadweight loss.

Adding up the social costs, it is no longer clear that the 1985 wheat program as depicted has the second-best property tentatively attributed to it earlier as compared to a simple production control or subsidy. However, before being tempted to draw practical implications or recommendations from this extended exercise on the wheat program, further complications must be considered that can make a big difference in social cost calculations. Unfortunately, some of them are quite difficult to deal with, which is why economic analysis of these programs is still a research area rather than a straightforward field of application of cut-and-dried methods.

First, it is necessary to bring in the nonparticipants, which account for about one-third of 1985 wheat production. Although discussed with reference to the restricted supply curve, the calculations centered on Fig. 3.1 have ignored them. Their presence signals a phenomenon that complicates almost every supply–demand analysis of farm programs: the heterogeneity of producers. Heterogeneity (in the sense of different costs of production, crop mix, off-farm opportunities, weather, and soil conditions) is not a problem in studying many supply and demand issues because we can assume that however different people's circumstances may be, they all respond to the same market price. (Of course, if people are heterogeneous in the sense of some of them not maximizing profits, say, there is more analytical work to be done even here.) The problems arise in policy analysis because when heterogeneity leads to some people participating in programs and others not, we have different people facing different price incentives. In the wheat example, nonparticipants do not respond to the $4.14 price, but to the expected market price. As mentioned earlier, this means that we really cannot draw an aggregate market supply curve that expresses output as a function of the (adjusted) target price. We need a model that first explains the supply behavior of participants, as shown in Fig. 3.1, and nonparticipants as a function of the market price. We have to have both specified before the demand side can be brought in. And because the market price depends on what both participants and nonparticipants do, we have to consider the behavior of all parties simultaneously. This can, in principle, be accomplished with a mathematical model, but there does not seem to be a good way to provide a graphic depiction. For purposes of calculating gains and losses once we have the constrained market equilibrium observations, as we do in points A' and B of Fig. 3.1, the calculation of gains and losses can be readily adjusted for nonparticipants. Thus, the $2.59 billion taxpayer cost is reduced by one-third to $1.74 billion when a third of output is produced by nonparticipants, and the receipts of producers are reduced correspondingly.

A second complication involves identifying the supply function relevant for policy analysis when there exist random disturbances, for example, due to weather, that influence output. A dynamic model incorporating these disturbances is necessary for a full treatment. If producers are risk averse, a guaranteed price, by stabilizing receipts, will shift the supply function. This complication is addressed in Chap. 10. But even in a static model, the question arises of how transitory yield variations should be handled. For example, in 1983 the PIK program idled 20 percent of cropland acres but output was down by closer to 30 percent because drought cut yields. Therefore if we use ex post output data to generate a curve like S' in Fig. 3.1, we would be accurately depicting the actual output corresponding to that year's expected price, but we would not be accurately depicting the effect of PIK. Instead of the ex post output, we should use the ex ante supply curve, showing output that should normally be expected, given the production incentive, at the time the crop is being planted. This creates complications because the ex ante supply must be estimated and cannot be located from an ex post observation of the year's output as we did in Fig. 3.1. The best simple approximation may be to multiply planted acres times trend yield to obtain the point like A'. The 1985 wheat crop was apparently not far from trend yield, and in such cases the problem may not be important. But in general, it complicates the analysis of program effects.

To see what difference it makes, consider the likely error in the assumption that 1985 wheat yield was actually at the trend level. A summary history of recent U.S. average wheat yield per acre is:

1970–1974	31.0 bushels per acre
1975–1979	31.3
1976–1980	32.0
1981	34.5
1982	35.5
1983	39.4
1984	38.8
1985	37.5

It could be that trend or normal yield has accelerated in the mid-1980s so the 1985 yield is actually below trend. Suppose that the true ex ante yield, given economic expectations as of spring 1985, was 5 percent above the actual ex post yield, that is, 39.4 bushels per acre instead of 37.5. Then the ex ante supply curve should have been specified with point A at 2.94 rather than 2.8 billion bushels, and the coefficient K_2 which locates the supply curve should have been 1.920 instead of 1.828. Solving for the no-program price under this altered assumption gives a no-program price of $2.36. This is 15 cents (6 percent) below the no-program price simulated earlier and makes a difference of $360 million in estimated producer gains and consumer losses from the program.

The simulation of alternative outcomes by varying key parameters over the range of our ignorance about them is called sensitivity analysis. It is a key step in useful policy analysis, not only because it gives us a feeling for the potential error in our estimate of program effects, but also because it helps in determining what parameters are important and what are unimportant in simulated results of policy changes.

A third complication concerns the length of run to which an estimate of policy effects pertains. The comparative statics may be quite different for the no-program situation one year as compared to 10 years after the policy is changed. Of course, comparative statics for a 10-year period are quite artificial in the sense that so many no-program changes are likely over this length of time that the effect of abandoning a particular program now are likely to be swamped by them. Nevertheless, it is often of interest to assess the likely consequences of a policy change, holding other things constant, beyond the initial year in which the change is made. This is accomplished in the context of a simple supply–demand model by using long-run, typically larger, elasticities of supply and demand. This can often make a substantial difference, but econometric evidence on long-run elasticities is so sketchy and incredible (not that it is entirely convincing for short-run elasticities) that about all we can do is sensitivity analysis over a fairly wide range, not neglecting the possibility of elasticities approaching infinity for many commodities.

An assumption that we should not neglect to examine is that the elasticities of supply and demand are fixed parameters, i.e., that the curves have constant elasticity form. This is a natural and simple approach for a mathematical model, especially when small changes are considered, as in Chap. 2. When we move relatively long distances along functions, however, it is necessary to be careful about assuming constant elasticities. On this point, graphic analysis has a definite advantage over an algebraic model. We can typically draw functional forms to reflect intuitions or observations about supply and demand (for example, that supply is quite elastic over a range of output but then becomes inelastic as a capacity constraint is approached) more easily than appropriate functional forms can be expressed algebraically. The flexible functional forms that have such promise econometrically in letting the data speak for themselves are quite useless for expressing particular prior notions about functional form.

A fourth complication involves the economics of the operation of programs as opposed to the problems in specifying the supply–demand structure that we have been discussing. The fact is that the CCC loan program does not support the market price at exactly the loan rate. For example, while the 1985 loan rate for wheat is \$3.30, the average price received by farmers in the 1985–1986 marketing year was nearer \$3.10 per bushel. How can this come about, when the CCC stands ready to pay \$3.30? Why would anyone sell at \$3.10? Even with many nonparticipants, the CCC would be expected to acquire enough of the participants' wheat to hold the market price up to the loan level, because participants would keep turning wheat over to the CCC until the quantity remaining cleared the market at that level. One source of nonexact support is simply a matter of calculation. The \$3.30 support price is a U.S. average, but most states' loan rates are above or below that average. Similarly, the U.S. average farm price is constructed from state average which can vary substantially. For example, in 1981 when the U.S. average farm price was \$3.66 per bushel, state averages ranged from \$3.15 (New York) to \$4.28 (Arizona). It is possible that different weights in the averaging for loan rates and farm prices, and different setting of the state loan rate relative to market prices, could make the U.S. average farm price lower than the average loan rate even though the farm price was actually at or above the loan rate in every state. It is difficult for the government to set state differentials because some states vary from year to year in local market conditions relative to the national average. For example, in 1980 the Maryland wheat price averaged 3 percent above the national figure, while in 1981 the Maryland price was 11 percent below the national average price.

Apart from these problems, there are economic reasons why a farmer would accept a market price lower than the loan rate even if eligible for a CCC loan. In order to receive the loan, the producer must put the loan in approved storage facilities and pay storage costs. A cash offer at a little less than the loan rate might be preferable.

Whatever the reason, a farm price less than the loan rate means that the calculations of gains to wheat producers are not accurate. Participating producers who do not place grain under loan receive the deficiency payment plus a market price averaging about 20 cents per bushel less than the loan rate. Thus, producer gains have been overstated earlier by about $400 million.

A fifth complication arises from the fact, so far neglected, that much of the wheat demand, about 45 percent in 1985–1986, is accounted for by exports. The curve D_d in Fig. 3.1 represents domestic demand, the remaining horizontal distance between D and D_d at each price showing the foreign demand for U.S. wheat. This diagram combines information in the "instigator" and "trade" diagrams in Fig. 2.7B. The equivalent of Fig. 3.1 could have been shown in Fig. 2.7 by adding quantity demanded (D) at each price from the trade sector to domestic demand in the instigator country, generating the total demand curve D_t in the left-hand panel in Fig. 2.6B. Dropping explicit representation of the sources of export demand in the rest of the world does not omit anything of importance for analyzing the U.S. policies, and indeed it is easier to see the deficiency payment's effect on market price as the intersection of D_t with the vertical line S'. As long as the function D_t is correctly drawn, the comparative statics of P and Q are unaffected by the existence of the exports as a component of demand. But the larger the share of exports in demand, the less likely we are to have an estimate of either the elasticity or ex ante position of D in which we can have confidence.

More important for assessing gains and losses is the fact that the counting of losses to foreign consumers may be quite different than for domestic consumer losses. In particular, a country is likely to be more favorably inclined to production controls, other things equal, if the consequent transfers of income are from foreign consumers to its own producers. This topic is important enough to repay detailed study, which will come in Chap. 11.

A sixth complication is that markets for many agricultural commodities are interrelated as mentioned earlier. We will not adequately analyze program alternatives for wheat if we fail to incorporate the consequences in related commodity markets. To provide an example of multicommodity policy analysis, consider corn and soybeans along with wheat. The assumed interactions are specified by cross-elasticities, which are difficult to estimate but have been stated in recent literature at values in the neighborhood of the following: On the demand side, in addition to the own-price elasticity of demand for wheat of -0.5, there is an elasticity of demand for wheat with respect to a change in the price of corn of 0.2. For corn, $\eta = -0.6$ and there is a cross-elasticity with respect to the price of wheat of 0.02 and with respect to soybeans of 0.1. For soybeans, $\eta = -0.7$ with a cross-elasticity with respect to the price of corn of 0.2. All other cross elasticities are assumed equal to zero.

On the supply side, the own-price supply elasticity of wheat is 0.5, the cross-elasticity with respect to the price of corn is -0.1 and with respect to soybeans, -0.05. For corn, the own-price elasticity is 0.4, the cross-elasticity with respect to wheat is -0.05, and with respect to soybeans, -0.2. For soybean supply, the own-price elasticity is 0.8 with a cross-elasticity with respect to the price of corn of -0.5 and respect to wheat of -0.05. (Wheat–soybean interaction is a particular problem because the increasing importance of double cropping these crops in the past 10 years should have introduced complimentarily—positive cross-elasticity of supply—for some southern producers while elsewhere the two crops would be substitutes competing for land.)

We locate the supply and demand functions for corn, which has a program similar to that of wheat, in the same manner as in Fig. 3.1. For soybeans, we equate supply and demand at ex ante market-clearing, no-program prices. The resulting supply–demand relationships are summarized as

$$
\begin{aligned}
\textit{Demand:} \quad Q_1 &= 3.11\ P_1^{-0.5}\ P_2^{0.2} \\
Q_2 &= 10.2\ P_1^{0.02}\ P_2^{-0.6}\ P_3^{0.1} \\
Q_3 &= 4.94\ P_2^{0.2}\ P_3^{-0.7} \\
\textit{Supply:} \quad Q_1 &= 1.63\ P_1^{0.5}\ P_2^{-0.1}\ P_3^{-0.05} \\
Q_2 &= 7.80\ P_1^{-0.05}\ P_2^{0.4}\ P_3^{-0.2} \\
Q_3 &= 0.94\ P_1^{-0.05}\ P_2^{-0.5}\ P_3^{0.8}
\end{aligned}
\tag{3.6}
$$

where the subscripts 1, 2, and 3 represent wheat, corn, and soybeans, respectively. The constant terms are chosen so that the supply and demand functions pass through the points as specified in Fig. 3.1 for wheat, but for soybeans, with no wedges created by policy, both supply and demand pass through the point $P_3 = \$5.10$ per bushel, $Q_3 = 1.9$ billion bushels.

The no-program equilibrium is simulated by solving this system of equations (which is linear in logarithms) for the prices and quantities that clear the three markets simultaneously. The resulting prices and quantities are shown in column 1 of Table 3.1. As compared to the market prices under the 1985 programs of \$3.20 for wheat, \$2.55 for corn, and \$5.10 for soybeans, the simulated no-program prices are down 60 cents (19 percent), 25 cents (10 percent), and 59 cents (12 percent), respectively.

The price of soybeans is estimated to fall by almost as large a percentage as directly supported crops. There are two reasons why soybean growers benefit from the corn and wheat programs. First, the higher market prices caused by the loan program increase the demand for soybeans as a substitute in feeds. Second, the target prices draw some land out of soybeans and into grains, notwithstanding the requirement that some of that land must be held idle in acreage-reduction programs. Thus, the grain programs increase soybean demand and reduce supply. The gains to soybean producers as compared to grains are less than the market price effects indicate, however, because of the lack of deficiency payments on soybeans.

Table 3.1   Simulation of U.S. Grain Policies, 1985

	(0) Base case (1985 policy)	No-program alternatives			
		(1) Short-run Assumptions base elasticity	(2) Elasticity Pessimism	(3) 10% demand increase	(4) Elasticity optimism (long run)
U.S. farm price ($ per bushel):					
1. Wheat	3.20	2.60	2.34	3.01	3.03
2. Corn	2.55	2.20	1.88	2.54	2.47
3. Soybeans	5.10	4.51	4.69	5.17	4.90
U.S. output (billion bushels):					
1. Wheat	2.4	2.3	2.2	2.4	2.2
2. Corn	8.0	7.5	7.7	7.7	7.8
3. Soybeans	1.9	2.0	2.0	2.1	2.0
Loss of producers (billion dollars):					
1. Wheat	—	− 3.6	− 3.9	− 2.7	− 1.9
2. Corn	—	− 5.5	− 6.4	− 2.8	− 3.0
3. Soybeans	—	− 1.2	− 0.8	+ 0.1	− 0.4
Total		− 10.3	− 11.1	− 5.4	− 5.3
Gains to consumers and taxpayers:					
1. Wheat	—	3.5	3.5	3.1	2.2
2. Corn	—	6.9	7.9	4.9	5.3
3. Soybeans	—	0.7	0.4	− 0.0	0.3
Total		11.1	11.8	7.9	7.8
Net gain to U.S.		0.8	0.7	2.5	2.5

The net gains simulated are shown in the lower half of Table 3.1. Producers of these commodities lose $10.3 billion with an end to the program. This is a rough producers' surplus calculation based on price changes times average (of with and without programs) output, minus costs of idled acreage as discussed earlier. However, consumers and taxpayers gain $11.1 billion. Therefore the United States as a whole is better off by $0.8 billion annually, the deadweight loss of the 1985 programs from the U.S. aggregate viewpoint.

In an attempt to judge the consequences of some of the many conjectural assumptions that had to be made to accomplish the simulated no-program situation, consider some sensitivity tests.

Elasticity Pessimism

Some have found export demand elasticities even lower than those used in the equations above, basically reflecting observations on the unresponsiveness of U.S. exports to price in the past decade or so. In Table 3.1, column 2, the own-price elasticities of demand for wheat, corn, and soybeans are −0.3,

−0.4, and −0.6, respectively, and the cross price elasticities are cut in half. The own-price supply elasticities are reduced to 0.3, 0.3, and 0.5. These are substantial reductions but the effects on prices and farmers' benefits are not as dramatic as might have been expected. One reason is the soybean interaction; with low cross-elasticities, soybean producers do not gain as much from the programs, so they don't lose as much when programs end.

Demand Optimism or Pessimism

On the other hand, the simulations so far may have been unduly pessimistic with respect to the weakness of demand. Export demand projections were reduced substantially during 1985, and the simulations locate the demand function at their lowest points up to that time, e.g., 1 billion bushels of wheat exports and 1.6 billion bushels of corn, down about 30 percent and 10 percent, respectively, from 1984 levels, even with lower nominal prices in 1985. Perhaps 1985 conditions were abnormally low, and the weakening dollar and other factors mean that normal (expected) demand is really higher. To simulate this possibility, we increase the constant terms in the demand equations of (3.6). Column 3 shows simulated no-program prices with demand 10 percent higher for all three crops. In this scenario, the no-program market prices are much closer to the 1985 loan rates, but still below them.

On the other hand, the export markets weakened still further in 1986, and perhaps this level of demand will continue. To simulate an outcome under this scenario, impose a 10 per demand decrease by reducing the constant terms appropriately. This generates prices even lower than those of column 2 of Table 3.1.

Long-Run Elasticities

Consider that the United States cannot influence world prices nearly so strongly for any long period because the price effects are swamped by even small percentage consumption and production adjustments elsewhere in the world. Not to go too far in this direction, let the own-price elasticity of demand for U.S. wheat, corn, and soybeans be −3, −2, and −2 respectively. Table 3.1, column 4, shows quite small market price effects of eliminating price supports, with wheat down 17 cents (5 percent), corn 21 cents (7 percent), and soybeans 20 cents (4 percent). Producers still lose $5 billion, however, mainly because of the loss of deficiency payments. Note that the net gain to the United States is highest in the long-run case. The reason is that with inelastic demand, a substantial fraction of the costs of higher price support is borne by foreign consumers, especially for wheat, so much so that under "elasticity pessimism" the wheat program generates a net gain to the United States. (This gives pause in identifying low elasticity with pessimism, in that the inelastic case transfers the most money to producers at the least cost to the nation.)

The comparative-static simulations of no programs can be summarized as follows. In the corn market, supply shifts to the right when acreage controls are lifted, and we move along the demand curve as loan rate falls and along the supply curve as the target price falls. But in addition, the supply curve of corn shifts to the right when the price of wheat falls; the coefficient of -0.05 means that the 22-percent decline in the wheat price increases the supply of corn by 1.1. percent (about 90 million bushels). Similarly, the 22 percent fall in the price of wheat reduces the demand for corn by 0.4 percent (about 30 million bushels) according to the 0.02 cross-elasticity used. The soybean market affects corn as well as being affected by elimination of the corn program. Soybean demand decreases and supply increases, and the resulting fall in price of soybeans of 17 percent increases the supply of corn by 3 percent and reduces the demand for corn by 2 percent. So we need to take the soybean–corn interactions into account even if our sole interest is in the corn market.

There are an indefinitely large number of simulations that could be undertaken for the purpose of sensitivity analysis. Knowing which ones to undertake requires an element of judgment that depends on familiarity and understanding of the market being studied, the econometric evidence on elasticities, and the policy issue of concern. For example, in the context of U.S. trade negotiations with the European Community, a contentious issue is whether U.S. farm programs have the effects on world markets that an export subsidy would. The EEC claims that they do, that U.S. programs are world-price decreasing. From our Chap. 2 discussion, we know that target prices are world-price decreasing, but acreage set-asides and CCC loans (which are equivalent to government purchases) are not. So it is an empirical question whether the EEC's claim is correct or not. In Table 3.1 we find less wheat and corn being produced with no programs than in the base case with 1985 programs. Thus, it appears that supply response to target-price incentives outweighs the effects of set-asides, so that U.S. programs are output increasing. But the programs are not price depressing. The base-case prices are higher over the whole range of assumptions. The CCC loan program keeps the larger supplies off the market. So the EEC's case turns on what the government does with stocks it controls. If it dumps them on the market, then the program will be world-price depressing, like an export subsidy; but as long as the CCC support price is maintained, the policy is world-price increasing. (This is why the Europeans were concerned with the CCC support-price cuts of 1986–1987.)

The simulations of Table 3.1 are crude (although no cruder than some of the evidence actually used in analyzing policy questions) but the discussion shows where econometric effort must be focused to answer the relevant questions. In judging the EEC's complaint we need to know with as much precision as possible what the producer incentive price really is, the elasticity of supply in response to it under program constraints, and the slippage in acreage controls. And we need to know what will be done with CCC stocks. Knowing the value of the elasticity of export or domestic demand is less important. For other questions, though, the elasticity of demand is the key parameter.

ALGEBRAIC SIMULATION

For some problems, it is simpler and the economics are clearer if we derive expressions like those of Chap. 2 that express, say, the price of corn as a function of a production control parameter, i.e., $\%\Delta P_2/\%\Delta C_2$, where C_2 is the control level. In order to simplify the derivation, let the cross-elasticities with respect to wheat in Eqs. (3.6) be zero, so we only have to worry about corn–soybeans interactions. But we will use algebraic parameters rather than numerical values to obtain a more general result (not dependent on particular parameter values). Dropping wheat from Eqs. (3.6), we have

Demand for corn: $Q_2 = K_2 P_2^{\eta_{22}} P_3^{\eta_{23}}$ (3.7)

Demand for soybeans: $Q_3 = K_3 P_2^{\eta_{22}} P_2^{\eta_{33}}$ (3.8)

Supply of corn: $Q_2 = C_2 P_2^{\epsilon_{22}} P_3^{\epsilon_{23}}$ (3.9)

Supply of soybeans: $Q_3 = C_3 P_2^{\epsilon_{32}} P_3^{\epsilon_{33}}$ (3.10)

where η_{ij} and ϵ_{ij} are the elasticities of quantity demanded or supplied of commodity i with respect to P_j. The analysis of a change in corn acreage controls is undertaken by differentiating with respect to C_2. This is readily accomplished by taking logs to obtain linear equations. There are four equations in four unknowns: P_2, P_3, Q_2, and Q_3. The differentiated equations, with primes denoting logs, can be solved by first equating (3.7) to (3.9), and (3.8) to (4.0):

$$\eta_{22}\frac{dP_2'}{dC_2'} + \eta_{23}\frac{dP_3'}{dC_2'} = 1 + \epsilon_{22}\frac{dP_2'}{dC_2'} + \epsilon_{23}\frac{dP_3'}{dC_2'} \qquad (3.11)$$

$$\eta_{32}\frac{dP_2'}{aC_2'} + \eta_{33}\frac{dP_3'}{dC_2'} = \epsilon_{32}\frac{dP_2'}{dC_2'} + \epsilon_{33}\frac{dP_3'}{dC_2'} \qquad (3.12)$$

This system can be rearranged and expressed in matrix form as

$$\begin{bmatrix} \eta_{22} - \epsilon_{22} & \eta_{23} - \epsilon_{23} \\ \eta_{32} - \epsilon_{32} & \eta_{33} - \epsilon_{33} \end{bmatrix} \begin{bmatrix} \dfrac{dP_2'}{dC_2'} \\ \dfrac{dP_3'}{dC_2} \end{bmatrix} = \begin{bmatrix} 1 \\ 0 \end{bmatrix} \qquad (3.13)$$

Applying Cramer's rule to solve for dP_2'/dC_2':

$$\frac{dP_2'}{dC_2'} = \frac{\eta_{33} - \epsilon_{33}}{(\eta_{22} - \epsilon_{22})(\eta_{33} - \epsilon_{33}) - (\eta_{32} - \epsilon_{32})(\eta_{23} - \epsilon_{23})} \qquad (3.14)$$

If all the cross-elasticities are zero, Eq. (3.14) becomes

$$\frac{dP_2'}{dC_2'} = \frac{1}{\eta_{22} - \epsilon_{22}} \tag{3.15}$$

a result like those of Chap. 2 for a simple supply–demand model. Using the values of Eqs. (3.6) we have

$$\frac{dP_2'}{dC_2'} = \frac{-0.7 - 0.8}{(-0.6 - 0.4)(-0.7 - 0.8) - (0.2 + 0.5)(0.1 + 0.2)}$$

$$= \frac{-1.5}{(-1)(-1.5) - (0.7)(0.3)} = \frac{-1.5}{1.5 - 0.21} = -1.16$$

Recalling that the primes indicates logs, these expressions show the percentage change in P_2 resulting from a given percentage change (horizontal shift) in the supply curve. Thus, the calculation indicates that a 10-percent leftwards shift in corn supply due to an acreage control program (that idles perhaps 15 percent of cropland) will increase the price of corn by 11.6 percent. Note that the same corn price elasticities in 3.10 would indicate a 10-percent corn price rise.

Price as Policy Instrument

Consider a policy that fixes the price of corn to producers and consumers without production controls, for example, by government purchases. To analyze this policy, replace Eq. (3.7) by the legislated price $\hat{P}_2$. The comparative statics then consists of varying $\hat{P}_2$. The result for output in the single-product case would be simply be $dQ'_2/d\hat{P}_2 = \epsilon_{22}$, that is, if $\hat{P}_2$ rises by 10 percent, $\hat{Q}_2$ rises by 10 percent times the elasticity of supply of corn.

To analyze soybean interactions, differentiate 3.8 to 3.10 with respect to $\hat{P}_2$. Equating 3.8 and 3.10 eliminates $\hat{Q}_3$, so the differentials constitute a system of two equations similar to Eq. (3.13), but different in key details, namely:

$$\begin{bmatrix} 1 & -\epsilon_{23} \\ 0 & \eta_{33} - \epsilon_{33} \end{bmatrix} \begin{bmatrix} \dfrac{dQ_2'}{d\hat{P}_2} \\ \dfrac{dP_3'}{d\hat{P}_2} \end{bmatrix} = \begin{bmatrix} \epsilon_{22} \\ \epsilon_{32} - \eta_{32} \end{bmatrix} \tag{3.16}$$

Solving for both variables:

$$\frac{dP_3'}{d\hat{P}_2} = \frac{\epsilon_{32} - \eta_{32}}{\eta_{33} - \epsilon_{33}} \tag{3.17}$$

$$\frac{dQ_2'}{d\hat{P}_2} = \frac{\epsilon_{22}(\eta_{33} - \epsilon_{33}) + \epsilon_{23}(\epsilon_{32} - \eta_{32})}{\eta_{33} - \epsilon_{33}} \tag{3.18}$$

$$= \epsilon_{22} + \epsilon_{23}\left(\frac{\epsilon_{32} - \eta_{32}}{\eta_{33} - \epsilon_{33}}\right)$$

Equation (3.17) shows the percentage change in the price of soybeans resulting from a 1-percent change in the (legislated) market price of corn. With the parameter values we have been assuming, $\%\Delta P_3/\%\Delta P_2 = (-0.5 -0.2)/(-0.7-0.8) = 0.46$. Note that as long as own and cross-elasticities have opposite signs, a rise in the corn support price increases the soybean price.

Equation (3.18) can be simplified by substituting from Eq. (3.17), obtaining

$$\frac{\%\Delta Q_2}{\%\Delta \hat{P}_2} = \epsilon_{22} + \epsilon_{23}\left(\frac{\%\Delta P_3}{\%\Delta \hat{P}_2}\right) \tag{3.19}$$

This result means that the full effect of changing the price of corn on the output of corn (taking into account adjustment in the soybean market) is smaller than would be estimated from the own-price elasticity of supply of corn. Using our parameter values, $\%\Delta Q_2/\%\Delta \hat{P} = 0.4 - 0.2 (0.46) = 0.308$. This expression can be called the multimarket (or "total," from the usage of Buse[6]) own-price elasticity of supply. If the commodities have the normal own-price elasticities and are gross substitutes in production and consumption ($\epsilon_{ij} < 0$, $\eta_{ij} > 0$), then the total elasticities are nearer zero than the ordinary partial elasticities which hold other commodity prices constant. Since policy changes do not hold other prices constant, when substitution between commodities in either consumption or production is important, we should use total rather than partial elasticities in comparative statics.

NUMERICAL SIMULATION OF NONLINEAR SUPPLY–DEMAND SYSTEMS

As in Chap. 2, algebraic expressions aid in the analysis of the consequences of changes in a single policy instrument. Note also that because the discussion uses derivatives, Eq. (3.14) is approximately correct for small changes even without the log-linear functional form. But to analyze large changes in several instruments simultaneously, as was done in the earlier analysis of the 1985 act, it is preferable to simulate the supply–demand system itself. This can only be done readily for linear or log-linear supply and demand equations, as in Eqs. (3.6). If the equations do not have constant elasticities or slopes, it will be much more difficult to simulate the system mathematically under alternative policies. In a single-market case, one can proceed with graphic analysis with any functional form that can be drawn; but with multimarket interactions, the graphic approach no longer works.

In assessing effects of big changes in policy, it is important to have flexibility in functional form on the supply side because neither a linear nor a log-linear equation makes economic sense. The predominance of empirical evidence indicates that, for particular commodities or agriculture as an aggregate, supply is inelastic in the neighborhood of market prices. This means that, if linear, the supply function cuts the horizontal (quantity) axis, which implies that some output is produced even at a zero price. This is absurd in a long-run context, and only slightly less so in the short run. A log-linear (constant elasticity) equation is only slightly less problematical in that it passes through the origin. We expect in any realistic assessment a supply "choke" price below which the commodity is no longer produced. But to get to such a point we need a functional form which changes from inelastic at normal prices (and increasingly inelastic in the short run as capacity constraints come into play) to elastic at some lower price range.

On the demand side, too, it is important to be able to work with nonlinear equations because some of the most common and important problems to be analyzed involve them. Often beliefs about demand functions for U.S. crops are expressed by stating that demand is composed of two additive components, domestic and foreign, with different elasticities. For example, assume the elasticity of demand for domestic rice is -0.5 and for exported rice is -3.0. If these components have constant elasticities, we can write the demand functions as

$$Q_x = K_4 P^{-3.0} \qquad Q_d = K_5 P^{-0.5}$$
$$Q = Q_x + Q_d = K_4 P^{-3.0} + K_5 P^{-0.5}$$

If we make this equation part of a system, we cannot solve for equilibrium price using linear solution methods because no simple transformation will make this equation linear.

Sometimes such equations can be solved algebraically, but with fast-working computers available the easiest way is to use iterative search methods to find market-clearing prices. Let us consider the rice example using 1985 data. We have about half of the 120 million hundredweights (cwt.) marketed through exports and half consumed domestically, so $Q_x = 60$ and $Q_d = 60$. The farm price is \$8.25 per cwt. Solving for the constant terms as earlier, we find $K_4 = 33,691$ and $K_5 = 172.3$, so the demand function for U.S. rice is

$$Q = 33,691\, P^{-3.0} + 172.3\, P^{-0.5} \qquad (3.20)$$

The supply function is

$$Q = 89.5\, P^{0.25} \qquad (3.21)$$

using the elasticity of supply estimated at 0.25 from Langley (1984), and estimates that the producer incentive price (adjusted target price) to get the 136 million cwt. observed in 1985 was \$11.00 per cwt. and that without acreage controls supply would have been 20 percent larger.

Equating (3.15) and (3.16) to solve for the no-program P_e we have

$$- 89.5\, P_e^{0.25} + 33{,}691\, P_e^{-3.0} + 172.3\, P_e^{-0.5} = 0$$

To find the solution for P_e we begin with an arbitrary guess. Since P_e should be less than the support price of \$8.25, try $P_e = 5$. The left-hand side is 213. At this price demand is greater than supply (because the demand components have positive signs and supply negative as the equation is set up). Therefore, P_e must be higher to clear the market. How much should P be raised for the next attempt? This is the key issue in any iterative solution process (given that there is a solution and the iterative process will find it). What we need to be efficient in solving the equation is an idea of how fast excess demand declines as P rises. This is given by the slope of the function, i.e., its derivative. The derivative, evaluated at $P = 5$, is -175. This suggests that raising P_e by $213/175 = 1.22$ would approximately reduce excess supply to zero (exactly if the functions were linear). Therefore, we try again, i.e. iterate, with $P = 6.22$.

The value of $P = 6.22$ yields excess demand of 68. The derivative at 6.22 is -80. This suggests that we increase P by a further $68/80 = 0.85$, i.e., to 7.07. Evaluating the equation at 7.07 yields excess demand of 16. Excess demand is much smaller. Two more iterations give us the result $P_e = \$7.37$ per cwt., implying equilibrium with 147 million cwt. produced, of which 84 million cwt. is exported and 63 million cwt. is domestically consumed (Fig. 3.2). This procedure for finding the no-program equilibrium, known as the Newton-Raphson method, is not as neat as solving linear equations, but it is readily accomplished for the functional forms typically used in supply–demand analysis and allows us to be more realistic in our specification.[7]

The next step is to consider a system of related markets with nonlinear demand or supply equations. Such systems can be solved iteratively also, but calculations naturally become more complicated. To see how such model can be solved, consider a joint corn and soybean model using structural elasticities from the FAPRI model.[8] The equations are

$$\text{Demand:} \quad Q_2 = 6.0\, P_2^{-0.2} + 1.4\, P_2^{-0.3}\, P_3^{0.4}$$
$$Q_3 = 10.6\, P_3^{-1.4} + 2.3\, P_2^{0.3}\, P_3^{-0.8}$$
$$\text{Supply:} \quad Q_2 = 7.8\, P_2^{0.13}$$
$$Q_3 = 0.84\, P_3^{0.50}$$

The subscripts 2 and 3 refer to corn and soybeans, in Eq. (3.6). Wheat is omitted here because no cross-elasticities are reported by FAPRI. The exponents (elasticities) are from the FAPRI report, but are rounded off to one decimal place, except for corn. "Supply" contains acreage response elasticities. The only cross-elasticities reported are in export demand. The constant terms are

$/cwt.

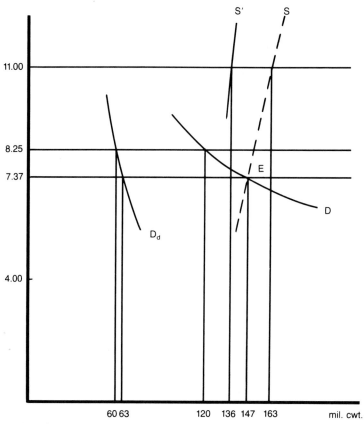

Figure 3.2 U.S. rice program.

inferred from the same base-period data and prices used earlier, and are not from FAPRI but are set to represent the situation with government programs in 1985.

How can we solve this system to find the no-program P's and Q's? Equating demand and supply in each market eliminates the Q's and gives us two equations in P_2 and P_3. But we can no longer use a logarithmic transformation to linearize the system. A useful approach for such situations is another iterative search technique.[9]

Begin by equating supply and demand for corn:

$$7.8\,P_2^{0.13} = 6.0\,P_2^{-0.2} + 1.4\,P_2^{-0.3}\,P_3^{0.4}$$

Try arbitrary prices near those found in the Table 3.1 simulations: $P_2 = \$2.00$ and $P_3 = \$5.00$ per bushel. This yields a right-hand side of 7.4 billion bushels and a left-hand side of 8.5, implying that excess supply exists. In the single-market case we proceeded by adjusting price until the market cleared. Here, however, there is a complication in that we could either raise the price of corn or lower the price of soybeans; and achieving equilibrium in the corn market does not achieve it in soybeans. So before iterating prices in corn, try the original P's in soybeans, where we have

$$0.84\, P_3^{0.50} = 10.6\, P_3^{-1.4} + 2.3\, P_2^{0.3}\, P_3^{-0.8}$$

When $P_2 = 2.00$ and $P_3 = 5.00$, the left-hand side is 1.88 (billion bushels) and the right-hand side is 1.90. Thus, we are very close to equilibrium, with a slight excess demand.

Going back to the corn market, use the Newton-Raphson method to find equilibrium P_2 given $P_3 = 5$. A value that comes close is $P_2 = 1.55$. Then we find P_3 to equilibrate soybeans given $P_2 = 1.55$. This turns out to require $P_3 = 4.94$. The next step in iteration is to go back to the corn market and solve for P_2 assuming $P_3 = 4.94$. This yields $P_2 = 1.32$.

After two more iterations, we end up with equilibrium in both markets simultaneously at $P_2 = \$1.30$ and $P_3 = \$4.88$ per bushel. The corresponding quantities are $Q_2 = 8.1$ billion bushels, with 5.7 billion consumed domestically and 2.4 billion exported, and $Q_3 = 1.84$ billion bushels, with 1.15 consumed domestically and 0.70 billion expected.

The results differ from the earlier constant-elasticity model mainly in that the no-program corn price is much lower. The economic reason is the low elasticity of export demand. The FAPRI publication does not present such drastic corn price declines, presumably because of other features of the model—stock-holding behavior or assumed demand levels different from those used here, perhaps. While FAPRI and other large policy models such as the USDA's FAP-SIM (Salathe et al., 1982) have many more commodities and variables than the corn–soybean model simulated here, the structure and solution methods are of the same kind. All are systems of interrelated supply and demand equations for agricultural commodities, simulated with changing policy instruments to forecast the effects of policy alternatives on commodity prices and quantities.

Linear Approximation

An alternative method of dealing with nonlinear systems is to construct a linear approximation to them. The benefit of this approach is that we can obtain analytical solutions in which the determinants of comparative static effects of policy changes are more transparent, as in Eqs. (3.14) and (3.15).

Consider the rice example of Eqs. (3.20) and (3.21). Using the E notation introduced in the subsidy analysis of Chap. 2, where $E(\cdot) = d \ln(\cdot) \cong \%\Delta(\cdot)$, we can write

$$EQ_d = \eta_d EP \quad \text{and} \quad EQ_x = \eta_x EP \tag{3.22}$$

where η_d is domestic demand elasticity and η_x is export demand elasticity. To obtain the linear approximation, use the fact that

$$EQ_t = \alpha_d EQ_d + \alpha_x EQ_x \tag{3.23}$$

where α_d is the share of output sold domestically and α_x is the share exported. For example, if $\alpha_d = 1/3$ and $\alpha_x = 2/3$, and Q_d rises 6 percent and Q_x rises 12 percent, then total demand Q_t rises $(2 + 8 =) 10$ percent.

Suppose we pay a subsidy to producers, as specified in Eq. (2.3) of Chap. 2. This implies

$$EQ_t = \epsilon EP + \epsilon EV \tag{3.24}$$

Equating (3.23) and (3.24) gives us with Eqs. (3.22) a system of three equations in three unknowns:

$$\begin{bmatrix} -\eta_d & 1 & 0 \\ -\eta_x & 0 & 1 \\ -\epsilon & \alpha_d & -\alpha_x \end{bmatrix} \begin{bmatrix} EP \\ EQ_d \\ EQ_x \end{bmatrix} = \begin{bmatrix} 0 \\ 0 \\ \epsilon EV \end{bmatrix} \tag{3.25}$$

Solving for EP and dividing by EV:

$$\frac{EP}{EV} = \frac{-\epsilon}{-\epsilon + \alpha_d \eta_d + \alpha_x \eta_x} \tag{3.26}$$

From Eq. (3.23), divide by EP to obtain the total elasticity of demand as $\eta_t = \alpha_d \eta_d + \alpha_x \eta_x$, the share-weighted average of the demand components. This means that Eq. (3.26) can be rewritten as $EP/EV = -1/(1 - \eta_t/\epsilon)$, which is the same as Eq. (2.8).

Since Eq. (2.8) is not an approximation, why is Eq. (3.26) an approximation? Because η in Chap. 2 was by construction a constant parameter, while the calculation of η_t is only good at an initial point. Why? Because α_d and α_x are not constants. Each component of demand is a constant-elasticity function, but the total demand function may be very far from it.

To see what difference it makes, note that in the rice example we began with $\alpha_x = \alpha_d = 0.5$, but that in the simulated no-program situation, $\alpha_x = 84/147 = 0.571$ and $\alpha_d = 0.429$. The value of η_t changes from $= -1.75$ at the initial equilibrium to -1.93 at the no-program equilibrium. If the approximation had been used, we would have simulated a price of $7.34, a decline of 11.0 percent compared to a decline of 10.7 percent using the exact nonlinear solution earlier. The approximation works quite well, because even though the two structural elasticities are not close in value, the demand-side price changes are relatively small.

The conceptual basis for measuring gains and losses is basically the same whatever the simulation method used. The separate specification of demand elasticity for exports does bring out that some of the gains accrue to foreigners. Consideration of the consequences of this fact for policy choice is postponed to Chaps. 7 and 11. Further analysis of multimarket equilibrium is developed in Chap. 5.

SUMMARY ON STRATEGY IN SIMULATION

This chapter has explored several ways of using information about policies, the observed market situations, and econometric evidence about supply and demand functions to assess the consequences of alternative policies. Because the alternatives considered are typically proposals that have not yet been tried, it is often necessary to make conjectures about counterfactual situations on little direct evidence. Sometimes policies are tried out on an experimental basis, but usually not. The best way to make the conjectures is with a simulation model of some kind. It forces the analyst to be systematic about inferences and conjectures made, explicit about facts used and assumptions maintained, and leads naturally to the quantitative statement of results.

Questions can be raised, however, about the type of simulation model that is most helpful in analyzing interventions in agricultural markets. Braverman et al. (1987) identify the following four approaches:

1. calculations of NPCs or PSEs (as discussed in Chapts. 1 and 2)
2. single-market, supply–demand analysis
3. multimarket supply–demand models
4. mathematical programming and computable general equilibrium (CGE) models

We generally cannot get very far with approach 1 beyond a rough assessment of the extent of existing intervention. Approach 2 allows us to do much more in modeling different types of intervention and the gains and losses resulting, but it has drawbacks when dealing with interventions in one or more closely related product markets. The problems of estimating price and quantity changes accurately were discussed in this chapter, but even more important are the difficulties in estimating welfare effects of policies in one market when there already exist policies in other markets. These issues are addressed in Chaps. 8 and 9.

Analysts who are committed to agricultural policy analysis on an ongoing basis have moved toward larger multimarket models and into approach 4. CGE models bring in nonagricultural sectors and may even have adjunct macroeconomic models explaining the economy's gross national product (GNP), rate of unemployment and so forth. Mathematical programming models go into more microeconomic detail, deriving results for particular types of farms or by regions of a country. In addition to the FAPRI and FAPSIM models already mentioned, examples of this approach are reported in Parikh et al. (1985) and Knutson et al. (1987).

While it is commendable to bring in as much completeness, detail, and realism into one's model as possible, and dangerous not to, there are drawbacks to approach 4. Braverman et al. (1987), pp. 339–340) state them as follows:

> First, elaborate models are essentially research tools which take a considerable amount of time and data to construct. Usually they cannot be done within the time horizon of operational work. Second, their complexity makes the incorporation of institutional detail more difficult (though not impossible). Similarly, changes in the model parameters for sensitivity analysis purposes are difficult to effect. Third, and perhaps most important, these models are frequently of such complexity that results are not intuitive—certainly not to a policymaker, and often not to the analyst!

To avoid the first problem, the four models cited earlier have been designed as general-purpose tools for policy analysis. The models have required up to 10 years work by many people (the publications cited each have at least four coauthors), but are intended to be adaptable to particular tasks of policy analysis with little additional investment of effort. Based on their review of general-purpose models, Rausser and Just (1981) argue against their use on the grounds that even if perfectly specified for the time of their construction, the agricultural economy's structure changes fast enough that they are unlikely to be trustworthy long enough to repay their setup costs.

The attempts to use large models to assess U.S. policy alternatives have produced results that appear just as reasonable as the small-model or single-product approach, and have greater claims to completeness. But their results have not provided definitive assessments of the policies analyzed. The particular problem areas seem to be:

1. Getting the policy instruments incorporated in the model. For example, in assessing acreage control programs the first and most important order of business is to determine how the program will alter the supply functions. But a large precooked structural model will have little or nothing directly applicable to this question, and will end up imposing an ad hoc shift on a structurally unchanged supply–demand system. The approach is weakest at answering the most crucial questions about the program.

2. Calibrating the model to the appropriate initial conditions. In the simple supply–demand model of Fig. 3.1, the model was easily calibrated to observed supply–demand–stocks conditions to show consequences of policy alternatives for 1985. We can be certain that substantial recalibration would be necessary to study the same alternatives in 1986 or 1987. (Corn prices in 1986 were already below the lowest no-program price in Table 3.1.) A large model must also be very often recalibrated so its initial state represents the appropriate supply–demand conditions, but this is a much bigger job.

3.　The consequences of many policies turn on a few key behavioral relationships, the nature of which may be changed by the policy. For example, when the government introduces a new CCC stock acquisition and release regime, this influences private stockholding behavior significantly, as discussed in Chap. 10. The most pertinent policy analysis would investigate in depth these behavioral changes, but large, general-purpose models do not seem amenable to this kind of work.

The problems seem to be the key reasons why, despite the evident limitations of simple, partial equilibrium models, they have been able to provide policy assessments just as valuable in most cases, and more valuable in some, as the larger and conceptually more adequate models.

Notwithstanding these problems, the point is well taken that many important features of agricultural policy are omitted from the commodity supply–demand models developed to this point. The following chapters develop the following elaborations: Chap. 4 brings in factor markets, particularly important for land as a recipient of policy benefits; Chap. 5 adds simultaneous effects at the wholesale or retail level; Chap. 6 discusses (but does not go far in formally modeling) differences between farms and other "structural" issues; Chaps. 7 and 9 incorporate general equilibrium, embedding the agricultural sector in the whole economy as an aggregate; Chaps. 8 and 9 model interventions and market imperfections for several commodities simultaneously; Chap. 10 considers issues in dynamics and uncertainty; Chap. 11 considers further complications arising from trade and international finance; and Chap. 12 endogenizes policies. When this is all finished, however, we will not have a recipe, outline, or skeleton of a grand model for policy analysis.

ENDNOTES

1.　Wheat growers rejected an acreage control approach in a watershed referendum in 1963. The situation may be different in the 1980s, since an advisory poll of wheat growers in 1986 found a majority in favor of mandatory supply controls.

2.　The congressionally designated names are used for historical reference. As a guide to the contents of the legislation they are quite misleading.

3.　See "Economic, Indicators of the Farm Sector: Costs of Production 1984," USDA-Econ. Res. Serv. *ECIFS 4-1*. Similar calculations for corn give $1.31 per bushel in variable costs assuming 112 bushels per acre yield. If corn grown could be sold at $2.00 per bushel, the farmer's cost of idling corn land is 69 cents per bushel that would have been produced.

4.　Provisions for changing acreage and yield bases have varied considerably between crops, over time for the same crop, and even from one area of the country to another at the same time for the same crop due to local variation in administration. Deficiency payments in the 1970s were initially tied to acreage bases from the 1950s and 1960s. The Food and Agriculture Act of 1977 changed this to a current acreage basis. The 1985 act attempts to freeze both acreage and yield bases.

5. This a difficult area to assess empirically, depending as it does on details of substitutability of inputs in the production function for wheat. This issue is addressed further in Chap. 4. It might be thought that the discussion is academic (in the pejorative sense) for wheat since wheat is not a big user of fertilizers and pesticides. However, the contrary is illustrated by the experience of recent immigrants from England growing wheat in Missouri. Used to higher wheat prices in England, they applied more intensive practices which increased wheat yields to about 100 bushels per acre. (*Washington Post,* March 1986).

6. R. C. Buse, Total elasticities—A predictive device, *J. Farm Econ.* 40:881–891, Nov. 1958: Buse derives an equation like (3.14) except he omits the supply equation and hence obtains a total demand elasticity.

7. For details on the Newton-Raphson method, see any of several texts on numerical analysis, e.g., S. S. Kuo, *Numerical Methods and Computers,* Addison-Wesley, Reading, Mass., 1965, pp. 90–94.

8. Food and Agricultural Policy Research Institute. For simulation of policy alternatives with this model see S. R. Johnson et al., Options for the 1985 farm bill, in: *U.S. Agricultural Policy,* B. Gardner, ed., American Enterprise Institute, Washington, D.C., 1985.

9. The procedure is analogous to the Gauss-Seidel method for solving systems of linear equations. It works for nonlinear equations like these when we know a priori that there is a unique solution, and the partial derivative of each function with respect to a particular variable is large compared to other partials (which is usually the case for own-price effects).

Part Two

Models of Program Effects

Chapter 4

Price Supports and Factor Markets

Some policies, such as subsidies paid to producers, can be readily analyzed in a satisfactory way with simple supply–demand models of commodity markets. But to provide a full analysis of policies like fertilizer subsidies or acreage controls, which affect output indirectly by regulating the use of a single input, it is necessary to model the relevant input markets. We need to consider input markets at least in sufficient detail to analyze the consequences of having two categories of inputs: regulated and unregulated. Explicit representation of input supply and demand is also important for investigating issues of who gains from policies of even the simple subsidy or control type. For example, some have argued that owners of agricultural land, not farmers as such, are the gainers from price supports. According to this view, a dentist who owned a farm that he leased to a tenant farmer would gain from a price-support program but the tenant would not.

In this chapter we consider the simplest model in which these issues may be addressed: a single-output, two-input model. In agricultural policy analysis, we are often interested in the land input as opposed to nonland inputs. But other issues involve human as opposed to nonhuman resources. And some issues cannot usefully be brought within the two-input framework at all. For present purposes it may be helpful to think of the quantity of one input, represented by the letter a, as acreage of land. The other input, b, represents a nonland aggregate. Figure 4.1 shows supply and demand curves for output, x, and two inputs under the special conditions that fixed quantities of a and b are required for

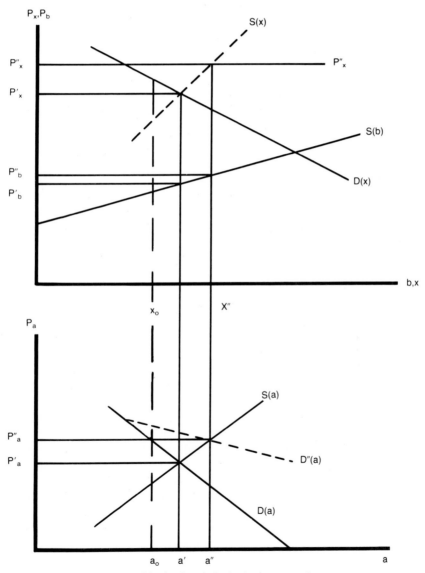

Figure 4.1 Derived demand for land under output price support.

each unit of x. For example, if x is corn, it might be that each 1000 bushels of corn requires 8 acres of land and a bundle of other inputs consisting of 2 days labor, 1200 lb. of anhydrous ammonia, and fixed quantities of other chemicals, machinery services, and so forth. The aggregate nonland input quantity b is represented as a quantity index. This representation of production conditions is unrealistic mainly in that it precludes the possibility of substituting inputs for one another, e.g., producing 1000 bushels of corn with 1000 lbs. of ammonia but on a larger land area. The benefit of this assumption is that with relationships among output and inputs fixed, it is easy to see how the demand for inputs is related to the output market.

Suppose we are interested in the demand for land's services (considering a rental market for land to avoid asset valuation problems). We know in general terms that the demand for agricultural land is a "derived" demand, derived from the demand for agricultural products. The fixed-proportions model permits a more exact specification of the sense in which the demand for land is a derived demand. The demand for x is shown in the top panel of Fig. 4.1. The demand for land can be derived by considering the maximum that a producer would pay for renting land. For any given quantity a_0 of land, the farmer can obtain no more than purchasers of the product will pay for the corresponding quantity x_0, as given by the demand function for x. Moreover, the farmer will have to use nonland inputs b_0 along with a_0 to produce x_0. He will have to pay for the nonland inputs (at least) the amounts given by the supply function for b in the same P, Q space, with price of b expressed as dollars per unit of x produced. The vertical difference between the demand for x and the supply b at x_0 thus measures the farmers' willingness to pay for a_0.

Tracing out these vertical differences for all possible values of x generates the demand function for a shown in the bottom panel of Fig. 4.1. The supply function of a, which depends on the alternatives available to landowners and the technical possibilities for creating and destroying farmland, is shown as $S(a)$. It determines equilibrium in the a market, with market clearing price P_a' (measured in terms of dollars per unit of x). The equilibrium value of a determines the equilibrium values of x and b in the upper diagram. There is an implied supply function of x, shown as a dashed line in Figure 4.1. The supply curve is a vertical sum of the supply functions of a and b. The demand for b is derived in the same manner as the demand for a. In short, we have a three-market supply-demand system, with three behavioral functions (the demand for x and the supplies of a and b) and three derived functions (the supply of x and the demands for a and b).

Consider a producer price support for x at level P_x', attained by paying a subsidy to producers. Equilibrium will be at output x''. To see that the equilibrium in the a market is $a = a''$, note that the vertical distance between P_x'' and $S(b)$ represents the derived demand price for a, given the policy. Tracing out the points implied by various levels of x, we obtain the new derived demand function for a shown as a dashed line in the lower panel of Fig. 4.1. Each time we raise the price support level we increase the derived demand for a.

These results give us a first model for analyzing the income distribution effects of a price support. We see that both P_a and P_b will rise, but not by equal amounts. The input least elastic in supply gains the most.

Consider a commodity program that restricts the use of land in commodity production. Figure 4.2 shows the equilibrium with less a; the supply function of a is replaced by the policy-determined quantity a''. Tracing the restricted equilibrium to the upper panel, we see a reduced P_b and an increased P_x. Thus, the distribution of program benefits is quite different for an acreage-control program than for a subsidy program that achieves the same P_x. The acreage-control program makes the owners of nonland inputs worse off.

The preceding result, however, ignores an important incentive created by acreage-control programs; namely, the inducement to substitute nonland for land inputs in production. For example, in response to the higher P_x, we would expect farmers to use more fertilizer per acre. But this substitution violates the fixed-proportion assumption on which Figs. 4.1 and 4.2 are based. In order to examine these issues, we need a model that relaxes this assumption. The simplest model that permits substitution in production is the single-output, two-input model used by Hicks (1932) to investigate issues in labor economics. The development of this model as applied to agricultural price supports is due to Floyd (1965). We follow Floyd's model almost exactly here.

The model consists of the following six equations:

Industry production function:	$x = f(a,b)$	(4.1)
VMP = factor price:	$f_a P_x = P_a$	(4.2)
	$f_b P_x = P_b$	(4.3)
Factor supplies:	$a = g(P_a)$	(4.4)
	$b = h(P_b)$	(4.5)
Product demand:	$x = D(P_x)$	(4.6)

In order to justify these equations as the representation of a one-output, two-input industry, we need the following assumptions: (1) the output market is competitive, (2) the input markets are competitive, (3) producers maximize profits, and (4) all firms are identical. The last assumption may be taken as meaning that all units of a and b have the same characteristics and only one least-cost technology is available, which can be represented as a twice differentiable, concave production function that generates the usual U-shaped average cost function. These conditions imply that at competitive equilibrium, all producers will be observed at the minimum of their average cost function so that the industry production function of Eq. (4.1) is linear homogeneous. This in turn implies the standard results that elasticities of x with respect to a and b are

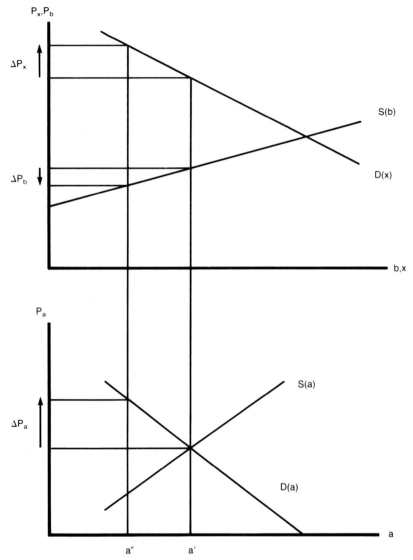

Figure 4.2   Effect of acreage control.

equal to the factor shares and that the sum of factor payments exhausts the value of output ($xP_x = aP_a + bP_b$).

The slopes of supply and demand equations are assumed to have the normal signs, and a single equilibrium with positive prices and use of both inputs is assumed to exist. The six equations can be solved to find this equilibrium since there are six mutually determined (endogenous) variables in the system.

Since we are interested in changes in the system, take the total differentials of Eqs. (4.1) through (4.6):

$$dx = f_a\, da + f_b\, db \qquad (4.1')$$

$$dP_a = df_a\, P_x + dP_x f_a \qquad (4.2')$$

$$df_a = f_{aa}\, da + f_{ab}\, db$$

$$dP_a = f_{aa}\, P_x\, da + f_{ab}\, P_x\, db + f_a\, dP_x$$

$$dP_b = f_{bb}\, P_x\, db + f_{ba}\, P_x\, da + f_b\, dP_x \qquad (4.3')$$

$$da = g_a\, dP_a \qquad (4.4')$$

$$db = h_b\, dP_b \qquad (4.5')$$

$$dx = D_x\, dP_x \qquad (4.6')$$

Next we convert Eqs. (4.1') to (4.6') to elasticity form and simplify. This requires four kinds of "tricks":

1. Convert differentials to percentage changes by dividing each by the relevant variable. Percentage changes are denoted by the E operator, e.g.,

$$EP_x = \frac{dP_x}{P_x}$$

2. Convert partials to elasticities, e.g.,

$$g_a = \frac{\partial a}{\partial P_a}$$

$$e_a = \frac{\partial a}{\partial P_a}\frac{P_a}{a}$$

Therefore,

$$g_a = e_a \frac{a}{P_a}$$

3. Eliminate all second partials of the production function by means of the relations

$$f_{aa} = -\frac{bf_a f_b}{ax\sigma} \qquad f_{ab} = f_{ba} = \frac{f_a f_b}{\sigma x}$$

where σ is the elasticity of substitution in production between a and b (Allen, 1938, p. 343, following from the assumption that the production function is linear homogeneous).

4. Eliminate f_a and f_b by substituting from Eqs. (4.2) and (4.3):

$$f_a = \frac{P_a}{P_x}$$

and

$$f_b = \frac{P_b}{P_x}$$

The resulting equations are

$$\frac{dx}{xab} = \frac{P_a}{P_x xb}\frac{da}{a} + \frac{P_b}{P_x xa}\frac{db}{b} \qquad \text{[divide (4.1') by } xab]$$

$$\frac{dx}{x} = \frac{P_a a}{P_x x}\frac{da}{a} + \frac{P_b b}{P_x x}\frac{db}{b} \qquad \text{(multiply by } ab) \qquad (4.1'')$$

$$EX = K_a Ea + K_b Eb$$

where K_a and K_b are the relative shares of a and b in total costs.

Dividing both sides of Eq. (4.2') by P_a, multiplying the right-hand side terms by a/a, b/b, and P_x/P_x, respectively, and substituting for f_{aa}, f_{ab}, f_a, and f_b as indicated in steps 3 and 4, we obtain

$$\frac{dP_a}{P_a} = -\frac{bf_a f_b}{ax\sigma}\frac{P_x a}{P_a}\frac{da}{a} + \frac{f_a f_b}{\sigma x}\frac{P_x b}{P_a}\frac{db}{b} + \frac{f_a P_x}{P_a}\frac{dP_x}{P_x}$$

$$EP_a = -\frac{bP_a P_b}{ax\sigma P_x P_x}\frac{P_x a}{P_a}Ea + \frac{P_a P_b}{\sigma x P_x P_x}\frac{P_x b}{P_a}Eb + \frac{P_a P_x}{P_x P_a}EP_x \qquad (4.2'')$$

$$EP_a = -\frac{bP_b}{\sigma x P_x}Ea + \frac{P_b b}{\sigma x P_x}Eb + EP_x$$

$$EP_a = -\frac{K_b}{\sigma}Ea + \frac{K_b}{\sigma}Eb + EP_x$$

Similarly, from Eqs. (4.3') to (4.6') we obtain

$$EP_b = -\frac{K_a}{\sigma}Eb + \frac{K_a}{\sigma}Ea + EP_x \qquad (4.3'')$$

$$\frac{da}{aP_a} = e_a\frac{a}{P_a a}\frac{dP_a}{P_a} \qquad (4.4'')$$

$$Ea = e_a EP_a$$

$$Eb = e_b EP_b \qquad (4.5'')$$

$$EX = \eta EP_x \qquad (4.6'')$$

where η is the elasticity of product demand.

We now have six linear equations in six mutually determined percentage change variables, Ex, Ea, Eb, EP_x, EP_a, and EP_b; three quantities and three prices. The relationships among them are determined by six parameters, the two factors shares and the four elasticity parameters σ, η, e_a, and e_b. Writing these equations in matrix form in preparation for solving via Cramer's rule, the right-hand side is a column of zeros. There are no constants in the equations. The only solutions are no percentage changes: $E(\cdot) = 0$. The economic meaning of this result is that we have a static system. The prices and quantities are all at given equilibrium levels, which we can obtain from Eqs. (4.1) to (4.6). In percentage change terms, however, while we have a system all set up to analyze changes, we have introduced nothing to cause a change. The changes of interest are introduced in two ways in this chapter, corresponding to the discussion in Chap. 2. First, we select one of the variables and, by regulating it, directly make it a policy instrument. Second, we introduce additional policy variables as policy instruments. Comparative statics is then conducted by differentiating the system with respect to the policy instrument.

PRICE SUPPORTS

Making one of the variables a policy instrument and changing it to some controlled level other than the equilibrium level causes one of the equations no longer to hold. (Graphically, we move off one function). We can use Eqs. (4.1″) to 4.6″) to trace through the effects on the other endogenous variables. These policy experiments pertain only to infinitesimal changes under the assumptions made thus far. They will be better approximations for large changes if the production function has the constant elasticity of substitution (CES) form and Eqs. (4.4) to (4.6) are constant-elasticity (log-linear).[1]

Suppose the government increases P_x by purchases of x. This moves us off the demand function. P_x is determined exogenously. The effects of a change in P_x are found by dividing Eqs. (4.1″) to (4.5″) by EP_x:

$$\frac{Ex}{EP_x} = K_a \frac{Ea}{EP_x} + K_b \frac{Eb}{EP_x} \tag{4.7}$$

For the factor markets, we first use Eqs. (4.4″) and (4.5″) to eliminate Ea and Eb. We then have, for the a market,

$$\frac{EP_a}{EP_x} = -\frac{K_b \, e_a}{\sigma} \frac{EP_a}{EP_x} + \frac{K_b \, e_b}{\sigma} \frac{EP_b}{EP_x} + 1 \tag{4.8}$$

and for the b market,

$$\frac{EP_b}{EP_x} = -\frac{K_a e_b}{\sigma}\frac{EP_b}{EP_x} + \frac{K_a e_a}{\sigma}\frac{EP_a}{EP_x} + 1 \tag{4.9}$$

These equations give us "cross-elasticities" which tell the effect of a change in P_x on P_a and P_b, i.e., the effects of a product price support on factor prices.

Unfortunately, the cross-elasticities are mutually determined. Equations (4.8) and (4.9) are solved simultaneously as follows:

$$1 = \left(1 + \frac{K_b e_a}{\sigma}\right)\frac{EP_a}{EP_x} - \frac{K_b e_b}{\sigma}\frac{EP_b}{EP_x}$$

$$1 = -\frac{K_a e_a}{\sigma}\frac{EP_a}{EP_x} + \left(1 + \frac{K_a e_b}{\sigma}\right)\frac{EP_b}{EP_x}$$

Applying Cramer's Rule:

$$\frac{EP_a}{EP_x} = \begin{vmatrix} \dfrac{1 - K_b e_b}{\sigma} \\[2ex] 1 + \dfrac{K_a e_b}{\sigma} \end{vmatrix} \div \begin{vmatrix} 1 + \dfrac{K_b e_a}{\sigma} & -\dfrac{K_b e_b}{\sigma} \\[2ex] -\dfrac{K_a e_a}{\sigma} & 1 + \dfrac{K_a e_b}{\sigma} \end{vmatrix}$$

$$= \frac{1 + K_a e_b/\sigma + K_b e_b/\sigma}{1 + K_a e_b/\sigma + K_b e_a/\sigma + K_a K_b e_a e_b/\sigma\sigma - K_a K_b e_a e_b/\sigma\sigma}$$

$$= \frac{\sigma + (K_a + K_b) e_b}{\sigma + K_a e_b + K_b e_a} = \frac{\sigma + e_b}{\sigma + K_a e_b + K_b e_a} \tag{4.10}$$

Similarly, solving the system for EP_b/EP_x gives

$$\frac{EP_b}{EP_x} = \frac{\sigma + e_a}{\sigma + K_a e_b + K_b e_a} \tag{4.11}$$

We have solved for two of the endogenous cross-elasticities. They are total or multimarket equilibrium elasticities because they allow for equilibration of related markets. The term "total" does not mean the elasticities are from a general equilibrium model in the sense of an economy-wide model in which factor payments provide income, which then affects commodity demand, and in which only relative prices are determined without a "numeraire" or money commodity.[2] The substantive point is that one must keep clear what is held constant and what is permitted to vary in the comparative statics that the elasticities describe.

To obtain Ea/EP_x and Eb/EP_x, note from Eqs. (4.4″) and (4.5″) that it is only necessary to multiply the results just derived by e_a and e_b, respectively. To obtain EX/EP_x, the last of the five endogenous variables, however, we can-

not simply use Eq. (4.6″). Why? Because by construction of the policy intervention which generated the comparative-static results, we have moved off the
market demand function which specifies Eq. (4.6″). Instead, we want the elasticity of supply of x as our value for Ex/EP_x. This is found by substituting
Ea/EP_x and Eb/EP_x in Eq. (4.7). The result is

$$\frac{Ex}{EP_x} = \frac{e_a e_b + \sigma(K_a e_a + K_b e_b)}{\sigma + K_a e_b + K_b e_a} \tag{4.12}$$

This equation is an algebraic decomposition of the determinants of elasticity of
supply of x, the same expression as derived by Muth (1965).

The preceding effects are the results of a policy that shifts the demand for
x to achieve a higher P_x. What if the deficiency payment approach were used
instead to achieve the same P_x support? From the producers' point of view, the
results are the same: they are allowed to produce all they like at the higher
price. Therefore, all the factor market effects are the same, too. The situation
differs, however, for consumers. In the former policy, P_x rises for consumers,
too, and their quantity consumed falls. In the payment approach, consumers'
consumption and producers' output both rise, and this is achieved by having
the producers' price rise while the consumers' price falls. P_x in Eqs. (4.7) to
4.9) is the producers' price; it is on the supply curve.

The change in the consumers' price of x, EP_d/EP_x, is analyzed as follows.
We already have the elasticity of supply from Eq. (4.12) and the elasticity of
demand is just the parameter η. Therefore, we can write

$$\frac{EP_d}{EP_x} = \frac{EP_d}{EX}\frac{EX}{EP_x} = \frac{\epsilon}{\eta} \tag{4.13}$$

where ϵ is the supply elasticity as analyzed in Eq. (4.12).

PRODUCTION CONTROL

In the simple supply–demand models of Chaps. 2 and 3, production control was
accomplished by regulating Q, the only quantity variable available. But here
we have three quantities: x, a, and b. Output x is the same as Q earlier. (We
retain the symbol Q as a generic quantity indicator, while x is used to refer
specifically to farm-level output.) Direct regulation of x can be depicted as earlier in Fig. 2.1, but now we are prepared to go into more detail on the factor
market consequences.

A complication is that while P_x, which is now price on the demand curve,
is received by producers, the rents generated do not necessarily go to either
factor of production. These rents go to the owner of rights to produce the re-

stricted quantity. The rights may be assigned to a factor owner, notably the land owner, but they need not be. In the U.S. tobacco program and in Canadian provincial dairy programs, the rights to market commodities are assigned to persons, who may even sell the rights, with or without land or cows. This means we have created a new factor of production that must be used in fixed proportions to output sold.

The rental price of "quota," as it is called in tobacco, is the difference between P_x and price on the supply curve at the restricted output level. Call this supply price C_x since it measures the cost (marginal and average) of x. Then the rental price of quota is $R_q = P_x - C_x$. The quantity of quota is stated in units of controlled output $\hat{x}$. When $\hat{x}$ changes, the percentage effect on C_x is just the reciprocal of the elasticity of supply from Eq. (4.12). (We do not move along a cost curve even though C_x measures cost at any point because factor prices are not fixed.) The change in R_q is

$$\frac{dR_q}{dx} = \frac{dP_x}{dx} - \frac{dC_x}{dx}$$

Expressing R_q as percentage of P_x (e.g., tobacco quota rents for 30 percent of the price of tobacco):

$$\frac{dR_q}{dx}\frac{x}{P_x} = \frac{dP_x}{dx}\frac{x}{P_x} - \frac{dC_x}{dx}\frac{x}{C_x}\frac{C_x}{P_x}$$

or,

$$\frac{ER_q}{Ex} = \frac{1}{\eta} - \frac{T_x}{\epsilon}$$

where T_x is the ratio C_x/P_x.

The effect of a change in $\hat{x}$ on factor prices can be analyzed using the results already obtained. The price support program gave us higher factor prices as we moved up the supply curve, and the production control program gives us lower factor prices as we move down the supply curve. To express the percentage changes in P_a in response to $E\hat{x}$, we have

$$\frac{EP_a}{Ex} = \frac{EP_a}{EP_x}\frac{EP_x}{Ex}$$

that is, we multiply Eq. (4.10) by the reciprocal of Eq. (4.12). This yields

$$\frac{EP_a}{Ex} = \frac{\sigma + e_b}{e_a e_b + \sigma(K_a e_a + K_b e_b)} \tag{4.14}$$

Multiplying Eq. (4.14) by e_a generates $Ea/E\hat{x}$, and comparable results for Eb and EP_b are obtained by exchanging a and b subscripts in the numerators.

ACREAGE CONTROLS

Consider a different policy regime in which the government does not control x directly but instead controls the quantity of a. Then we modify the system of Eqs. (4.1″) to (4.6″) by dropping Eq. (4.4″), the supply function of a, and divide all equations by Ea.

First, from Eq. (4.2″) we have

$$\frac{EP_a}{Ea} = -\frac{K_b}{\sigma} + \frac{K_b}{\sigma}\frac{Eb}{Ea} + \frac{EP_x}{Ea}$$

Second, Eqs. (4.3″) and (4.5″) are equated to obtain

$$\frac{1}{e_b}\frac{Eb}{Ea} = -\frac{K_a}{\sigma}\frac{Eb}{Ea} + \frac{K_a}{\sigma} + \frac{EP_x}{Ea}$$

$$\frac{K_a}{\sigma} = \frac{K_a e_b + \sigma}{\sigma e_b}\frac{Eb}{Ea} - \frac{EP_x}{Ea}$$

Third, by equating (4.1″) and (4.6″) we obtain

$$\eta\frac{EP_x}{Ea} = K_a + K_b\frac{Eb}{Ea}$$

The three preceding equations are linear in three unknowns, EP_a/Ea, Eb/Ea, and EP_x/Ea. Solving for EP_a/Ea:

$$\frac{EP_a}{Ea} = \frac{\begin{vmatrix} \dfrac{K_a}{\sigma} & \dfrac{K_a e_b + \sigma}{\sigma e_b} & -1 \\[2mm] \dfrac{-K_b}{\sigma} & \dfrac{-K_b}{\sigma} & -1 \\[2mm] -K_a & K_b & -\eta \end{vmatrix}}{\begin{vmatrix} 0 & \dfrac{K_a e_b + \sigma}{(\sigma e_b)} & -1 \\[2mm] 1 & \dfrac{-K_b}{\sigma} & -1 \\[2mm] 0 & K_b & -\eta \end{vmatrix}}$$

The numerator's determinant is

$$\frac{K_a K_b \eta}{\sigma\sigma} + \frac{K_a (K_a e_b + \sigma)}{\sigma e_b} + \frac{K_b^2}{\sigma} + \frac{K_a K_b}{\sigma} + \frac{K_a K_b}{\sigma} - \frac{K_b \eta (K_a e_b + \sigma)}{\sigma\sigma e_b}$$

The determinant of the denominator is

$$-K_b + \frac{\eta (K_a e_b + \sigma)}{\sigma e_b}$$

Multiplying the numerator and denominator both by e_b and using the facts that $K_a + K_b = 1$ and $K_a^2 + K_b^2 + 2 K_a K_b = (K_a + K_b)^2$, EP_a/Ea simplifies to:[3]

$$\frac{EP_a}{Ea} = \frac{e_b + K_a \sigma - K_b \eta}{\eta\sigma + e_b (K_a\eta - K_b\sigma)} \tag{4.15}$$

Solving for EP_x/Ea,

$$\frac{EP_x}{Ea} = \frac{K_a (e_b + \sigma)}{\sigma\eta - e_b (K_b \sigma - K_a\eta)} \tag{4.16}$$

If we now divide Eq. (4.15) by Eq. (4.16) we will have the effect of an increase in a policy-determined commodity price on the input price, *given that the product price change is now achieved by input quantity control*. The expression is

$$\frac{EP_a}{EP_x} = \frac{e_b + K_a\sigma - K_b\eta}{(\sigma + e_b)K_a} \tag{4.17}$$

Compare Eq. (4.17) with Eq. (4.10), which shows the effect of P_x on P_a when the price support is achieved by government purchases without production controls. The comparative-static effects are obviously quite different.

The preceding discussion spells out the derivation of some comparative statics results for the one-product, two-input model. These and related results are presented as Table 4.1. Each entry is an elasticity. For example, the lower left-hand corner is $\%\Delta b/\%\Delta P_x$ or Eb/EP_x. Used as an approximation for finite changes, the table tells what information we need in order to answer such questions as, if a price support program for wheat raises the price of wheat by 10 percent, what effect will it have on the price of nonland inputs? We see from the entries in the bottom row of Table 4.1 that the answer depends on what kind of price support mechanism is used, but that in either case, the answer depends on the values of the parameters K_a, K_b, σ, and e_b, and on η if we use acreage controls, or e_a if we use subsidy payments without production controls.

Table 4.1   Effects of P_x Support Using Different Support Mechanisms*

Program	Deficiency payments†	Production control	Acreage control
Effect on:			
x	$\dfrac{e_a e_b + \sigma e_2}{\sigma + e_1}$	η	η
P_d	$\dfrac{e_a e_b + \sigma e_2}{\eta(\sigma + e_1)}$	1	1
P_a	$\dfrac{\sigma + e_b}{\sigma + e_1}$	$\dfrac{\eta(\sigma + e_b)}{e_a e_b + \sigma e_2}$	$\dfrac{e_b + K_a \sigma - K_b \eta}{K_a(\sigma + e_b)}$
P_b	$\dfrac{\sigma + e_a}{\sigma + e_1}$	$\dfrac{\eta(\sigma + e_a)}{e_a e_b + \sigma e_2}$	$\dfrac{\sigma + \eta}{\sigma + e_b}$
a	$\dfrac{e_a(\sigma + e_b)}{\sigma + e_1}$	$\dfrac{e_a \eta(\sigma + e_b)}{e_a e_b + \sigma e_2}$	$\dfrac{\eta\sigma - e_b(K_b \sigma - K_a \eta)}{K_a(\sigma + e_b)}$
b	$\dfrac{e_b(\sigma + e_a)}{\sigma + e_1}$	$\dfrac{e_b \sigma(\sigma + e_a)}{e_a e_b + \sigma e_2}$	$\dfrac{e_b(\sigma + \eta)}{\sigma + e_b}$

*Each entry is an elasticity, $E(\cdot)/EP_x$, where $(\cdot)$ is x, P_d, P_a, P_b, a, or b.
†$e_1 = K_a e_b + K_b e_a$ and $e_2 = K_a e_a + K_b e_b$.

The signs of all the expressions are unambiguous except for the effect of acreage controls on P_b and b. Here the sign depends on whether σ is greater than or less than $-\eta$. This is the same condition for the cross-elasticity of input demand being positive or negative. Thus, a purely graphic approach will not be sufficient even to give qualitative effects of commodity programs on factor markets. Whether nonland input suppliers gain or lose from acreage controls depends on the magnitude of σ and η.

SIMULATION OF POLICY OPTIONS

To see the empirical implications of these elasticity relationships, consider the U.S. corn program discussed in Chap. 3. Suppose a desired 20 percent increase in P_x (farm price of corn) can be achieved by either a target price increase or acreage controls. Let $\eta = -0.6$, $e_b = 0.2$, $e_a = 1.0$, $K_a = 0.3$, $\sigma = 1.0$ (Cobb-Douglas). The share of land of 0.3 is based on land rental value of about $55 per acre and $135 per acre in nonland costs (fertilizer, seed, etc.). Letting these nonland inputs be aggregated in b, we have $K_b = 0.7$. The elasticities are conjectural but are chosen to be roughly consistent with available empirical work (which is really quite sketchy on factor supply and substitution elasticities).

Using parameter values in the equations of Table 4.1, we find that the 20 percent target price increase would cause: a (corn acreage) to rise 5.6 percent; b (nonland inputs) to rise 16.7 percent; P_a (the rental value of land) to rise 27.8

percent, P_b to rise 16.7 percent; and x (corn output) to rise 13.3 percent. On the other hand, if the 20-percent increase in P_x were obtained by means of acreage controls, the changes would be: a falls by 49.3 percent, b rises by 4.0 percent, P_a rises by 90.7 percent, P_b rises by 4.0 percent, and x falls by 12 percent.[4]

The two policies are depicted in supply–demand curves in Fig. 4.3. Because X, a, and b, are not in fixed proportions we cannot solve for the multi-market equilibrium graphically. But we can show what the constrained equilibrium looks like. For either of the policies, labeled 1 and 2, we obtain the same product price, and can see the differences in factor prices that are associated with each of the two programs.

One of the most widely accepted beliefs about price support programs is that their benefits accrue predominantly to landowners. This occurs in the deficiency payment program with no output controls because land is less elastic in

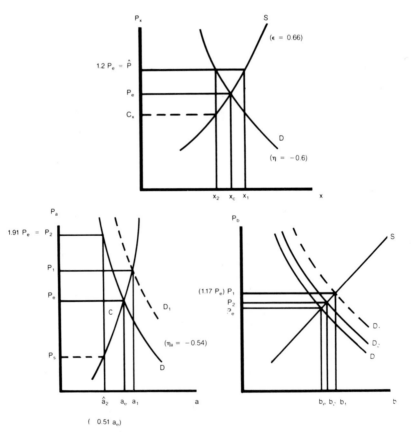

Figure 4.3 Target price and acreage control.

supply than nonland inputs. But dominance of land is not total. In this example the elasticity of nonland input supply is five times that of land, but the rental value of land rises 28 percent compared to a 17-percent rise in nonland inputs. This is not so heavily favored for land as might have been expected. The reason is the substitution possibilities between land and nonland inputs in production. If $\sigma = 0$, P_a would have risen five times as much as P_b. To derive this result formally, divide $E(P_a, P_x)$ by $E(P_b, P_x)$ using the expressions from Table 4.1, first column. When $\sigma = 0$, the ratio is e_b/e_a; with elasticities of 1.0 and 0.2, we have $1.0/0.2 = 5$.

Some economists' discussions tie the idea of land's predominance to acreage control policies. Tweeten (1971) states that "economic theory and observed behavior suggest that the monetary benefits of federal programs controlling land would be capitalized into land values over time" (p. 260). Cochrane and Ryan (1976, p. 371) assert more generally that

> The ultimate gainer from a net income increase in agriculture whether resulting from an increase in demand, a farm technological advance, or a farm program, is the land owner. Any income gain tends to get capitalized into the limiting input, land, through the competitive process. And that is where the income benefits of the farm programs had to come to rest.

The idea of capitalization in both these quotations is that a permanent and expected increase in the rental returns to land would result in an increase in the market price equal to the discounted present value of the increased future rental returns. The issue here is not the capitalization of return, but that the returns have to accrue to *land*.

The simulation of acreage controls in Fig. 4.3 suggests that acreage controls may provide even less of a predominance of benefits to land than deficiency payments. True, the rise in P_a is higher, and in P_b lower under acreage controls than under deficiency payments. But we have to consider the loss to landowners from having to divert acreage from the supported crop. If we measure this loss analogously to the producers' loss of economic rents in Fig. 2.1 in our earlier discussion of production controls, we should subtract the area labeled C in Fig. 4.3 from the gains from obtaining $\hat{P}_2$ on the restricted acreage $\hat{a}_2$. Setting the no-program land receipts, P_e times a_e, at an index value of 100, the upper rectangle of gains is 45 and the area C of losses is about 20. The net gain to a owners is 25, i.e., 25 percent of no-program revenue.

The use of area C as the loss from diverting land presumes that the acreage is shifted to its next-best use. That is the meaning of not counting as loss the area under the supply curve of land, which measures the opportunity costs of using land in agriculture. But some programs require land to be left idle. This means the area under the supply curve is also lost to landowners. In our example, the loss to be subtracted from the gains of 45 is now $(a_e - \hat{a}_2)P_e$, which is

49. Thus, landowners incur a net loss from the program. Meanwhile the b owners reap their modest gain from the 5.6 percent increase in P_b. This is far from a situation in which land is the "ultimate gainer."

It can still turn out that land is the big gainer, but this depends on the empirical situation: the elasticities of land's supply and demand, the elasticity of substitution between land and nonland inputs, and the characteristics of the program. Land may be helped by being permitted employment in alternative uses which may not be the best alternative use, but still do not yield a zero return. More importantly, some diversion programs pay farmers a rental payment per acre idled, as discussed in Chap. 2. If the government pays P_e per acre diverted, the losses we have been calculating do not exist. Indeed, in some programs the government pays *more* than the no-program rental price of land, in order to induce participation. In this case, landowners' gains are very likely to dominate the gains of nonland inputs.

In analyzing acreage controls algebraically, we proceeded by eliminating the supply curve of a, replacing it with $\hat{a}$ as a policy instrument, then finding P_a as a point on the demand function for a. The graphic depiction in Fig. 4.3 shows that the supply curve of a has not simply disappeared, nonetheless. And there exists a point on the supply curve, at price P_s, where $\hat{a}_2$ is consistent with this supply price as the rental price of land; it is what landowners would have to be paid to plant the acreage $\hat{a}_2$. Why isn't this the price of a under the acreage-control program? It would be if farmers rented all their land from absentee landlords. Under the acreage-control program, farmers are granted rights to plant acreage $\hat{a}_2$. Since they rent only acreage $\hat{a}_2$, instead of a_e, the rental rate paid to the landlords falls to P_s. So P_s is the relevant factor price, and the landowners lose from the program. The value of land in crop production is still $\hat{P}_2$. The difference between $\hat{P}_2$ and P_s can now be seen as the rental value not of land as such, but of the right to use land. An acreage control program can be seen as introducing a new, artificially created factor of production, fixed in supply, that conveys the right to use land. Its price is a pure rent, which goes to zero in the absence of the program (when everybody has the right to grow the crop in unrestricted quantities). It is only the historical fact that rights to plant under acreage controls are allocated to landowners that allows us to view the rents created as returns to land, and that results in some—but not all or even necessarily most as we have seen—of the program's benefits being capitalized in land's price as an asset.

This discussion has been abstract in that we have not considered a particular program for a particular crop, or even stated whether we are referring to a crop or the whole agricultural sector. Any of these alternatives will do, so long as the relevant elasticities can be specified (and the necessary aggregation is legitimate). The expected result about land's gains as compared to nonland inputs will depend on these particulars. Some general tendencies can be hypothesized, however. For example, the more aggregated the program we are considering—reducing all cropland 10 percent as opposed to reducing soybean land 10 percent—the less elastic we expect the supply function of land to be, because there are fewer alternative uncontrolled uses. Also, the longer the run, the more elastic the supply function of nonland inputs (farmers' labor and manufactured goods). In fact, the idea that implicitly lies behind some depictions of land's dominance of program benefits is that in the long run the supply of nonland inputs is perfectly elastic. This is a case in which all other variables are overridden and all program benefits accrue to (the right to use) land.

It is instructive to confirm these results using the elasticities of Table 4.1. Looking at the P_b row, the denominators of all three formulas go to infinity as $e_b \rightarrow \infty$, so EP_b is zero. It is not so straightforward to see what happens to the formulas in the P_a row as $e_b \rightarrow \infty$ because e_b appears in both the numerator and denominator of each of them. Using the trick of dividing through by e_b before taking the limit, we find $EP_a/EP_x = 1/K_a$ for the deficiency payment and acreage control programs. If P_x rises 1 percent and K_a is 1/4, then P_a rises 4 percent: all the increase in commodity receipts goes to land. However, the production control still makes land worse off. All the gains go to quota rents.

Another extreme case is when $e_a = 0$, land is fixed in supply. In this case EP_a/EP_x rises, but not so much as to absorb all the program benefits. The reason is that as P_a rises, nonland inputs are substituted for land, which tends to drive up P_b. If $\sigma = 0$ and $e_a = 0$, then $EP_a/EP_x = 1/K_a$ for the deficiency payment program, and land gets all the benefits.

Other Input Market Regulation

Although acreage control is the commonest form of input intervention, the quantities of other inputs could be regulated, too. If we limit input b, the resulting formulas for changes in other endogenous prices are just as already derived for land, except that the a and b subscripts are exchanged in all equations. We obtain different results only because the parameter values are different for nonland inputs. We are inclined to believe that limiting fertilizer or tractor production would not be a useful basis for a price-support program, but there is no reason in principle why it could not be. The main parameter-value problem is that σ between particular purchased inputs and all other inputs is high so that P_x would not be increased much. More importantly, the rents created might go predominantly to nonfarm suppliers of these inputs. The input regulation that we do observe, such as on quantities of pesticides, appears designed to aid neither farmers nor input suppliers. This is clear for a ban on a chemical, since cutting quantity to zero cannot increase rents for either its consumers or producers, although it can increase rents of other farm inputs.

As these examples suggest, it is important to keep factor ownership in mind when translating input price changes into income gains and losses. Also, varying our concentration over different inputs makes it plain that the two-input restriction in our model is quite confining for some applications. Many-input models are discussed below.

Factor prices could also be regulated, but there are not many examples. One is minimum-wage legislation, applicable in the United States to sugar workers and employees of large farms generally. Requiring that workers be paid a wage $\hat{P}_b$ above the no-intervention wage is equivalent to reducing hours worked to the point that the wage is bid up to $\hat{P}_b$. Thus the formulas for a regulated P_b are essentially the same as the formulas for input quantity regulation. The income distribution results are more complicated for wage regulation than for acreage controls for reasons which fall outside the model. Under acreage controls each farmer might reduce plantings by 10 percent, but under equivalent minimum wage legislation, 90 percent of the workers might work the same hours as with no program while 10 percent of them do not work at all. Thus, minimum-wage regulation is likely to cause gainers and losers within the set of workers, while acreage controls have closer to the same effects on all landowners. Nonetheless, the effect of minimum wages on all workers as a group is analytically the same as the effect of acreage controls on all landowners as a group.

COMPLEX ELASTICITIES

Sometimes we are interested in how a function of endogenous variables changes when a support price changes. For example, what happens to the relative factor price ratio P_a/P_b. To express the answer to such questions compactly, we can construct "complex" elasticities using the properties of the percentage change operator E:

$$
\begin{aligned}
\frac{E(P_a/P_b)}{EP_x} &= \frac{d(P_a/P_b)/(P_a/P_b)}{dP_x/P_x} \\
&= \frac{P_b dP_a - P_a dP_b}{P_b^2} \frac{P_b}{P_a} \frac{P_x}{dP_x} \\
&= \frac{dP_a}{dP_x} \frac{P_x}{P_a} - \frac{dP_b}{dP_x} \frac{P_x}{P_b} \\
&= \frac{EP_a}{EP_x} - \frac{EP_b}{EP_x}
\end{aligned}
$$

Thus, we reduce complex to simple total elasticities. It is then easy to analyze the determinants of the complex elasticity. In the present case we subtract Eq. (4.11) from Eq. (4.10) to obtain

$$
\frac{E(P_a/P_b)}{EP_x} = \frac{e_b - e_a}{\sigma + K_a e_b + K_b e_a} \tag{4.18}
$$

This shows that for the government-purchase or target-price policy, the relative price of the factor least elastic in supply always increases.

But what if the policy generating the changes were acreage controls? Then we obtain the appropriate comparative statics from the appropriate elasticities in the right-hand column of Table 4.1. The result is

$$\frac{E(P_a/P_b)}{EP_x} = \frac{e_b - \eta}{K_a(\sigma + e_b)} \tag{4.19}$$

which is positive regardless of relative supply elasticities.

An issue that often arises in acreage controls is their effect on yields. Yield is not explicitly a variable in our six-equation system, so we cannot solve for the relevant elasticity directly. But we can find it indirectly. Yield is x/a. The elasticity of yield with respect to a, when the supply function of a is replaced by controlled $\hat{a}$, is

$$\frac{E(x/a)}{Ea} = \frac{d(x/a)/(x/a)}{\dfrac{da}{a}} = \frac{adx - xda}{a^2}\frac{a}{x}\frac{a}{da}$$

$$= \frac{dx}{da}\frac{a}{x} - \frac{da}{da}\frac{a}{a}$$

Since the actual quantity a is equal to the controlled $\hat{a}$

$$\frac{E(x/a)}{Ea} = E(x,a) - 1$$

From Eq. (4.1″), divide through by Ea to obtain

$$E(x,a) = K_a + K_b E(b,a) \tag{4.20}$$

From the system of Eqs. (4.10) to (4.12), we solve to find

$$E(b,a) = \frac{K_a(\sigma + \eta)}{\eta\sigma/e_b + K_a\eta - K_b\sigma} \tag{4.21}$$

Substituting in Eq. (4.14) yields

$$E(x,a) = K_a\left[1 + \frac{K_b(\sigma + \eta)}{\eta\sigma/e_b + K_a\eta - K_b\sigma}\right] \tag{4.22}$$

Note that if $e_b = 0$, that is, nonland inputs are fixed in quantity, Eq. (4.22) reduces to $E(x,a) = K_a$. Moreover, in the general case, whether $E(x,a) \lessgtr Ka$ depends on $\sigma \lessgtr -\eta$.

These results are helpful in explaining the phenomenon of "slippage" in acreage-control programs. If a 10 percent acreage reduction reduced output by 10 percent, there would be no slippage. Consider the scenario for U.S. corn in which K_a (land's share) is 0.3 $K_b = 0.7$, $\sigma = 0.5$, $e_b = 1$, and $\eta = -0.6$. Equation (4.22) is then

$$E(x,a) = 0.3\left[1 + \frac{0.7\,(0.5 - 0.6)}{-0.3 -0.18 -0.35}\right] = 0.28$$

Thus, if acreage is cut by 10 percent, output falls by only 2.8 percent.

The key variable in slippage is σ. Note that in the fixed proportions case, $\sigma = 0$. In Eq. (4.22), we then have

$$E(x,a) = K_a\left[1 + \frac{K_b}{K_a}\right] = 1$$

that is, there is no slippage.

EXOGENOUS POLICY INSTRUMENTS IN THE SYSTEM

In order to analyze shifts in policy parameters, such as subsidy rates or government purchases, we need to add exogenous variables to Eq. (4.1″) to (4.6″). The resulting system of equations is

$$\begin{bmatrix} 1 & -\eta & 0 & 0 & 0 & 0 \\ 1 & 0 & -k_a & -k_b & 0 & 0 \\ 0 & 0 & k_b/\sigma & -k_b/\sigma & 1 & 0 \\ 0 & 0 & -k_a/\sigma & k_a/\sigma & 0 & 1 \\ 0 & 0 & -1/e_a & 0 & 1 & 0 \\ 0 & 0 & 0 & -1/e_b & 0 & 1 \end{bmatrix} \begin{bmatrix} Ex \\ EP_x \\ Ea \\ Eb \\ EP_a \\ EP_b \end{bmatrix} = \begin{bmatrix} EG \\ 0 \\ 0 \\ 0 \\ ET_a \\ ET_b \end{bmatrix} \quad (4.23)$$

Where EG, ET_a, ET_b are changes in policy control variables, respectively, government purchases and taxes on inputs a and b, with a subsidy being represented as $-T_a$ or $-T_b$. Note that Eq. (4.6″), the product demand function, is moved to the first row, and that the factor supply equations (fifth and sixth rows) are specified in price-dependent form.

In this model, the choice of a policy, e.g., $\hat{G}$ does not fix any market quantities or prices directly, but all must adjust to the change to maintain supply–demand equilibrium. To analyze a change in $\hat{G}$, we divide all variables by EG, so that the percentage changes become cross-elasticities, Ex/EG, EP_x/EG, etc., and the right-hand side becomes $[1, 0, 0, 0, 0, 0]^T$.

The preceding system of equations can be expressed as $B_{6\times6} X_{6\times1} = Z_{6\times1}$. We solve for the variables $X = B^{-1}Z$. This gives reduced form equations which explain the variables X as a function of the parameters B and exogenous variables Z. The results are shown in Table 4.2.

Market interventions as modeled in the system (4.23) are a generalization of the earlier results in Table 4.1. For example, a change in G has effects isomorphic with the effects of fixing P_x via government purchase, as discussed in Chap. 2. The implication here is that the formulas shown in Table 4.1 are implicit in, and can be derived from, corresponding formulas in Table 4.2. Consider government purchases G. Government purchases increase P_x and P_a by amounts given in the top two formulas of the first column of Table 4.2. The fourth row of the first column of Table 4.1 gives relationships between P_a and P_x when we move along the supply curve of X, which we denote as EP_a/EP_x. The two formulas cited in Table 4.2 are EP_a/EG and EP_x/EG. Therefore, dividing EP_a/EG by EP_x/EG gives EP_a/EP_x, i.e.,

$$\frac{(\sigma + e_b)/D}{(\sigma + K_b e_a + K_a e_b)/D} = \frac{\sigma + e_b}{\sigma + e_1}$$

where e_1 is defined as in Table 4.1. Similarly, each column of Table 4.2 can be used to derive any desired set of cross-elasticities relating endogenous variables for the given policy.

Table 4.2 Effects of Exogenous Policy Variables on Endogenous Variables*

Endogenous variables	Exogenous variable		
	G	**T_a**	**T_b**
P_x	$\dfrac{\sigma + K_b e_a + K_a e_b}{D}$	$\dfrac{K_a e_a(e_b + \sigma)}{D}$	$\dfrac{K_b e_b(e_b + \sigma)}{D}$
P_a	$\dfrac{\sigma + e_b}{D}$	$\dfrac{e_a(e_b + K_a\sigma - K_b\eta)}{D}$	$\dfrac{K_b e_b(\sigma + \eta)}{D}$
P_b	$\dfrac{\sigma + e_a}{D}$	$\dfrac{K_a e_a(\sigma + \eta)}{D}$	$\dfrac{e_b(e_a + K_b\sigma - K_a\eta)}{D}$
X	$\dfrac{e_a e_b + \sigma(K_a e_a + K_b e_b)}{D}$	$\dfrac{K_a \eta e_a(e_b + \sigma)}{D}$	$\dfrac{K_b \eta e_b(e_a + \sigma)}{D}$
a	$\dfrac{e_a(\sigma + e_b)}{D}$	$\dfrac{e_a\sigma\eta - e_b(K_b\sigma - K_a\eta)}{D}$	$\dfrac{K_b e_a e_b(\sigma + \eta)}{D}$
b	$\dfrac{e_b(\sigma + e_a)}{D}$	$\dfrac{K_a e_a e_b(\sigma + \eta)}{D}$	$\dfrac{e_b\sigma\eta - e_a(K_a\sigma - K_b\eta)}{D}$

*Entries show effect of percentage changes in the exogenous variables on percentage changes in the endogenous variables, e.g., $\%\Delta P_x/\%\Delta G$, or the elasticity EP_x/EG.

$D = \det B = e_a e_b - \eta\,(\sigma + K_a e_b + K_b e_a + \sigma(K_a e_a + K_b e_b)$.

$D > 0$ for $\eta < 0$, $e_a \geq 0$, $e_b \geq 0$.

For a simple supply–demand model, Eq. (2.17) gives the result that a demand shift, EG, would yield

$$\frac{EP}{EG} = \frac{1}{\epsilon - \eta} \tag{4.24}$$

In the current context, ϵ is the derived elasticity of supply, Ex/EP_x from Eq. (4.12). Substituting Eq. (4.12) into Eq. (4.24)

$$\frac{EP_x}{EG} = \frac{1}{[e_a e_b + \sigma (K_a e_a + K_b e_b)]/[\sigma + K_b e_a + K_a e_b] - \eta} \tag{4.25}$$

$$= \frac{\sigma + e_1}{e_a e_b + \sigma e_2 - \eta (\sigma + e_1)}$$

where $e_1 = K_a e_b + K_b e_a$, the weighted factor supply elasticity defined in Table 4.1, and e_2 reverses the weights: $e_2 = K_a e_a + K_b e_b$. Note that Eq. (4.25) is the upper left-hand entry in Table 4.2. Thus, there is a direct correspondence between the simple supply–demand model of Chap. 2 and comparative statics of this one-product, two-input model.

If we had used a price-dependent specification, we would have

$$\frac{EP}{EV} = \frac{\epsilon}{\eta - \epsilon} \tag{4.26}$$

where V is a subsidy (as a percentage of price). Note that P could be either on the demand or supply function, but as specified [in Eqs. (2.10) to (2.13)], it is the demand price. Supply price (price received by purchasers) is $P_d + V$ ($= P_s$). Thus, multiplying EP/EG by ϵ yields EP/EV; we can convert directly from the price effect of a government purchase to the price effect of a subsidy payment.

Applying this result to Eq. (4.25), multiplying it by Eq. (4.12) gives the corresponding result for the two-input model:[5]

$$\frac{EP_x}{EV} = \frac{\sigma + e_1}{e_a e_b + \sigma e_2 - \eta (\sigma + e_1)} \frac{e_a e_b + \sigma e_2}{\sigma + e_1} \tag{4.27}$$

This is the fourth entry in the first column of Table 4.2. That is, we have

$$\frac{EX}{EG} = \frac{EP_x}{EV} \tag{4.28}$$

The total effect of a horizontal demand shift on X is the same as that of vertical shift of the same proportion on P_x. The reason is apparent graphically in that we are taking the horizontal (X) axis as the "dependent" variable in the first case, and the vertical (P) axis in the second.

Input Subsidies

Developing countries commonly subsidize fertilizer, irrigation, or other "modern" inputs, and industrial countries also subsidize irrigation projects, credit for farmers, and, by special tax treatment, some forms of investment. Also some input users are taxed or regulated, for example, in environmental policies banning certain pesticides. Quantitative regulation of an input is, in our model, equivalent to acreage control, with the input referred to as "a" suitably changed. Input subsidies, however, have not yet been explicitly discussed.

Consider a subsidy paid to farmers for each ton of fertilizer used. This is analyzed by means of a reduction in T_a using the elasticities in the middle column of Table 4.2, with input a being fertilizer and b all other inputs as an aggregate. Assume that $K_a = 0.15$, $\eta = -0.4$, $e_a = 2.0$, $e_b = 0.5$, and $\sigma = 1.0$. The elasticities imply that for each 1-percent increase in the fertilizer subsidy (i.e., the price to farmers is reduced by 1 percent) the following price and quantity changes result: P_x falls by 0.16 percent, P_a falls by 0.70 percent, P_b falls by 0.06 percent, X rises by 0.06 percent, a rises by 0.60 percent, and b falls by 0.03 percent. The effects for this case are sketched in Fig. 4.4. The qualitative effects would be the same for all (normally signed) parameter values in the a and x markets. However, the direction of effects in the b market would be reversed if $\sigma < |\eta|$, in which case subsidizing input a will increase the use of b.

Note the contrast between input quantity controls and input subsidies. Reducing the quantity of input a is beneficial to suppliers of input b if $\sigma > -\eta$, but a subsidy of input a is beneficial to suppliers of input b if $\sigma < -\eta$. The reason is that the former policy raises P_a, so the better are the substitution possibilities, the better off is b; but the subsidy lowers P_a, so a high σ leads to substitution away from b.

Equivalence of Input and Output Subsidies

Tolley et al. (1982) consider this topic in the context of a model consisting of Eq. (4.1') to (4.3') only. It omits consideration of product demand and input supply. It is thus best construed as a firm-level model. The production function is accordingly not restricted to be linear homogeneous. They consider three policy disturbances to this system: first, changing P_x as a policy variable, holding P_a and P_b constant; second, changing P_a as a policy variable, holding P_x and P_b constant; third, changing P_b as a policy variable, holding P_x and P_a constant.

For the first policy change, divide Eq. (4.1') to (4.3') by dP_x to obtain the system of equations:

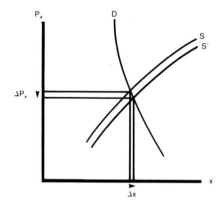

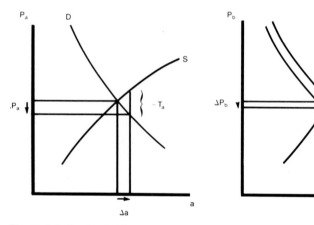

Figure 4.4 Input subsidy.

$$
\begin{bmatrix}
f_a & f_b & -1 \\[2ex]
P_x f_{aa} & P_x f_{ab} & 0 \\[2ex]
P_x f_{ba} & P_x f_{bb} & 0
\end{bmatrix}
\begin{bmatrix}
\dfrac{da}{dP_x} \\[2ex]
\dfrac{db}{dP_x} \\[2ex]
\dfrac{dx}{dP_x}
\end{bmatrix}
=
\begin{bmatrix}
0 \\[2ex]
-f_a \\[2ex]
-f_b
\end{bmatrix}
$$

Solving for dx/dP_x yields

$$
\frac{dx}{dP_x} = \frac{f_b(f_b f_{aa} - f_a f_{ab}) + f_a(f_a f_{bb} - f_b f_{ab})}{P_x(f_{ab}^2 - f_{aa} f_{bb})}
\tag{4.29}
$$

which is an expression for the (firm-level) elasticity of supply.

Solving the corresponding systems of equations for the second and third policy changes, the results are

$$\frac{dx}{dP_a} = \frac{f_b f_{ab} - f_a f_{bb}}{P_x (f_{ab}^2 - f_{aa} f_{bb})} \tag{4.30}$$

$$\frac{dx}{dP_b} = \frac{f_a f_{ab} - f_b f_{aa}}{P_x (f_{ab}^2 - f_{aa} f_{bb})} \tag{4.31}$$

Substituting Eqs. (4.30) and (4.31) into Eq. (4.29):

$$\frac{dx}{dP_x} = -f_a \frac{dx}{dP_a} - f_b \frac{dx}{dP_b} \tag{4.32}$$

Converting to elasticities by the usual manipulations yields

$$\left.\frac{EX}{EP_x}\right|_{\bar{P}_a, \bar{P}_b} = -\left.\frac{EX}{EP_a}\right|_{\bar{P}_x, \bar{P}_b} - \left.\frac{EX}{EP_b}\right|_{\bar{P}_x, \bar{P}_a} \tag{4.33}$$

The vertical lines indicate that these are *partial* elasticities, holding prices constant as indicated. These are conceptually quite different from the total elasticities we have been using. Equation (4.33) says that an increase in output price is equivalent to an equal percentage decline in both input prices. This seems too simple a result to require such a complicated derivation, and indeed it is a straightforward result in the dual approach to the theory of the firm. The profit function at the firm's optimum is

$$\pi^*(P_x, P_a, P_b) = P_x X^* - P_a a^* - P_b b^* \tag{4.34}$$

where at the optimum $X^* = X^*(P_x, P_a, P_b)$ and similarly for a^* and b^*.

The envelope theorem yields

$$\frac{\partial \pi^*}{\partial P_x} = X^* \qquad \frac{\partial \pi^*}{\partial P_a} = -a^* \qquad \frac{\partial \pi_z}{\partial P_b} = -b^*$$

which gives production and input use at the optimum. Assuming the profit function is twice continuously differentiable, we know that

$$\frac{\partial^2 \pi^*}{\partial P_x \partial P_a} = \frac{\partial^2 \pi^*}{\partial P_a \partial P_x} \quad \text{and} \quad \frac{\partial^2 \pi^*}{\partial P_x P_b} = \frac{\partial^2 \pi^*}{\partial P_b \partial P_x} \tag{4.35}$$

Substituting the envelope results for the first partials in Eq. (4.35), the second partials can be expressed as

$$\frac{\partial x}{\partial P_a} = -\frac{\partial a}{\partial P_x} \quad \text{and} \quad \frac{\partial x}{\partial P_b} = -\frac{\partial b}{\partial x}$$

Now going back to Eq. (4.1′) expressed as derivatives with respect to P_x, substitute these results in its right-hand side to obtain Eq. (4.32) directly.

Recall that these results are derived at the level of the competitive firm. Does a variant of Eq. (4.33) hold at the industry level? At the industry level we cannot change P_x and expect P_a and P_b to remain unchanged. The issue is whether a subsidy $-T_a$ and $-T_b$ of the same size has the same effects as a subsidy on output, V. Using the fact that $Ex/EV = \epsilon\, EP_x/EV$ (using ϵ, instead of η because we are moving along the supply function of x), we have, from endnote 5 and using ϵ from Eq. (4.12),

$$\frac{EX}{EV} = \frac{-\eta\,(\sigma + e_1)}{e_a\,e_b + \sigma e_2 - \eta\,(\sigma + e_1)}\;\frac{e_a\,e_b + \sigma e_2}{\sigma + e_1} \tag{4.36}$$
$$= \frac{-\eta\,[e_a\,e_b + \sigma\,(K_a\,e_a + K_b\,e_b)]}{D}$$

using definitions of D and e_2 given above. Now taking minus the sum of Ex/ET_a and Ex/ET_b from Table 4.2,

$$-\frac{EX}{ET_a} - \frac{EX}{ET_b} = \frac{-K_a\,\eta e_a\,(e_b + \sigma) - K_b\,\eta e_b\,(e_a + \sigma)}{D} \tag{4.37}$$
$$= \frac{-\eta\,[e_a\,e_b + \sigma\,(K_a\,e_a + K_b e_b)]}{D}$$

Since the right-hand sides of Eqs. (4.36) and (4.37) are equal, the equivalence between output and equal input subsidies holds.

Note that Eq. (4.36) could also be expressed as $\eta \cdot EX/EG$, using the expression in the fourth line of column 1 of Table 4.2, yielding the same right-hand side as in Eq. (4.36).

Effective Protection

These results allow a fuller consideration of the effective rate of protection, the idea that a country's nominal protection in commodity markets can be offset or augmented by intervention in some (but not all) input markets. Of particular interest is the situation in a developing country that taxes agricultural output but subsidizes modern inputs. The effect of the tax on the producer price P_s is obtained by changing the sign of the equation in endnote 5 (because the tax on x, T_x, is a negative subsidy), that is,

$$\frac{EP_s}{ET_x} = \frac{\eta\,(\sigma + e_1)}{e_a\,e_b + \sigma e_2 - \eta\,(\sigma + e_1)} \tag{4.38}$$

The effect of a change in the input subsidy $V_a (= -T_a)$ on P_s, is obtained by multiplying EX/ET_a by $- 1/\epsilon$, which yields

$$\frac{EP_s}{EV_a} = \frac{-K_a \eta e_a (e_b + \sigma)}{e_a e_b + \sigma e_2 - \eta (\sigma + e_1)} \frac{\sigma + e_1}{e_a e_b + \sigma e_2}$$

$$= \frac{- \eta (\sigma + e_1) \left(K_a \left[\dfrac{e_a e_b + \sigma e_a}{e_a e_b + \sigma (K_a e_a + K_b e_b)} \right] \right)}{e_a e_b + \sigma e_2 - \eta (\sigma + e_1)} \qquad (4.39)$$

The change in effective rate of producer protection is $EP_s/ ET_x \cdot \Delta T_x + EP_s/EV_a \Delta V_a$. Equations (4.38) and (4.39) would be equal and opposite in sign if $K_a = 1$. That is, if we were subsidizing all inputs, then the change in effective protection is zero if $\Delta T_x = \Delta V_a$, the change in tax rate equalled the change in the subsidy. But generally, a bigger percentage subsidy increase is needed. A helpful special case occurs when $\sigma = 0$, i.e., subsidized and unsubsidized inputs are used in fixed proportions. Then, the effective rate of protection change is

$$\Delta EPR = \frac{EP_s}{ET_x} \Delta T_x + \frac{EP_s}{EV_a} \Delta V_a$$

$$= \frac{\eta e_1}{e_a e_b - \eta_1} \Delta T_x - \frac{\eta e_1 K_a}{e_a e_b - \eta e_1} \Delta V_a \qquad (4.40)$$

$$= \frac{\eta e_1}{e_a e_b - \eta e_1} (\Delta T_x - K_a \Delta V_a)$$

Thus, if K_a is 1/4, a 10-percent tax on output is just offset by a 40-percent subsidy on modern inputs.

But, of course, the idea of subsidizing modern inputs is to encourage their use, which must mean that substitutability between a and b is expected, i.e., $\sigma \neq 0$. Suppose $\sigma = 1$. How far wrong will we be in using 4.40? The answer depends on the size of the term in square brackets in Eq. (4.39), which multiplies K_a in (4.40) if $\sigma \neq 0$. Consider that modern inputs are more elastic in supply than traditional inputs ($e_a = 0.3$, $e_b = 2.0$). Let $K_a = 0.25$ and $K_b = 0.75$. Then the term in square brackets is equal to 0.424. Equation (4.40) is (using $\eta = -0.5$):

$$\Delta EPR = -0.377 (\Delta T_x - 0.106 \Delta V_a)$$

If we were assessing a 10-percent output tax increase accompanied by a 20-percent input subsidy increase, the change in the effective rate of protection would be $-0.377 [10 - 0.106(20)] = -2.97$, i.e., a 3-percent decrease in producer protection. If we had simply taken the tax increase minus subsidy increase weighted by input share we would have $-[10 - 0.25 (20)] = -5$, i.e., a 5-percent decrease in protection. Depending on the size of the tax and subsidy and the particular parameters, crude methods of calculating effective rates of protection could be seriously in error.

MANY-INPUT MODELS

The firm-level results of Eqs. (4.33) to (4.35) are readily extended to cover any number of inputs. Since the two-input restriction of our industry model is too restrictive for some issues, consider extending the model to contain more. In Eqs. (4.1) to (4.6), we add a *VMP* equation and an input supply equation for each additional input. To solve for comparative statics of in terms of percentage changes, the system of Eq. (4.23) must be expanded accordingly. This requires adding two new rows for each new input, and new parameters: the factor share, the elasticity of supply, and the elasticities of substitution for the each added input.

The elasticities of substitution cause added complexity when we move beyond two inputs. For example, if we add fertilizer as an input to a model containing land and labor, we need to allow for the possibility that fertilizer substitutes less well for labor than it does for land. For a three input model, Eqs. (4.23) become

$$
\begin{bmatrix}
1 - \eta & 0 & 0 & 0 & 0 & 0 & 0 \\
1 & 0 & 0 & 0 & 0 & -K_a & -K_b & K_c \\
0 & 0 & -\gamma_{aa} & -\gamma_{ab} & -\gamma_{ac} & 1 & 0 & 0 \\
0 & 0 & -\gamma_{ba} & -\gamma_{bb} & -\gamma_{bc} & 0 & 1 & 0 \\
0 & 0 & -\gamma_{ca} & -\gamma_{cb} & -\gamma_{cc} & 0 & 0 & 1 \\
0 & 0 & 1 & 0 & 0 & -1/e_a & 0 & 0 \\
0 & 0 & 0 & 1 & 0 & 0 & -1/e_b & 0 \\
0 & 0 & 0 & 0 & 1 & 0 & 0 & -1/e_c
\end{bmatrix}
\begin{bmatrix}
Ex \\
EP_x \\
EP_a \\
EP_b \\
EP_c \\
Ea \\
Eb \\
Ec
\end{bmatrix}
=
\begin{bmatrix}
EG \\
0 \\
0 \\
0 \\
0 \\
ET_a \\
ET_b \\
ET_c
\end{bmatrix}
\quad (4.41)
$$

where $\gamma_{ij} = K_j (\sigma_{ij} - \eta)$ with σ_{ij} the Allen partial elasticity of substitution (see Allen, 1938, p. 504). The γ_{ij} are partial elasticities of demand in the sense that they show the effect of a change in the jth input price on the ith input quantity holding prices of other inputs constant.

An algebraic solution for, say, EP_a/ET_b, is now much more complicated than the formulas shown in Table 4.2. The structure of determinants of policy effects is not apparent. Simulation of policies in this model can just as well use the system (4.41) directly. We plug in the values of parameters and then solve the system using a computer to invert the coefficient matrix.

For calculating purposes, it is convenient to equate supply and demand for output and each input, yielding the four-equation system:

$$
\begin{bmatrix}
\eta & -K_a & -K_b & -K_c \\
0 & 1-\gamma_{aa}/e_a & -\gamma_{ab}/e_b & -\gamma_{ac}/e_c \\
0 & -\gamma_{ba}/e_a & 1-\gamma_{bb}/e_b & -\gamma_{bc}/e_c \\
0 & -\gamma_{ca}/e_a & -\gamma_{cb}/e_b & 1-\gamma_{cc}/e_c
\end{bmatrix}
\begin{bmatrix}
EP_x \\
Ea \\
Eb \\
Ec
\end{bmatrix}
=
\begin{bmatrix}
EG \\
\gamma_{aa}ET_a \\
\gamma_{ba}ET_a \\
\gamma_{ca}ET_a
\end{bmatrix}
\qquad (4.42)
$$

To analyze a change in T_a, divide all equations by ET_a, let $EG = 0$, and solve for $E(\cdot)/ET_a$ for all four variables. From these results, the effects on other variables are straightforward to estimate. For example, we know that $EX = \eta EP_x$. The input prices are found from $EP_a = 1/e_a\,Ea + ET_a$, or $EP_a/ET_a = 1/e_a(Ea/ET_a) + 1$. To investigate changes in T_b, which were zero in Eq. (4.42), we place $\gamma_{ab}ET_b$, $\gamma_{bb}ET_b$, and $\gamma_{cb}ET_b$ on the right-hand side. Note that although $\sigma_{ij} = \sigma_{ji}$, it is not true that $\gamma_{ij} = \gamma_{ji}$ unless $K_i = 1/3$ for all three inputs.

As an example, consider a fertilizer subsidy program. Let a be fertilizer; b, labor; and c, land. Suppose we learn that fertilizer substitutes well for land but less well for labor, specifically $\sigma_{ab} = 0.3$, $\sigma_{ac} = 1.0$, and $\sigma_{bc} = 0.5$. For factor shares, $K_a = 0.2$, $K_b = 0.5$, and $K_c = 0.3$. The σ_{ij} are not all independent of one another. In particular,

$$
\sigma_{aa} = \frac{K_b\,\sigma_{ab} + K_c\,\sigma_{ac}}{-K_a} \qquad (4.43)
$$

(This result is derived in the n $-$ input case in Allen, pp. 503–505.) Using analogous equations for the other own-elasticities, we have our example $\sigma_{aa} = -2.25$, $\sigma_{bb} = -0.42$, and $\sigma_{cc} = -1.5$. Fertilizer is elastic in supply, but labor and land less so: $e_a = 2.0$, $e_b = 1.0$, and $e_c = 0.2$. Output has inelastic demand, $\eta = -0.4$. Calculating the γ_{ij} and substituting in Eqs. (4.42), the system becomes

$$
\begin{bmatrix}
-0.4 & -0.2 & -0.5 & -0.3 \\
0.0 & 1.26 & 0.05 & -0.09 \\
0.0 & 0.01 & 1.41 & -0.15 \\
0.0 & -0.06 & -0.05 & 3.85
\end{bmatrix}
\begin{bmatrix}
EP_x/ET_a \\
Ea/ET_a \\
Eb/ET_a \\
Ec/ET_a
\end{bmatrix}
=
\begin{bmatrix}
0 \\
-0.53 \\
-0.41 \\
-0.57
\end{bmatrix}
\qquad (4.44)
$$

Using Cramer's rule to solve the system, we find that a 10-percent subsidy ($ET_a = -10$) causes the following percentage changes: $Ea = 4.2$, $Eb = 3.1$, $Ec = 1.6$, and $EP_x = -7.2$. The corresponding changes in the remaining variables are $Ex = 2.9$, $EP_a = -7.9$, $EP_b = 3.1$, $EP_c = 8.0$. Note that the fall in P_a refers to price paid by farmers for fertilizer (price on the demand curve) due to the specification of the equation containing T_a. The increase in price received by fertilizer sellers is $-7.9 + 10 = 2.1$ percent. Thus, land owners gain most from the fertilizer subsidy despite fertilizer and land being good substitutes. The story would have been different if land had been more elastic in supply. The model permits the analysis of such possibilities. Of course, the most difficult part of this type of policy analysis is obtaining reliable estimates of the appropriate parameter values. The simulations can be quite valuable, however, in indicating which parameters matter most, and how much they matter.

Solving the model for expressions, such as those in Table 4.2, would make these matters even clearer, except that the additional parameters, especially σ's, make the equations too complicated for their economic content to be accessible. Welch (1970c) analyzes a model in which there are three inputs, but the marginal rate of substitution between two of them (land and labor) is independent of the quantity of the third (purchased inputs). He then uses separability properties to generate a model having only two elasticities of substitution—between land and labor, and between purchased inputs and a land-labor aggregate. This yields results only a little more complicated than those of Table 4.1. However, it is questionable whether the assumed structure of production is applicable. Equations (4.42) are more general.

Equations (4.42) are especially helpful as compared to the earlier two-input model in that it is apparent how to extend Eqs. (4.42) to accommodate still more inputs. For example, in the case of the fertilizer subsidy, we might want to separate out nonfertilizer inputs purchased by farmers. This can be done by adding a row and column to the coefficient matrix and a new variable, Ed. Then respecifying the K's appropriately and adding appropriate parameter values for e_d, γ_{da}, γ_{db}, and γ_{dc}, we are ready to simulate a four-input model.

ENDNOTES

1. Policy experiments will be approximations even where these assumptions hold because factor shares may change. For the results to be exact, we need Eq. (4.1) to be CES with $\sigma = 1$, i.e., Cobb-Douglas, in which case factor shares are constant.
2. Confusion between this multimarket model and a general equilibrium model has misled some economists, as in the irrelevant critique of Floyd contained in a note by Auerbach (1970).
3. This is the same as Floyd's Eq. (14) (Floyd, 1965, p. 153). Note that it is the reciprocal of the elasticity of the derived demand function for the factor a, as given in Hicks (1932).
4. Checks on the calculations can be made using Eq. (4.1''), the fact that $EP_x = K_a P_a + K_b P_b$, and the constancy of K_a and K_b when $\sigma = 1$. (None of these checks is exact when $\sigma \neq 1$ because then K_a and K_b changes when P_x changes.) Using Eq. (4.1'') in the second policy, $Ex = K_a Ea + K_b Eb$, or $-12 = 0.3(-49.3) + 0.7(4.0)$.
5. If price were defined as supply price P_s, we obtain EP_s/EV by multiplying Eq. (4.25) by $-\eta$ to obtain

$$\frac{EP_s}{EV} = \frac{-\eta(\sigma + e_l)}{e_a e_b + \sigma e_2 - \eta(\sigma + e_l)}$$

Chapter 5

Models of Related Markets

In studying the one-product, n-input situation, we have been using a particular multimarket model. In this chapter, policy issues are studied that require multimarket models at the product level. To begin with the simplest cases, a model for analyzing joint products (like honey and beeswax) is laid out and applied to some issues that cannot be properly analyzed using a single-product model. Second, we consider the consequences of marketing costs and middlemen, explicitly differentiating between the supported farm-level product and the final product that consumers buy. The structure of the model is the same as in Chap. 4, but the introduction of imperfect competition adds complications. Third, a model is developed for the study of multiple products and multiple inputs simultaneously. Chapter 3 provided a start in considering three products simultaneously, but it omitted the input markets, which Chap. 4 has shown to be a requirement for analyzing acreage controls or input subsidies.

The essential multimarket economics can be studied without undue complexity in two-product, two-input model where all four markets are competitive. Since neither the commodities nor the inputs exhaust the economy, we do not have a full general equilibrium model, and we have a ''real'' (relative) price for each commodity and each input.

Complicated models can incorporate more realistic assumptions about the markets, but quickly become too complex to grasp the details intuitively. The more complex models are used mainly in simulation or as a framework for econometric work.

JOINT PRODUCTS

Joint products are two or more commodities produced in a single production process. Many of the traditional examples of joint products are agricultural: wool and mutton, beef and cowhides, sugar and molasses, soybean oil and soybean meal, honey and pollination services, and many others. Joint products raise interesting and important problems in economic analysis of market intervention, particularly in predicting the consequences of a change in the market for one of a pair of joint products. Consider recent proposals for large-scale production of agricultural synfuels, notably grain alcohol (ethanol) and edible fats and oils as substitutes for diesel fuel. Ethanol production, for example, yields substantial quantities of distillers' dried grain (DDG) as a by-product. (*By-products* are a subset of joint products taken to be in some sense less important than the *main* product, but the economic analysis of by-products is identical to that of joint products.) We want to be able to analyze the consequences in the feed market. Is it possible, for example, that feed prices could be driven down enough by the by-products that the cost of producing food could be decreased even though the diversion of grain to alcohol is expected to raise grain prices?

An argument of this sort was given by the soybean processors in making the case for restricting imports of palm oil, which competes with soybean oil. They argued that increased U.S. imports of palm oil would reduce the price of U.S. soybean oil, and because soybean production costs must be covered by either meal or oil value, that this in turn would increase soybean meal prices, hence, the price of meat and consumers' food bills. Consequently, it was said that U.S. consumers would be made better off by restricting palm oil imports! A simple model of market equilibrium for the joint products will show that this argument is invalid.

Before proceeding to details of the model, it is necessary to define joint products more precisely, in two respects. First, we define jointness *at the margin*. Consider dairy production as a single process. Before it can produce milk, a cow must normally give birth to a calf. Therefore, milk and veal are joint products in the dairy production process. This fits Pasinetti's (1980) definition of joint products as "those goods that cannot be produced separately from each other" (p. xii). However, in our simplest model defining jointness at the margin, two commodities are joint products only if *changing* the output of one of them necessarily changes the output of the other. Milk and veal are not joint products in this sense; a cow's milk production can be increased (for example, by increased feeding during lactation) without having any effect on the output of veal.

Second, our simple model considers jointness in the strict sense that the products are necessarily produced in fixed proportions, so that a 1-percent increase in one implies a 1-percent increase in the other. Many pairs of commodities such as those listed above approach being joint products in the strict sense in the short run, but in the long run, the proportions may be and have been varied, often by changing the nature of the animal or process that produces the joint products. Changes in factor and product proportions within a given multiproduct production function are discussed below, e.g., changing the ration or length of fattening period of steers in order to change the product mix of beef carcasses. Changes in the nature of the process, such as the development of leaner hogs or bald sheep, would be instances of induced innovation which are not discussed further.

To develop the model in terms of an intuitive example, consider the discovery that soybean oil can be used directly, with simple engine modifications, as diesel fuel. In the strict joint product case, the demand for a given quantity of soybeans can be decomposed into a joint demand for specific quantities of oil and meal. That is, the maximum that will be paid for any given quantity of soybeans is the sum of the maximum that will be paid for oil from these beans plus the maximum that will be paid for meal from these beans. This case is diagrammed in Fig. 5.1, with the demand curve for soybeans being the vertical sum of the demand curves for oil and meal. The effect of increased synfuels demand for soybean oil is to shift the demand for oil, and therefore the demand for beans, to the right, while leaving the demand curve for meal and the supply curve of soybeans unchanged. At the new equilibrium, the price of oil and beans is higher and the price of meal is lower. The sizes of these changes relative to one another depend on the elasticities of demand for oil and meal, the elasticity of supply of beans, and the technical coefficients relating quantities of soybeans to quantities of oil and meal.

The model in Fig. 5.1 can be written algebraically as follows. First, demand functions for the products are written as

$$X = D_1 (P_x, Z_1) \tag{5.1}$$
$$Y = D_2 (P_y, Z_2) \tag{5.2}$$

where X is the quantity of one joint product (e.g., soybean oil), with P_x the price of soybean oil. Z_1 is an exogenous variable (e.g., in the case of soybean oil as fuel, the price of petroleum-based diesel fuel). Similarly, Y is the quantity of the other joint product (e.g., soybean meal), with price P_y and Z_2 is an exogenous variable in this equation (e.g., the quantity of livestock). (All equations may contain other variables, but they are assumed held constant for present purposes.)

Supply of the raw material or common resource (e.g., soybeans):

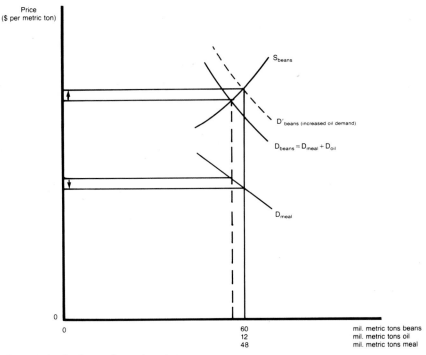

Figure 5.1 Soybean oil–meal market.

$$a = g(P_a, Z_3) \tag{5.3}$$

where a is the quantity produced, P_a is its price, and Z_3 is an exogenous variable such as a fertilizer price index.

Production relation for each product:

$$a = \gamma_x X \tag{5.4}$$

$$a = \gamma_y Y \tag{5.5}$$

where γ_x and γ_y are, for example, the tons of beans necessary to produce 1 ton of oil and meal, respectively. Although Eqs. (5.4) and (5.5) may be interpreted as separate production functions, they do not violate the definition of joint technology because the same value of a is common to them.

Price equation:

$$P_a = \frac{1}{\gamma_x} P_x + \frac{1}{\gamma_y} P_y - P_s \tag{5.6}$$

where P_s is the price of processing services necessary to crush 1 ton of soybeans.

To illustrate, if 1 ton of soybeans yields 0.2 ton oil and 0.8 ton meal (so that $\gamma_x = 5$ and $\gamma_y = 1.25$), the price of crushing services is \$4.00 per ton, and the price of soybean meal is \$130 per metric ton and oil \$375 per ton, then

$$P_a = 0.2(375) + 0.8(130) - 4 = 175$$

that is, the implied price of soybeans if \$175 per metric ton (\$4.77 per bushel). The price so derived is the maximum that would be paid for the bean equivalent of oil and meal. It would be the market price if crushing costs were zero. If crushing costs are a constant amount per bushel, they are subtracted to get the wholesale price of soybeans (and transportation and handling costs would be subtracted as well to get the farm price). In what follows, crushing costs are taken to be a constant so that P_s is exogenous and $dP_s = 0$.

These six equations contain six endogenous variables: the prices and quantities of the two products and their source raw material. After introducing an exogenous change in any of the exogenous variables, Z_1, Z_2, or Z_3, the determinants of resulting changes in the remaining variables can be analyzed.

Price Relationships in the Model

To examine the effects of an exogenous change, first differentiate each equation totally:

$$dx = \frac{\partial x}{\partial P_x} dP_x + \frac{\partial x}{\partial z_1} dz_1 \tag{5.1}$$

$$dy = \frac{\partial y}{\partial P_y} dP_y + \frac{\partial y}{\partial z_2} dz_2 \tag{5.2}$$

$$da = \frac{\partial a}{\partial P_a} dP_a + \frac{\partial a}{\partial z_3} dz_3 \tag{5.3}$$

$$da = \gamma_x dx \tag{5.4}$$

$$da = \gamma_y dy \tag{5.5}$$

$$dP_a = \frac{1}{\gamma_y} dP_x + \frac{1}{\gamma_y} dP_y \tag{5.6}$$

Next, these changes are expressed in terms of percentage changes, for which elasticity notation will be used; i.e., Ex means dx/x or $\%\Delta x$. The elasticity relationships are

$$Ex = \eta_x EP_x + \eta_{xz_1} Ez_1 \tag{5.7}$$

$$Ey = \eta_y EP_y + \eta_{yz_1} Ez_2 \tag{5.8}$$

$$Ea = e_a EP_a + e_{az_3} Ez_3 \tag{5.9}$$

$$Ea = Ex \tag{5.10}$$

$$Ea = Ey \tag{5.11}$$

$$EP_a = K_x EP_x + K_y EP_y \tag{5.12}$$

where η_x and η_y are the own-price elasticities of demand for each of the joint products x and y, e_a is the elasticity of supply of the common raw material or resource, K_x and K_y are the shares of the value of a accounted for by x and y, and η_{xz1}, η_{yz2}, and e_{az3}, are partial elasticities of endogenous with respect to exogenous variables.

The reason why γ_x and γ_y disappear in moving from Eqs. (5.4) and (5.5) to Eqs. (5.10) and (5.11) may be illustrated with reference to Eq. (5.4). Multiplying by a/a and x/x and substituting $\gamma_x = a/x$ from Eq. (5.4) transforms Eq. (5.4) as follows:

$$\frac{da}{a}\,a = \frac{a}{x}\frac{dx}{x}\,x$$

$$\frac{da}{a} = \frac{dx}{x} \qquad (\text{i.e., } Ea = Ex)$$

Similar manipulations of Eq. (5.6) are as follows:

$$\frac{dP_a}{P_a}\,P_a = \frac{x}{a}\frac{dPx}{P_x}\,P_x + \frac{y}{a}\frac{dP_y}{P_y}\,P_y$$

$$\frac{dP_a}{P_a} = \frac{xP_x}{aP_a}\frac{dPx}{P_x} + \frac{yP_y}{aP_a}\frac{dP_y}{P_y}$$

which in $E\,(\cdot)$ notation is Eq. (5.12).

Formulas for Application

A change in the availability of diesel fuel would constitute an exogenous change in the variable EZ_1 in Eq. (5.7). To analyze the effects of such a change, let $EZ_2 = EZ_3 = 0$, and divide each equation by EZ_1. This produces a system of six equations in six unknowns, where each variable is an elasticity with respect to Z_1 which can be solved as a function of the parameters of the equations. For example, solving for the elasticity of the soybean price, P_a, with respect to Z_1 yields

$$\frac{EP_a}{EZ_1} = \frac{K_x\,\eta_x\,Z_1\,\eta_y}{-\eta_x\,\eta_y + e_a\,(K_x\,\eta_y + K_y\,\eta_x)} \qquad (5.13)$$

The total elasticity given by Eq. (5.13) is a function of the partial elasticities from Eqs. (5.7) to (5.12). Suppose we want to consider the effects of alternative quantities of soybean oil shifted to diesel fuel. Then Z_1 is the quantity of diesel fuel. Equation (5.13) will provide a mechanism for an assessment of the consequences of changes in Z_1. Assume the following values: $K_x = 0.4$ and $K_y = 0.6$, from the prices and quantities of oil and meal used above; $\eta_x = 1.3$, η_y

$= 0.7$, and $e_a = 0.8$ (values from Adams, 1975, and Heady and Řao, 1967). Unfortunately, there is a wide range of econometrically estimated values for η_x, η_y, and e_a. Perrin (1980, p. 450) finds plausible demand elasticity estimates from -4.0 to -0.3 for oil and from -0.9 to -0.14 for meal. Sensitivity of results to alternative parameter values is explored below. The value of η_{xz1} depends on the substitutability of diesel fuel and soybean oil and the size of the market for each. Assuming that their fuel value is equivalent on a pound-for-pound basis and that the soybean oil market is 10 times the diesel fuel market (i.e., 10 times the quantity is traded), $\eta_{xz1} = 10$. Using these parameter values, Eq. (5.13) yields $\%\Delta P_a = 1.8$ from using soybean oil to replace 1 percent of the nation's diesel fuel.

The system can also be solved to obtain the effect of increased diversion of soybean oil to fuel uses on soybean oil and meal prices, as follows:

$$\frac{EP_x}{EZ_1} = \frac{\eta_{xz1}(\eta_y - K_y e_a)}{-\eta_x \eta_y + e_a(K_x \eta_y + K_y \eta_x)} \tag{5.14}$$

$$\frac{EP_y}{EZ_1} = \frac{K_x \eta_{xz1} e_a}{-\eta_x \eta_y + e_a(K_x \eta_y + K_y \eta_x)} \tag{5.15}$$

Using the same elasticities, we obtain $\%\Delta P_x = 7.7$ and $\%\Delta P_y = 2.1$. Thus, we estimate that replacing 1 percent of diesel fuel by soybean oil will increase the price of soybean oil 7.7 percent, reduce the price of soybean meal 2.1 percent, and increase the price of soybeans 1.8 percent. Consistency of these answers can be checked by means of Eq. (5.12), which says that a change in the price of beans has to be accounted for by a change in oil and meal prices: $1.8 = 0.4(7.7) - 0.6(2.1)$.

For some problems, simpler relationships than Eqs. (5.13) through (5.15) may be more useful. For example, suppose that the issue is not a policy determining the quantity of soybean oil used as diesel fuel but rather the response of the U.S. soybean and soybean product markets to a change in the world price of a substitute vegetable oil, such as palm oil. Z_1 now represents the price of palm oil. To analyze the effects of a change in the palm oil price, divide Eqs. (5.13) and (5.15), respectively, by Eq. (5.14) to obtain

$$\frac{EP_a}{EP_x} = \frac{K_x \eta_y}{\eta_y - K_y e_a} \tag{5.16}$$

and

$$\frac{EP_y}{EP_x} = \frac{K_x e_a}{\eta_y - K_y e_a} \tag{5.17}$$

Using the same parameter values as for Eq. (5.13), according to Eq. (5.17), a

10-percent rise in the price of soybean oil (caused by a 10-percent rise in the world price of palm oil) will decrease the price of soybean meal 3.5 percent. Equation (5.17) indicates that the prices of oil and meal must always move in opposite directions. This result can be confirmed geometrically by reference to Fig. 5.1, where a rightward shift in oil demand leads to a decrease in the price of meal. Note, however, that Eq. (5.16) is always positive, meaning that a decline in the price of oil must be associated with a decline in the price of soybeans. Since the cost of oil plus meal is equal to the cost of beans plus the crushing margin, it is not possible for the meal price decrease to more than offset the oil price increase, thus generating lower food prices as a result of higher oil prices.

This last "impossibility" result has practical importance in view of the position of the National Soybean Processors Association in pressing their case for legislation to restrict U.S. palm oil imports, which were rapidly expanding in the mid-1970s. They argued that increased U.S. imports of palm oil would reduce the price of U.S. soybean oil, and that this in turn would increase soybean meal prices, hence the price of meat, hence consumers' food bills. Consequently, it was said that U.S. consumers would be made better off by restricting palm oil imports. The point is quite correct that meal prices are expected to rise. But Eq. (5.16) implies that the sum of oil and meal costs will not rise, as there is never a reason to fear upward pressure on consumer food costs overall. The case closest to this occurs when $e_a \to \infty$, when soybeans are produced at constant cost. In this case, Eq. (5.16) is zero. A rise in the value of oil from a bushel of soybeans is exactly offset by a decline in the price of meal.

For illustrative purposes, Table 5.1 shows how the price of soybeans changes in response to a change in the price of soybean oil under various parameter values.

Table 5.1   Percentage Change in Price of Soybeans Due to a 10-Percent Fall in Price of Soybean Oil*

Elasticity of demand for meal	Elasticity of supply of soybeans		
	0.02	1.0	2.0
−0.3	−2.9	−1.3	−0.8
	(1.8)	(4.5)	(5.3)
−0.7	−3.3	−2.2	−1.5
	(1.2)	(3.5)	(4.2)
−1.5	−3.7	−2.9	−2.2
	(0.5)	(1.8)	(3.0)

*Figures in parentheses are associated percentage changes in the price of soybean meal.

Note: Oil is assumed to account for 40 percent of bean product value. The 40-percent share puts an upper limit on the effect of an oil price change on the bean price. In this table, the maximum possible value would be −4.0 [if bean supply were fixed ($e_a = 0$) or if demand for meal were perfectly elastic ($\eta_y \to \infty$)]. If the share of soybean product value due to oil were 30 percent, the maximum possible effect of a 10-percent fall in oil price on bean price would be 3 percent.

The maximum meal price change occurs when supply is perfectly elastic ($e_a \to \infty$). In this case the price of beans does not change, but the price of meal rises by K_x/K_y, or 6.66 percent, when the price of oil falls 10 percent. In this case the rise in the value of meal exactly offsets the fall in the value of oil.

Other Elasticities

The preceding relationships pertain to an exogenous change in the demand for soybean oil. Basically similar results can be derived for a change in the demand for the other joint product, soybean meal. Elasticities of P's with respect to Z_2 are symmetrical with those for Z_1. However, somewhat different effects are obtained by changing the exogenous shifter Z_3, which shifts the supply of the common resource (soybeans) in Eq. (5.9). Holding Z_1 and Z_2 constant, dividing Eqs. (5.7) through (5.12) by EZ_3, and then calculating the effects of soybean price changes yields

$$\frac{\%\Delta P_x}{\%\Delta P_a} = \frac{\eta_y}{K_x\eta_y + K_y\eta_x} \tag{5.18}$$

$$\frac{\%\Delta P_y}{\%\Delta P_a} = \frac{\eta_x}{K_x\eta_y + K_y\eta_x} \tag{5.19}$$

Note that Eq. (5.18) is not the reciprocal of Eq. (5.16), since the exogenous changes that influence both P_x and P_a are different. An example of a policy change generating Eqs. (5.18) and (5.19) would be price supports or supply restrictions in soybeans. A policy-induced rise in the price of soybeans causes an increase in the price of both oil and meal, the price of the product least elastic in demand rising most. This result can be affirmed geometrically by shifting the supply curve in Fig. 5.1.

RETAIL PRICES AND FARM PRICE SUPPORTS

Equations (5.18) and (5.19) show the effect of a regulated farm price change on products at a higher stage of processing. A generally interesting issue is the effect of farm price supports at the consumer level. To this point we have followed the usual practice in agricultural policy of identifying a $1 rise in the farm price as a $1 increase in consumers' costs. This assumes that retailers, processors, other middlemen, and livestock producers (if a feed price is supported) simply pass through farm price changes, and neither absorb nor magnify them. Is this plausible?

The essential economic issues can be analyzed most simply by collapsing the stages of processing so that there are only two levels: farm and retail. Marketing then consists of combining the farm commodity with a bundle of marketing inputs to produce a retail food product. The markup between farm and retail is viewed as the price of these marketing services. If the cost of these marketing services per unit of final product stays constant, then farm-level price changes will be passed through to consumer on a dollar-for-dollar basis.

Discussion of the food marketing bill typically assumes that there exists a given recipe-like process by which the raw farm product is transported, transformed, packaged, and distributed to consumers. This implies that the final product can be expressed as the output of a fixed-coefficient production process in which farm products are combined with marketing services to yield retail output. This two-input, one-output model is formally identical to the one presented graphically in Fig. 4.1 and 4.2 of the preceding chapter. But now input a is agricultural raw material, b is marketing services, and x is the retail product. Figure 4.2 shows a reduction in the quantity of a, which is the result of a farm program that restricts output. From the construction of the derived demand for a (which the reader should review), it is apparent that $\Delta P_a = \Delta P_x - \Delta P_b$, that is, $\Delta P_x = \Delta P_a + \Delta P_b$. Consequently, the dollar-for-dollar pass through can occur only if $\Delta P_b = 0$. The diagram indicates that ΔP_b will not be zero; it will be negative, so that the retail price will rise less than the farm price. The program-generated price increase at the farm level will in part be absorbed by suppliers of marketing services. The economic reason for this result is that with less agricultural output, the demand for marketing services and their price falls (just as grain ocean freight rates for grain fell when declining exports in 1980s reduced the demand for shipping). The limiting case is when the supply of b is perfectly elastic. Then $\Delta P_b = 0$ and we do observe $\Delta P_a = \Delta P_x$.

Consider a target price and deficiency payment program. This program is shown in Fig. 5.2. The irregularly shaped S and D curves are used just to remind ourselves that this model does not depend on the linearity assumed in Figs. 4.1 and 4.2. The key to the model is that the derived demand in the a market is the vertical distance between $D(x)$ and $S(b)$ in the upper panel.

The representation of equilibrium in the a market given the price guarantee at $\hat{P}_a$ has one possibly confusing element, namely that $\hat{P}_a$ is *not* the price carried forward to the retail market. The market price is P_a, the price at which output $\hat{P}_a$ induced by the price guarantee clears the market. One way to keep straight the location of the program-caused equilibrium is to draw in the supply curve that the program generates. It is the hatched curve $S(a)$, showing production as a function of market price. When the *market* price falls below $\hat{P}_a$, the producer price stays at that level, so production stays at $\hat{a}$ and does not respond to market prices below $\hat{P}_a$. Carrying the quantity $\hat{a}$ through to the retail level, we see that more marketing services are required, bidding up P_b (especially if the industry is near the capacity level at which $S(b)$ becomes inelastic). At the same time P_x falls. But again, we have the result that the fall in P_x is less than the fall in P_a.

The fixed-proportions model can be generalized to allow substitution between farm commodities and marketing inputs in the production of retail goods. For example, if wage rates fell, more services might be provided in grocery stores, or if beef became expensive, cheaper soy proteins might be introduced to cut the a share of costs in x. The formal model for analyzing this situation is Eqs. (4.1) to (4.6), with the variables redefined as for Fig. 5.2. The elasticities of Tables 4.1 and 4.2 can, therefore, be used to analyze the passthrough of policy-induced farm price changes to the retail level.

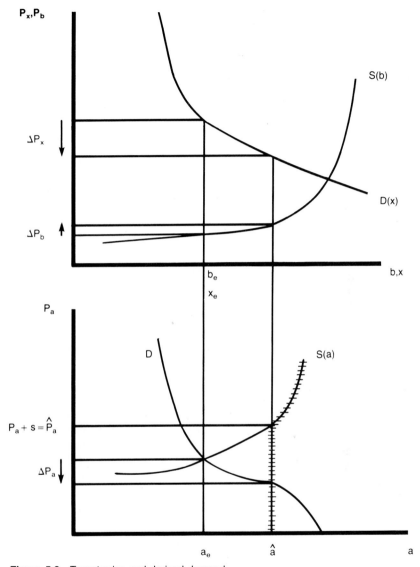

Figure 5.2 Target price and derived demand.

The effect of a deficiency payment program is analyzed using the elasticities for a subsidy of a, in the middle column of Table 4.2. Dividing the elasticities of the first two rows of this column yields

$$\frac{EP_x}{EP_a} = \frac{K_a(e_a + \sigma)}{e_a + K_a\sigma - K_b\eta} \quad . \tag{5.20}$$

Let K_a, the farmers' share of retail food expenditure, be 0.4; η, the elasticity of demand for retail food, is taken as -0.25; $e_b = 2.0$; $e_a = 0.3$; and $\sigma = 0.2$ (quite limited substitution possibilities). Using elasticities from Table 4.2, a 10-percent increase in the payments to farmers (equivalent to a decrease in a tax) causes a fall of 5.95 percent in P_a and a fall of 2.35 percent in P_x. The passthrough in Eq. (5.20) is, accordingly, 0.39, a 10-percent fall in P_a causing a 3.9-percent fall in P_x. A sufficient condition for Eq. (5.20) to be less than 1, i.e., that a rise in P_a narrows the P_x/P_a margin, is that $\eta < 0$ and $e_b > 0$.

These percentage changes do not tell the dollar passthrough. That can be approximated using the share data. Thus a 6.0-percent rise in P_a, which accounts for 40 percent of retail costs, amounts to $6.0 \times 0.4 = 2.40$ percent at the retail level; so the 2.35 change in P_x in this example is almost a full dollar-for-dollar passthrough.

The effect of a production-control program in the farm-retail context is the same as the effect of an acreage-control program on the prices of output compared to land in Chap. 4. Therefore, the equation we want to replace (5.20) for this program is the reciprocal of Eq. (4.17). But this reciprocal is what we already have for Eq. (5.20). Thus, the passthrough relationship is the same for a production control or production subsidy. Graphically, to generate either program in Fig. 5.2, we are effectively shifting the supply curve of a, and this is why the algebra is the same.

Complex elasticities can be used to estimate the effect of policy changes on the farm-retail price ratio. For example, consider the effects of a change in government purchases of processed products under Section 32 of the Agricultural Act of 1949, used to support prices of commodities found to be in surplus, at the Secretary of Agriculture's discretion. In Table 4.2 such purchases were analyzed as if the government were purchasing farm-level products (which in some programs it does). Under what circumstances will government purchase of retail products be just as effective as purchasing farm products? If the ratio of retail to farm price remains constant, i.e., if $E(P_x/P_a)/EG = 0$. Using our earlier results on complex elasticities, this is $EP_x/EG - EP_a/EG$, or the difference between the first and second expressions in the "G" column of Table 4.2. The result is

$$\frac{E(P_x/P_a)}{EG} = \frac{K_b(e_a - e_b)}{e_a e_b - \eta(\sigma + K_a e_b + K_b e_a) + \sigma(K_a e_a + K_b e_b)} \qquad (5.21)$$

The sign of Eq. (5.21) depends on whether e_a is greater than or less than e_b, the denominator being positive. A sufficient condition for Eq. (5.21) to be zero is $e_a = e_b$. In general there is no reason for intervention in a processed goods market to have the same effect on the farm price as the same percentage removal of the farm product.

MULTIPLE OUTPUTS WITH SUBSTITUTION

Policy issues involving effects of intervention in one commodity market on
price and output in related commodity markets require two extensions of the
joint-product model to be analytically helpful. The first is to relax the assumption that the products be produced in fixed proportions. The second is to incorporate more than one raw material input, since if the ratio of final products can
be varied, there must be something other than a common raw material involved
in their production. These changes can be made using a modest generalization
of the model used in Chap. 4, adding one more product, called y. The quantity
of corn could be x, while y is soybeans.

The two-product, two-input model is expressed in differential form as follows. The demand equation for x now has included the price of y, P_y. This
permits substitution in demand as well as supply, which may not be important
in some cases (corn and cotton) but will be important in other cases (corn and
grain sorghum), notably where both outputs are used in livestock feed.

$$Ex = \eta_x EP_x + \eta_{xy} EP_y \tag{5.22}$$

The letter η still refers to demand elasticity but now requires subscripts. For
own-price elasticity we simply use the commodity identifier; for cross-price
elasticity, the first subscript identifies the quantity and the second the price
which is changing. Thus, η_{xy} is the elasticity of demand for x in response to a
change in the price of y. Note that this is a *partial* elasticity, a parameter in the
usual sense of measuring the effect of a change in P_y holding constant all other
prices.

We also have a demand equation for y:

$$Ey = \eta_y EP_y + \eta_{yx} EP_x \tag{5.23}$$

In doing simulations with cross-elasticities, choosing a value for η_{xy} in Eq.
(5.22) already determines a value for η_{yx} in Eq. (5.23). We have from demand
theory the symmetry results $\partial x/\partial P_y = \partial y/\partial P_x$. Multiplying both sides by
$P_x P_y/Z$, where Z is expenditures on all commodities, and multiplying $\partial x/\partial y$ by
x/x and $\partial y/\partial P_x$ by y/y, yields $k_x\, \eta_{xy} = k_y\, \eta_{yx}$, where k_x and k_y are the shares of
x and y in expenditures on both. Thus, if y is sorghum grain and x is corn, we
have $k_y = 0.1$ and $k_x = 0.9$. If η_{xy} is 0.2 (a 10-percent rise in the sorghum
price increases corn demand by 2 percent), then $\eta_{yx} = (0.9/0.1)\, 0.2 = 1.8$. A
change in the price of corn has to have a much bigger *percentage* impact on the
demand for sorghum simply because the sorghum market is so much smaller.

Maintaining the Chap. 4 assumptions about industry production functions, we have

$$Ex = K_{ax}Ea_x + K_{bx}Eb_x \tag{5.24}$$

$$Ey = K_{ay}Ea_y + K_{by}Eb_y \tag{5.25}$$

Equation (5.24) is Eq. (4.1″) of Chap. 4, but it is necessary here to complicate the notation. The parameter K_a can be different in the two commodities, for example, the share of fertilizer in production costs is different for corn and wheat. The second subscript of K identifies the product whose cost share K measures. Similarly, we need a subscript on the input quantities to indicate which commodity the input is being used to produce.

Next we have the VMP = factor price conditions, the same as in Eqs. (4.3″) and (4.4″) of Chap. 4.

$$EP_a = \frac{K_{bx}}{\sigma_x}Ea_x - \frac{K_{bx}}{\sigma_x}Eb_x + EP_x \tag{5.26}$$

$$EP_b = \frac{K_{ax}}{\sigma_x}Eb_x - \frac{K_{ax}}{\sigma_x}Ea_x + EP_x \tag{5.27}$$

$$EP_a = \frac{K_{by}}{\sigma_y}Ea_y - \frac{K_{by}}{\sigma_y}Eb_y + EP_y \tag{5.28}$$

$$EP_b = \frac{K_{ay}}{\sigma_y}Eb_y - \frac{K_{ay}}{\sigma_y}Eb_y + EP_y \tag{5.29}$$

Subscripts are added to σ to distinguish between the elasticity of substitution between a and b in x production and in y production.

Finally, we have the input supply functions, which are

$$EP_a = \frac{\alpha_x}{e_a}Ea_x + \frac{\alpha_y}{e_a}Ea_y \tag{5.30}$$

$$EP_b = \frac{\beta_x}{e_b}Eb_x + \frac{\beta_y}{e_b}Eb_y \tag{5.31}$$

The α parameters are fractions of the inputs used in each output, for example, $\alpha_x = a_x/(a_x + a_y)$. Consequently, $\alpha_x + \alpha_y = 1$; and $\beta_x + \beta_y = 1$. [Note also that $K_{ax} = a_xP_a/(a_xP_a + b_xP_b)$, so that $K_{ax} + K_{bx} = 1$ and $K_{ay} + K_{by} = 1$.]

Equations (5.22) through (5.31) are a system of 10 linear equations in 10 unknowns. The unknowns are percentage changes in four prices (P_x, P_y, P_a, P_b) and six quantities (x, y, a_x, b_x, a_y, b_y). We assume that a solution exists having positive values of all the variables. As it is, all variables are determined, so there are no comparative statics to do. We can make one of the variables policy-determined, say x, eliminate the appropriate behavioral equation (the one that is overridden by the policy) and find the elasticities $E(\cdot, \hat{x})$ where each of the other nine variables in turn takes the place of $(\cdot)$. More generally (because we can calculate all the elasticities just mentioned plus others), we can introduce exogenous variables in each equation, and treat these as policy instruments. Equation (5.32) shows the resulting system of equations in matrix form. This matrix is used to solve for comparative statics of exogenous changes. Because the variable EG_x in demand has effects the same as $-EG_x$ in supply, Eqs. (5.22) and (5.24) are equated, as well as Eqs. (5.23) and (5.25), eliminating x and y as variables. This leaves eight equations in eight unknowns.

$$
\begin{bmatrix}
-\eta_x & -\eta_{xp\,y} & 0 & 0 & K_{ax} & 0 & K_{bx} & 0 \\[2mm]
-\eta_{yp\,x} & -\eta_y & 0 & 0 & 0 & K_{ay} & 0 & K_{ay} \\[2mm]
-1 & 0 & 1 & 0 & \dfrac{K_{bx}}{\sigma_x} & 0 & -\dfrac{K_{bx}}{\sigma_x} & 0 \\[3mm]
-1 & 0 & 0 & 1 & -\dfrac{K_{ax}}{\sigma_x} & 0 & \dfrac{K_{ax}}{\sigma_x} & 0 \\[3mm]
0 & -1 & 1 & 0 & 0 & \dfrac{K_{by}}{\sigma_y} & 0 & -\dfrac{K_{by}}{\sigma_y} \\[3mm]
0 & -1 & 0 & 1 & 0 & -\dfrac{K_{ay}}{\sigma_y} & 0 & \dfrac{K_{ay}}{\sigma_y} \\[3mm]
0 & 0 & 1 & 0 & -\dfrac{\alpha_y}{e_a} & -\dfrac{\alpha_y}{e_a} & 0 & 0 \\[3mm]
0 & 0 & 0 & 1 & 0 & 0 & -\dfrac{\beta_x}{e_b} & -\dfrac{\beta_y}{e_b}
\end{bmatrix}
\begin{bmatrix}
EP_x \\ EP_y \\ EP_a \\ EP_b \\ Ea_x \\ Ea_y \\ Eb_x \\ Eb_y
\end{bmatrix}
=
\begin{bmatrix}
-EG_x \\ -EG_y \\ ET_{ax} \\ ET_{bx} \\ ET_{ay} \\ ET_{by} \\ ET_a \\ ET_b
\end{bmatrix}
\quad (5.32)
$$

The right-hand column vector in Eq. (5.32) represents policy instruments. EG_x and EG_y are most readily thought of as quantities removed from the market by government—a nonprice responsive component of demand.

The remaining six policy instruments represent price-dimension variables, equivalent to taxes, with subsidies being negative taxes. ET_a and ET_b represent an input tax or subsidy in all uses, for example, a general subsidy on fertilizer. The other four ET variables represent taxes on an input in only one of the two commodities. Note that the bottom two rows are input supply equations while the middle four represent input demands. Thus, as in the simple supply–demand model, a general tax on a of 10 percent could be represented as either $-ET_a = 10$ or $ET_{ax} = ET_{ay} = -10$, but not both. Generally, to conduct comparative statics of a policy intervention, we make the minimum number of right-hand-side variables nonzero to represent the policy, with all others zero.

A quantity intervention in an input market is represented by replacing ET by ET times the appropriate input supply or demand elasticity if the intervention does not override any of the behavioral equations. If the intervention does override a behavioral equation, as with an acreage-control program, it is necessary to make appropriate changes in the equation system. This can be tricky. It is best to begin by sketching in graphic form the intervention contemplated. A sufficient (but not necessary) condition for the system of equations to have a single solution is that all factor and product supply and demand functions have normally signed own-price elasticities. A policy or set of policies simulated by substituting assumed or estimated parameter values in the left-hand-side coefficient matrix, values of percentage change in policy variables in the right-hand-side, and solve for the percentage changes in the eight endogenous variables. Strictly speaking, the changes imposed must be infinitesimal, since the equations are generated from differentials; small finite changes yield approximations. The approximations will usually be not as good for larger changes, like 30 percent.

Figure 5.3 illustrates the kinds of interrelationship the model incorporates. Suppose a subsidy is paid on the use of a single input in a single product, say subsidizing by 15 percent the use of grassland (a) for race horses (x) but not for dairy cattle (y), both of which use pasture and other inputs (b) in production. This can be represented as a value of -0.15 for ET_{ax} in Eq. (5.32), the other right-hand-side variables being zero. Diagrammatically, we have a 15-percent wedge in the market for a_x (or alternatively as a 15-percent vertical fall in the postsubsidy supply curve of a_x). This reduces the cost of using a in x and the cost of x, so that the supply curve of x shifts to the right. Consequently P_x falls. The increase in x tends to increase the demand for other inputs b, but this will be offset by substitution of a for b if $\sigma > -\eta$. Shown is a case where $\sigma < -\eta$ so the demand for b shifts to the right, increasing P_b by an amount depending on the elasticity of supply of b to x.

We cannot determine the price rises for P_a and P_b, however, without reference to the y (dairy) market. Inputs a and b have to bring their owners the same price in x and y, so they are drawn into horse breeding and away from dairy. This shifts the input supplies to the left in y, which shifts the supply of y to the left, hence increasing P_y. These changes in the y market feed back to the x market, shifting supply functions there. Indeed, there is a question of how to specify these input supply functions. The supply of a_x, given P_a in y, is perfectly elastic. But allowing P_a in y to change means we can't specify the supply of a_x without knowing all the effects in the y market. This leads to specifying multi-market supply functions analogous to those of Chap. 3 but more complicated in the present model.

The simulation would be still more involved if there were significant cross-

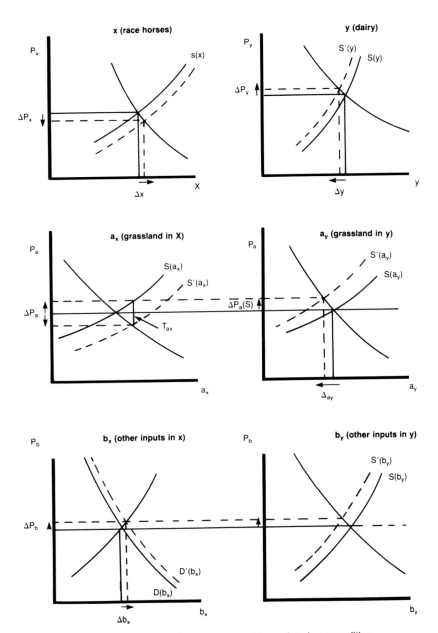

Figure 5.3 Subsidy of one input for use in one of two related commodities.

elasticities of product demand, for example, if x and y were hogs and cattle. Then the subsidy of a_x would end up shifting both product demand curves, and this would have further effects in all four factor markets.

A diagrammatic supply–demand description of these six markets can be helpful in comparing the situation before and after a policy change, where the comparative statics are actually carried out using Eq. (5.32) calculations. But the interactions are too complicated to permit even qualitative (directional) effects on some variables, notably b_x, y, a_x, and b_y, to be found with a graphic analysis. The system of Eq. (5.32) indicates what information is needed and how to use it.

Consider a policy of supporting the price of x, but not y, by means of deficiency payments to achieve target price $\hat{P}_x$. To obtain the output and input effects, we drop Eqs. (5.22) and (5.24) and divide all the others by $E\hat{P}_x$. Equating input supply appropriately with each of Eqs. (5.26) to (5.29) eliminates the factor prices, and equating (5.23) and (5.25) eliminates y. This leaves us with the following system of five linear equations in five unknowns:

$$
\begin{bmatrix}
-\eta_y & 0 & K_{ay} & 0 & K_{by} \\[2ex]
0 & \dfrac{\alpha_x}{e_a}+\dfrac{K_{bx}}{\sigma_x} & \dfrac{\alpha_y}{e_a} & -\dfrac{K_{bx}}{\sigma_x} & 0 \\[2ex]
-1 & \dfrac{\alpha_x}{e_a} & \dfrac{\alpha_y}{e_a}+\dfrac{K_{by}}{\sigma_y} & 0 & -\dfrac{K_{by}}{\sigma_y} \\[2ex]
0 & -\dfrac{K_{ax}}{\sigma_x} & 0 & \dfrac{\beta_x}{e_b}+\dfrac{K_{ax}}{\sigma_x} & \dfrac{\beta_y}{e_b} \\[2ex]
-1 & 0 & -\dfrac{K_{ay}}{\sigma_y} & \dfrac{\beta_x}{e_b} & \dfrac{\beta_y}{e_b}+\dfrac{K_{ay}}{\sigma_y}
\end{bmatrix}
\begin{bmatrix}
\dfrac{EP_y}{E\hat{P}_x} \\[2ex]
\dfrac{Ea_x}{E\hat{P}_x} \\[2ex]
\dfrac{Ea_y}{E\hat{P}_x} \\[2ex]
\dfrac{Eb_x}{E\hat{P}_x} \\[2ex]
\dfrac{Eb_y}{E\hat{P}_x}
\end{bmatrix}
=
\begin{bmatrix}
-\eta_{ypx} \\[2ex]
1 \\[2ex]
0 \\[2ex]
1 \\[2ex]
0
\end{bmatrix}
\quad (5.33)
$$

Solving this system involves complicated algebra to write out the determinant of the coefficient matrix (using expansion by alien cofactors); but after solving for $Ea_x/E\hat{P}_x$ and $Eb_x/E\hat{P}_x$ and substituting into Eq. (5.24), the results can be "simplified" to

$$
\frac{Ex}{E\hat{P}_x} = [e_a e_b + K_{ax} e_a \sigma_1 + K_{bx} e_b \sigma_2 - \phi \sigma_y e_1
$$
$$
- \eta_y (e_2 + \sigma_3) - \eta_{ypx}(e_3 + \sigma_3)] \qquad (5.34)
$$
$$
/ [\alpha_x \sigma_1 + e_4 + (K_{bx} \sigma_y + \phi \eta_y)(\beta_x - \alpha_x)]
$$

where $e_1 = \beta_y e_a + \alpha_y e_b$, $e_2 = \beta_y K_{by} e_a + \alpha_y K_{ay} e_b$, $e_3 = \beta_y K_{bx} e_a + \alpha_y K_{ax} e_b$, $e_4 = \beta_x K_{bx} e_a + \alpha_x K_{ax} e_b$, each of these being weighted sums of

e_a and e_b; $\sigma_1 = \beta_x\,\sigma_x + \beta_y\,\sigma_y$, $\sigma_2 = \alpha_x\,\sigma_x + \alpha_y\,\sigma_y$, and $\sigma_3 = a_y\,K_{ax}\,\sigma_1 + \beta_y\,K_{bx}\,\sigma_2$ (weighted elasticities of substitution); and $\phi = K_{ax} - K_{ay}$, a factor intensity coefficient. The formula (5.34) is a total supply elasticity of x, anologous to ϵ as found in Eq. (4.12) for the one-product case, but expanded to consider simultaneous equilibrium in the x and y markets. This extension makes things more complicated than might have been supposed. The parallel between Eq. (4.12) and Eq. (5.34) can be seen, however, in the special case in which both products have the same factor intensity. In this case $K_{ax} = K_{ay}$, which implies that $\phi = 0$ and $\alpha_x = \alpha_y$.[1] The elasticity formula simplifies to

$$\frac{Ex}{E\hat{P}_x} = \frac{e_a e_b + \sigma_1(K_{ax}e_a + K_{bx}e_b)}{\alpha_x(\sigma_1 + K_{bx}e_a + K_{ax}e_b)} - \frac{\alpha_y}{\alpha_x}(\eta_y + \eta_{ypx}) \qquad (5.35)$$

Equation (5.35) breaks down total supply elasticity into two additive components. The first pertains to factor supply and production conditions, the second to adjustments induced by simultaneous equilibration of the market for y when P_x changes. If x is the only product, we have $\alpha_x = 1$ and $\alpha_y = 0$, and Eq. (5.34) reduces to (4.12).

This model permits analysis of the effects of a price support for x upon the market for y. The cross-price effect is found by solving Eqs. (5.33) for $EP_y/E\hat{P}_x$:

$$\frac{EP_y}{E\hat{P}_x} = \frac{e_5 + \beta_x\,\alpha_x\,\sigma_x + (\beta_y\,\alpha_y\,K_{by} + \beta_y\,\alpha_x\,K_{ay})\,\sigma_y - (\beta_x - \alpha_x)\,\phi\eta_{ypx}}{D} \qquad (5.36)$$

where $e_5 = \beta_x K_{by}e_a + \alpha_x K_{ay}e_b$, and D is the denominator of Eq. (5.34). In the special case of identical factor intensity of x and y, Eq. (5.36) reduces to 1. Thus, P_y rises by the same percentage as $\hat{P}_x$: supporting the price of corn supports soybeans equally well. The reason for this result is that with industry-level CES production functions having equal factor intensities, the relative prices of the two goods are cost-determined and are independent of demand. The production possibilities curve for x and y is linear. Given an initial rise in $\hat{P}_x$, the equalization of opportunity costs will result in a new equilibrium at unchanged relative product prices. This result is the two-product analog of perfectly elastic supply in a single-product model.

The effect of a change in $\hat{P}_x$ on the quantity produced of y can be calculated from the cross-elasticity of supply, $Ey/E\hat{P}_x$. This elasticity is obtained by substituting Eq. (5.36) into (5.23). It might be expected that increasing the support price of x would cause the output of y to fall, i.e., that the cross-elasticity of supply is negative. The economics of the negative cross-elasticity is basically that an increase in a product's price bids resources away from alternative products. However, when less of the alternative product is produced, its price in turn will rise. Since both product prices rise, how do we know that resources will not be drawn into the industry such that production of both products rises when the demand for one of them increases? The reason is that when the demand for the alternative product is stable, the market can only clear at higher prices with less of the alternative product being consumed.

The exceptional case in which $Ey/E\hat{P}_x$ can be positive requires that x and y be substitutes in consumption. A positive partial cross-elasticity of demand is not sufficient for a positive $Ey/E\hat{P}_x$, however. It is also necessary that y be relatively intensive in the use of the input which is most elastic in supply. An an illustrative example, let x be vegetable oils and y be animal fats. Vegetable oils are relatively intensive in the use of land ($K_{ax} > K_{ay}$), which is inelastic in supply. Suppose the values of the relevant parameters are $e_a = 0.2$, $e_b \rightarrow \infty$ (nonland input perfectly elastic in supply), $K_{ax} = 0.6$, $K_{ay} = 0.2$, $\eta_y = -.8$, and $\eta_{ypx} = 0.5$. Then the cross-elasticity is 0.23, i.e., a 10 percent increase in the price of vegetable oils increases the output of animal fats 2.3 percent.

Input Market Policies

The two-product model also helps in analyzing the consequences of some input-market interventions. In a single-product model, increasing an input price by taxing it or by means of a quantitative restriction always increases product price and reduces production. But in a two (or more) product case, an input price increase can result in more of one of the products being produced. An interesting example is provided by Swanson and Taylor (1976). In their model, an increase in energy price increases the production of soybeans. The essential reason is that corn is relatively energy-intensive, so that land shifts out of corn to a next-best alternative of soybeans (or other crops) even though it is more expensive to produce these other crops, too. An immediate implication is that because more soybeans will only clear the market at a lower price, other inputs, presumably land, must fall in price by more than enough to offset the cost increase caused by higher energy prices.

These propositions may be derived formally in terms of a fixed-proportions version of the basic model of Eq. (5.32) (to be consistent with Swanson and Taylor who use a linear programming model). The effect of a given percentage change in price of an input, P_a, on the outputs of the products, x and y, are

$$\frac{Ex}{E\hat{P}_a} = \frac{\eta_x K_{ax} e_b - \phi\beta_y \eta_y}{e_b - K_{bx}\beta_x \eta_x - K_{by}\beta_y \eta_y} \tag{5.37}$$

$$\frac{Ey}{E\hat{P}_a} = \frac{\eta_y K_{ay} e_b + \phi\beta_x \eta_x}{e_b - K_{bx}\beta_x \eta_x - K_{by}\beta_y \eta_y} \tag{5.38}$$

All the denominator terms are positive. Often both numerators would be negative, so that Ex/Ep_a and Ey/EP_a are negative: higher input prices generate production cutbacks.

However, in certain cases the sign is reversed. Let P_a be the price of energy and P_b the price of other inputs (principally services of land). Let the product x be corn, which is energy-intensive relative to soybeans, with $K_{ax} = 0.5$, $K_{ay} = 0.2$. Let the elasticity of supply of land be zero, the elasticity of demand for corn be -0.40 and the elasticity of demand for soybeans be -0.67 (values used by Swanson and Taylor), and the relative importance of corn, β_x, be 0.6. Inserting these values in Eq. (5.37) and (5.38) yields $Ex/E\hat{P}_a = -0.096$ and $Ey/E\hat{P}_a = 0.144$. An increase in the price of energy reduces the energy-intensive crop output about 0.1 percent for each 1-percent increase in the price of energy, but increases the less energy-intensive crop by 0.14 percent. This result is dependent on the low elasticity of supply of alternative inputs, e_b, which "traps" these resources into producing either one crop or the other despite lower returns.[2] If e_b were 0.5 instead of zero and the other parameter values remained the same, $Ex/E\hat{P}_a$ would be -0.19 and $Ey/E\hat{P}_a$ would be -0.02.

A more complete treatment of this issue requires going back to the Eq. (5.32) model. We do not have algebraic expressions for the relevant elasticities but after plugging in the necessary parameter values the effects of all the endogenous variables can be found numerically.

ENDNOTES

1. The relative factor intensity of the two products can be defined equivalently in terms of either factor. The basic definition of ϕ is $\phi = K_{ax} K_{by} - K_{by} K_{ay}$; but, using the fact that the factor shares for each commodity sum to 1, this can be simplified to either $\phi = K_{ax} - K_{ay}$ or $-\phi = K_{bx} - K_{by}$.

   To see that $K_{ax} = K_{ay}$ implies $\alpha_x = \beta_x$, note that equal factor shares implies equal ratios of factor quantities, because factor prices are the same for both products. If x is using, say, 30 percent of the total a available, x must also be using 30 percent of b, i.e., $\alpha_x = \beta_x$.

2. Because more soybeans are produced, they must sell for a lower price, even though energy prices have risen. Therefore, the price of nonenergy inputs must fall. This can be seen formally by deriving the elasticity of P_b with respect to P_a, which is

$$\frac{EP_b}{E\hat{P}_a} = \frac{K_{ay}\beta_y\eta_y + K_{ax}\beta_x\eta_x}{e_b - K_{by}\beta_y\eta_y - K_{bx}\beta_x\eta_x}$$

This equation is always negative. However, it will approach zero as $e_b \to \infty$. The more elastic is the supply of e_b (the less "trapped" are nonenergy inputs), the less the burden imposed on owners of farm inputs b.

Chapter 6

Distributional Consequences
of Farm Policy

Rises in commodity prices and returns to inputs affect different people differently. A changed system of price support can influence the overall structure of an industry, such as the relative numbers of big and small farms, their degree of commodity specialization, the nature of contracting, and price-making. These effects are sometimes accidental and sometimes the objects of policies. Some wish to preserve traditional "family" farms. The view cited in Chap. 1 that the U.S. farm programs have aided the largest farms most has caused political pressure to trim the benefits of large-scale producers. A cap was placed on deficiency payments, currently $50,000 per farm, but it has not proved effective as larger operators have been able to subdivide their farms for program purposes.

Before addressing the normative question of why the government would wish to target benefits to particular classes of farm people, it is important to conduct the positive economics of the income distributional consequences, or more broadly, the "structural" consequences, of agricultural policy. This issue is less settled, more of an ongoing research area than the sectoral price and quantity effects of policies that we have been studying in Chaps. 1 through 5.

There does not exist a widely accepted counterpart to the supply–demand model for use as a conceptual framework in thinking about structural-distributional issues. This chapter, thus, has a more ad hoc and tentative character. Nonetheless, standard neoclassical economics does provide some help in addressing distributional issues, and the chapter proceeds by extending the results obtained to this point as far as possible into the structural domain.

The chapter first analyzes factor shares, which can be accomplished with a straightforward extension of the earlier factor price models. Then we consider the consequences for the size distribution of income implied by factor share changes, along with issues in the inequality of factor ownership. Finally, the chapter discusses the broader structural issues of concentration of production on larger farms, land tenure and debt patterns, and the interaction of these characteristics of agriculture with technical progress as well as a broader range of policies than the price supports we have so far concentrated on.

FACTOR SHARES

The study of the income accruing to different groups of factor owners once constituted the major part of the income distribution story. Under the traditional system of economic organization of agriculture in Europe or in the colonial plantation systems around the world including the U.S. South, landowners accounted for little of the labor input, and those who supplied labor owned little land. Thus, factor shares determined the distribution of income among economic classes of people, so rigidly designated that they become social classes also, each with identifiable characteristics of noneconomic behavior. Consequently, a large literature developed on the shares of labor, land, and capital in a country's income.

In this situation, the analysis of how a price support program for cotton, say, affected the rental value of land and the returns of laborers (including share tenants) would constitute an analysis of the main income distributional consequences. Today matters are more complex in that farmers own much of their own land (more than half in the United States), and own most of the capital used. Nonetheless, farmers vary greatly in the factor origin of their income, and in size of incomes. The first step toward an economic understanding of income distribution as related to farm program is still to consider factor shares.

We have been considering factor shares, denoted as K in the preceding two chapters, as parameters. This is only strictly correct in the case of a Cobb-Douglas production function (CES with $\sigma = 1$). To begin to investigate the behavior of factor shares when policy changes, consider K_a in the one-product, two-input model of Chap. 4. The definition of a's share is

$$K_a = \frac{aP_a}{xP_x} \qquad (6.1)$$

Using multiplication and division rules

$$dK_a = \frac{xP_x(adP_a + P_a\,da) - aP_a(xdP_x + P_x\,dx)}{(xP_x)^2} \qquad (6.2)$$

Now, expand; multiply both sides by xP_x, and divide by aP_a:

$$\frac{xP_x\,dK_a}{aP_a} = \frac{adP_a}{aP_a} + \frac{P_a\,da}{aP_a} - \frac{dP_x}{P_x} - \frac{dx}{X} \qquad (6.3)$$

which by definition of E notation ($E = \%\Delta$) is

$$EK_a = EP_a + Ea - EP_x - Ex \qquad (6.4)$$

[This result, as many with elasticities, can be derived more straightforwardly by taking the natural logarithm of Eq. (6.1) and using the fact that $d\,(\ln x) = Ex$.]

To consider effect of price support without production controls, divide through by EP_x:

$$\frac{EK_a}{EP_x} = \frac{EP_a}{EP_x} + \frac{Ea}{EP_x} - 1 - \frac{Ex}{EP_x} \qquad (6.5)$$

The first right-hand-side elasticity, from Chap. 4, is

$$\frac{EP_a}{EP_x} = \frac{\sigma + e_b}{\sigma + K_a e_b + K_b e_a}$$

The second right-hand-side elasticity is

$$\frac{Ea}{EP_x} = \frac{(\sigma + e_b)e_a}{\sigma + K_a e_b + K_b e_a}$$

The last right-hand-side term is the elasticity of supply (not demand because the policy moves the sector off the original demand curve and along the supply curve):

$$\frac{Ex}{EP_x} = \epsilon_x = \frac{e_a e_b + \sigma(K_a e_a + K_b e_b)}{\sigma + K_b e_a + K_a e_b}$$

Substituting these elasticities back into Eq. (6.5):

$$\frac{EK_a}{EP_x} = [\sigma + e_b + (\sigma + e_b)\,e_a - \sigma - K_b\,e_a$$

$$- K_a\,e_b - e_a\,e_b - \sigma(K_a\,e_a + K_b\,e_b)]\, / \tag{6.6}$$

$$[\sigma + K_b\,e_a + K_a\,e_b]$$

Noting that $K_a = 1 - K_b$, the numerator reduces to

$$- K_b\,e_a + K_b\,e_b + K_b\,\sigma e_a - K_b\,\sigma e_b$$
$$= K_b(-e_a + e_b + \sigma e_a - \sigma e_b)$$
$$= K_b(e_a - e_b)(\sigma - 1)$$

Thus, Eq. (6.6) simplifies to

$$\frac{EK_a}{EP_x} = \frac{K_b(e_b - e_a)(1 - \sigma)}{\sigma + K_b\,e_a + K_a\,e_b} \tag{6.7}$$

The most interesting implications of this equation concern the elasticity of substitution in production and the elasticities of factor supplies. If $\sigma = 1$, then Eq. (6.7) is zero; changing P_x leaves factor shares unchanged. This is true no matter what the values of the other parameters. Thus, it shows a surprising predominance of a technical characteristic of agricultural production in the distributional issue. This result is especially noteworthy in view of the fact that at least until flexible functional forms based on "dual" models of production began to be the standard empirical approach, much econometric work in agricultural production assumed the Cobb-Douglas production function in which $\sigma = 1$. Thus distributional effects were assumed away.

If σ is greater than or less than 1, the sign of Eq. (6.7) is not determined until we know whether e_a is greater than or less than e_b. It is almost axiomatic that land is less elastic in supply to agriculture than is labor or purchased inputs. Letting the land supply elasticity be e_a, this means $(e_a - e_b)$ is negative. Then, if σ is less than one, which the limited empirical work on the substitutability between land and other inputs suggests that it is for individual crops and for agriculture as an aggregate, Eq. (6.7) is positive. A rise in a commodity's support price increases land's share. On the other hand, if σ turned out to be greater than 1, land's share would decrease as the support price increased. The intuitive economic reason is that, while the relative price of land would rise so long as $e_a < e_b$, when $\sigma > 1$ the demand for nonland inputs would rise sufficiently that aggregate income (price times quantity) would rise faster for the nonland inputs than for land.

Acreage Controls

Using elasticities from the right-hand column of Table 4.1, substitute into Eq. (6.5) to obtain

$$\frac{EK_a}{EP_x} = \frac{e_b + K_a \sigma - K_b \eta}{K_a (\sigma + e_b)} + \frac{\eta \sigma - e_b (K_b \sigma - K_a \eta)}{K_a (\sigma + e_b)} - 1 - \eta \qquad (6.8)$$

$$= \frac{K_b (e_b - \eta)(1 - \sigma)}{K_a (\sigma + e_b)}$$

Again, when $\sigma = 1$, the factor shares are unchanged. But the other parameters enter differently. The sign of Eq. (6.8) depends on σ being greater than or less than 1. Acreage controls decrease land's share if $\sigma > 1$, because then the increase in demand for b is large enough to offset the gains in aP_a as we move up the demand function for a. Consider parameter values that are plausible for U.S. crops as an aggregate, with a being land and b nonland inputs. Let $\eta = -0.6$, $e_a = 0.2$, $e_b = 2$, $\sigma = 0.5$, and $K_a = 0.3$. Then Eq. (6.8) yields an elasticity of 1.21; a 1-percent increase in P_x increases K_a by 1.21 percent, or from 0.3 to 0.304. In contrast, Eq. (6.7) indicates that a 1-percent increase in P_x increases K_a by 0.51 percent, less than half as much.

It may seem strange that in Eqs. (6.7) and (6.8) we are generating changes in K_a, yet K_a and K_b are taken as parameters in the right-hand-side. The factor share changes depend on the initial values from which a change is taken, just as the derivative of a function depends on the point at which the derivative is calculated. This means that, even given the earlier list of assumptions for this model, the elasticities are exact only at the point calculated. For finite changes they are approximations. A special case in which the elasticities are exact even for large changes is when all the behavioral functions have constant elasticity and the production function is Cobb-Douglas. The further the system departs from these assumptions, the less good the approximation for finite changes.

Equation (6.7) provides a convenient way to check on the sensitivity of the Chap. 4 elasticities to $\sigma \neq 1$. For example, we calculate the effect on P_b of a 10 percent change in P_x according to the Table 4.1 formula, using the given initial factor shares. Then we use Eq. (6.7) to estimate the change in K_a and K_b from a 10-percent change. Then we recalculate EP_b/EP_x using the estimated end-point factor shares. The range of the two estimates of EP_b/EP_x indicates the maximum approximation error. [The same approach can be used to assess the approximation error in Eq. (6.7) itself.]

THE SIZE DISTRIBUTION OF HOUSEHOLD INCOME

In today's agriculture, whether composed of small farms in the developing countries or large family farms in the industrialized countries, it is usual that a farmer is the supplier of some of each of the labor, land, capital, and management of the farm. In these circumstances, it is not immediately apparent what knowledge about factor shares has to contribute to an understanding of the inequality of the personal distribution of income. It is this latter aspect of income distribution that we are usually most interested in when it comes to public policy issues. To see how the functional and personal distributions of income are connected, let us start with an accounting definition of household income.

The income of the ith income receiving unit is

$$Y_i = w_i H_i + r_i V_i + e_i$$

where w is the wage rate, H is human capital, r is the rate of return on capital, V is the value of nonhuman resources owned, and e is transitory income not contracted for or allocatable to either factor. (Note that some of these letters stood for different economic concepts in the earlier chapters, an unavoidable inconvenience due to the fixed supply of readily accessible symbols.)

The variance (Var) of Y_i, one measure of inequality, is

$$\text{Var } (Y) = \text{Var } (wH) + \text{Var } (rV) + 2 \text{ Cov } (wH,rV) + \text{Var } (e) \quad (6.9)$$

assuming covariance (Cov) of e_i with $w_i H_i$ and $r_i V_i$ to be zero (i.e., transitory income is not systematic.)

Let w_i be the same for all labor of given quality (differences in skills are incorporated in the variance of H). Likewise, r_i is taken as a market rate of return which is the same for everybody. Differences in wealth are measured in V. Any disequilibrium or chance returns are included in e. Thus $w_i = \overline{w}$ and $r_i = \overline{r}$ for all i.

The first term of Eq. (6.9) can be rewritten as

$$\text{Var } (\overline{w}H) = \frac{\sum_{i=1}^{n} (\overline{w}H_i - \overline{w}\overline{H})^2}{n}$$

$$= \frac{\sum_{i=1}^{n} [\overline{w}(H_i - \overline{H})]^2}{n}$$

$$= \frac{\sum_{i=1}^{n} (\overline{w}^2(H_i - \overline{H})^2}{n}$$

$$= \overline{w}^2 \frac{\sum_{i=1}^{n} (H_i - \overline{H})^2}{n}$$

$$= \overline{w}^2 \text{ Var } (H)$$

The same transformation of Var (rV), and Cov (wH, rV) permits us to rewrite Eq. (6.9) as:

$$\text{Var}(Y) = \overline{w}^2 \, \text{Var}(H) + \overline{r}^2 \, \text{Var}(V) + 2\,\overline{rw}\, \text{Cov}(H,V) + \text{Var}(e) \qquad (6.10)$$

Subtracting Var (e) from Eq. (6.10) gives us the variance of *permanent* income.

The variance of income is not a useful measure of inequality for many purposes. Its main defect is that it is not invariant to the unit of monetary account used. For example, if all prices and incomes fall by one-half, inequality as we usually think of it is unchanged; yet the variance of income will decrease.

The squared coefficient of variation of Y gives us a measure of relative income inequality. It will not change, for example, if everyone's income doubled. It is defined as:

$$C^2(Y) = \left(\frac{\text{S.D. }(Y)}{\overline{Y}}\right)^2 = \frac{\text{Var}(Y)}{\overline{Y}^2}$$

Therefore, we can analyze $C^2(Y)$ by dividing Eq. (6.10) by $\overline{Y}^2$

The first term of Eq. (6.10), divided by $\overline{Y}^2$, can be usefully expanded by multiplying and dividing by $\overline{H}^2$, i.e.,

$$\frac{\overline{w}^2 \, \text{Var}(H)}{\overline{Y}^2} = \frac{\overline{w}^2 \, \overline{H}^2}{\overline{Y}^2} \frac{\text{Var}(H)}{\overline{H}^2}$$
$$= K_H^2 \, C^2(H)$$

where K_H is the relative share of labor earnings in total income, and $C^2(H)$ is the squared coefficient of variation of H.

The second term of Eq. (6.10) can be handled in exactly the same way. To analyze the third term of Eq. (6.10), first recall that the correlation coefficient between H_i and V_i is

$$\rho = \frac{\text{Cov}(H,V)}{\sqrt{\text{Var}(H)}\,\sqrt{\text{Var}(V)}}$$

Substituting for Cov (H,V) in Eq. (6.10) gives us the third term:

$$2\,\overline{rw}\,\rho\,\sqrt{\text{Var}(H)}\,\sqrt{\text{Var}(V)}$$

Dividing this expression, as the first and second terms, by $\overline{Y}^2$, and multiplying by $\overline{H}/\overline{H}$ and $\overline{V}/\overline{V}$, yields

$$2\rho\,\frac{\overline{rV}}{\overline{Y}}\frac{\overline{wH}}{\overline{Y}}\frac{\sqrt{\text{Var}(H)}}{\overline{H}}\frac{\sqrt{\text{Var}(V)}}{\overline{V}} = 2\rho\,K_H\,K_V\,C(H)\,C(V)$$

Omitting Var (e) from Eq. (6.10), which means again that we are looking at the inequality of permanent income, we get

$$C^2(Y) = K_H^2 C^2(H) + K_V^2 C^2(H) + 2\rho K_H K_V C(H) C(H) \qquad (6.11)$$

Equation (6.11) reveals the connection between functional shares and the inequality of the personal distribution of income. The measure of inequality is a weighted average of the inequality of factor ownership, the weights being functions of factor shares. [Note: the sum of the weights equals 1. We have $K_H^2 + K_v^2 + 2K_H K_v = K_H^2 + (1 - K_H)^2 + 2K_H(1 - K_H) = 1$].

Consider what happens when a factor share changes. For a small change in K_H, we have, using the fact that $K_V = 1 - K_H$,

$$\frac{\partial C^2(Y)}{\partial K_H} = 2K_H C^2(H) - 2C^2(H) - 2C^2(V) + 2K_H C^2(V)$$

$$+ 2\rho C(H) C(V) - 4K_H \rho C(H) C(V)$$

$$= 2K_H C^2(H) - 2K_V C^2(V) + 2(1 - 2K_H)\rho C(H) C(V) \qquad (6.12)$$

The first two terms of Eq. (6.12) indicate that when land's share of income goes up, the inequality of the distribution of income by households goes up so long as land ownership is more unequally distributed than nonland inputs, i.e., $C^2(V) > C^2(H)$. But the third term could upset this result, the likelihood of this case increasing as ρ moves toward its maximum or minimum possible values of ± 1. Empirical work is necessary to obtain the relevant information: factor shares, the inequality of ownership of each factor, and the correlation between land and nonland ownership (negative if those with more than average land have less nonland inputs).

EVIDENCE ON U.S. FARM INCOME DISTRIBUTION

The U.S. Census of Agriculture and the Economic Research Service of the USDA provide much economic data for farms classified by value of sales. Key data are shown in Table 6.1. The direct government payments increase with size of farm, with the largest farms receiving an average of $33,000 in 1984. Since these farms have an average income greater than $400,000 and net worth more than $2 million, it is hard to see the programs as contributing to equality. Yet the payments are smaller as a percentage of total income for large farms than for the average farm, and payments provide the biggest percentage boost to farm income in the sales class with the lowest total income per farm (the $40,000 to $100,000 sales class).

The Table 6.1 data indicate many farms, perhaps a majority of all farms,

Table 6.1   Income by Sales Class of Farm, United States, 1984

	Annual sales (10³ $)					
	Less than 20	20 to 40	40 to 100	100 to 250	250 to 500	500 and more
Number of farms (x10³)	1,391	247	353	229	77	31
(percent of all farms)	(59.7)	(10.6)	(15.2)	(9.9)	(3.3)	(1.3)
Net farm Income per farm (10³ $)	−1,580	390	6,070	31,880	81,880	423,060
Off-farm income per farm (10³ $)	19,830	21,080	9,720	10,690	11,470	14,440
Total Income per farm (10³ $)	18,250	21,470	15,790	42,560	93,350	437,500
Government payments per farm (10³ $)	288	2,200	5,310	13,000	20,560	33,420
(percent of total income)	(1.5)	(10.2)	(33.6)	(30.5)	(22.0)	(7.6)
Addendum: Net worth per farm ($ th.)	133	273	427	735	1,250	2,392

should not really be thought of farms in an economic or commercial sense at all. The 1.4 million farms with sales less than $20,000, as a group, get all their net income (and pay off their farm losses) through off-farm income, mostly from employment at off-farm jobs. There is no economic reason for them to be considered in agricultural policy discussion, any more than suburbanites' week-end building activities should be counted part of the construction industry. Leaving them in or out does not make much difference for sectoral output, re-ceipt or cost accounting, but it can make a substantial difference in distribu-tional calculations.

   The fact that the lowest total income group is not the lowest sales group illustrates a problem in using sales as the classification criterion for measuring inequality to serve as the empirical basis for Eqs. (6.9) to (6.11). Most of the real inequality is within the sales classes.

   In any case, government payments tell only part of the story of program effects. Much of the economic impact (for some programs, all of it), results from higher market prices rather than payments.

Data are available on the size distributions of total income of farm families, from the Current Population Survey of the U.S. Bureau of the Census. But these data do not identify government payments or provide other economic data about the farm operation that would permit an assessment of farm program effects.

The only empirical work available to place data in Eq. (6.11) is synthetic, estimating the size distribution of ownership of land and other assets, and then using factor share changes due to farm programs. One study estimated that farm programs increased the coefficient of variation of farm income $[C(Y)]$ by 6.5 percent, i.e., increased inequality (Gardner and Hoover, 1975). For illustrative calculations, we have $C^2(H)$ at 0.6, $C^2(V)$ at 2.0, ρ at 0.4, and K_v at 0.4. Now suppose that from a study of the functional distribution of farm income we know that if government price supports are eliminated, Eq. (6.7) yields an estimate that K_v will fall from 0.4 to 0.35. Plugging the estimated values into Eq. (6.11), we get the inequality of income distribution with farm programs as

$$C^2(Y) = (0.36)(0.6) + (0.16)(2.0) + (2)(0.5)(0.6)(0.4)(\sqrt{2})(\sqrt{6}) = 0.80$$

When the programs are eliminated and K_V falls to 0.35, we get

$$C^2(Y) = (0.42)(0.6) + (0.12)(2) + (2)(0.5)(0.65)(0.35)(\sqrt{2})(\sqrt{6}) = 0.74$$

POLICY AND THE STRUCTURE OF AGRICULTURE

The analysis to this point has concerned the distribution of income among a given set of people having given initial wealth and skills. Another set of issues has been of more widespread interest among agricultural economists, although the discussion has been more diffuse and less tied in with applied price theory. These issues involve the effects of policy on the number and kinds of people in farming, and on the economic organization of farm enterprises, in short, on characteristics of the industry we have so far taken as given, which can be referred to loosely as the structure of the industry.

In order to do full justice to these issues, it is necessary to have an applicable theory of the structure of competitive industry, and farming in particular. What determines the number of firms, their size, their choice of enterprise diversification or specialization, their use of hired or family labor, their use of forward contracting or direct marketing to sell products, or the form of land tenure? In what circumstances do farms expand, acquire debt, or incorporate? Why do some products, notably broilers, become dominated by forms of contracting in which the farmer is essentially a salaried employee, perhaps paid

piece-rate wages, of a large corporation? Why is there so much capital investment by nonfarm individuals in certain types of farming, notably cattle feedlots? What are the primary forces causing farms to go out of business; and what
happens to the land and capital equipment of those who do? We need to know
the determinants of these events in order to assess how farm policies alter the
picture.

The supply–demand model of the industry that we have been elaborating
has nothing to contribute to this topic. Individual firms have been ignored. The
assumption of constant returns to scale for the industry production function limits the structure of industry to an undetermined number of identical firms. The
firms have U-shaped cost curves, and may have different outputs that minimize
costs, but they must all be identical in the sense of having the same minimum
average cost (even though this cost will change for all of them whenever factor
prices change). This assumed structure has the negative consequence that it affords no reason for a price-support program to have any structural consequences. A higher support price draws in more firms and bids up the price of
specific factors in the new equilibrium, but there is no reason for any firm to
have larger or smaller output than it did before.

HYPOTHESES ABOUT POLICY AND STRUCTURE

Many possibilities exist for including heterogeneity among farms in policy
modeling. For example, in considering what would happen to the U.S. sugar
or dairy industries in the absence of current policies, geographic differences in
production costs would be important. Within geographic areas, differences from
farm to farm in efficiency or costs can be important. The quality of inputs,
including managerial ability, varies. For given cost conditions, the institutional
characteristics of marketing and contracting can make a difference, especially
in conjunction with payments targeted to particular groups, such as tenants as
opposed to landlords. Of the many possible structural issues, a few have been
emphasized by agricultural economists. This section samples the arguments in
the literature for U.S. farm policy.

Cochrane and Ryan (1976, p. 364) state that

> Farm price and income support programs interacting with rapid commercial and
> technological development result in a situation in which the larger, more aggres-
> sive, more alert commercial farmers cannibalize the smaller, less aggressive, less
> alert commercial farmers.

This picture of the farm sector differs from our industry model in emphasizing
the existence of technical change and in postulating two types of firms: aggressive ones which are well adapted to a rapidly changing environment and passive
ones, which are not so well adapted, become relatively high-cost producers,

and are cannibalized. Being cannibalized is not necessarily bad for these firms because they may well be bought out at higher prices for their assets due to the aggressiveness of the aggressive farmers. But the high-cost producers who stay in business may see their income decline.

The simplest extension of our industry model that permits an investigation of this issue is one in which there are two types of firms, low-cost and high-cost, and the only specific factor to the industry is a fixed supply of low-cost producers (the aggressive ones who are ahead, at any given point in time, in adopting new technology). For the moment, we ignore land or other inputs as specific factors causing the supply function to slope upward. The resulting industry supply function is S_1, in Fig. 6.1. The existence of high-cost producers creates Ricardian rents for the low-cost producers, but the good fortune of the low-cost producers does not influence the income of the high-cost producers (nor, as we expect from pure rents, do these rents influence the market price). Further gains of the low-cost producers to generate the dotted segment of S_1 would have similar null effects. The market would be affected only if the low-cost producers expanded output so much as to drive out the high-cost producers, as in supply curve S_1'.

To elaborate the model slightly, suppose that, instead of two types of producers, we had a continuum of managerial ability among producers generating supply curve S_2. The Cochrane-Ryan situation could result from the costs of the better managers falling more in the dynamic world of technical change. Then

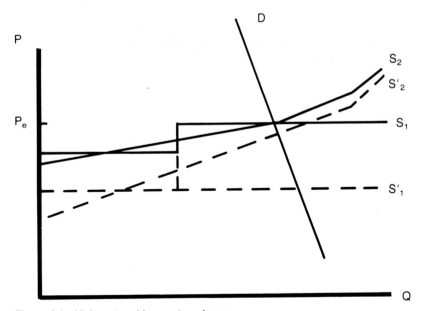

Figure 6.1   High-cost and low-cost producers.

the supply curve shifts to a position like S'_2 each year as compared to the year before, with marginal producers forced out and the newly marginal producers having their rents eroded.

Further elaboration by including land and perhaps other inputs in the model as specific factors makes S_2 steeper and increases the loss of rents by formerly intramarginal farms when low-cost farms expand. The economics of the specific factors in the heterogeneous firm case is that making land more valuable to the low-cost firms also makes it more costly to the high-cost firms; but as land owners, all farmers gain, even those who exit the industry.

With respect to land of varying quality, it should be kept in mind that low quality land cannot be identified with high-cost production—production that leaves the industry first when the price of output falls. It could, for example, be relatively cheap to produce wheat on low-yielding, dry land because the land has few alternatives and a low price. So if the demand for wheat fell, the land to leave wheat first would be better land, and the high-yielding acreage would be the high-cost acreage.

We have been discussing dynamics, which requires an explicitly dynamic model explaining the time paths of variables for a satisfactory analysis. Nonetheless, the supply–demand snapshot, or temporary equilibrium for a particular crop year in the midst of this process, helps in obtaining a grasp of these structural issues.

Missing from the Fig. 6.1 story so far is price supports. How do we obtain the result that price supports intensify the process of adjustment favoring low-cost farmers? One factor emphasized by Cochrane and Ryan is that as price supports increase land prices, this further strengthens the financial position of the low-cost producers and enables them to expand faster. But price supports also strengthen the position of high-cost producers, indeed may make it possible for them to survive when they otherwise would not. So there is no a priori case for expecting price supports to cause structural change in one direction or the other. This returns us to the null results on structure and farm policy that the homogeneous-firm model implied. But now we have reasons why there might be structural effects favoring either aggressive, low-cost or passive, high-cost producers.

A second reason emphasized by Cochrane and Ryan to explain why farm programs have caused structural change favoring our low-cost farmers is that

> The farmer with superior commercial ability and superior technical skill *used the price-income stability provided by the government programs* to borrow capital, invest in new and improved technologies, and reduce unit costs, and increase his net return on each unit of product sold (p. 365; *italics added*).

Why does stability favor large over small farms? Couldn't one as easily argue that an uncertain environment is relatively better suited to the aggressive entrepreneurial types? Pope and Gardner (1978) discuss three ways in which policies that reduce risk can increase farm size: (1) increased output by risk-averse producers with given factor and product prices, (2) increased input supply by factor owners, and (3) encouragement of adoption of decreasing cost technologies. In addition, risk reduction under a given technology has been hypothesized to induce increased specialization (among farm enterprises as well as specialization in commercial agriculture as opposed to a mix of on- and off-farm work by the operator). The fact that the ratio of net family income to gross receipts becomes smaller as we move to larger-scale operations means that risk increases with size, ceteris paribus. Example: A one-man operation on 200 acres of owned land in corn might have $40,000 in normal sales and $25,000 in normal expenses for a $15,000 return to operator labor and land. By adding rented land and larger machinery and/or hired labor, the operation might have $100,000 in normal sales and $80,000 in normal expenses for a $20,000 operator return. If there is a 10-percent chance of corn revenues being 20 percent below normal, the small operation bears a 10-percent risk of net income of $7,000, while the large operator bears a 10-percent risk of net income of zero. Thus, the risk of severe financial pinch is greater for the large than for the small operation, despite the higher normal income for the large farm. Price stabilization by means of commodity programs reduces the risk in moving to a larger-scale, specialized operation, and might therefore encourage such shifts. However, it is necessary to consider the structural consequences of risk-bearing in the absence of commodity programs. Many private-market substitutes for government stabilization programs, such as forward sales, involve investment of time and money, which may itself contribute to observed economies of size. Thus, it is not clear that risk reduction through government stabilization will induce more rapid structural change than its absence.

MODELING STRUCTURAL ISSUES

A full analysis of these issues requires going back to first principles to model the characteristics of farming and farmers that have been discussed. Much more detail is needed on firm-level economics. Instead of an industry production or supply function, we need firm-specific production or cost functions. Models incorporating heterogeneous firms have been developed which add a firm-specific variable that measures each farm's efficiency to its production or cost function (for example, see Chambers, 1987). This parameter comes into play in the industry-level assessment of price supports only when the nature and distribution among firms of the parameter is specified. Is it fixed for each firm or can it be changed by investment (e.g., technical training of the farmer)? Is it uniformly distributed through the population of farms, normally distributed, or what; and what are the characteristics of new firms that may be drawn into the industry if price supports are raised?

Although a more formal and detailed development of this idea might be fruitful, it is not undertaken here. An approach to heterogeneity that is more in keeping with the industry model of Chaps. 4 and 5 is to introduce input supply functions for the feature that makes firms heterogeneous. If farmers differ in ability, we introduce managerial ability as an input. It may be supplied jointly with labor, but it may not. Farms can purchase managerial services in marketing or financial management, or can even have hired farm managers. In terms of Eqs. (4.41), we add an input, m. The analytical and empirical issues then involve the elasticity of supply of m and its substitutability with other inputs. We can examine how a proposed policy influences the rents received by management services, and how the existence of scarce management changes the gains to labor compared to land from a policy.

Alternatively, we could disaggregate labor into two inputs, high-quality labor, which includes managerial skills, and low-quality labor, which does not. Then we can study the effects of policies on the distribution of income between the two types of labor.

A related but distinct cause of heterogeneity is that people who supply labor to agriculture have varying preferences for farm living. Such preferences play a role in labor supply and returns generally, as is well recognized going back to Adam Smith. The relevance of these preferences is that they may create nonpecuniary benefits to farmers who greatly prefer farming to the next best opportunity and thus would work in agriculture at a relatively low wage. The nonpecuniary benefits are rents, conceptually identical to rents of land and similarly dependent for their existence on heterogeneity; if there were 3 million people willing to be farmers for $3.00 per hour, then that is all any farmer could expect to earn, but if heartless money grubbers who can obtain $5.00 per hour elsewhere are receiving the $5.00 necessary to induce them to be farmers, the ones who like farming receive a $2.00+ rent. The more instances of this type of heterogeneity there are, the less elastic are long-run supply curves of inputs and hence of output. This means that output-expanding policies will generate more producer benefits, and that output-reducing policies will be less attractive. (Areas like C in Fig. 2.2 will be larger.)

This way of structural modeling has the limitation that it can incorporate only a few sources of heterogeneity and each one must be specified narrowly. The model becomes more general but only in a quite limited respect and only by making still further assumptions. This is a useful limitation because it recognizes the nonexistence of a truly general presuppositionless model that could be used in policy analysis. Attempting to be more general, we can criticize an assertion that policy A will have consequences B by pointing out that the inference came from a model that made unrealistic assumptions (that all farms are identical, say). But if we go beyond this criticism to assert that the consequences of A will be C, we will have to make assumptions of our own. Formal modeling forces us to do this explicitly.

Adding inputs to represent managerial ability, say, is not sufficient to analyze hypotheses like that of Cochrane and Ryan that it is the interaction between price support and uncertainty that causes structural changes, or that the short-run effects may be quite different from long-run effects. To examine these issues fully we need a dynamic model with random prices and output. Some such models are developed in Chap. 10, but they are not developed far enough to address structural issues. We can fall back on the informal application of basic economic principles, which indeed was the approach used earlier in discussing Cochrane and Ryan. However, this proved unsatisfactory in that the issues were not resolved.

It should also be noted that incorporation of heterogeneity in a conceptual model, and even the inclusion of empirically validated behavorial parameters, does not provide all the machinery to answer structural questions. Also necessary is information on the distribution of structurally relevant characteristics of farms. The importance of the distribution of wealth endowments in Eq. (6.11) is an example. A model bringing in managerial skills can be helpful, but to carry out an analysis of how farm programs change the results of skills, we need to know the distribution of these skills among farmers.

Evidence on Policies and Structure

Evidence to establish farm programs as empirically important determinants of the structure of agriculture is difficult to develop. With respect to commodity programs generally, the empirical issue is counterfactual: how the size or other characteristics of farms would have changed historically in the absence of programs. The best empirical study available is that of Sumner (1985). He finds no generalizable structural consequences of past U.S. farm commodity programs.

Apart from the question of the average size of farms, other aspects of structure seem more likely to be influenced by agricultural policies. And the policies most influential may not be commodity price supports. Subsidized credit offers a clear inducement to expand the size of farming operations. Liberal terms and eased access to credit have been provided for farms in financial trouble under the Economic Emergency Loan Program and other lending by the Farmers Home Administration should tend to keep some high-cost producers in business. Also, the existence of these programs encourages farmers to take financial risks they might otherwise avoid. Similarly, subsidized crop insurance encourages the growing of riskier crops (corn instead of grain sorghum) in some areas. The Disaster Payments Program (insurance with no premiums charged) caused expanded grain planting in marginal areas of West Texas. (For empirical evidence on this, see Gardner and Kramer, 1985.)

FARM PROGRAM INSTITUTIONS

Structural and distributional consequences of farm programs can arise from features that are left out altogether from aggregate supply–demand models. The problems of monitoring and enforcing program provisions have been mentioned with reference to price ceilings, price floors, and acreage controls, but these problems did not play a role in the depictions of program-constrained market equilibrium. When it comes to the welfare economics of program choice these issues and the related implementation and administrative costs of policy cannot be ignored, and are briefly discussed in Chaps. 9 and 12. The issue here is the possibility of structural effects of these problems. In the United States, inter-state differences in tobacco taxes bred an industry of cigarette smuggling. Would sustained acreage limitations on corn, say, generate an industry of illicit corn growing?

In some cases, programs can cause nominal structural change even though little has really happened. Under U.S. grain and cotton programs of the 1980s, a limit of $50,000 is placed on the deficiency payment that any farm can re-ceive. This caused a substantial reduction in the number of farms of size large enough to be subject to the limit. (In 1986–1987, with a payment of $1.11 per bushel, a farmer with 140 bushel per acre corn yield reaches the limit at 322 acres.) However, this reduction took place almost entirely in USDA records without corresponding changes in the actual structure of farming, as family members were each assigned new farms small enough to qualify for full pay-ments on an original larger farm. But even here, "farming the programs" can have real structural effects, too.

A related issue arises under acreage (or other input quantity) controls, con-cerning owners as compared to renters of the input. U.S. farm program pay-ments tied to acreage have often been required to be split between landlord and tenant in proportion to crop shares. This allocation requirement was intended, when introduced in the 1930s, to make sure crop-share tenants received pro-gram benefits. Under cash rental arrangements, payments are sometimes made to the tenant, sometimes to the landlord. In terms of a supply–demand model, it makes no difference who receives the government check, as discussed in Chap. 2 with reference to consumer versus producer subsidies. If the landlord receives the payments, then the tenant will pay a lower rental price. If the ten-ants receive the payments, they will bid up the rental price of land carrying payments so that the net position of landlord and tenant will be the same in either case. The incidence of gains depends only on the elasticities of supply and demand for land rental.

A real issue exists about who gains, nonetheless, even though it does not matter who receives the government's checks. The issue is who owns the *right* to receive checks, or if there are no checks, to the right to plant limited acreage. If the landowner owns the right, landowners gain from the program and tenants lose. If the tenant owns the right, landowners lose. We cannot tell who owns the rights by observing the supply–demand equilibrium. We have to observe what happens when landlord and tenant part company. If the right to plant or receive checks stays with the particular parcel of land, then the landlord reaps the gains, no matter who gets the checks. Tenants have to compete to use the scarce rights to plant. On the other hand, if the tenants carry the right to plant their historical acreage with them when they move, then the tenants reap the gains. Landlords have to compete to get the tenants to use scarce planting rights on their land; otherwise it stays idle. Under U.S. policy, planting rights reside on farms, on parcels of land, and not with farmers. So no matter who receives checks, landowners reap the program benefits that accrue to land.

A similar complication arises with production controls. The production control that limits output to $\hat{Q}$ results in a supply price of P_s, as in Fig. 2.1. This means that all inputs, including land and the farmer's own labor could be had at cost P_s. Who gets the rents of $(\hat{P} - P_s)$ per unit output? The owners of the program-created asset which carries the right to produce the commodity do. While it is often true that the rights are tied to land, this need not be the case, and often is not in fact. For example, the dairy programs of Ontario and British Columbia allocate rights to sell fixed quantities of milk. These are allocated according to farmers' historical cow numbers, but newcomers can buy quota, independently of cows. The right to sell a cow's output in perpetuity sold for about eight times the price of a cow in the early 1980s. This kind of program involves a transfer to quota owners at the expense of consumers and "real" factor owners. Since the quota owner is typically also the owner of at least some of the farm-supplied resources, this may not be important in changing the personal redistribution caused by a quota program. But when quota can be sold and rented, the way is opened for quota-owners to become a separate interest group. The U.S. flue-cured tobacco program provides a good example. Marketing quotas have been traded, passed on to descendents, or held by retired farmers to the point that the majority of tobacco is now grown on acreage for which quota is rented. The growers rent quota from other farmers or nonfarmowners of quota. Sumner and Alston (1984) estimate the gains to quota owners, area $A + D$ in Fig. 2.1, at $800 million annually, and the loss of rents to other inputs, area $D + C$, at $200 million.

Algebraically the quota rents R are

$$R = \hat{P}\hat{Q} - P_s \qquad (6.13)$$

and the change in R when the controlled output level $\hat{Q}$ changes is

$$\frac{dR}{d\hat{Q}} = \hat{P} + \frac{d\hat{P}}{d\hat{Q}}\hat{Q} - P_s\frac{dP_s}{dQ}\hat{Q} \qquad (6.14)$$

Rearranging, and dividing R by QP_s to express rents as a fraction of factor income:

$$\frac{ER}{E\hat{Q}} = T\left(1 + \frac{1}{\eta}\right) - \left(1 + \frac{1}{\epsilon}\right) \qquad (6.15)$$

where T is the ratio $\hat{P}/P_s$.

Capitalization and Wealth

The rents received are a flow of income to owners of quota. The expectation of future rents generates a program-created asset. The value of the asset is

$$W_0 = \sum_{t=1}^{T} \frac{1}{1 + i_t} R_t \qquad (6.16)$$

where W_0 is the value of a unit of quota at the beginning of year 1, R_t are returns received at the end of each year, i is the relevant interest rate for discounting purposes, and T is the length of the program. In the first year, T and future values of R_t are unknown. Each person's assessment of future R_t is subjective and determines willingness to pay for quota. With a market for quota (often but not always sold jointly with land), the market price of quota provides a market estimate of W_0, revealing the market's expectations about the future of the program that generates the rents.

Even if there is no market for buying and selling quota, the right to produce has value and is part of its owner's nonhuman wealth. Therefore, when P_x is changed, for example, by reducing acreage as in Eq. (6.8), this will change not only factor prices and factors shares, but also wealth. This change could leave $C^2(V)$ unchanged in Eq. (6.11) if all farmers had an equal fraction of their wealth in the form of quota ownership. But generally this will not be the case. Some will own no quota or land to which quota is tied, and have to rent it from others. So an increase in P_x will tend to raise $C^2(V)$, increasing the inequality of wealth ownership. In addition, wealth will be created for people who own quota but do not farm—quota lords—who, the earlier data suggest, are an important component of the U.S. tobacco program. Their addition can either increase or decrease the inequality of wealth ownership. In the case of the flue-cured tobacco program, quotas are based on historically small tobacco acreages of the 1950s averaging less than 1 acre per farm. The renters of quota are the aggressive, expanding farmers often thought to be the big gainers from price supports. It is more likely in tobacco, however, that the program hinders the structural transformation of tobacco growing.

Farm Tax Breaks

Special income tax provisions for agricultural enterprises also have structural consequences. During 1980–1985, the farm sector as a whole reported farm losses to the Internal Revenue Service (as compared to $20 billion to $30 billion net income according to the USDA). The reporting of losses makes sense only in balancing losses against nonfarm income to reduce tax liability. The structural aspects in part involve heavier subsidies for certain enterprises (e.g., breeding cattle, race horses, orchards, cattle feedlots), hence, redirecting investment toward those commodities and driving down their prices. On an overall basis, a USDA study attributes 20 percent of recent investment in agriculture to tax provisions (Le Blanc and Hrubovcak, 1986). The inducement of nonfarm capital into agriculture drives down rates of return in agriculture, placing the farmer with no outside income in a position like that of a low-income person drawing income from tax-exempt bonds.

This issue can be analyzed in more depth using our two-factor model. Let a be the farmer-supplied resources and b capital goods from outside the sector, owned by nonfarmers. The tax breaks on investment in agriculture constitute a subsidy on the use of b in producing agricultural output X. The formulas of Table 4.2 allow the calculation of consequences of the subsidy, given the parameter values σ, η, k_a, e_a, and e_b. Suppose $e_b \to \infty$, i.e., the rate of return to capital in agriculture is set by the rate of return elsewhere, so that the supply of b to X is perfectly elastic at that rate. The elasticities show that X rises and P_x falls: consumers receive more food products at lower prices. If e_a were large, as it may be for particular products that are especially favored, the consumers' costs fall by almost the full amount of the subsidy. The economic reasoning is that if producers can readily switch land and labor to growing almonds, when tax breaks bring in more capital farmers end up earning not much more than before because they enter the business until their returns are driven down to the same level as elsewhere in agriculture. Thus, the benefits of tax breaks, and the costs of tax reform in this area would be borne primarily by the consumers of almonds, or avocadoes, or other favored commodities.

When capital is drawn into agriculture generally, then the relevant e_a is smaller, and P_a, the (rental) price of farmers' labor and land, can share in the gains. However, farmers may lose. If $\sigma > -\eta$ the subsidy of b will reduce the demand for a and hence reduce P_a. The Table 4.2 elasticity for EP_a/ET_b with $e_b \to \infty$ is $K_b (\sigma + \eta)/(e_a - K_a\eta + K_b\sigma)$. In the Cobb-Douglas case ($\sigma = 1$), with $\eta = -0.25$, $e_a = 0.3$, and $K_a = 0.5$, this implies that a 10-percent subsidy of b would reduce P_a by 4 percent. Thus, farmers are made worse off by the tax-code subsidies of capital in agriculture. If $\sigma < -\eta$, the sign of the effect on P_a is reversed, in intuitive economic terms because now the additional demand for a, as output of X increases, outweighs the substitution of the subsidized b for a inputs in production. For some commodities, notably exported ones, η may be quite large, and so the b subsidy is more likely to be beneficial to farmers. There may also be cases where σ is very low, and again a owners would benefit.

Two complications should be added. First, farmers themselves supply capital to agriculture. With $e_b \to \infty$, this makes no difference for gains and losses since P_b is unchanged in any case. However—the second complication—e_b is unlikely to be perfectly elastic under the tax-break scenario. Nonfarmers in higher tax brackets will accept a lower rate of return in agriculture, but those just at the margin of indifference in tax-shelter searching, in lower brackets, require a higher return. Also, if farmers with little or no off-farm income to shelter keep their assets in agriculture, they must be willing to accept a lower post-tax rate of return than the marginal nonfarm investor. This implies a rising supply of b to X. Suppose e_b is still elastic, say, 2.0. Then, other parameters remaining as specified earlier, the 10-percent subsidy of b would reduce P_a less, by 3.3 percent instead of 4.0 percent.

More importantly, there would now be gains to b owners. The formula for EP_b/ET_b implies that a 10-percent subsidy would reduce P_b on the demand curve by 8 percent, which means that with the subsidy, b owners' returns rise by 2 percent. Consumers still get the major gains as P_x falls.

The difference between specialists in farming and outside investors has important structural implications. Figure 6.2 shows the b market as just described. Owing to the tax breaks, the returns to b have fallen by 8 percent to P_b'. This means that farmers who can't take advantage of the tax breaks and, hence, do not get the subsidy, would be supplying capital to agriculture only if their willingness to invest in agriculture put them to the left of b_1 on S. They are thus losing considerable rents that they would have if there were no subsidy to b and the market was at b_0, P_0. These losses are in addition to those from declines in P_a as analyzed earlier.

In the long run, as S approaches being perfectly elastic, all farm capital that cannot take advantage of tax breaks goes to other (nonsheltered) sectors. This is the structural worry about the favorable tax treatment of nonfarm investment in agriculture.

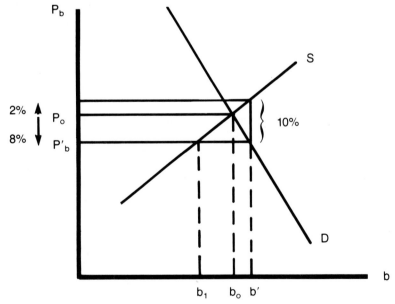

Figure 6.2 Effect of subsidy on input b.

The Structure of Farm Decision-Making

Another and perhaps more fundamental structural issue involves the "control" of agriculture—whether farm decision-making is done by individual owner-operators as opposed to farmers being hired employees of off-farm owners. It is easy to overstate the autonomy of the traditional "family" farmer. In the strict sense of control as determination of events, it is hard to find any instances of control when social interaction is involved. Farmers may be said to control their use of fertilizer or purchases of feeder cattle, but they are constrained by actions of the fertilizer supplier, the price of fertilizer, the requirements of their bankers, their health, and so forth. It would also not be correct to say that the fertilizer supplier controls a farmer's fertilizer use because the farmer may take his or her business elsewhere or change production plans, or the economics of fertilizer availability to the supplier may change. An agent's control of an event may be thought of quantitatively as the probability that the event occurs according to the agent's intentions. Control seems to become a policy issue when an individual's ability to influence events involving on-farm activities is reduced or threatened.

Analysis of control in this sense requires consideration of elements of the economic organization of agriculture other than the concentration of production on large farms. When economic activity is undertaken jointly, any individual involved loses control. Suppose two owner-operator farms combine. Even if one of the farmers becomes a hired employee of the other, both would be expected to have less control over the joint operation than either had over his or her own (although the employee presumably gives up more control than the employer). If an owner-operator sells his or her land to an urban resident, and then becomes the urban resident's cash or share tenant, there is a real sense in which farm residents have lost control of agriculture. If a farmer accepts contracting arrangements, such as have become the norm in some commodities, notably poultry and vegetables, there is an even greater loss of control.

Whatever the policy issues involved in these events, it is not possible to tie them to commodity policies. Indeed, the movement toward nontraditional farm organization appears to have gone furthest in commodities with relatively little intervention.

In developing countries, the argument has been made that new technologies accompanying improved crop varieties and other innovations have changed the structure of agriculture by selecting for the farmers in these countries corresponding to Cochrane-Ryan's U.S. aggressive commercial farmers. This is a policy-caused rather than market event because of the role of governments in developing and disseminating new technologies, and in subsidizing fertilizer, irrigation projects, and other inputs suited to these technologies.

Similarly, U.S. public research and extension is thought by some to have increased the size of farm operations. In a proper examination of this issue, the effects of public research and extension must be compared with the relevant alternative. The relevant alternative is the conduct of research and extension in the absence of public activities in these areas. If agricultural research and extension were left in private hands, there would be two kinds of consequences which work in opposite directions. First, because of its public good character, there would be a smaller commitment of resources to research, which would slow down the rate of technical advance and associated structural change. Second, there would be a less wide distribution of research results and instructions for implementing these results, which would increase incentives for large-scale ventures to cover the fixed costs of acquiring information on new techniques for which the producer must pay the full price in a private market. Which set of consequences would dominate is not clear a priori, and the relevant empirical evidence does not exist. Welch (1970b) finds that public research has a small effect taken by itself, but that, in conjunction with education, it accounts for about a quarter of the measured economies of scale that can be explained. However, it is not clear whether farm size growth would be associated with increasing concentration of production, or whether small and large farms would tend to grow at the same rate. The key element in structural change in agricultural production may well be the human agent. Welch (1970a) and Huffman (1974) have provided empirical evidence on the importance of education in determining responses to technical innovation and economic change. The characteristics of farm operators are likely as well to be an important determinant of responses to change in the policy environment. In this context, the structural consequences of policy operate by influencing the demand for human capital. Equally important, from this point of view, are policies that influence the supply of human capital in agriculture. It could be that the most important governmentally directed influence on the structure of agriculture is the number and quality of graduates from land-grant colleges who enter farming. In the absence of government programs and policy intervention, there would be a demand for skills in dealing with uncertainty and disequilibria (see Schultz, 1945, 1975). In the presence of the complex set of policy interventions outlined above, the same type of demand exists. The factor limiting structural change in either case could well be the supply of these skills.

In sum, while there appears to be no doubt that technical progress and its diffusion has changed the structure of agricultural production toward larger-scale farming, it is not clear that the marginal contribution of public research and extension has been to accelerate or decelerate the rate of change to larger units, or the movement to increased concentration of production.

REGIONAL ISSUES IN STRUCTURE

Commodity policies can influence the regional patterns of production for two reasons: the policy may vary regionally or the policy may be uniform nationally but have different effects in different regions. Some U.S. programs have regional provisions intended to reduce regional effects, that is, to make the policy effect more uniform nationally. For example, CCC loan rates vary by state, being higher in states where prices are higher (typically states that import the commodity from other states). The idea is that farmers should use the CCC loan program, and acquire stocks, in roughly the same proportion of each state's output. Because regional price patterns vary, this can be difficult to accomplish.

The policies that have more notable regional consequences are ones in which regional pricing intentionally departs from market pricing patterns. U.S. dairy policy sets minimum prices for fluid milk sold for drinking purposes in more than 40 different marketing-order areas. These are supposed to reflect transportation cost between the upper Midwest producing areas and the various consuming areas. But it is doubtful whether this is accomplished. It is also doubtful whether it should be accomplished since under unrestrained trade it is not clear that all regions would import milk from the upper Midwest. In any case, the established regional fluid milk prices, together with the marketing-order price differential between fluid milk and manufacturing milk (the same milk used for cheese, butter, and so forth), has fostered a substantial shift in production of milk away from the traditional producing areas. With manufactured milk products in surplus during the 1980s and selling at CCC support prices, we find processing plants being built in the western United States just to handle surplus milk from new producers that will go into CCC stocks.

Production-control policies can have even more direct regional impacts by hindering the transfer of quota from traditional producing areas. The unmet incentives to transfer cotton allotments from the Gulf states to West Texas in the early 1960s were so great that Billy Sol Estes estimated it to be worth his while to risk prosecution to bend USDA regulations to make such transfers. In the later 1960s, U.S. law liberalized cotton growing but geographically restricted acreage allotments remain in place for tobacco and peanuts in the 1980s.

Tobacco affords an example of geographic restriction favoring producers in an area excluded from production quotas. Tobacco grown in Maryland has a different curing process and slightly different characteristics from the dominant flue-cured and burley types. Both flue-cured and burley tobaccos have stringent production quotas which cannot be transferred to Maryland. Maryland had an allotment program for its own type of tobacco, but the Maryland producers voted to end it. This worked to their advantage because Maryland tobacco is a good substitute for other tobacco in cigarette manufacturing. So the more restrictive the quotas on other tobaccos, the more the demand for Maryland tobacco increases. Maryland moves along its supply curve and earns a larger increase in rents for a given price than could be obtained through production controls. Maryland is essentially a free rider on flue-cured and burley producers' cartel.

Policies that are uniform nationally may nonetheless have regional effects. U.S. target price guarantees to producers and the sugar support level are the same everywhere. However, supply conditions vary. The differences are typically expressed in terms of cost of production. Hawaii is said to be a high-cost area in sugar, so that higher support prices are needed to keep sugar viable there.

Cost comparisons are notoriously slippery, however. Measuring cost as the sum of factor payments, it is a condition of competitive equilibrium that cost equals revenue. Therefore, cost per unit output equals price (revenue per unit output). To isolate the appropriate element of cost, we could look only at opportunity cost, omitting rents. Then we could say that Hawaii's being a high-cost area means that if sugar prices were to fall, Hawaiian resources would go into other activities. High cost is synonymous with elastic supply and low cost with inelastic supply. In this sense, cost does not measure efficiency or productivity differences between regions. Moreover, at the margin opportunity cost equals price in every region, indeed for every farm.

These considerations make it difficult to use accounting cost data in policy analysis. For example, Table 6.2 USDA (1984) shows cost of production for corn in 1982. The Corn Belt is the low-cost area, looking either at variable expenses or total unit cost excluding residual return to management. This residual plays a rent-like role in the USDA accounting, making up the difference between cost and price. The residual can be negative because of transitory events (low prices or yields), because other owned inputs (labor, old equipment, general farm overherd) are overpriced, or because some receipts are excluded, notably government payments.

How can this cost information be used in policy analysis? Suppose we cut the support price of corn. The lower purchased input costs in the Corn Belt suggest that farmers there won't be financially squeezed as much as in the Southeast. But this does not mean that corn production will fall by the largest percentage in the Southeast. It could be, for example, that there are better alternative uses for land in the Corn Belt so that land rent cannot be reduced much by a drop in the corn price; whereas in the Southeast there are less good alternative uses. Then when the corn price falls, corn land rent falls most in the South-

Table 6.2   Cost of Production for Corn, 1982*

	Corn Belt ($)	Southeast ($)
Cost per bushel:		
Purchased inputs and labor	1.35	1.66
Capital	0.51	0.37
Land rent	0.58	0.53
Management	−0.35	−0.42
Price received	2.09	2.14

*Data from USDA (1984).

east, notwithstanding that southeastern rents are already lower in the initial situation.

The analytical problem is that the accounting categories of cost do not divide costs into economic rents and opportunity costs; and even if they did, we would not have information on how opportunity costs change with output. We also have no information on how the input mix changes with output.

Attempts to model regional effects of policies have been made by using programming models containing input/output coefficient, given input prices for variable factors and given quantity constraints for fixed factors. This approach has the same problems as the use of cost-of-production data, with the additional one of determining which factors are variable and which fixed. The former assumes an input supply elasticity of zero, the latter an infinite elasticity. The actual values are in between. With sufficient creativity, programming models can build in flexible input quantity constraints and input–output coefficients that respond to prices. The model then approximates a regionally specific supply–demand model, which is what we really want. Nothing short of such a model is really adequate for analyzing the regional consequences of commodity policies.

CONCLUDING REMARKS

The distributional and structural issues discussed in this chapter generally introduce complications and pitfalls into the comparative statics. Comparative statics of policy instruments consists of changing a policy, holding other things constant, and analyzing the consequences for variables like farm prices, rents, and incomes. The things held constant are parameters in the models (e.g., elasticities and factor shares) and exogenous variables (like population, aggregate GNP, the weather) assumed not to be significantly influenced by agricultural policies. We can get into serious trouble when policies affect "exogenous" variables or the parameters. Several issues discussed in this chapter open up possibilities for such analytical mischief.

The first parameter is factor shares. They are a prime example of a parameter that changes (endogenously) when policy instruments change. Ways of dealing with this problem analytically have already been discussed.

A second part of things held constant is technology, not input choices and consequent yield changes, but the underlying production function. If this changes with policy instruments, we have a serious error of omission in comparative statics that ignores such changes. The importance of endogenous technology becomes more important with length of run. In a short period of time, within a year or two, it is not plausible that research and technical development in response to changed commodity policies have a big effect. In the long run, however, matters may be different. If supporting the price of cotton, say, leads to technical progress in cotton growing, then this will influence the price-quantity effects of a cotton program. A CCC storage program will result in bigger effects on output, and hence larger CCC stocks to support a given $\hat{P}$, than would have been estimated neglecting the induced technical change. A deficiency payment program would result in low market prices and larger government outlay than the short-run model would predict. Assuming that a long-term average market-induced price rise (a permanent shift in demand) has the same effects on induced innovation as a policy-induced price rise, we can modify the short-run model by incorporating higher own-price elasticities of supply in the long run. If we have an estimate of the long-run as well as short-run elasticity, we can accordingly do the comparative-statics exercise twice, once for short run and once for long-run effects.

An especially troublesome possibility is that the induced technical changes might be so large as to reduce the marginal cost of producing a price-supported commodity even though factor prices are bid up. That is, the long-run supply curve is downward sloping. If this occurs, however, it must have been unanticipated. It is contradictory to postulate an *expectation* of a lower-price outcome resulting from technical change induced by expectations of permanently higher prices!

Of course, it could be rational for a country to invest in technological research despite expectations of lower market prices. And high price supports would not not necessarily cause policy-induced technical progress. Indeed, if in deciding how much to appropriate for dairy research, it were taken as a given that the milk support price would remain fixed, this would reduce the social returns to the research and might lead public decision-makers to direct research efforts elsewhere.

A third structural element held constant in the discussion so far is the demand for imports of U.S. commodities abroad. This is very important for grains, rice, cotton, tobacco, and other minor commodities. Foreign countries' demand for commodities depends on their import policies. If these policies change when U.S. policy instruments change we have another factor that we have been treating as exogenous not turning out to be so. It might seem far-fetched that other countries' policies would respond to U.S. farm policy instruments, but the large share of some U.S. commodities in world markets makes it a real issue. When in 1986, the United States reduced wheat and feed grain loan rates by 25 to 30 percent, this added hundreds of millions of dollars to the EEC'S export restitution (subsidy) costs. So it is not at all out of the question for the EEC to adjust one or more policy parameters in response. Such responses, if systematic, should be included in the model and not held constant in the comparative statics of U.S. policy changes. The issue of endogeneity of policies is pursued further in Chaps. 11 and 12.

A related issue exists with respect to U.S. nonagricultural policies. For example, suppose the U.S. stopped supporting sugar prices, and in consequence, cane workers in Florida and the Gulf States lost their jobs. This would cause an increase in unemployment in the affected areas and a rise in outlays for unemployment compensation. However, if the unemployment policy regime remained the same before and after the sugar policy change, comparative statics that ignored this policy might still be appropriate. The reason is that the supply curve of labor to the sugar cane industry would reflect the existence of the unemployment policy. It would probably make the supply of labor more elastic because if demand were reduced, the workers have an additional alternative in unemployment compensation to ease the transition to another industry. As long as the policy is stable, its existence influences the elasticity of supply just as the existence of alternative industries does, and the effects of both would be captured by econometric evidence on supply elasticity that we would use in our comparative statics.

Part Three

Normative Economics
of Intervention

Chapter 7

Welfare Economics of Price Supports

From the positive to the normative—making recommendations about what ought to be done—is generally reckoned a big step. Yet often it is not. Suppose I look at your physical condition, the prescription that has been issued to you, and the prognosis for ailments of your type, and conclude: (1) You should take your pill. My diagnosis may be very intricate and require a lot of expertise, leading to the conclusion: (2) If you don't take your pill you will die. Statement (1) is normative, (2) is positive. Is it really a big leap from one to the other? No. The real and perhaps debatable issues involved arriving at (2). From there the inference to (1) is easy. It is true that the inference is not a logical one, but this point is academic in the disreputable sense of the term, at least as far as economic policy is concerned. If economists can make the case that if action A is not taken, the economy will collapse, it would be taken as terminal foolishness for an economist to refrain from stating that A ought to be done on the grounds that a value judgment is necessarily implied in such a statement.

The more prevalent case, however, is a deficiency rather than an excess of professional modesty. Economists addressing policy issues often are inclined to place themselves in the position of solvers of society's economic problems.

Agricultural economists are no exception, being tempted to see the task of agricultural policy analysis as diagnosing problems, analogous to diagnosing illness in a person or malfunctioning of a machine. Undertaking farm programs is then analogous to curing an illness or fixing a machine.[1]

The idea of policy research as diagnosing a "farm problem" and recommending remedies is dangerous because it can obtain normative results without explicitly making value judgments. Who could object to curing an illness? If social problem-solving is really what agricultural policy is all about, then the normative component of what agricultural economists assert may well be as innocuous as in the introductory paragraph's case. But there is an alternative view of what policy is all about, the view that its central feature is conflict between interest groups—producers or landowners as against consumers or taxpayers. If this view is correct, then recommendations to solve a "farm problem" are far from normatively innocuous. Problems can be solved but conflict can only be resolved, and the resolution typically consists of involuntary transfers of wealth. Without concluding that interest-group conflict is the only impetus of governmental intervention in agriculture, the possibility that it is an important impetus impells us to the study of welfare economics. The purpose is to clarify how far the economic analyst can go in the direction of recommending policies while using only the tools and presuppositions of standard (neoclassical) economics.

We presume in considering policy alternatives that individuals are the best judges of what is good for them, and that they are rational in choosing among alternatives in such a way as to make themselves as well off as possible given the constraints they face. We also assume that more goods, in the present instance goods made from agricultural products, are preferred to less goods by everyone. These presumptions imply that if policy A increases the real income of everyone as compared to policy B, it makes everyone better off. Our first normative judgment is that a policy alternative that makes everyone better off should be chosen. In fact, we can extend this slightly to obtain the "Pareto criterion" that a policy that makes at least one person better off and no one worse off should be chosen. Such a policy is said to be a Pareto improvement. If no such policy exists, the economy is said to be at Pareto optimum.

Restating the introductory paragraph in these terms, if solutions to the farm problem made everyone better off, then the burden of normative policy analysts would be light indeed, and they would receive the type of acclaim that goes to those experts who find cures for dread diseases. But because every policy alternative we have considered makes some people better off and others worse off, we are unable, on an objective basis, to provide policy advice unless we can find a method objectively to measure and weigh against one another the gains and losses that result from policy options. The history of welfare economics is largely the search for such a method. As the codification of the results of this search, theoretical welfare economics has set forth loftier aims, and achieved fewer of them, than any other branch of economics.

At the more modest level of methods for measuring gains and losses, applied welfare economics has been helpful. This chapter reviews the results and considers the issue of how to aggregate and compare these gains and losses to obtain a measure of the overall gains or losses (the "national interest").

QUANTIFYING WELFARE GAINS

In Chaps. 1 through 3, the gains and losses from intervention in commodity markets were measured as areas in price–quantity space, calculated with reference to market supply and demand curves. The use of these surplus areas—economic rents for producers and consumers' surplus for buyers—makes sense intuitively. But questions can be raised about these areas as welfare measures. The most serious of them include:

1. The intuition for areas such as those in Fig. 2.1 dissipates when we consider price changes in more than one commodity at a time, because the demand or supply curve for commodity A may shift when the price of commodity B changes. If a price support in A is what causes the change in the B market, how do we calculate appropriate areas in the A market?

2. A related issue is how we can identify consumers' gains or losses with areas behind farm-level demand functions when, as we already know, some farm-level price changes may be absorbed by marketing inputs and never reach the consumer.

3. Basic intuitions about welfare, at least for economists, are expressed in terms of an individual's utility, or revealed preference for alternative bundles of goods. Market demand and supply functions may not serve as an appropriate basis for such calculations because: (a) they depend not only on preferences but on income and wealth (which policies can change), (b) they depend on our being able to represent gains of all individuals with reference to aggregate behavior, and (c) they may not measure the concepts that they must in order to serve as welfare measures—the supply price may not measure marginal social cost at each output and demand price might not measure the full social benefit, because of externalities.

The points under number 3 have been most fundamental to economists, and have been the concern of much ingenious thought from Marshall and Pigou through Hicks to many recent authors. Many of the problems have been solved, so much so that if we accept the neoclassical assumptions about demand and utility, costs, and competitive markets, we can with sufficient econometric information provide a quantitive assessment of each individual's gains and losses (although aggregating them to obtain a single indicator of social welfare is a different matter).

But before proceeding to discuss in detail how to estimate gains, losses, and welfare, we should give due respect to fundamental questions about whether welfare calculations can be adequately grounded in measures of individual preferences. One point often asserted is that preferences themselves are caused by social factors. If these factors are unaffected by the policy alternatives being considered, however, they will not influence the comparison of policies and can be ignored. Although some policies can perhaps influence preferences (e.g., policies concerning advertising or education), this seems unlikely to be an issue with commodity price supports and the like. Moreover, even in agricultural cases in which endogenous preferences can be made plausible, such as subsidized turkey in school lunches changing the children's desire for turkey in later years, it seems possible to control for the effect on market demand rather than rejecting the whole approach to welfare measurement that uses market demand.

In agricultural policy, the broader issues also concern the supply side, the role of farming as a vocation or rural living as a way of life. In their pastoral letter on the economy, the U.S. Catholic bishops pose three questions about the economy:

"What does the economy do for people?"
"What does it do to people?"
"And how do people participate in it?"[2]

Neoclassical welfare economics ignores the last two questions. In their discussion of the situation of migrant workers and family farms, the bishops give prominence to these questions. They are good questions.

Another pitfall in individual preferences as a basis for welfare measurement is that my utility may be a function of your situation (even though nothing you do affects me directly). For example, some may believe that absentee corporate ownership of farms is an inherently bad thing. The practical import of this kind of interdependence is that it can justify intervention in the affairs of individuals that would be income-reducing for everyone. Following the standard economic approach, we will ignore the utility gains or losses of the onlookers. It can be argued that this is a reasonable approach not only for practical reasons but also because of another pitfall in the normative use of individual preferences, the idea that directly involved individuals have rights that override others' preferences.

The notion of individual rights raises broad questions about justifying farm policies; for example, some citrus growers have challenged quantitative marketing restrictions in court on the ground that each grower has the right to choose the quantity of oranges that growers sells. The generalization of this argument would rule out any market intervention that mandated any particular behavior by any individual (absent externalities). Nonetheless, we will count only the economic gains and losses from policies and not the psychological gains or losses of individuals who desire or oppose intervention apart from an economic stake in the outcome. Having with due respect attended to both the libertarians who rule out most intervention on grounds of individual rights and the modern liberals who call for general intervention on grounds of social responsibility, let us pass on.

Returning to the questions raised under item 3, think of welfare as each individual's utility, expressed as a function of goods and services used,

$$U_j = U_j (X_{ij}) \qquad i = 1, n \qquad (7.1)$$

where j is an index number for each individual and X_{ij} is the quantity consumed of each of the n products in the economy. The consumer's problem is to maximize Eq. (7.1) subject to the budget constraint, $I_j = \sum_i P_i X_{ij}$, where I_j is given in money terms for each individual. The reason for consumer welfare losses when a price is raised by a support program is that less can be bought with the given income. The change in welfare is then measured as the resulting change in U_j. The change in U_j when consumption of X_i changes is the marginal utility of good i. Since this determines willingness to pay for X_i, which is measured by the demand curve, the demand curve is a natural indicator of the utility of each additional unit of X_i. But if P_1 goes up, this in general changes not only X_1 but also $X_2, \ldots, X_n$. So how can we look at just the demand for X_1 in calculating welfare?

The simplest way of proceeding is to use the expenditure function, derived by solving the problem dual to Eq. (7.1), i.e., minimizing expenditures required to attain a given level of utility. The resulting expenditure function is helpfully thought of as a cost-of-utility function. The minimization problem is solved by choosing, for given prices and utility level, the same X's as in the maximization problem. But now X's are conditional on the given level of U_j. Thus, we have

$$C_j (P_i, U_j) = \sum_i P_i X_{ij}(P_i, \ldots, P_n; U_j) \qquad (7.2)$$

where X_{ij} is the utility-constant (Hicksian) demand function for the jth person. Now, when we introduce a change in P_i, we will get the change in the cost of attaining the initial level U_j^0, and the partial derivitive of X_i with respect to P_i gives the slope of the utility constant (Hicksian) demand function for X_i (see, for example, Varian, 1978, Chap. 3), i.e.,

$$\frac{\partial C_j (P_i, U_j^0)}{\partial P_i} = D_h(P_i, U_j^0)$$

We typically do not know the cost function, any more than we know the utility function itself, but now we know that the change in cost caused by a change in P_i can be measured by an appropriately specified demand function. Moreover, this change in cost is invariant to a monotonic transformation of the utility function, which is helpful given our need to aggregate over individuals despite our ignorance of the utility function. In short, the Hicksian demand function gives us the willingness-to-pay measure that we want for the kind of gain and loss calculations that we have been doing.[3]

The ordinary (Marshallian) demand functions that market data generate are not utility-constant, but the parameter that is most crucial, the Hicksian elasticity of demand, can be estimated from the Slutsky equation. In elasticity form it is

$$\eta_i^h = \eta_i^m + K_i \, \eta_{il} \tag{7.3}$$

where the h superscript denotes the Hicksian elasticity for the ith good, m denotes the Marshallian elasticity, K_i is the budget share, and η_{il} is income elasticity. In industrial countries, K_i is typically 0.3 or lower, even for food as an aggregate, and is much less for individual items. η_{il} is typically less than 1 (Engel's law) and often near zero. However, the Marshallian elasticity is often small, too. In developing countries, K_i and η_{il} can both be relatively large, so that η^h can be substantially smaller (in absolute value) than η^m. For example, if η^m is estimated at -0.6, while $K_i = 0.5$ and $\eta_{il} = 0.8$, we find $\eta^h = -0.2$. This will typically not make much difference in consumer loss calculations ($A + B$ in Fig. 2.1) but it can make a big difference in the size of deadweight loss triangles (see Dodgson, 1985, for some relevant case studies). In any case, as long as we have estimates of the right-hand-side variables of Eq. (7.3), we can obtain the Hicksian elasticity and calculate appropriate consumer losses. Things get more complicated when two or more prices change simultaneously, or intervention exists in other markets, but the conceptual basis for welfare change calculations remains as outlined here.

The preceding technical concerns about surpluses as measures of welfare, though important, are not the source of the main criticisms that agricultural economists have made of using sums of surpluses as indicators of social cost of farm programs. More pressing concerns are those expressed in the following survey of agricultural policy issues published by the American Agricultural Economics Association (and thus presumably a mainstream view) (Brandow, 1977, p. 271):

> Economic evaluation of social costs associated with partricular policies has frequently employed partial equilibrium analysis and the concepts of consumers' and producers' surplus. Reservations on theoretical grounds often are based on a reluctance to aggregate personal utilities and on second-best considerations.
>
> This reviewer is unwilling to aggregate personal utilities indiscriminately. He is particularly unwilling to accept the assumption that there exist empirical counterparts of either the perfect competition situation or the equivalent situation under

the constraints of a program. As the general model of the agricultural sector discussed earlier indicates, agriculture has been and is in chronic disequilibrium. The neat alignment of resources, output, and prices specified by the perfect competition model is far from duplicated in free markets, and the equally neat alignment assumed under the constraints of a program is not experienced when programs are in effect. In particular, areas under empirically determined supply curves are unlikely to represent opportunity costs. The basic theory is invaluable in providing a conceptual orientation for the analysis of programs, but the assumptions implicit in the literal use of simple forms of it for policy conclusions are breathtakingly heroic.

The absence of perfect competition in the absence of programs is an instance of market failure. Market failures, and government intervention in nonagricultural markets, do change the picture considerably, and Chap. 9 is devoted to "second best" policy analysis in their presence. The point made by Brandow that is taken up in this chapter is the question of aggregating over individuals' utilities. What warrant do economists have to do this "indiscriminately"? Of course, discrimination to favor some people over others requires justification, too, maybe even stronger justification.

The intuitively appealing approach taken in welfare economics is to search for compensation principles. Let policy A be introduced, replacing policy B. Some people will be made better off, some worse off. If the people who are made better off can compensate those who are made worse off and still be better off, then both groups are at least as well off after as before, the Pareto criterion is satisfied, and policy A should be chosen.[4] A characteristic of all of the calculations made in Chaps. 1 to 3 was that elimination of the interventions would cause gains for consumers or taxpayers that were larger than the losses of producers. Recalculating with the appropriate Hicksian demand functions would change the magnitude of the net gains (generally decreasing the net gains from removing price distortions and increasing the net gains from removing quantity restrictions). But there would still be net gains, since there are still deadweight-loss triangles, and usually other net losses as well due to administrative costs and idled land, for example. This is not to say that a dollar is equally valuable to everyone—that the marginal utility of income is constant over individuals—but that everyone can in principle be restored at least to that person's no-intervention utility level, with money left over. In this sense, eliminating interventions is a Pareto-improving move.

However, it is usually impossible to make the compensation without introducing further distortions in the market. The point of the compensation idea is that if we want to transfer $10 billion to farmers it would be cheaper (for non-farmers) simply to write checks than to transfer the $10 billion by means of price supports. The idea of net social cost or deadweight loss calculations is to indicate how much cheaper. But the very acts of deciding who qualifies as a farmer, which farmers get how much, and how adjustments are to be made in future years inevitably bring administrative costs and program incentives back in.

Perhaps it is enough that compensation is in principle possible to conclude so that eliminating the dairy program would be Pareto-improving? No, because if compensation were not paid in fact, then the program change would not be Pareto-improving (dairy farmers would be worse off). So the practicalities of compensating transfers are relevant, just as relevant as the triangular dead-weight areas of the program.

If compensation is feasible and is paid, then we pay off the dairy farmers and eliminate the program. Conversely, if we start with no program, we just pay the farmers a lump sum. But why should this be done? Why should even a costless (no deadweight loss) transfer be made? There must be some higher weighting of the recipients' well-being than of the taxpayers' well-being. The normative problem then is to justify this weighting.

WELFARE ECONOMICS AND REDISTRIBUTION

To make redistributional choices we need a collective choice criterion or social welfare function (SWF) that will rank distributional alternatives in which some people are better off and some are worse off. The concept of a SWF has been thoroughly developed expositionally in the context of a two-sector general equilibrium model of the economy. The model is explained in depth in many texts and expository articles. For present purposes, consider the two sectors as agriculture and nonagriculture. The constraints caused by the economy's resource endowment and technology available generate a production possibilities curve (PPC) which shows the maximum combination of agricultural products A and nonagricultural products N obtainable from the economy's resources. Let us add an additional assumption, implicit in dividing the economy's interests into producers of A and producers of N. Within these two groups it is assumed that everyone's tastes or utility functions are identical so that we can specify aggregate utility functions for each group. Given the utility functions for the two groups, $U_A (A, N)$ and $U_N (A, N)$, we can map indifference curves for the two groups in a box diagram whose sides are quantities of commodities, as in Fig. 7.1. For any arbitrary combination of commodities, such as A_0 and N_0, we can construct indifference maps starting from O_N and O_A. Points of tangency between indifference curves define a contract curve running from O_A to O_N, at which the relative prices P_A/P_N are the same for both groups.

If one or more points on the contract curve has the same P_A/P_N as the slope of the PPC, then the production of A_o, N_0 is a possible competitive general equilibrium for the economy. Assuming that the economy has at least one competitive equilibrium, let it be the position shown in Fig. 7.1. Then the A group will consume A_A and N_N, generating utility U_A^0, and the N group will consume A_N

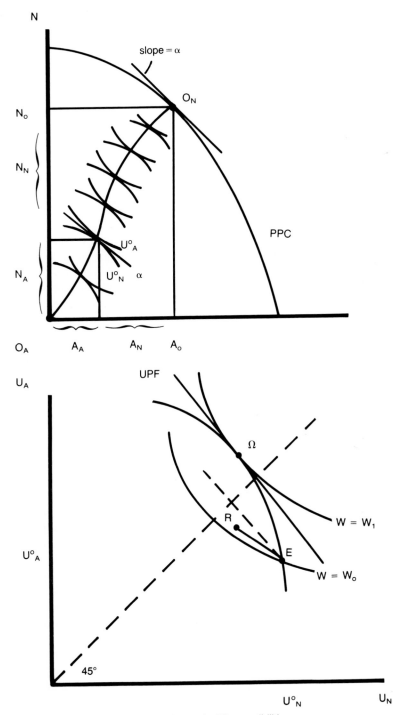

Figure 7.1 Production possibilities and utility possibilities.

and N_N with utility U_N^0. Assuming we have a numerical indicator of utility (a big assumption), we can plot the equilibrium point as E in utility space, as in the lower panel of Fig. 7.1.

Suppose now that we can make lump-sum transfers of income from the N group to the A group. This will move us along the contract curve toward O_N. In general, this will change the relative commodity demands and, hence, generate a new production point. Before analyzing this change, consider the special case in which both the A and N groups have the same utility function, and it is homothetic: income elasticities of both goods are 1. This means that the contract curve will be a diagonal line from O_A to O_N and P_A/P_N will be unchanged, as will equilibrium outputs. Although the economy still produces A_0, N_0, we move northwest from E, with U_A increasing and U_N decreasing. If the common utility function has constant marginal utility of income, we move along a line with slope of -1 in utility space (the dashed line in Fig. 7.1).

It is typically presumed that the marginal utility of income declines with increasing income. In this case, if A is the relatively low-income group, U_A will rise more than U_N falls, so we move along the utility possibility frontier (UPF) sketched in Fig. 7.1. On the other hand, if the marginal utility of income is greater for the N group than for the A group, the UPF extended northwest from point E would lie inside the dotted line. In either case the UPF will be concave to the origin so long as the marginal utility of income is nonincreasing for both groups.

So much for the special case of identical utility functions for A and N. More generally, imagine a small income redistribution from N to A which does change commodity demands. Since the consumption of A is likely to follow Engel's law, an increase in the A group's income will result in an increase in their demand for N relative to A. But the corresponding decrease in the N group's income will reduce the demand for N relative to A. Which effect dominates is an empirical question. On a priori grounds we cannot forecast whether the redistribution will move us northwest or southeast along the PPC. It is not implausible that the range of combinations of A and N generated would be quite small, with some pairs appearing at more than one income distribution endowment as we move from O_A along the contract curve (whose O_N end is constantly moving as income is redistributed). Thus, only a limited range of the PPC is attainable by means of income redistribution. Nonetheless, redistribution toward the A group will move the economy steadily northwest from E along the utility possibility frontier. Presumably, though, there is some lower limit of U_A and U_N, perhaps corresponding to subsistence income, below which the economy cannot be pushed. Thus we do not extend the UPF all the way to either axis.

The UPF defines Pareto-optimal points. At all points on the UPF the marginal rates of substitution in consumption are the same for all consumers and equal to the marginal rate of transformation (ratio of marginal costs) in production. And because we are on the PPC, we know that resource allocation is efficient. At any point inside the UPF a Pareto improvement is possible, but on the UPF we can make one group better off only at the expense of the other.

A theoretical device for choosing among Pareto optima is the social welfare function,

$$W = \phi\ (U_A,\ U_N) \tag{7.4}$$

The SWF permits us to rank alternative allocations of U_A and U_N. It can be represented by social indifference curves (SIC) analogous to a consumer's indifference curves. But for the SWF there are no theoretical constraints on the function. We usually assume that $\partial\phi/\partial U_A$ and $\partial\phi/U_B$ are non-negative. Impartiality might be taken as an additive SWF where $W = U_A + U_N$. This would imply linear SICs having a slope of -1. Then the economy's optimum would be at the point on the UPF where its slope is -1, assuming there exists such a point. Alternatively, there might be a social preference for equality of utilities but with the lower-utility group being favored when utilities are unequal. This implies SIC curves convex to the origin such as $W = W_1$ in Fig. 7.1, which implies the economy's optimum at Ω. In Fig. 7.1, either the impartial or egalitarian SWF would recommend redistribution of income from the N group to the A group, moving away from the competitive equilibrium at E.

Unfortunately, we have no way to prescribe the proper SWF. Modesty suggests accepting the actual choices of governments as revealing the SWF. Even if we don't think governments work well—which in this context means being an appropriate an arbiter of distributive justice—governmental decisions will, in fact, determine the redistributions that are made. So the revealed SWF is at least a political preference function.

Once a SWF is defined, Pareto optimality loses what little value it had as a social decision generator. For now, it is quite possible for a non-Pareto optimal point (inside the UPF) to be socially preferred to the full competitive equilibrium point E. This can be true even if the sum of utilities is less than at E. For example, in Fig. 7.1, point R is on a higher social indifference curve (SIC) than E.

The preceding point is especially important because lump-sum transfers that have no resource allocation effects are impossible as an ongoing means of public finance. When we attempt to move away from E, we will violate one or more of the marginal conditions (often with respect to labor–leisure choice) and hence move inside the UPF.

REDISTRIBUTION IN A COMMODITY MARKET

The remainder of this chapter considers the application of welfare economics concepts to intervention in the market for a single product. The analysis is partial in the sense that incomes and policies elsewhere are held constant as we engage in fine-tuning policy in this one market. When the principles for this activity are established, we then move back to multiple-product and general equilibrium considerations in Chaps. 8 and 9. In this chapter, the emphasis is on specifying the welfare economics concepts narrowly enough that they can be applied using econometric information about a commodity market. The calculating equations for this purpose are conceptually straightforward but algebraically sometimes clumsy and require consideration of special cases. But because some of the results needed are not available in published literature they are derived in detail here.

Specific topics are taken up in the following order:

1. Intervention by means of production controls is analyzed, because it is the simplest policy that brings out the key issues, in five steps:
    a. After the surplus concepts are defined, calculating formulas are derived for marginal changes in surpluses in the case of linear supply and demand, and then a more general functional form.
    b. Efficiency in redistribution and deadweight losses are measured.
    c. Optimal redistribution for a given a SWF is derived.
    d. Total (finite) redistribution calculating formulas (more complicated than marginal calculations, and requiring assumptions about functional form of supply and demand) are developed for the constant-elasticity case.
    e. Marginal and total redistributional concepts are reformulated entirely in terms of changes from an initial no-intervention state.
2. Having analyzed a particular type of intervention (production controls), alternative policies are more briefly considered: target price and deficiency payments, and redistribution from producers to consumers.
3. Application and approximation of the formulas derived is discussed.

Redistribution Using Production Controls

Concepts analogous to the UPF and SWF can be specified for the single-product context, but the arguments in both functions are no longer the utility levels of two groups that exhaust the economy. Instead, policy redistributes gains and losses between producers and consumers of the product. Gains and losses are generated by intervention in the commodity market rather than lump-sum transfers. Let the policy variable be a controlled level of production $\hat{Q}$. Changing $\hat{Q}$ over its range of possible values generates a sequence of market equilibria just as lump-sum redistribution did above. The gains of producers and consumers are measured as changes in their respective surpluses. The combinations of PS and CS attainable by changing $\hat{Q}$ define the surplus transformation curve, which is analogous in the single product framework to a utility possibilities curve.

To quantify the losses and gains from production controls, we proceed as follows. The inverse (price-dependent) Hicksian demand and supply curves are

$$P_d = D\,(Q) \tag{7.1}$$
$$P_s = S\,(Q) \tag{7.2}$$

It is assumed that D and S have the usual slopes, i.e., $D'(Q) < 0$ and $S'(Q) > 0$, and that D and S both cross the P axis at positive P. The surpluses at regulated $\hat{Q} < Q_0$ are

$$CS = \int_0^{\hat{Q}} D\,(Q)\,dQ - D\,(\hat{Q})\,\hat{Q} \tag{7.3}$$

$$PS = D\,(\hat{Q})\,\hat{Q} - \int_0^{\hat{Q}} S\,(Q)\,dQ \tag{7.4}$$

where CS is consumers' surplus. (Or more precisely, since the demand function is utility constant, CS can be identified with "compensating" surplus as defined by Hause, 1975.) PS is the sum of all economic rents.

Linear Case. In order to see more concretely how surplus redistribution works, consider the special case of linear demand and supply functions. Then Eqs. (7.1) and (7.2) become

$$P_d = a_0 + a_1\,Q \qquad a_1 < 0 \tag{7.5}$$
$$P_s = b_0 + b_1\,Q \qquad b_1 > 0,\ a_0 > b_0 > 0 \tag{7.6}$$

The surpluses resulting from production controls are

$$CS = \int_0^{\hat{Q}}(a_0 + a_1\,\hat{Q})\,dQ - (a_0 + a_1 + a_1\,\hat{Q})\,\hat{Q} \tag{7.7}$$

$$= a_0\,\hat{Q} + \frac{1}{2}a_1\,\hat{Q}^2 - a_0\hat{Q} - a_1\hat{Q}^2$$

$$= -\frac{1}{2}a_1\,\hat{Q}^2$$

$$PS = (a_0 + a_1\,\hat{Q})\,\hat{Q} - \int_0^{\hat{Q}}(b_0 + b_1\,Q)\,dQ \tag{7.8}$$

$$= a_0\hat{Q} + a_0\,\hat{Q}^2 - b_0\,\hat{Q} - \frac{1}{2}b_1\,\hat{Q}^2$$

$$= (a_0 - b_0)\,\hat{Q} + (a_1 - \frac{1}{2}b_1)\,\hat{Q}^2$$

The effects of changing $\hat{Q}$ can be analyzed by differentiating Eqs. (7.7) and (7.8):

$$\frac{dCS}{d\hat{Q}} = -a_1 \hat{Q} \tag{7.9}$$

$$\frac{dPS}{d\hat{Q}} = (a_0 - b_0) + (2a_1 - b_1) \hat{Q} \tag{7.10}$$

When $\hat{Q}$ is reduced (production controls tightened), CS falls since $-a_1$ is positive. However, the effect on PS can be either positive or negative since $(a_0 - b_0)$ is positive but $(2a_1 - b_1)$ is negative.

Suppose we want to choose $\hat{Q}$ to maximize the economic rents of producers. This is accomplished by setting $dPS/d\hat{Q} = 0$, which requires

$$a_0 - b_0 + (2 a_1 - b_1) \hat{Q} = 0 \tag{7.11}$$

$$\hat{Q} = \frac{b_0 - a_0}{2 a_1 - b_1}$$

This expression can be simplified by using the fact that competitive equilibrium output, Q_0, obtained by equating (7.5) and (7.6), is

$$Q_0 = \frac{b_0 - a_0}{a_1 - b_1} \tag{7.12}$$

This result can be used to simplify the expression for rent-maximizing output. Since $b_0 - a_0 = Q_0 (a_1 - b_1)$, we have

$$\frac{\hat{Q}}{Q_0} = \frac{a_1 - b_1}{2 a_1 - b_1} \tag{7.13}$$

Thus, the producer-otpimal production control relative to no-program output depends only on the supply and demand slopes. For example, suppose $a_1 = -1$ and $b_1 = 1$. Then $\hat{Q}/Q_0 = 2/3$; producers' rents are maximized by a production control that reduces output by one-third from competitive equilibrium output.

The welfare economics of production controls requires consideration of the consumers' losses that must be given up to achieve the producers' gains. In Fig. 7.1, the trade-offs are summarized in the utility possibilities frontier. Here the trade-offs are PS gains and CS losses caused by policy determination of $\hat{Q}$. The surplus transformation curve (STC) is obtained by solving Eq. (7.7) for $\hat{Q}$ and substituting in Eq. (7.8) to yield

$$PS = \frac{a_0 - b_0}{\sqrt{-\frac{1}{2} a_1}} \sqrt{CS} + \frac{2 a_1 - b_1}{- a_1} CS \tag{7.14}$$

Examples of Eq. (7.14) are shown in Fig. 7.2 as the solid curves to the left of point E. This point is attained when $Q = Q_0$, so that it is analogous to point E in the two-sector model of Fig. 7.1, and the STC is analogous to the UPF. The diagram helps us to see what is gong on as $\hat{Q}$ is reduced. Maximizing PS places us at point M. Levels of $\hat{Q}$ between Q_0 and Q_M trace out the economically rational surplus possibilities for a production control. Further reductions in $\hat{Q}$, say a 40-percent output cutback when the rent-maximizing cutback was one-third, causes both PS and CS to fall. This is the economic meaning of the indeterminacy of the sign of $dPS/d\hat{Q}$.

General Case (Unrestricted Functional Form of S and D).   Relaxing the assumption of linear supply and demand curves will aid in developing our economic intuition about the optimal $\hat{Q}$. To find the effect on PS of change in $\hat{Q}$, differentiate Eq. (7.4),

$$\frac{dPS}{d\hat{Q}} = D'(\hat{Q})\hat{Q} + D(\hat{Q}) - S(\hat{Q}) \qquad (7.14a)$$

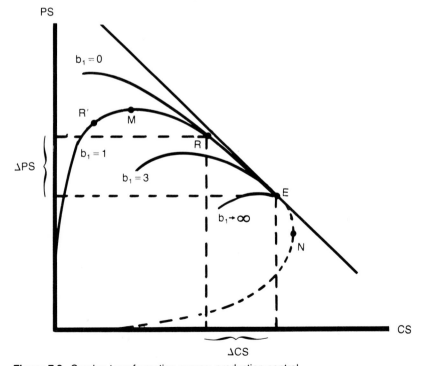

Figure 7.2 Surplus transformation curves: production control.

To obtain a unit-free measure, normalize PS by dividing by $\hat{P}\hat{Q}$, where $\hat{P}$ is $D(\hat{Q})$. The effect of a percentage change in $\hat{Q}$, i.e., $d\hat{Q}/\hat{Q}$, is obtained by dividing the right-hand side of Eq. (7.14a) by $D(\hat{Q})$:

$$\frac{dPS/PQ}{d\hat{Q}/\hat{Q}} = \frac{D'(\hat{Q})\hat{Q}}{D(\hat{Q})} + 1 - \frac{S(\hat{Q})}{D(\hat{Q})}$$

Recalling that $D(Q)$ is price on the demand function and $S(Q)$ is price on the supply function at Q, using the definition of inverse elasticity of demand, we have

$$\frac{dPS/\hat{P}\hat{Q}}{d\hat{Q}/\hat{Q}} = \frac{1}{\eta} + \frac{P_d - P_s}{P_d} \qquad (7.15)$$

Note that $1 - P_s/P_d = (P_d - P_s)/P_d$. The economic meaning of Eq. (7.15) is shown in Fig. 7.3. A reduction in $\hat{Q}$ has two effects, opposite in sign. The first term of Eq. (7.15) indicates the gain on production of $\hat{Q}$ when price rises ($\eta < 0$ and $d\hat{Q} < 0$). The second term is the loss on being able to produce less. Figure 7.3 is representing infinitesimal changes, so the small triangular areas are negligible. The cumulation of such changes from an initial competitive equilibrium generates total PS gains such as those shown in Fig. 2.1.

The change in CS when Q changes is

$$\frac{dCS}{dQ} = D(Q) - D'(Q)Q - D(Q) = -D'(Q)Q \qquad (7.16)$$

which placed in relative terms as in Eq. (7.15) yields

$$\frac{dCS/PQ}{dQ/Q} = -\frac{1}{\eta} \qquad (7.17)$$

It is not possible to specify the functional form of the STC without making assumptions about the functional form of the demand and supply curves. We can, however, learn something about the STC in general by considering its slope. The slope is found by dividing Eq. (7.14a) by Eq. (7.16):

$$\frac{dPS}{dCS} = \frac{dPS/dQ}{dCS/dQ} = \frac{D'(Q)\hat{Q} + D(\hat{Q}) - S(\hat{Q})}{-D'(Q)\hat{Q}} \qquad (7.18)$$

Alternatively, we can express the slope in relative terms, that is, measuring surpluses as percentages of revenues, by dividing Eq. (7.15) by Eq. (7.17):

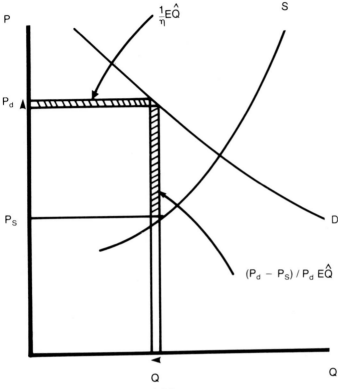

Figure 7.3 Changes in PS and CS.

$$\frac{dPS}{dCS} = \frac{1/\eta + (P_d - P_s)/P_d}{-1/\eta} \qquad (7.19)$$

$$= -\eta\tau - 1$$

where $\tau = (P_d - P_s)/P_d$, the wedge between demand and supply price as a fraction of the demand price—an implicit tax rate or markup caused by the production cutback.

In the special case of linear demand and supply functions, the slope looks different. Dividing Eq. (7.10) by Eq. (7.9):

$$\frac{dPS}{dCS} = \frac{a_0 - b_0 + (2a_1 - b_1)Q}{-a_1\hat{Q}} \qquad (7.20)$$

$$= \frac{a_0 + 2a_1Q - b_0 + b_1Q}{-a_1\hat{Q}}$$

$$= \frac{a_1\hat{Q} + a_0 + a_1\hat{Q} - b_0 + b_1\hat{Q}}{-a_1\hat{Q}}$$

Dividing the numerator and denominator by $\hat{P}$, we obtain

$$\frac{dPS}{dCS} = \frac{a_1 (\hat{Q}/\hat{P}) + (P_d - P_s)/\hat{P}}{- a_1 (\hat{Q}/\hat{P})} \qquad = -1 - \eta\tau \qquad (7.21)$$

since $a_1 = dP_d/dQ$, and $\hat{P}$ is the price on the demand curve. Thus, Eq. (7.20) is identical to Eq. (7.19). This identity is worth establishing because using Eq. (7.12) to eliminate $a_0 - b_0$ in Eq. (7.20), we can also rewrite Eq. (7.20) as

$$\frac{dPS}{dCS} = \frac{Q_0 (a_1 - b_1)}{\hat{Q}a_1} - \frac{a_1 - b_1}{a_1} - \frac{a_1}{a_1} \qquad (7.22)$$

$$= \frac{a_1 - b_1}{a_1} \left(\frac{Q_0}{\hat{Q}} - 1\right) - 1$$

The economic difference between Eqs. (7.19) and (7.22) is that the former specifies the production control policy in terms of τ, the price wedge caused by it, while Eq. (7.22) specifies the policy, more directly, in terms of the percentage cutback in output, $Q_0/\hat{Q} - 1$. But in Eq. (7.22) we need both the supply and demand slopes to determine the surplus tradeoffs, while in Eqs. (7.21) or (7.19) we need only the demand slope. How can we get away with throwing away the supply-side information in Eqs. (7.19) and (7.21)? We cannot. We need to know the supply as well as demand slope in order to calculate the τ resulting from any proposed $\hat{Q}$. So Eq. (7.19) is not as simple to apply as it at first appears.

Consider the problem of maximizing PS, done in Eq. (7.13) for the linear case, with the general functional form. This is accomplished by setting Eq. (7.15) equal to zero, i.e.,

$$\tau = -\frac{1}{\eta} \qquad (7.23)$$

This rule, equating the price wedge to the absolute value of the inverse demand elasticity, is the condition for profit maximization by a monopolist, $-1/\eta$ being Lerner's measure of the degree of monopoly. However, in order to know the value of τ, we need to know more about supply and demand, namely how much of a production cutback is required to achieve the desired price wedge. The information is not available from the elasticity at $\hat{Q}$. We can go further only if we know the functional form of the supply and demand curves between $\hat{Q}$ and Q_0. In the linear case, we have the rule given by Eq. (7.13). If we want to have a criterion expressed in terms of elasticities rather than slopes, we must assume a constant-elasticity functional form. This case is taken up below. Before going further, however, we still must complete the job of relating the surplus transformation curve to the more usual welfare economics concepts.

Efficiency in Redistribution and Deadweight Losses. Perfectly efficient redistribution through production controls would increase PS by a dollar for every dollar that CS fell. This condition is expressed graphically by means by the line segment with slope of -1 passing through point E in Fig. 7.2. The extent to which the STC falls inside the efficient redistribution line indicates how far the production control falls short of perfect efficiency. For a marginal change in $\hat{Q}$, we can measure the shortfall as the sum of $dPS/d\hat{Q}$ and $dCS/d\hat{Q}$. Using the results for the general functional form, summing Eqs. (7.14a) and (7.16),

$$\frac{d(PS + CS)}{d\hat{Q}} = P_d - P_s = DM \qquad (7.24)$$

where DM stands for marginal deadweight loss. Graphically, it is the vertical slice in Fig. 7.3.

Cumulating the vertical slices generates area $B + C$ in Fig. 2.1. This roughly triangular area is thus a geometric depiction of the deadweight loss caused by production control at $\hat{Q}$ as compared to Q_0. The cumulated deadweight loss is depicted in Fig. 7.2 as the (horizontal or vertical; both simply measure dollars) distance between any point on the STC and the efficient redistribution line. The quantitative results obtained so far have pertained to the slope of the STC and not to this distance. The slope is related to the distance, since the closer to zero (further from -1) the slope becomes, the greater will be the accumulated distance between the STC and the efficient redistribution line. But we have an equation for the STC itself only in the linear case, in Eq. (7.14). In order to identify the STC and, hence, the total redistribution and deadweight loss, we have to make some assumptions about the functional forms of demand and supply. It is easiest to continue with the linear case.

Following the procedure used to define marginal deadweight loss in Eq. (7.24), calculate the sum of CS and PS resulting from any given $\hat{Q}$. Using Eqs. (7.7) and (7.8), and (7.12) to eliminate $a_0 - b_0$, this is

$$CS + PS = \frac{1}{2} a_1 \hat{Q}^2 + (a_0 - b_0)\hat{Q} + (a_1 - \frac{1}{2} b_1)\hat{Q}^2 \qquad (7.25)$$

$$= (b_1 - a_1) Q_0 \hat{Q} - \frac{1}{2} (b_1 - a_1)\hat{Q}^2$$

The total deadweight loss, DW, is the difference between Eq. (7.25) and the sum of surpluses at competitive equilibrium, which is $-\frac{1}{2}(b_1 - a_1)Q_0^2$. Subtracting this last expression from Eq. (7.25) yields

$$DW = (b_1 - a_1)(Q_0\hat{Q} - \frac{1}{2}\hat{Q}^2 - \frac{1}{2}Q_0^2) \qquad (7.26)$$

$$= -\frac{1}{2}(b_1 - a_1)(\hat{Q} - Q_0)^2$$

If $\hat{Q} = Q_0$, then $DW = 0$. Differentiating Eq. (7.26) with respect to $\hat{Q}$ gives the marginal deadweight loss,

$$DM = (b_1 - a_1)(\hat{Q} - Q_0) \qquad (7.27)$$

This expression is equal to Eq. (7.24), which can be confirmed by substituting Eqs. (7.5) and (7.6) into (7.24).

For an example of the use of these results, suppose that we have the demand and supply functions:

$$P_d = 120 - 2Q$$
$$P_s = 30 + Q$$

where Q is millions of tons of a crop and P is in dollars per ton. The competitive equilibrium is $Q_0 = 30$ and $P_0 = \$60$. Suppose a production control makes $\hat{Q} = 20$. Then from Eq. (7.26) we have the deadweight loss,

$$DW = -\frac{1}{2}(1 + 2)(100) = -\$150 \text{ million}$$

(The calculated negative value means the sum of surpluses falls.) The marginal deadweight loss, from Eq. (7.27), is $30. From the demand and supply prices at $\hat{Q}$, which are $P_d = 80$ and $P_s = 50$, we confirm that $MD = P_d - P_s$, as Eq. (7.24) indicates. The surplus transformation curve, from Eq. (7.14) is

$$PS = 90\sqrt{CS} - 2.5\,CS \qquad (7.27a)$$

This is the STC plotted in Fig. 7.2 for $b_1 = 1$. The surplus redistributions and deadweight losses can be read off from this curve. The particular point on it corresponding to $\hat{Q} = 20$, can be calculated using Eq. (7.7) to find CS:

$$CS = 0.5\,(2)\,(20)^2 = \$400 \text{ million}$$

Substituting in the STC, Eq. (7.27a),

$$PS = 90\sqrt{400} - 2.5\,(400) = \$800 \text{ million}.$$

At the competitive equilibrium, we have $CS_0 = \$900$ million and $PS_0 = \$450$ million. Thus, the production control causes gains of \$350 million for producers and losses of \$500 million to consumers. The difference is the \$150 million in deadweight losses.

For a given finite change in $\hat{Q}$, we often are interested to analyze this total redistribution, $\Delta PS/\Delta CS$. It is this trade-off, not the marginal redistribution, that is most directly comparable to the areas and calculations of Chaps. 1 to 3. Since $DW = \Delta PS + \Delta CS$, we can estimate ΔPS or ΔCS in addition to DW. Rosine and Helmberger (1974) estimated that in 1970, \$4829 million was distributed away from consumers and taxpayers in order to give farmers \$2140 million. This implies that $\Delta PS/\Delta CS = 0.44$, but it does not provide an estimate of the marginal rate of surplus transfer (dPS/dCS) at the restricted equilibrium point.

Returning to the linear example, using Eqs. (7.7) and (7.8), algebraic expressions for ΔPS and ΔCS can be derived which yield the following calculating equation for total redistribution:

$$\frac{\Delta PS}{\Delta CS} = \frac{(b_1/a_1)\left(1 - \hat{Q}/Q_0\right) - 2}{1 + \hat{Q}/Q_0} \tag{7.28}$$

Also, using Eq. (7.13), we can calculate the level of $\hat{Q}$ that maximizes PS. The maximizing $\hat{Q}/Q_0$ is 0.6, implying $\hat{Q} = 18$. This places the market at point M in Fig. 7.2. The deadweight loss is now \$216 million, substantially larger than when $\hat{Q} = 20$—the output reduction increased from 10 to 12 million tons, by 20 percent, while the deadweight loss increased from 150 to 216, or 44 percent. The increased rate of deadweight loss is implied by the concavity of the STC. The slope of the STC is given by Eq. (7.22), which at $\hat{Q} = 20$ is

$$\frac{dPS}{dCS} = \frac{-3}{-2}\left(\frac{30}{20} - 1\right) - 1 = -0.25$$

This means that, at the margin, a dollar given up by consumers yields only 25 cents to producers. This implies a different measure of marginal deadweight loss than in Eq. (7.27); the economy's loss per additional dollar taken from consumers rather than per unit output reduction. In general, we have

$$\frac{dDW}{dCS} = \frac{dPS}{dCS} + \frac{dCS}{dCS} = \frac{dPS}{dCS} + 1$$

that is, we simply add 1 to Eq. (7.22) to obtain the marginal deadweight loss. In our example with $\hat{Q} = 20$, this is 0.75; for each dollar transferred, 75 cents is wasted.

This measure of marginal deadweight loss equals 1 at point M in Fig. 7.2; correspondingly, Eq. (7.22) is zero when $\hat{Q} = 18$.

The efficiency of redistribution depends not only on the size of the production cutback but also on the demand and supply slopes, a_1 and b_1. Equation (7.22) is closer to -1, i.e., more efficient redistribution is possible, the smaller is b_1 and the larger is a_1. A small b_1 corresponds roughly to an elastic supply curve, and a large a_1 to inelastic demand. Thus, deadweight losses per dollar redistributed to producers using production controls are smaller, the less elastic is demand and the more elastic is supply.

Figure 7.2 shows the effect of a change in supply elasticity for the linear case from perfectly elastic ($b_1 = 0$) to perfectly inelastic ($b_1 \rightarrow \infty$). Note that when $b_1 \rightarrow \infty$ (perfectly inelastic supply) in Fig. 7.2, it is impossible to redistribute much surplus to producers. This occurs because PS is equal to total revenue and the elasticity of demand is only a little less than 1. For elastic demand curves at E, producers' surplus is reduced by output control when supply is perfectly inelastic. Fixed supply can generate corner solutions at E. The slope of the transformation curve at E is not -1 when $b_1 \rightarrow \infty$. Generally, there will be corners in the surplus transformation curve if output restriction is capable of driving supply price to zero.

Why not Lump Sum Transfers?   The existence of deadweight losses from commodity market intervention implies that the losers should be able to pay the gainers a bribe that exceeds their surplus gains, while the losers are better off paying the bribe than enduring the intervention. The maximum size of the net gain is the deadweight-loss triangle. This reasoning, based on the compensation principles mentioned earlier, suggests lump-sum transfers as a policy reform that provides a Pareto improvement. In terms of surplus transformation curves, we move outside them to a point on the line through the no-program point with slope of -1. If this is feasible, this line is the correct single-market analog to the UPF of the general equilibrium model, not the STC.

One problem with this approach is that lump-sum transfers are in practice impossible. They are almost inevitably tied to some characteristic of an individual or of economic behavior that can be changed in response to the economic incentive of receiving the transfer. Exceptions in agriculture are payments tied to an acreage or yield base from the past. For example, the Rice Production Act of 1975 tied deficiency payments to output bases from the 1950s. After 1 year of payments, this program was replaced by a program basing payments on current output, thus abandoning the more efficient lump-sum approach.

The reason is the second problem with lump-sum payments, that in a growing or changing industry fixed payments lead to arbitrary exclusions from the program. In the case of rice, producers who had long since given up rice growing received payments while growers in new areas of the Mississippi Delta and California received nothing. The fairness of this result does not affect the surplus calculations but it does pertain to the political viability of such payments, and hence whether they should be treated as a live option. It is possible that rice-growers of 1955–1960 could form a politically viable interest group in 1975, but there are reasons to expect problems, and they, in fact, seem to be insuperable. In part, this is a matter of costs of organization for such groups, but more importantly, it is the difficulty such groups have in mitigating opposition. The general public, even if sympathetic with farmers generally, is harder to bring along in support of payments to nonproducers. More importantly, perhaps, a portion of the commodity producers themselves is brought into opposition. Therefore, we continue to consider the STC as the proper analog to the UPF, and the appropriate constraint facing redistributional policies.

The Social Welfare Function and Optimal Redistribution

Given an analog to the SWF for the single-market context, we can find an optimal intervention in the commodity market just as we specified optimal redistribution in the two-sector model. Here the SWF aggregates CS and PS,

$$W = W\,(PS,\ CS) \tag{7.29}$$

With the controlled production level $\hat{Q}$ as the policy instrument, the social indifference curves are defined by

$$dW = W_p \frac{dPS}{dQ} + W_c \frac{dCS}{dQ} = 0$$

so that

$$\frac{dPS}{dCS} = \frac{dPS/dQ}{dCS/dQ} = -\frac{W_c}{W_p} \tag{7.30}$$

where W_c and W_p are the marginal contributions of CS and PS to social welfare. If a dollar is equally socially valuable to the two groups, then $W_c/W_p = 1$.

We do not have an objective means of claiming that a dollar has more social value in the hands of one group or the other, so we are inclined to make $W_c = W_p$, or $W_c/W_p = 1$. But political choices often redistribute income, involving implicit political weights that we can interpret as W_c/W_p. Since the only property of the W function used in policy analysis is the weights it places on the interest groups relative to one another, let us simplify by letting consumers' (the general public's) welfare weight be 1, and represent producers' welfare weight as the parameter Θ (although Θ will not always be taken as a fixed, exogenous parameter). For a given Θ we can rewrite Eq. (7.29) as

$$W = CS + \Theta PS \qquad (7.31)$$

so that $dPS/dCS = -1/\Theta$ all along each linear SIC.

Now we can specify the social optimum corresponding to Ω in Fig. 7.2 in terms of equal slopes of an SIC and STC. The STC, in general, is

$$W = T(PS, CS) \qquad (7.32)$$

which for given supply and demand conditions can be solved for PS as a function of CS, as Eq. (7.14) does for linear supply and demand. For the slope of the STC in the general case, we have Eq. (7.19). Equating (7.19) to the SIC slope of $-1/\Theta$ and solving to find the first order condition for the social optimum,

$$\tau^* = -\frac{1}{\eta}\left(1 - \frac{1}{\Theta}\right) \qquad (7.33)$$

where τ^* is the optimal price wedge, $(P_d - P_s)/P_d$. The optimal wedge is a surprisingly simple function of η and Θ. If $\Theta = 1$ (equal welfare weights for producers and consumers) the optimal wedge is zero. That is, $P_s = P_d$, the competitive no-intervention equilibrium. At the other extreme, let $\Theta \to \infty$ (consumers are socially valueless). Then the optimal wedge is $-1/\eta$. This is the equilibrium for a monopoly producer of the commodity, the same result derived earlier in Eq. (7.23).

Note also that for given Θ, the elasticity of demand makes a big difference in optimal intervention. Even if $\Theta \to \infty$, if η is also very large (very elastic demand) the wedge becomes small, approaching zero as $\eta \to \infty$.

Equation (7.33) characterizes the optimum, but it does not tell how to find the optimal restricted output level, Q^*. For this purpose, we need to know how both P_s and P_d change as intervention moves the market from Q_0 to $\hat{Q}$. This requires more information than the slopes or elasticities at Q^*. The simplest approach is to assume a particular functional form for $D(Q)$ and $S(Q)$. Having already explored the linear case, let us consider constant-elasticity functions.

$$P_d = AQ^n \qquad (7.34)$$
$$P_s = BQ^e \qquad (7.35)$$

where n is inverse elasticity of demand $(1/\eta)$ and e is inverse elasticity of supply $(1/\epsilon)$. P_s/P_d at any regulated $\hat{Q}$ is

$$\frac{P_s}{P_d} = \frac{P_s/P_0}{P_d/P_0} = \frac{B\hat{Q}^e/BQ_0^e}{A\hat{Q}^n/AQ_0^n} = \left(\frac{\hat{Q}}{Q_0}\right)^{e-n} \qquad (7.36)$$

Substituting Eq. (7.25) for P_s/P_d in Eq. (7.24), we obtain

$$\frac{Q^*}{Q_0} = \left[n\left(1 - \frac{1}{\Theta}\right) + 1 \right]^{1/(e-n)} \tag{7.37}$$

Recall that $n = 1/\eta$ and $e = 1/\epsilon$. When $\Theta = 1$, we have $Q^*/Q_0 = 1$, i.e., no intervention.

The corresponding formula for the linear case is obtained by multiplying Eq. (7.8) by Θ and maximizing the weighted sum of Eqs.(7.7) and (7.8). This is accomplished by finding Q^* such that the weighted derivatives (7.9) and (7.10) sum to zero:

$$- a_1 Q^* + \Theta (a_0 + b_0) + \Theta (2a_1 - b_1) Q^* = 0$$

$$\frac{Q^*}{Q_0} = \frac{a_1 - b_1}{(2a_1 - b_1) - a_1/\Theta} \tag{7.37a}$$

Again, when $\Theta = 1$, then $Q^*/Q_0 = 1$. And when $\Theta \to \infty$, consumers' weight shrinks to zero importance and Eq. (7.37a) reduces to Eq. (7.13), the monopoly solution.

Total Redistribution. Consider total redistribution in the constant-elasticity case. A complication here is that the constant-elasticity demand curve does not meet the price axis. We cannot count on integrating from zero to $\hat{Q}$ to obtain CS, although this integral is defined if $-\eta > 1$. Instead, we integrate over $\hat{Q}$ from some arbitrarily small value α instead of zero.

$$CS = \int_{\alpha}^{\hat{Q}} AQ^n \, dQ - P_d \hat{Q}$$

$$= \frac{1}{n+1} A\hat{Q}^{n+1} - \frac{1}{n+1} A\alpha^{n+1} - A\hat{Q}^{n+1} \tag{7.38}$$

$$= - \frac{n}{n+1} A\hat{Q}^{n+1} - \frac{1}{n+1} A\alpha^{n+1}$$

Solving for $\hat{Q}$

$$\hat{Q} = \left(- \frac{1}{n} \alpha^{n+1} - \frac{n+1}{nA} CS \right)^{1/(1+n)} \tag{7.39}$$

Producers' surplus is

$$PS = P_d \hat{Q} - \int_0^{\hat{Q}} BQ^e \, dQ$$

$$= A\hat{Q}^{n+1} - \frac{1}{1+e} B\hat{Q}^{1+e} \tag{7.40}$$

Substituting Eq. (7.39) into Eq. (7.40), we get the surplus transformation curve

$$PS = -\frac{1}{n} A\alpha^{1+n} - \frac{1+n}{n} CS - \frac{B}{1+e}\left(-\frac{1}{n}\alpha^{1+n} - \frac{n+1}{nA} CS\right)^{(1+e)/(1+n)}$$

(7.41)

The first additive term is a constant, the second is linear in CS, and the third provides the curvature.

To calculate finite changes in surpluses, we use Eqs. (7.38) and (7.40) at $\hat{Q}$ and at the market equilibrium, Q_0, subtracting in each case to obtain

$$\Delta CS = -\frac{n}{n+1} A\hat{Q}^{n+1} + \frac{n}{n+1} AQ_0^{n+1}$$

(7.41a)

$$= \frac{An}{n+1}\left(Q_0^{n+1} - \hat{Q}^{n+1}\right) \qquad n \neq -1$$

$$\Delta PS = A\hat{Q}^{n+1} - \frac{1}{e+1} B\hat{Q}^{e+1} - AQ_0^{n+1} + \frac{1}{e+1} BQ_0^{e+1}$$

(7.41b)

$$= \frac{1}{e+1} B\left(Q_0^{e+1} - \hat{Q}^{e+1}\right) + A\left(\hat{Q}^{n+1} - Q_0^{n+1}\right)$$

Using the fact that $B/A = Q_0^{n-e}$, obtained by equating (7.34) and (7.35), we divide ΔPS by ΔCS to obtain

$$\frac{\Delta PS}{\Delta CS} = \frac{[1/(e+1)] Q_0^{n-e} (Q_0^{e+1} - \hat{Q}^{e+1}) + (\hat{Q}^{n+1} - Q_0^{n+1})}{[n/(n+1)] (Q_0^{n+1} - \hat{Q}^{n+1})}$$

$$= \left(1 + \frac{1}{n}\right)\frac{1}{e+1} Q_0^{n-e}\left(\frac{Q_0^{e+1} - \hat{Q}^{e+1}}{Q_0^{n+1} - \hat{Q}^{n+1}}\right) - 1$$

Multiplying out the expressions containing the Q's and then dividing numerator and denominator by Q_0^{n+1} yields the simplification

$$\frac{\Delta PS}{\Delta CS} = \left(\frac{1}{n} + 1\right)\left[\frac{1}{e+1}\left(\frac{1 - T^{e+1}}{1 - T^{n+1}}\right) - 1\right] \qquad n \neq -1$$

(7.42)

where T is the ratio $\hat{Q}/Q_0$. Thus, given values for n and e, we can calculate the redistribution possibilities for the range of possible T, and having found the optimal T^* from Eq. (7.37), we can calculate the corresponding redistribution using Eq. (7.42).

The total deadweight loss is

$$DW = \Delta CS + \Delta PS$$

(7.43)

$$= \frac{1}{n+1} A (\hat{Q}^{n+1} - Q_0^{n+1}) - \frac{1}{e+1} B (\hat{Q}^{e+1} - Q_0^{e+1})$$

Eliminate A and B by substituting $A = P_0/Q_0^n$ and $B = P_0/Q_0^e$. Then divide through $P_0 Q_0$ to obtain the normalized deadweight loss $D_n = DW/P_0 Q_0$ as

$$D_n = \frac{1}{n+1}(1 - T^{n+1}) - \frac{1}{e+1}(1 - T^{e+1}) \qquad (7.43a)$$

To analyze marginal redistribution in the constant-elasticity case, differentiate Eqs. (7.38) and (7.40) with respect to $\hat{Q}$:

$$\frac{dCS}{dQ} = - nA\hat{Q}^n$$

$$\frac{dPS}{dQ} = (n+1)A\hat{Q}^n - B\hat{Q}^e$$

The slope of the surplus transformation curve for given $\hat{Q}$ is

$$\frac{dPS}{dCS} = \frac{(n+1)A\hat{Q}^n - B\hat{Q}^e}{- nA\hat{Q}^n} \qquad (7.44)$$

$$= \frac{(n+1)P^d - P^s}{- nP^d}$$

$$= \frac{n + (P^d - P^s)/P^d}{- n} \qquad (7.45)$$

which is identical to Eq. (7.19) for the general case. To express the STC slope in terms of $\hat{Q}$, divide the numerator and denominator of Eq. (7.44) by A and use the facts that $B\text{-}A = Q^{n-e}$ and $Q_0 = (B/A)^{1/(n-e)}$:

$$\frac{dPS}{dCS} = \frac{(n+1)\hat{Q}^n - B/A\,\hat{Q}^e}{- n\hat{Q}^n}$$

$$= \frac{(n+1)\hat{Q}^n - Q_0^{n-e}\,\hat{Q}^e}{- n\hat{Q}^n}$$

$$= \frac{(n+1) - Q_0^{n-e}\,\hat{Q}^{e-n}}{- n}$$

$$= - \frac{1}{n}\left[1 - \left(\frac{\hat{Q}}{Q_0}\right)^{e-n}\right] - 1$$

In terms of elasticities of demand and supply as usually expressed, we have $\eta = 1/n$ and $\epsilon = 1/e$, and the slope of the STC is

$$\frac{dPS}{dCS} = - \eta\left[1 - \left(\frac{\hat{Q}}{Q_0}\right)^{1/\epsilon - 1/\eta}\right] - 1 \qquad (7.46)$$

Equation (7.46) has the same implications as found earlier for the linear case, but here explicitly in terms of elasticities rather than slopes of supply and demand functions. The effect of an increase in ϵ is to make the bracketed term of Eq. (7.46), which is always positive, smaller. Therefore, the slope of the surplus transformation curve, for any given restriction $\hat{Q}$, becomes closer to -1. This means that the marginal deadweight loss per dollar transferred is reduced. The effect of an absolute increase in η is to make Eq. (7.46) larger. Consequently, the marginal deadweight loss per dollar transferred is increased. Thus, the social cost of redistribution to producers is reduced by a lower demand elasticity or a higher supply elasticity.

Table 7.1 shows how much difference the elasticities can make for the efficiency of tradeoffs between CS and PS both at the margin and in total for a finite intervention. For example, if the elasticity of demand is -0.2 and the elasticity of supply is 1.0, the table shows that a 20-percent production cutback increases PS by 90 cents for every dollar of CS given up. But at the margin, if more redistribution is attempted by reducing output by 21 percent, we obtain only 85 cents for the next dollar of CS given up. For a given η, variations in ϵ change the efficiency of redistribution, but variation in η is more important. With an elastic demand curve, a 20-percent production cutback becomes quite inefficient, as shown by the case of $\eta = -1$ and $\epsilon = 0.2$. Then PS rises only 55 cents for each dollar of CS given up. The situation is even worse for more elastic demand, in which case a 20-percent cutback can make producers and consumers both worse off.

Table 7.1 Simulated Results of Production Controls

$\lvert \eta \rvert$	ϵ	Marginal PS benefits*	Average PS benefits[†]	Optimal cutback[‡] (%)
0.2	0.2	-0.82	-0.87	16
	1.0	-0.85	-0.90	26
	5.0	-0.86	-0.91	29
1.0[§]	0.2	-0.26	-0.55	3
	1.0	-0.64	-0.81	9
	5.0	-0.77	-0.88	14
5.0	0.2	2.4[‖]	0.99	1
	1.0	0.17	-0.40	3
	5.0	-0.57	-0.79	8

*dPS/dCS from Eq. (7.46). $\hat{Q}/Q_0 = 0.8$.
[†]$\Delta PS/\Delta CS$ from Eq. (7.42). $\hat{Q}/Q_0 = 0.8$.
[‡]$(1 - Q^*/Q_0)$ from Eq. (7.37), $\times$ 100; $\Theta = 1.2$.
[§]The case of $\eta = -1$ is special in that Eqs. (7.41a) and (7.42) are undefined. In this case we have $\Delta CS = A$ (ln Q_0 $-$ ln $\hat{Q}$) and

$$\frac{\Delta PS}{\Delta CS} = \frac{1}{1+e}\left[\frac{1 - (\hat{Q}/Q_0)^{1+\epsilon}}{\ln (Q_0/\hat{Q})}\right]$$

[‖] The positive sign means that when consumers' surplus is reduced, producer's surplus is reduced also.

Still, as long as demand is not perfectly elastic, some production cutback increases W if $\Theta > 1$. Table 7.1 shows the optimal policy for $\Theta = 1.2$. The 20-percent cutback is not optimal for any of the elasticities. The closer to -1 is dPS/dCS at a given $\hat{Q}$, the larger the optimal cutback. In the least-favorable case for intervention, where $\eta = -5$ and $\epsilon = 0.2$, optimal production control still exists, even if the cutback is only 1 percent of no-program output.

The cases of extreme elasticities are not of practical interest but they may aid in understanding the economics of these equations. If demand is perfectly elastic ($\eta \to \infty$ or $n = 0$), Eq. (7.37) is zero—it is not possible to increase PS via production controls because P_d does not rise. If supply is perfectly elastic, we obtain the largest optimal intervention for a given η because no rents are lost when resources are shifted to other uses. If supply is perfectly inelastic, Eq. (7.42) reduces to $-\eta -1$; that is, PS can be increased if and only if $-\eta < 1$. Otherwise Eq. (7.42) is zero or positive.

An especially noteworthy special case occurs when demand is perfectly inelastic. If $\eta = 0$, then Eq. (7.46) equals -1. The same is true of Eq. (7.22)—representing the linear case—when $a_1 \to \infty$. The economic meaning of these results is that if demand were perfectly inelastic, production controls could transfer income to producers without deadweight loss; indeed an infinitesimal cut in production would generate an indefinitely large rise in PS, and an equally large fall in CS. Thus the STC coincides with the efficient redistribution line in Fig. 7.2.

AN ALTERNATIVE REPRESENTATION OF SURPLUS TRANSFERS

In the discussion of the "general" case at beginning of this section, it was assumed that $D(0) < \infty$, that is, the demand function meets the vertical axis. This was done in order to assure that CS was finite. (Actually all that is necessary is for the demand function to converge to the P axis, which as mentioned earlier occurs in the constant-elasticity case if $-\eta > 1$ but not if $-\eta \leq 1$.) The main instance when $D(0) \to \infty$ is the Hicksian demand function for a good that has a subsistence (required) component of demand, as in LES demand specifications. This is a real possibility for food commodities. But even when total CS is undefined, we can and have proceeded with well-defined dCS and dPS expressions. To handle these cases graphically, and to see the STC conceptually from a different angle, we can translate point E to the origin and plot changes in CS and PS from that point. This curve is shown in Fig. 7.4 with points E, R, and M corresponding to the STC in the linear case with $b_1 = 1$ as in Fig. 7.2. The point C_0 is reached when all the consumers' surplus is exhausted, i.e., Q is driven to zero. For Hicksian demand functions for necessities, C_0 will not exist.

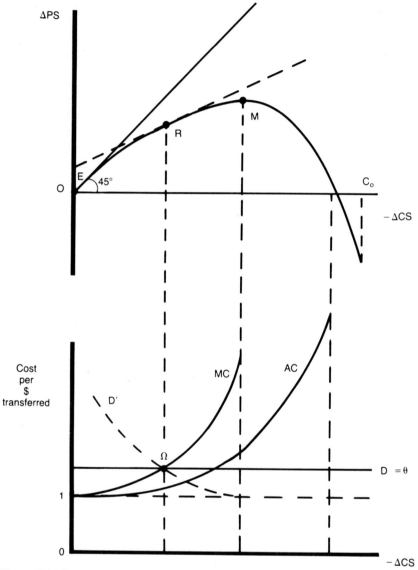

Figure 7.4 Surplus transfers and the cost of redistribution.

The irrelevance of points to the right of M is apparent from the implied cost function for redistribution. The average cost of redistribution is $\Delta PS / -\Delta CS$, and the marginal cost is $-dPS/dCS$. The former becomes indefinitely large when ΔPS is zero (i.e., PS at $\hat{Q} = PS$ at Q_0) and the latter when $dPS =$

0 (i.e., at point M). Both cost curves are shown in the bottom panel of Fig. 7.4, as AC and MC. Since the deadweight loss is $DW = \Delta CS + \Delta PS$, the AC function is $AC = -DW/\Delta CS + 1$; the average cost of transferring a dollar is a dollar plus the deadweight loss per dollar taken from consumers. We can also define the marginal deadweight loss as $DM = dD/dCS = dPS/dCS + 1$; the marginal cost function is then $MC = DM + 1$. The cost of transferring an additional dollar is that dollar plus the marginal deadweight loss. Thus, the deadweight loss is conceptually the "price of redistribution" over and above the amount redistributed. When $dPS = 0$ at point M, the price becomes infinite. The area under MC is the total deadweight loss from redistribution plus the amount redistributed.

Points corresponding to Ω in Fig. 7.2 are found by using the SWF for this context, for example Eq. (7.31). Point R would be an Ω point if $1/\Theta$ were the slope of the STC in the upper panel of Fig. 7.4. A fixed Θ would be represented in the lower panel of Fig. 7.4 as a horizontal line segment at Θ. If $\Theta = 1$, then there are no transfers. If $\Theta > 1$, then we have a perfectly elastic social demand for transfers, labelled D. The optimum (Ω) point occurs where D intersects MC.

In the more general case in which if Θ changes with redistribution, e.g., Θ falls as producers have more and more transferred to them, we would have convex social indifference curves and a social demand for transfers that is negatively sloped as in the dashed curve D' in Fig. 7.4. Thus, we can think of D and MC in such a diagram as supply and demand functions for redistribution as quite analogous to market supply and demand for private goods. An increased demand for redistribution increases this activity, but deadweight losses act as a real constraint. These losses are particularly binding when using production controls for a product with elastic demand, in which case MC rises quite sharply and little can be transferred without exceeding the monopoly price.

With the introduction of a SWF and corresponding Ω point, the deadweight loss loses any normative content it may have had. It is the cost of not being able to redistribute by means of costless lump-sum transfers. A normatively meaningful deadweight loss measure for production controls would be possible if alternative policies existed which generated STCs closer to the efficient redistribution line in Fig. 7.2. In 1987, the Reagan administration proposed a reform of target price payments that would make them independent of current output. This can be viewed as an attempt to approximate lump-sum transfers along the efficient redistribution line. If this policy is feasible, the efficient redistribution line, and not the production-control STC, is the proper analog to the utility possibilities-frontier of welfare economics. The STC is inside the UPF, and there are deadweight losses that imply that a Pareto-improving change in policy is possible. We now turn to a consideration of the main policy alternative.

TARGET PRICE/DEFICIENCY PAYMENT PROGRAM

Guaranteeing producers the difference between a legislated target price, P_T, and the market price brings in a third interest group, taxpayers. For simplicity, assume that taxpayers get the same welfare weight as consumers. Consider the optimum program as one that maximizes

$$W = CS + \Theta PS - T \tag{7.47}$$

subject to

$$CS = \int_0^{\hat{Q}} D(Q)\, dQ - P_d Q \tag{7.48}$$

$$PS = P_s \hat{Q} - \int_0^{\hat{Q}} S(Q)\, dQ \tag{7.49}$$

$$T = (P_T - P_d)\, \hat{Q} \tag{7.50}$$

where $\hat{Q}$ is output forthcoming when P_T is guaranteed. The first-order condition for the maximum is obtained by substituting the preceding three expressions into Eq. (7.47) and setting the derivative with respect to $\hat{Q}$ equal to zero. The result is (before simplifying)

$$\frac{dW}{d\hat{Q}} = D(Q) - D(Q) - \hat{Q}D'(Q) + \Theta\,[S(Q) + \hat{Q}S'(Q) - S(Q)]$$
$$- S'(\hat{Q})\,\hat{Q} - S(Q) + D(\hat{Q}) + \hat{Q}D'(\hat{Q}) = 0$$

Using the notation that $P_d = D(Q)$, $P_s = S(Q)$, and $P_T = S(\hat{Q})$, we divide through by P_s and convert $D(Q)$ and $S(Q)$ to elasticities:

$$\frac{\Theta}{\epsilon} - 1 - \frac{1}{\epsilon} + \frac{P_d}{P_T^*} = 0 \tag{7.51}$$

$$\frac{P_d}{P_T^*} = 1 - \frac{1}{\epsilon}(\Theta - 1) \qquad P_d > 0$$

where P_T^* is the optimum P_T. This then becomes the supply price, P_s, under the policy.

Equation (7.51) contains all the information necessary to describe the optimal policy. Why isn't the demand elasticity involved? It is, in determining how P_T^* compares to the no-program price. To express Eq. (7.51) in terms of the policy instrument P_T as compared to the no-program price P_0, assume we have constant-elasticity S and D curves,

$$\frac{P_d}{P_T^*} = \frac{P_d/P_0}{P_T^*/P_0} = \frac{A\hat{Q}^n/AQ_0^n}{P_T^*/P_0} = \frac{(Q/Q_0)^n}{P_T^*/P_0} \tag{7.52}$$

Since e is inverse elasticity of supply, we have

$$\frac{\hat{Q}}{Q_0} = \left(\frac{P_T^*}{P_0}\right)^{1/e}$$

substituting into Eq. (7.52), we have

$$\frac{P_d}{P_T^*} = \left(\frac{P_T^*}{P_0}\right)^{n/e - 1} \tag{7.53}$$

Substituting Eq. (7.53) into Eq. (7.51), and solving for P_T^*/P_0, using the fact that $1/(n/e - 1) = e/(n - e)$,

$$\frac{P_T^*}{P_0} = [1 - e(\Theta - 1)]^{e/(n - e)} \tag{7.54}$$

Note that if $\Theta = 1$, then $P_T^* = P_0$ (no intervention is optimal, the same result as for production controls). Note also that if $e = 0$ (infinitely elastic supply) then $P_T^* = P_0$; no intervention is optimal because no rents can be created using a subsidy (though they can be with production controls). If demand is perfectly elastic ($n = 0$), then (7.54) is the reciprocal of Eq. (7.51), i.e., $P_0 = P_d$ since P_d is the same at all outputs. At the other extreme, if $n \rightarrow -\infty$ (perfectly inelastic demand) $P_T^* = P_0$, i.e., the optimal subsidy is zero. Here Eq. (7.51) could lead us astray. We need the constraint that $P_d > 0$. Similarly, as Θ increases, anomalous results are obtained when $\Theta > 1/e + 1$, again because the implied P_d is negative.

To see more directly what is going on in these transfers, consider the STC between consumers-and-taxpayers and producers. In the linear case, we have

$$CS - T = (a_0 - b_0)\hat{Q} + \left(\frac{1}{2}a_1 - b_1\right)\hat{Q}^2$$

$$PS = \frac{1}{2}b_1\hat{Q}^2$$

These imply the transformation curve,

$$CS - T = \frac{\frac{1}{2}(a_0 - b_0)}{\sqrt{b/2}}\sqrt{PS} + \frac{(a_1 - 2b_1)}{b_1}PS \tag{7.55}$$

Figure 7.5 compares the surplus transformation curve from Fig. 7.2 with that for Eq. (7.55), using the same supply and demand functions. The dashed line running northwest from point E shows the trade-off between producers' surplus and consumers' surplus minus taxpayers costs. If the SIC curve is flat enough (Θ high enough) the tangency between SIC and STC can occur where $CS - T \leq 0$ (not shown in Fig. 7.5).

The marginal rate of surplus transformation in the linear case is obtained by differentiating Eq. (7.55) with respect to PS.

$$\frac{d(CS - T)}{dPS} = \frac{\frac{1}{4}(a_0 - b_0)}{\sqrt{b_1/2}} \frac{1}{\sqrt{PS}} + \frac{(a_1 - 2b_1)}{b_1} \tag{7.56}$$

In the case of constant-elasticity supply and demand curves, note that Eqs. (7.48) and (7.50) yield

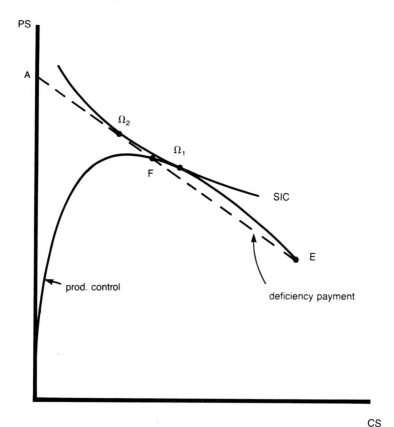

Figure 7.5 Production control compared to deficiency payment program.

$$M = CS - T = \int_0^{\hat{Q}} D(Q)\, dQ - P_T \hat{Q}$$

The ratio $dPS/dM = (dPS/dQ) / (d(CS - T)/dQ)$. Thus,

$$
\begin{aligned}
\frac{dPS}{dM} &= \frac{eB\hat{Q}^e}{A\hat{Q}_0^n - (1+e)B\hat{Q}^e} \\
&= \frac{e\hat{Q}^e}{Q_0^{e-n}\hat{Q}^n - (1+e)\hat{Q}^e} \\
&= \frac{e}{(Q_0/\hat{Q})^{e-n} - (1+e)} \\
&= \frac{1}{(1/e)(Q_0/\hat{Q})^{e-n} - (1/e + 1)}
\end{aligned}
\tag{7.57}
$$

Figure 7.5 provides a convenient diagrammatic depiction of the relative efficiencies of production controls and deficiency payments. If political preferences are such that tangency between the SIC and STC lies to the right of point F, then production controls are preferred. Note that the STC frontier defined by the maximum sum of surpluses available from either policy regime is no longer strictly concave to the origin. This raises the possibility of multiple equilibria, as for example with the SIC as sketched in. If the curve AFE is the appropriate composite STC, then both Ω_1 and Ω_2 are social optima.

The calculations reported in Table 7.2 show how the efficiency of redistribution depends on elasticities. Efficient redistribution is fostered by having either supply or demand be inelastic. If demand is inelastic, production controls are preferred (left-hand column). If supply is inelastic, deficiency payments are preferred. However, if demand is inelastic, so that production controls are chosen, efficiency is increased the more elastic is supply (look at the left-hand number of each pair moving down any column). Similarly, given inelastic supply, elastic demand is preferable (look at the right-hand number of each pair moving across any row).

REDISTRIBUTION TO CONSUMERS

In Fig. 7.2, an extension of the surplus transformation curve to the right of point E involves intervention to redistribute income from producers to consumers. The mechanism could be a price ceiling below the unregulated market price. This STC also has a slope of -1 at point E. The maximum consumers' surplus is at point N, the monopsony outcome. Equilibria favoring consumers lie between points E and N.

We expect the area of rational policy to involve an optimum somewhere

Table 7.2   Marginal Rate of Transformation of Surpluses*

	Elasticity of demand (η)				
	-0.2	-0.5	-1.0	-5.0	$-100.$
0.2	$-0.82, -0.85^{\dagger}$	$-0.60, -0.86$	$-0.26, -0.87$	$2.4, -0.88$	$66, -0.89$
0.5	$-0.84, -0.73$	$-0.70, -0.77$	$-0.51, -0.80$	$0.93, -0.84$	$35, -0.85$
ϵ 1.0	$-0.85, -0.57$	$-0.76, -0.67$	$-0.64, -0.73$	$0.17, -0.81$	$19, -0.83$
5.0	$-0.86, -0.22$	$-0.81, -0.34$	$-0.77, -0.40$	$-0.57, -0.70$	$4, -0.71$
100	$-0.87, -0.01$	$-0.82, -0.03$	$-0.79, -0.05$	$-0.77, -0.18$	$-.55, -0.69$

*All values are calculated for a 20-percent quantity intervention ($\hat{Q}/Q_0 = 0.8$ or 1.2).

†The first number in each pair is the value from Eq. (7.46) (production control) and the second is from Eq. (7.57) (deficiency payments).

between points M and N as the SWF varies from ignoring consumers completely to ignoring producers completely (Θ varies from ∞ to 0).

A possible exception with equilibrium to the left of M would arise if for some reason the SWF placed a negative value on consumers' benefits. This might occur if consumption of the good considered is thought to be a nuisance by enough people. An example might be tobacco. Production would not necessarily be reduced to zero because the loss of producers' benefits would be taken into account, yielding equilibrium at a point like R' in Fig. 7.2. Assuming that unregulated equilibrium would occur at E, there must be some people who do not see the good as a nuisance (otherwise they would not buy it). So this case must involve some important differences in consumers' utility functions, which violates the initial assumptions above. We need at least two kinds of consumers. Also, it might be said that if social indifference curves had a positive slope, then it would be more efficient to simply buy out the producers. This is an instance of the general question why we don't always use cash transfers.

In Fig. 7.5, the dashed transformation curve FE could also be extended rightward from point E to generate redistribution favoring consumers. This might involve an all-or-none offer to producers to produce output $\hat{Q}$ ($>Q_0$) to be sold at a regulated price $\hat{P}$ ($<P_0$). Stalinist delivery quotas at state-specified prices could approximate such a policy. This is a difficult policy administratively because producers must be forced to supply more than the supply function specifies at the regulated price. The situation of a price ceiling, where producers are on the supply curve, but excess demand exists, is the more usual type of regulation favoring consumers. The administrative problem here is the prevention of illegal or "black market" transactions, which are seen as beneficial since both consumers and producers at the margin benefit by sales at prices just above the regulated price.

PERFECT DISCRIMINATION AND NONLINEAR PRICING

The mention of delivery quotas opens up a more complex set of policy options which involve practical difficulties but theoretically can be as efficient as lump-sum transfers. Suppose we know a consumer's demand function for a commodity. The area under the demand curve up to competitive output Q_e measures willingness to pay for Q_e. Calculate

$$\frac{\int_0^{Q_e} D(Q)\, dQ}{Q_e}$$

that is, the area under $D(Q)$ divided by Q_e. Call the resulting price P^*. It will be higher than the competitive price by CS/Q_e. The policy consists of offering the consumer quantity Q_e at price P^*, or else nothing (a "package deal"). This policy captures essentially all the consumer's surplus and does not reduce demand. The administrative problems are, first, that since each consumer has a different demand function, a different package must be offered to each; and second, lump-sum payments of the proceeds or else production controls at Q_e are necessary to place the CS in farmers' hands without causing overproduction. Conceptually, though, it is possible to obtain the effect of perfect price discrimination via the all-or-none offers (see, Patinkin, 1963).

Delivery quotas coupled with producer prices below P_e could similarly be used to extract all of the producers' surplus and redistribute it to taxpayers. Indeed, the true Stalinist quota would not offer a (P, Q_e) pair or nothing, but a (P, Q_e) pair or exile to Siberia. This permits offer of still lower prices—an amount greater than PS can be extracted. With many producers having different cost functions, this type of policy would become quite complicated, too. Chambers (1987) develops a policy of this type that does not require identifying particular individuals but offers a nonlinear price schedule with a range of (P, Q) pairs, of which each producer can choose the one desired. This approach in general cannot extract all the producers' surplus but is always more efficient than the establishment of a single price and movement along the consumer-favoring STC of Fig. 7.2.

APPLICATION AND APPROXIMATION

The application of principles of welfare economics to actual and proposed policies should take into account two features of the agricultural economy that have so far been neglected: first, interactions between closely related commodities such as corn and soybeans, and between commodity and input markets; and second, the existence of distortions in regulated markets other than the intervention being analyzed. Chapters 8 and 9 address these features. However, the complications brought in do not change the conceptual basis for normative judgments that has been developed. In order to promote a better intuitive grasp of the conceptual relationships of this chapter, and their practical implications, this section deals with applications and introduces approximation methods for deadweight loss and surplus transfer measurement.

Approximations are often necessary because of the weakness of econometric information about commodity markets. Typically we have estimates of supply and demand elasticities, but these pertain to the mean of some data set. We know much less about the functional form of supply or demand, in particular how supply or demand elasticities change as we move along the functions. Three approaches are considered to deal with this situation:

  1. Assume constant-elasticity functions.
  2. Assume linear functions.
  3. Use an approximation formula (which may be equivalent to assuming linear functions).

The purpose here is not to choose among these approaches but to explore the sensitivity of welfare calculations to the choice of one or another of them.

Suppose we have an initial no-program (competitive) equilibrium of $Q_0 = 10$ billion bushels and $P_0 = 1$ (dollar per bushel), and that we have estimates of the elasticities of supply and demand at that point of $\eta = -2/3$ and $\epsilon = 0.5$. An output-reduction program is proposed, to bring output to $\hat{Q}/Q_0 = 0.8$ or $Q_0/\hat{Q} = 1.25$. What are the surplus transfers and deadweight loss?

Approach 1 proceeds by assuming that the supply and demand curves are linear. The given data imply that the inverse demand slope is $a_1(10/1) = 1/-0.667$, or $a_1 = 0.15$. The inverse supply slope is $b_1(10/1) = 1/0.5$, or $b_1 = 0.20$. The data yield the results shown in Table 7.3, using the calculating equations from this chapter as numbered in the table. Price rises 30 percent with deadweight losses of $700 million, and other results occur as shown.

Approach 2 proceeds by assuming that the supply and demand curves have constant elasticity. Table 7.3 lists appropriate calculating equations for this case. We obtain a higher estimate of the price increase. The reason is that with the linear demand curve, elasticity rises as price rises, so the price effects of further output reductions are diminished as compared to the constant elasticity case. Or to put the point the other way around, both demand curves have the same slope at competitive equilibrium, but in the constant elasticity case the slope becomes steeper as price rises.

Approach 3 involves a two-step approximation. First, the production cutback is expressed as a percentage by letting it be 22.5 percent, the midpoint of 2/8 and 2/10. Thus, the approximation can be viewed as using Fisherian crossed weights as a base for calculating percentage changes. Dividing by the demand elasticity yields $0.225/0.667 = 0.3375$, a 33.75 rise in P_d.

Second, the formula for the deadweight loss triangle with base given by ΔQ is:

$$DW \cong \frac{1}{2} P_0 Q_0 \, \eta \tau^2 \left(1 - \frac{\eta}{\epsilon} \right) \qquad (7.58)$$

Table 7.3   Alternative Estimates of Production Control Effects*

Variable	Approach 1 (linear S and D)		Approach 2 (log-linear S and D)		Approach 3 (approximation)	
	Eq. no.	Program effect	Eq. no.	Program effect	Ref.	Program effect
P_d	(7.5)	0.30	(7.34)	0.40		0.3375
ΔCS	(7.7)	−2.7	(7.41a)	−3.6		
ΔPS	(7.8)	2.0	(7.41b)	2.8	Wallace, 1962 [Eq. (8)]	2.0
DW	(7.26)	0.70	(7.43)	0.80	Wallace, 1962 [Eq. (1)]	0.88
$\dfrac{\Delta PS}{\Delta CS}$	(7.28)	−0.74	(7.42)	−0.79		
$\dfrac{dPS}{dCS}$	(7.22)	−0.42	(7.46)	−0.64		
$\dfrac{Q^*}{Q_0}$	(7.37a)	0.875	(7.37)	0.82		

*Program effects given in billions of dollars, except P_d, which is in dollars.

where τ is the percentage increase in P_d (not the wedge $P_s - P_d$ used earlier). This result is derived in Wallace (1962, p. 594). The values for the current problem give $DW = (0.5) (1) (10) (-0.667) (0.3375)^2 (1 + 0.667/0.5) = -0.88$. This formula is exact for linear demand and supply and would have yielded $DW = 0.70$ if $\tau = 0.30$ as it was in approach 1.

In the spirit of optimal surplus transfers, Table 7.3 also shows the difference made by different approaches in specifying the optimal controlled output ratio, Q^*/Q_0, with the SWF specified as additive with $\Theta = 1.5$ for producers. In the linear case, this ratio is 0.875, or $Q^* = 8.75$ billion bushels, while in the constant elasticity case $Q^* = 8.2$ billion bushels. This is a substantial difference reflecting how much more quickly dPS/dCS changes toward zero from -1 in the linear case.

It is not clear how an ad hoc approximation method would proceed in the optimization question. This method finds areas of triangles and trapezoids readily but does not help in the choice of *which* of the many possible triangles to measure, i.e., what value of τ to pick. This feature of the approximations can lead to misleading judgments of efficiency in comparing alternative policies. For example, it leads to comparisons such as asking whether production controls or deficiency payments with no controls are most efficient at attaining a given target price level for farmers. One such result is that when linear supply and demand have slopes that are equal (in absolute value), a production control or deficiency payment program to achieve a given price $\hat{P} > P_0$ both have the same deadweight loss. It is easily seen that this is so by diagraming this situation. The two deadweight loss triangles have equal base and height and so are equal in area. So why don't we have equal rates of surplus transformation in each pair along the diagonals of Table 7.2? The reason is that here we measure deadweight loss *per dollar transferred,* and in the situation described, the deficiency payment transfers more rents to producers for a given $\hat{P}$. This points up the crucial importance of evaluating policies with reference to the purpose they are intended to serve. The presumption of welfare economics is that the objectives of policies—the arguments in the SWF—are utilities or incomes or surpluses, which are indicators of people's well-being, and not prices.

SUMMARY

The essential issues in the normative economics of agricultural policies involve measuring individuals' welfare gains and aggregating them to obtain measures of a group's and a whole nation's gains. Besides technical questions about proper ways of making these measurements, there are methodological questions about how far we can go in welfare analysis without bringing in value judgments. The first part of the chapter considered individual welfare measurement. Assumptions have to be made for such measurement but they are politically innocuous. The more troublesome questions involve aggregating over gains and losers from a policy change. The SWF accomplishes this formally but it is scientifically empty; it only specifies value judgments more precisely than might otherwise be done. We proceeded by considering what optimal policies would be *given* a SWF, particularly one that weighted producers' gains above consumers' and taxpayers' losses.

The bulk of the chapter studied the quantitative effects of policy alternatives, and the determination of optimal policies given such a SWF. Two kinds of problems were solved, the first finding the redistribution and deadweight losses resulting from any arbitrary intervention, and the second finding optimal intervention. It is important to keep these distinct conceptually, for when intervention is optimal as dictated by a SWF, the notion of deadweight loss has no normative force. It is just the price that must be paid for redistribution in the same sense as hiring people to administer the programs is a cost of these policies.

For each type of problem, three kinds of equation were developed. First, without assuming a particular functional form, we have equations to give a conceptual basis for the *PS* and *CS* transfers, such as Eqs. (7.15) to (7.17). Second, we have particular calculating equations for the case of linear supply and demand functions; and third, calculating equations for the log-linear (constant-elasticity) case. The last case has especially messy algebra, some of which is spelled out in the hope that it will assist those who wish to work through the details without hopelessly interrupting the flow of the discussion. Although working through this material can be tedious, especially considering that the single-product case has to be generalized before it is useful for many practical policy issues, it is worth doing because the conceptual basis for more complex welfare calculation is essentially the same.

Table 7.3 provides a guide to the main results for a production-control policy. Some, but fewer, analogous equations for a target-price and deficiency payment program were also derived. Policies of other kinds outlined in Chap. 2 have not been analyzed here. Fortunately, many of them are isomorphic with production controls or deficiency payments as far as surplus transfers are concerned. The main policies that generate different surplus transfers are those involving international trade and border interventions. The policies are analyzed in Chap. 11.

ENDNOTES

1. "Economic problems, like medical problems, have symptoms, causes, and cures. The objective of this paper is to diagnose and suggest treatment for farm economic ills" (Tweeten, 1985, p. 1).
2. Quotation from the bishops' letter as excerpted in the *New York Times,* November 14, 1986.
3. We do *not* have a money metric for utility itself that could be aggregated over individuals, but only an estimate of how much it would cost to compensate individuals for their loss of utility when a price rises. For discussion of a money metric and many other interesting technical and conceptual issues that have been glossed over here, some of the more illuminating sources are Deaton and Muellbauer, 1980 (Chap. 7); Hause, 1975; Just et al., 1982; Patinkin, 1963; McKenzie and Pearce, 1982; and Morey, 1984.
4. The possibility exists that this criterion could be satisfied and that nonetheless the losers could bribe the gainers *not* to make the change, so not making the change would also be Pareto optimal. Scitovsky argued that both conditions have to be met for a change to be unambiguously welfare-improving (see the discussion in Just et al., 1982, pp. 37–38). The compensation here is all potential, i.e., it assumes that costless lump-sum redistribution between interest groups is feasible. The falsity of this assumption is seen below to be important in explaining why it can be efficient to transfer income through commodity markets.

Chapter 8

Income Redistribution through Multimarket Commodity Programs

The preceding chapter analyzed the efficiency of redistribution in a single commodity market, and brought out the relationships between neoclassical welfare economics and the gains and losses from market intervention. It is not sufficient, however, to consider only producers, consumers, and taxpayers of a single commodity. In Chaps. 4 and 6 we traced through the input market and factor income consequences of policy, and in Chaps. 3 and 5 we examined the complications that arise with interrelated commodity markets. This chapter considers some topics in social optimization and efficiency in these situations.

RELATED AGRICULTURAL COMMODITIES

Suppose that the goal of policy is to aid crop farmers as a group ($\Theta > 1$ in a linear SWF), but not to favor producers of one commodity over another. Different farmers grow different products, however, and price supports must be established for all of them. It might seem a sensible supposition that efficient redistribution under these circumstances would involve the same rate of protection for all commodities, that is, an equal percentage difference between the supported price $(\hat{P})$ and no-program price (P_0) for each farm product. This supposition is incorrect. A key to obtaining a good analytical grasp of multimarket welfare economics is to understand why.

Consider the case in which farmers produce two crops, say, food, x_1, and nonfood raw materials, x_2. Consumers have demand functions for each of the goods (neglecting marketing for the present). The demand and supply function for each good contains the price of the other. Our first analytical difficulty in this case is that we cannot simply add up the surplus gains from changing each price separately to obtain the gains from changing both prices jointly. The economic reason is clearest with respect to consumers' gains. If either commodity's price were raised, holding the other price constant, the loss might not be great because the product whose price had not risen would be substituted for the commodity whose price had risen. But when both commodities' prices rise, this avenue of escape is not available, so the loss is greater. How much greater depends on the substitutability of the products in consumption. In analyzing producers' rents, the same problem arises on the supply side, depending on the substitutability of the products in farmers' production activities.

By working through the multimarket equilibrium effects of each price change, all the price and quantity effects can be added up. To see how this works, return to the constant elasticity model of Chap. 3 [Eqs. (3.2) to (3.5)], and consider the effects of subsidy payments to producers. For two commodities, x and y, the demand and supply functions are

$$\text{Demand for } x: \qquad x = z_1 \, P_x^{\eta_x} \, P_y^{\eta_{xy}} \tag{8.1}$$

$$\text{Supply of } x: \qquad x = z_2 \, (V_x \, P_x)^{\epsilon_x} \, (V_y \, P_y)^{\epsilon_{xy}} \tag{8.2}$$

$$\text{Demand for } y: \qquad y = z_3 \, P_x^{\eta_{yx}} \, P_y^{\eta_y} \tag{8.3}$$

$$\text{Supply of } y: \qquad y = z_4 \, (V_x \, P_x)^{\epsilon_{yx}} \, (V_y \, P_y)^{\epsilon_y} \tag{8.4}$$

where $V_x = 1 + v_x$, with v_x the subsidy as a percentage of market price, so that the producer's price is $C_x = V_x \, P_x$. The cross-price elasticity, η_{xy}, means the percentage change in x resulting from a 1-percent change in the price of y.

Taking logs of Eqs. (8.1) to (8.4) yields linear equations whose differentials are percentage change equations:

$$Ex = \eta_x \, EP_x + \eta_{xy} \, EP_y \tag{8.1'}$$

$$Ex = \epsilon_x \, EP_x + \epsilon_{xy} \, EP_y + \epsilon_x \, EV_x + \epsilon_{xy} \, EV_y \tag{8.2'}$$

$$Ey = \eta_{yx} \, EP_x + \eta_y \, EP_y \tag{8.3'}$$

$$Ey = \epsilon_{yx} \, EP_x + \epsilon_y \, EP_y + \epsilon_{yx} \, EV_x + \epsilon_y \, EV_y \tag{8.4'}$$

The effect of changing the subsidy rate by 1 percent of the market price is found by dividing through by EV_x, holding $EV_y = 0$. Then equating (8.1) and

(8.2) and (8.3) and (8.4) yields two equations in two unknowns, EP_x/EV_x and EP_y/EV_y. Solving for EP_x/EV_x,

$$\frac{EP_x}{EV_x} = \frac{\epsilon_x(\eta_y - \epsilon_y) - \epsilon_{yx}(\eta_{xy} - \epsilon_{xy})}{(\eta_x - \epsilon_x)(\eta_y - \epsilon_y) - (\eta_{xy} - \epsilon_{xy})(\eta_{yx} - \epsilon_{yx})} \tag{8.5}$$

Assuming x and y are substitutes in both production and consumption, η_{xy} and η_{yx} are positive, and ϵ_{xy} and ϵ_{yx} are negative. The numerator and the denominator can be either positive or negative, but as long as own-price effects outweigh cross-price effects, Eq (8.5) is negative.[1] Increasing the subsidies reduces the market price. If all cross-price effects are zero, Eq (8.5) reduces to $EP_x/EV_x = \epsilon_x/(\eta_x - \epsilon_x)$, the result obtained in Chap. 4, Eq. (4.26).

Solving the system for EP_y/EV_x gives the effect of a change in the subsidy paid on x on the price of the substitute product.

$$\frac{EP_y}{EV_x} = \frac{\eta_y \epsilon_{yx} - \epsilon_x \eta_{yx}}{D} \tag{8.6}$$

where D is the denominator of Eq. (8.5).

From Eq. (8.1') we have the effect on quantity of x:

$$\frac{EX}{EV_x} = \eta_x \frac{EP_x}{EV_x} + \eta_{xy} \frac{EP_y}{EV_x} \tag{8.7}$$

Substituting Eqs. (8.5) and (8.6) into Eq. (8.7) tells how the elasticity parameters determine the effects of V_x on output. Similarly, from Eq. (8.3'), the effect of V_x on y can be found. The same expressions with all x's and y's interchanged show the consequences of a subsidy of V_y, i.e., EP_x/EV_y, EP_y/EV_y, EX/EV_y, and Ey/EV_y.

The effect of a change in V_x on the producer price is derived as follows:

$$C_x = V_x P_x$$
$$\frac{dC_x}{dV_x} = V_x \frac{dP_x}{dV_x} + P_x$$
$$\frac{EC_x}{EV_x} = \frac{1}{P_x} \frac{dC_x}{dV_x} = \frac{V_x}{P_x} \frac{dP_x}{dV_x} + 1 = \frac{EP_x}{EV_x} + 1$$

Thus, if a 1-percent increase in V_x reduces P_x by 0.3 percent, it must raise C_x by 0.7 percent.

In calculating gains and losses from price and quantity changes, a convenient approximation method is to use a second-order Taylor's series expansion around the expenditure function (7.2) when all prices change (see Boadway and Bruce, 1984, pp. 217–218). This yields consumers' gains, ΔG_c as

$$\Delta G_c = -\sum_i x_i \Delta P_i + \frac{1}{2} \sum_i \sum_j \frac{\partial x_i}{\partial P_j} \Delta P_j \Delta P_i$$

Since $\Delta X_i = -\sum_j \frac{\partial X_i}{\partial P_j} \Delta P_j$, this reduces to

$$\Delta G_c = \sum_i X_i \Delta P_i + \frac{1}{2} \sum_i \Delta X_i \Delta P_i \qquad (8.8)$$

These gains are analogous to ΔCS in the single-product case.

In the present two-good case we have

$$\Delta G_c = -X\Delta P_x - Y\Delta P_y + \frac{1}{2}(\Delta X\Delta P_x + \Delta Y\Delta P_y) \qquad (8.9)$$

Or in relative terms, dividing through by $(XP_x + yP_y)$,

$$EG_c = -K_x\, EP_x - K_y\, EP_y + \frac{1}{2}(K_x\, ExEP_x + K_y\, EyEP_y) \qquad (8.10)$$

For producers, the gains are:

$$\Delta G_p = X\Delta C_x + Y\Delta C_y + \frac{1}{2}(\Delta X\Delta C_x + \Delta Y\Delta C_y) \qquad (8.11)$$

The changes in expenditures on subsidies are $\Delta V_x = (C_x + \Delta C_x - P_x - \Delta P_x)$ $(X + \Delta X)$ and similarly for ΔV_y. Subtracting these costs from the sum of Eqs. (8.9) and (8.11) gives the deadweight loss of the subsidies:

$$\Delta DW = -\Delta X\,(C_x - P_x) - \Delta Y\,(C_y - P_y) + \frac{1}{2}\,[\Delta X\,(\Delta C_x - \Delta P_x)$$
$$+ \Delta Y\,(\Delta C_y - \Delta P_y)] \qquad (8.12)$$

This would be the change in social welfare if producers', consumners', and tax-payers' gains were all weighted equally.

These calculations give the same results as the common-sense counting of gains and losses in the wheat–corn–soybean example of Chap. 3—taking the price gain times the original quantities plus the price gains times half the change in quantity. The only difference is that x and y are the new (postchange) quantities, from which we subtract the triangular area. The Chap. 3 measure was a compensating variation welfare indicator while Eqs. (8.8) to (8.11) give equivalent variations. The two are the same because our structural demand elasticities are real-income constant, but the latter measure would be larger if we used ordinary demand functions.

Graphically, Fig. 8.1 shows the gains and losses. In the x market, area A is ΔG_p, area C is ΔG_c, $A + B + C$ is the taxpayers loss, and B is the added deadweight loss, ΔDW. If the policy change generating these changes were a subsidy only in the x market, while $V_y = 0$, then the dashed curves $\tilde{S}$ and $\tilde{D}$ would pass through point E as shown. These are "total" elasticities, derived in Chap. 3, which account for shifts in demand and supply of x owing to adjustments in the y market. There would be gains and losses, but no deadweight losses, in the y market.

However, if $V_y \neq 0$, there are also deadweight losses in the y market. Moreover, if we have simultaneous changes in V_x and V_y, the curves $\tilde{S}$ and $\tilde{D}$ will shift so that areas like A and B, or the hatched areas of gains and losses in the y market, are not defined with reference to any single supply or demand function. For example, the upper hatched area is the producers' gains but involves no implication that any specification of a supply curve of y has a negative slope. What is going on is that there is a much bigger subsidy in x (48 percent) than in y (18 percent), as a result of which the supply curve of y shifts to the left. (With roughly equal subsidies or unequal subsidies but small cross-elasticities of supply, it is more likely that the output of both x and y would be increased.

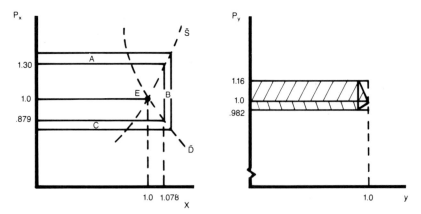

Figure 8.1 Gains and losses in two related markets.

Optimal Subsidy Rates

To find the optimal subsidies, we maximize welfare by equating the sum of the marginal gains aggregated in Eq. (8.12), each appropriately weighted, to zero. With equal weights, we already know that the sum, as given in Eq. (8.12), is negative. Its maximum value is zero.

Using the earlier notation of $\Theta > 1$ as a weight for producers' welfare, with $\Theta = 1$ for consumers and taxpayers, we do not obtain such a simple result. A solution for V_x in the two-good case could be found numerically using parameter values in Eqs. (8.5) to (8.7) to find the V_x that makes $\Delta w = 0$. An easier method is available, however, referring back to the deficiency payment as optimized in Eq. (7.51) of Chap. 7. The ratio of market price to target price there is just $P_x/V_xP_x = 1/V_x$ in the notation of this model. The difference is that now e is the (inverse) multimarket elasticity of supply. This can be derived from Eqs. (3.2) to (3.5) as

$$\tilde{\epsilon}_x = \epsilon_x + \epsilon_{xy}\frac{\epsilon_{yx} - \eta_{yx}}{\eta_y - \epsilon_y} \tag{8.13}$$

Then from (7.51), we have the condition for the optimum being

$$\frac{1}{\tilde{\epsilon}_x}(\Theta - 1) = 1 - \frac{1}{V_x^*} \tag{8.14}$$

or

$$V_x^* = \frac{1}{1 - (1/\tilde{\epsilon}_x)(\Theta - 1)} \qquad \Theta < \tilde{\epsilon}_x + 1$$

If $\Theta = 1$, then $V^* = 1$, i.e., no intervention. Otherwise, the optimal subsidy rate depends on the supply and demand parameters in Eq. (8.13).

Now consider a subsidy for y production. It will give the same results using the multimarket elasticity of supply for y,

$$\tilde{\epsilon}_y = \epsilon_y + \epsilon_{yx}\frac{\epsilon_{xy} - \eta_{xy}}{\eta_x - \epsilon_x} \tag{8.15}$$

and we have

$$V_y^* = \frac{1}{1 - (1/\tilde{\epsilon}_y)(\Theta - 1)} \qquad \Theta < \tilde{\epsilon}_y + 1 \tag{8.16}$$

When we subsidize *both* x and y, the optimum is found at the point where a subsidy on y and on x each adds the same marginal contribution to the SWF. That is,

$$\frac{1}{\bar{\epsilon}_x}(\Theta - 1) - 1 + \frac{1}{V_x^*} = \frac{1}{\bar{\epsilon}_y}(\Theta - 1) - 1 + \frac{1}{V_y^*}$$

Rearranging,

$$\left(\frac{1}{\bar{\epsilon}_x} - \frac{1}{\bar{\epsilon}_y}\right)(\Theta - 1) = \frac{1}{V_y^*} - \frac{1}{V_x^*}$$

Note that if $\Theta = 1$, $V_y^* = V_x^*$, that is, the optimal subsidy rate is the same for both commodities, as in our original supposition; but from Eq. (8.14), $V_x^* = V_y^* = 1$, that is, the optimal subsidy rates are both zero. If $\bar{\epsilon}_x = \bar{\epsilon}_y$, it is also true that $V_y^* = V_x^*$. Generally, though, it is not optimal to have the same subsidy rates for both commodities. Solving for V_y^*,

$$V_y^* = \frac{1}{1/V_x^* + (1/\bar{\epsilon}_x - 1/\bar{\epsilon}_y)(\Theta - 1)} \tag{8.17}$$

If x is more elastic in supply ($\bar{\epsilon}_x > \bar{\epsilon}_y$) and $\Theta > 1$, then the denominator is smaller than $1/V_x^*$ and the reciprocal is bigger than V_x^*. That is, $V_y^* > V_x^*$ if $\bar{\epsilon}_x > \bar{\epsilon}_y$. This parallels the Ramsay-pricing result that it is optimal to charge a higher price, or tax on the product with least-elastic demand (Baumol and Bradford, 1970). Here it is optimal to pay a higher subsidy on a product with less elastic (multimarket equilibrium) supply.

Case Study.　To illustrate, let x and y be corn and soybeans, with parameter values used in Chap. 3 for corn (x) and soybeans (y): $\eta_x = -0.6$, $\epsilon_x = 0.4$, $\eta_y = -0.7$, $\epsilon_y = 0.8$, $\eta_{xy} = 0.1$, $\eta_{yx} = 0.2$, $\epsilon_{xy} = -0.2$, $\epsilon_{yx} = -0.5$. These values imply from Eqs. (8.13) and (8.15), that $\bar{\epsilon}_x = 0.307$, and $\bar{\epsilon}_y = 0.650$. To find the optimal subsidy, assume that $\Theta = 1.1$ (producers' income valued at 10 percent more than consumers' and taxpayers' incomes).[2] From Eq. (8.14) we get $V_x^* = 1.48$, i.e., the optimal subsidy is 48 percent of the market price. Then from either Eq. (8.16) or (8.17), we obtain $V_y^* = 1.18$, an 18-percent subsidy. The reason is the lower value of $\bar{\epsilon}_x$ as compared to $\bar{\epsilon}_y$.

To find the effects on X, P_x, C_x, Y, P_y, C_y, and the gains G_c, G_p, and DW we go back to Eqs. (8.5) to (8.12). Since these are based on percentage change equations involving derivatives, yet EV_x and EV_y are quite large, it is also instructive to solve the original system (8.1) to (8.4) for $V_x = V_y = 1$ and again for $V_x = 1.48$ and $V_y = 1.18$ to see if approximation errors are significant.

The percentage changes are:
from the change in V_x:[3]

$$EP_x = \frac{0.4\,(-0.7-0.8) + 0.5\,(0.1+0.2)}{(-0.6-0.4)\,(-0.7-0.8) - (0.1+0.2)\,(0.2+0.5)}\,(0.392) = -0.137 \qquad (8.5')$$

and from the change in V_y:

$$EP_x = \frac{(-0.6)\,(-0.2) - (0.8)\,(0.1)}{1.29}\,(0.166) = \frac{0.04}{1.29}\,(0.166) = 0.005$$

Adding the two effects gives $EP_x = -0.132$, i.e., P_x falls by 13.2 percent. The change in producer price is found by adding 1 to EP_x as shown earlier:

$$EC_x = \left(\frac{(-0.132)}{0.392} + 1\right)(0.392) = 0.259$$

The effect on P_y is,
from the change in V_x using Eq. 8.6:

$$EP_x = \frac{(-0.7)\,(-0.5) - (0.4)\,(0.2)}{1.29}\,(0.392) = 0.082 \qquad (8.6')$$

and from the change in V_y:

$$EP_y = \frac{0.8(-0.6-0.4) + 0.2\,(0.2+0.5)}{1.29}\,(0.166) = -0.085$$

Adding the two effects gives $EP_y = -0.003$, i.e., P_y falls by 0.3 of 1 percent. The change in the producer price of y is

$$EC_y = \left(\frac{-0.003}{0.166} + 1\right)(0.166) = 0.163$$

The changes in x and y are, using Eq. 8.7:

$$EX = -0.6\,(-0.132) - 0.1(0.003) = 0.079 \qquad (8.7')$$
$$EY = 0.2\,(-0.132) + 0.7(0.003) = -0.024$$

To sum up these results, the optimal subsidies of 48 percent of P_x and 18 percent of P_y causes P_x to fall 13.2 percent, P_y to fall 0.3 percent, x to rise 7.9 percent, and y to fall 2.4 percent.

To solve the problem without approximating percentage changes, in Eqs. (8.1) to (8.4), let initial values of P_x, P_y, x, and y all take on index value of 1.00, with $V_x = V_y = 1$ (no intervention). Taking logs, we obtain linear equations in which initial values are zero (hence the Z's are zero). Then inserting ln 1.48 = 0.392 and ln 1.18 = 0.166, we obtain constant terms of 0.124 in Eq. (8.2) and -0.063 in Eq. (8.4). Then we solve for the logs of prices and quantities given the subsidies. The antilogs give: $P_x = 0.879$, $P_y = 0.982$, $x = 1.078$, and $y = 0.981$; also $C_x = P_x(1.48) = 1.30$ and $C_y = P_y(1.18) = 1.16$. These values are shown in Fig. 8.1

Thus applying the percentage-change approximations to initial unit values, we obtained prices and quantities all quite close to the "true" values. Of course, this assumes that the constant-elasticity model of Eqs. (8.1) to (8.4) is the true functional form. The only approximation error is in using ln $(1 + V_x)$ as the percentage change in V_x. (The approximation errors would be much larger if we used the subsidy rate itself as the percentage-change approximation, e.g., multiplying EP_x by 0.48 instead of 0.392.)

Note that the percentage changes could also have been derived from the relationship used in Chap. 4, $EP = \epsilon/(\eta - \epsilon) \cdot EV$, but here $\bar{\epsilon}$ and $\bar{\eta}$ would be used. For example, for our parameter values, we found $\bar{\epsilon}_x = 0.307$ using Eq. (8.13). The analogous equation for $\bar{\eta}_x$ (derived in Buse 1958) is

$$\bar{\eta}_x = \eta_x + \eta_{xy} \frac{\epsilon_{yx} - \eta_{yx}}{\eta_y - \epsilon_y} \qquad (8.18)$$

Its value is -0.553 (less elastic than $\eta_x = 0.6$). Using EV_x of 0.392, $EP_x = [0.307/(-0.553 - 0.307)]0.392 = -0.140$.

To calculate the changes in benefits from the subsidy on x, we have, for consumers, using equation 8.9

$$\begin{aligned} G_c &= 1.078\,(1.0 - 0.879) + 0.981\,(1.0 - 0.982) \\ &\quad - \frac{1}{2}[(1.078 - 1.0)\,(0.879 - 1.0) + (0.981 - 1.0)(0.982 - 1.0)] \\ &= 0.153 \end{aligned}$$

$$(8.9')$$

which is 7.6 percent of base-period expenditure $(1 + 1 = 2)$. For producers,

$$G_p = 1.078\,(0.30) + 0.879\,(0.16) - \frac{1}{2}[(0.078)\,(0.30)$$
$$+ (-0.019)\,(0.16)] \tag{8.11'}$$
$$= 0.454$$

or 23 percent of base-period revenue. For taxpayers

$$G_g = -1.078\,(1.30 - 0.879) - 0.981\,(1.16 - 0.982)$$
$$= -0.629$$

Summing up the gains for all three groups, we have -0.022. This deadweight loss from optimal subsidization is 1/4 of 1 percent of base-period expenditures. Another way of putting this result is that it costs consumers and taxpayers jointly $1.011 for each $1.00 transferred to producers. This means that if $\Theta > 1.011$ for producers, the weighted welfare index is increased by the taxation scheme.

The optimal subsidy rates in this example were found by assuming $\Theta = 1.1$ for producers, so the welfare gain is

$$\Delta w = 0.153 + (1.1)\,0.454 - 0.629 = 0.023$$

This is the maximum welfare gain. In particular, the gain is larger than that resulting from any pair of equal subsidy rates, e.g., $V_x = V_y = 1.25$.

Diagrams to illustrate the nature of the social optimum are not as helpful as in Chap. 7 because of the difficulty of showing trade-offs between producers' and consumers' gains with reference to two policy instruments simultaneously. What we can do is plot the contours of a "welfare hill" for any given value of Θ. Such a diagram is shown in Fig. 8.2. The subsidy rates are measured along the axes; equal rates place us on the 45° line, and zero rates for one input or the other place us on one of the axes. For $\Theta > 1$, we know that the social optimum (maximum W) is achieved with a higher subsidy rate on the product less elastic in supply, assumed to be x. This yields an Ω point as shown. If we hold V_x constant and change V_y, we move along the dashed horizontal line. Since we started at Ω, we know that W must be lower as we move in either direction. Reducing V_y to zero places us at point A. Increasing V_y sooner or later generates the same welfare level, as at point B. Thus at A and B we have points of equal welfare, $W = W_1$. We could also find points where $W = W_1$ by increasing or decreasing V_x while holding V_y at V_y^*. This yields points C and D which also have $W = W_1$. Indeed, we can alter both V_x and V_y to obtain the ellipsoid shown of points where $W = W_1$. This is a social indifference curve (SIC) in subsidy-rate space, which will be called an indirect SIC. As in surplus space or goods space, we can trace out a whole contour map of

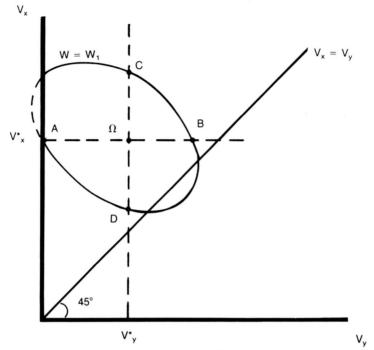

Figure 8.2 Welfare contour for subsidies, $\Theta > 1$.

such curves. They imply an indirect social welfare function, a concept analogous to the indirect utility function in the theory of demand in which utility is expressed as a function of prices.

Note that Ω is at the origin when $\Theta = 1$. The indirect SICs then are concave to the origin. When $\epsilon_x = \epsilon_y$ the Ω point is on the 45° line, where $V_x = V_y$. As Θ increases, Ω moves further from the origin along this line. The dotted part of the indirect SIC curve outside the positive quadrant of V_x, V_y refers to the results of taxing one commodity and subsidizing the other.

PRICE DISCRIMINATION AND MARKETING ORDERS

A related but distinct issue arises when the market for a single product can be broken up into two or more submarkets with different demand elasticities. The idea is that, starting from a situation in which price is the same in two submarkets, revenue from selling any given quantity of the product can be increased by reallocating some of the product from the submarket with relatively inelastic demand to the submarket with relatively elastic demand. A discriminating monopolist would reallocate until marginal revenue was the same in both submarkets, and would choose an output level such that marginal cost was equal to the common marginal revenue. The submarkets could be different regions, different uses of the product (raw versus processed), or consumers at different income or age levels (lower prices for senior citizens). Since the prices may be quite different in the two submarkets, the monopolist must be able to prevent resale from the low-priced one to the high-priced one. This necessity creates an insuperable obstacle for many potential discriminating monopolists.

Strange to say, some of the purest cases to be found of price discrimination are in marketing orders for U.S. agricultural commodities. It is strange because these commodities have many producers, and would be easy to transfer to high-price from low-price submarkets. With many producers, a cartel is necessary to duplicate a monopoly result. All must agree to limit sales in the high-price market. Marketing orders achieve the necessary discipline by means of legal procedures under which a majority of producers can force all producers, under penalty of law, to limit sales in high-price uses. A many-member cartel with legal authority to punish noncooperators is more viable than a few-member cartel whose firms are subject to antitrust penalties if they are caught in a conspiracy in restraint of trade.

Market separation is achieved because in marketing orders, a regulatory body can not only set minimum prices (in milk) or maximum quantities in (oranges and lemons) in the high-price submarket, but can also proscribe transfers from the low-price to the high-price market at discounted prices. The main problem to be solved in administering marketing orders is how to establish and enforce this proscription.

U.S. marketing orders typically do not control entry by producers. They are price-discriminating cartels with free entry. This means that the price discrimination activity acts like a rightward or upward shift in demand, since any given quantity is sold at a higher price. But the creation of rents for producers depends on product supply being less than perfectly elastic. For a complete description of this model as applied to milk marketing orders, see Ippolito and Masson (1978).

FACTOR MARKET REDISTRIBUTION

This section considers surplus redistribution with simultaneous equilibrium in output and input markets. We begin with acreage-control programs. The issue in this context is how increases in rents to landowners due to an acreage-control program are related to changes in rents to nonland resources in agriculture and to changes in consumers' gains in the product market. To analyze this issue, we apply the model of Chap. 4, treating input a as land services, b as nonland inputs, and x as farm-level output. Consider a policy intended to make farmers better off by means of acreage control. It consists of setting a control level $\hat{a}$ less than a_0, which is competitive equilibrium. The resulting rents are

$$R_a = \hat{a}P_a - \int_0^{\hat{a}} S(a) \, da \qquad (8.19)$$

where P_a is the rental value of a as given by the demand for a at $\hat{a}$. Graphically, R_a is the hatched area in Fig. 8.3. To investigate surplus redistribution, we analyze changes in R_a as the differential of Eq. (8.19), substituting $P_a = f_a P_x$ from the profit-maximization condition.

$$
\begin{aligned}
dR_a &= d\,(aP_x f_a) - S(a) \, da \qquad (8.20)\\
&= aP_x\,(f_{aa} \, da + f_{ab} \, db) + P_x f_a \, da + af_a \, dP_x - S(a) \, da
\end{aligned}
$$

We expand $df_a = (f_{aa} \, da + f_{ab} \, db)$ because we cannot assume f_a to be a constant. Collecting terms, and using the facts for a linear homogeneous production function that $f_{aa} = bf_a f_b / ax\sigma$ and $f_{ab} = f_{ba} = f_a f_b / x\sigma$, where σ is the elasticity of substitution; and using VMP = factor price to eliminate f_a and f_b :

$$dR_a = -\frac{b P_a P_b}{\sigma X P_x} \, da + \frac{a P_a P_b}{\sigma X P_x} \, db + \frac{a P_a}{P_x} \, dP_x + P_a - S(a) \, da \ (8.21)$$

This expression can be simplified by placing it in relative terms. Define $ER_a = dR_a/aP_a$, that is, the change in rents as a percentage of factor payments. Dividing through by aP_a yields

$$ER_a = -\frac{k_b \, da}{\sigma a} + \frac{k_b \, db}{\sigma b} + \frac{dP_x}{P_x} + \left(1 - \frac{S(a)}{P_a}\right) \frac{da}{a} \qquad (8.22)$$

This can be written as an elasticity by dividing through by da/a. The first three right-hand-side terms are components of the derived demand for a (see Chap. 4). Recalling that P_a is price on the demand curve at $\hat{a}$ and $S(a)$ is price on the supply curve, Eq. (8.22) can be expressed as

$$\frac{ER_a}{Ea} = \frac{EP_a}{Ea} + T_a \qquad (8.23)$$

where EP_a / Ea is the price flexibility (elasticity of inverse derived demand func-

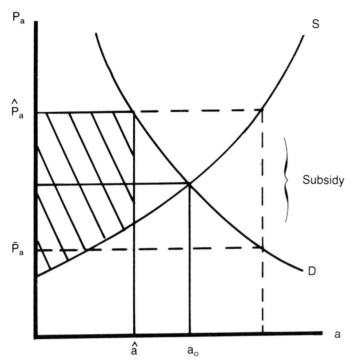

Figure 8.3 Rent creation by input control.

tion) of a, and T_a is the relative markup of demand price over supply price at $\hat{a}$, defined as $(P_a - S(a))/P_a$.

Making landowners as well off as possible involves choice of $\hat{a}$ to maximize R_a. The first-order condition is that Eq. (8.23) must equal zero, so that

$$- \frac{EP_a}{Ea} = T_a \qquad (8.24)$$

that is, the markup equals the absolute value of the inverse demand elasticity. This gives the analog for the present context of Lerner's results for monopoly pricing. His measure of monopoly power here is a measure of potential surplus extraction by a owners, in both cases the key factor being the inverse demand elasticity.

In order to explicitly solve for the extent of reduction in $\hat{a}$ from a_0, recall from Eq. (7.36) that with constant-elasticity supply and demand functions,

$$\frac{P_s}{P_d} = \left(\frac{\hat{Q}}{Q_0} \right)^{e-n}$$

where e is inverse elasticity of supply and n is inverse elasticity of demand. In the present context this means, substituting into Eq. (8.23):

$$\frac{ER_a}{Ea} = \frac{EP_a}{Ea} + 1 - \left(\frac{\hat{a}}{a_0}\right)^A \tag{8.25}$$

Where $A = 1/e_a - EP_a/Ea$. Thus, all we need to know to calculate the landowner optimal percentage cutback in acreage $(\hat{a}/a_0)$ is the elasticity of demand for and supply of land.

Trade-offs with Other Surpluses

Consider the rents to purchased inputs:

$$R_b = bP_b - \int_0^{\hat{b}} S(b)\,db \tag{8.26}$$

where $\hat{b}$ is the level of b that results in full equilibrium when $\hat{a}$ is chosen. Differentiating as above,

$$\frac{dR_b}{bP_b} = -\frac{K_a}{\sigma}\frac{db}{b} + \frac{Ka}{\sigma}\frac{da}{a} + \frac{dP_x}{P_x} + \left(1 - \frac{S(b)}{P_b}\right)\frac{db}{b} \tag{8.27}$$

The main analytical difference in the b market is that supply price equals demand price, $P_b = S(b)$, so that the far right-hand side term is zero. Consequently we have

$$\frac{ER_b}{Ea} = \frac{EP_b}{Ea} \tag{8.28}$$

Consider next the gains to consumers of X, called buyers' surplus, BS (it would be consumers' surplus if the buyers were final consumers).

$$BS = \int_0^{\hat{x}} D(x)\,dx - XP_x \tag{8.29}$$

$$dBS = P_x\,dx - XdP_x - P_x\,dx \tag{8.30}$$

$$EBS = \frac{dBS}{XP_x} = -\frac{dP_x}{P_x} \tag{8.31}$$

$$\frac{EBS}{Ea} = -\frac{EP_x}{Ea} \tag{8.32}$$

To make the relative surplus changes comparable, they must be normalized in terms of common-base dollar amounts. A convenient base for reference is expenditures on the agricultural product, XP_x. This leaves Eq. (8.32) unchanged, but requires multiplying Eq. (8.25) by K_a and Eq. (8.28) by K_b. The resulting three equations define a surplus transformation surface, generated by changes in $\hat{a}$.

What determines the characteristics of the transformation surface? Elasticities in Eqs. (8.25), (8.28), and (8.32) can be expressed in terms of underlying parameters as follows:

$$\frac{EP_a}{Ea} = \frac{e_b + K_a \sigma - K_b \eta}{D} \tag{8.33}$$

$$\frac{EP_b}{Ea} = \frac{K_a (\sigma + \eta)}{D} \tag{8.34}$$

$$\frac{EP_x}{Ea} = \frac{K_a (\sigma + e_b)}{D} \tag{8.35}$$

where the common denominator D is $\eta\sigma + e_b (K_a \eta - K_b \sigma)$. These results have been derived in Chap. 4. The changes in surpluses (normalized on XP_x) can thus be expressed as

$$\frac{ER_a}{Ea} = K_a \left[\frac{e_b + K_a \sigma - K_b \eta}{D} + 1 - \left(\frac{\hat{a}}{a_0} \right)^A \right] \tag{8.36}$$

$$\frac{ER_b}{Ea} = \frac{K_a K_b (\sigma + \eta)}{D} \tag{8.37}$$

$$\frac{EBS}{Ea} = - \frac{K_a (\sigma + e_b)}{D} \tag{8.38}$$

where

$$A = \frac{1}{e_a} - \frac{EP_a}{Ea} = \frac{D - e_a (e_b + K_a \sigma - K_b \eta)}{e_a D}$$

Assuming that $\eta < 0$, $e_a > 0$, and $e_b > 0$, we know that $D < 0$. This implies that Eq. (8.38) is positive. Thus, when policy reduces $\hat{a}$ [carets (hats) were omitted from Ea expressions for convenience], BS declines. The sign of Eq. (8.37) is negative if $\sigma > - \eta$, i.e., reducing $\hat{a}$ increases rents to b owners if b is a good enough substitute for a in production.

The sign of Eq. (8.36) is indeterminate, so it is uncertain whether a reduction in $\hat{a}$ will increase rents to a owners, contrary to what might be expected. The expression $1 - (a/a_0)^A$ is positive (and between 0 and 1), but the other term in brackets is negative. Note that when $\hat{a} = a_0$, i.e., no intervention, the right-hand part is $1 - 1 = 0$. Therefore, Eq. (8.36) is negative, and reducing $\hat{a}$ makes a owners better off. So if there has been no intervention, a owners can always be made better off by a sufficiently small reduction in a. As $\hat{a}$ decreases, the positive component of Eq. (8.36) increases. When does the whole expression become positive? Referring back to Eq. (8.24), maximum R_a is attained when the positive term equals the absolute value of the negative term. Thus, the a owners are made worse off when $\hat{a}$ is reduced below the monopoly quantity. Note also that the largest the positive term can be is 1, so that R_a always increases with a decline in $\hat{a}$ if the derived demand function for a is inelastic.

The deadweight loss from a reduction in $\hat{a}$ is the sum of surplus gains: $ER_a + ER_b + EBS$. From Eqs. (8.36) to (8.38), this is

$$\frac{EW}{Ea} = \frac{K_a(e_b + K_a\sigma - K_b\eta + K_b\sigma + K_b\eta - \sigma - e_b)}{D}$$
$$+ K_a\left[1 - \left(\frac{\hat{a}}{a_0}\right)^A\right] \tag{8.39}$$
$$= K_a\left[1 - \left(\frac{\hat{a}}{a_0}\right)^A\right]$$

There is a deadweight loss if $\hat{a}/a_0 < 1$. For very small interventions, policy redistributes surpluses with only a small EW, but as the intervention becomes larger, EW increases at an increasing rate. To show this, divide Eq. (8.39) by Eq. (8.37) plus Eq. (8.38) to find the marginal deadweight loss per dollar redistributed from nonlandowners:

$$\frac{EW}{ER_b + EBS} = \frac{D[1 - (\hat{a}/a_0)^A]}{K_a\sigma + K_b\eta - e_b} = -\frac{Ea}{EP_a}\left[1 - \left(\frac{\hat{a}}{a_0}\right)^A\right] \tag{8.40}$$

The derivative of this expression with respect to $\hat{a}/a_0$ is negative, meaning that the rate of increase of deadweight loss increases as $\hat{a}/a_0$ decreases.

Examples to show how redistribution possibilities and associated deadweight losses depend on parameter values are given in Table 8.1. The first five columns show values for the basic parameters of the system. Their values are chosen in line 1 to be plausible for U.S. agriculture: inelastic product demand (-0.4), inelastic land supply (0.2), more elastic nonland supply (1.2), and limited possibilities for substituting land for nonland inputs in farm production $(\sigma = 0.5)$. The results of a 15-percent reduction in land use are a gain in rents to land of 6.4 (percent of free-market commodity revenue), a gain of 0.4 in nonland rents, and a loss of 8.3 in buyers' surplus (consumers' surplus plus middlemen's rents). This adds up to a deadweight loss of 1.5. In dollar magnitudes, for a $60 billion crop sector, the gains to landowners would be $3.8 billion and the deadweight loss, $1.2 billion.

The second line of Table 8.1 shows what happens if we double the percentage land diversion to 30 percent. The gains to landowners less than double, while the deadweight loss more than doubles. The increasing rate of deadweight loss is also shown in the marginal rate of surplus transfer (MST) column which shows the *marginal* trade-off between gains to landowners and losses to others. Thus, the value of -0.7 means that for a marginal acre diverted, landowners gain 70 cents per $1 given up by all others; equivalently, there is a deadweight loss of 30 cents per dollar transferred to landowners.

Successive lines of Table 8.1 show what happens as η and σ vary. A more elastic product-demand curve reduces the efficiency of redistribution, as does a greater elasticity of substitution. Note that the sign of ΔR_b varies. This reflects the standard result that when $\sigma > -\eta$, the cross elasticity of factor demand is positive, but when $\sigma < -\eta$, it is negative. The last line shows a case meant to represent an exported crop, such as U.S. wheat. Here we have a very elastic demand function, Cobb-Douglas substitution possibilities, and more elastic land and other input supplies, since we are considering a single crop. The efficiency of redistribution through land controls is quite low, but the possibility of gains to land still exists. The 1.7-percent increase in land rents amounts to $1.7 \times 4 = 6.8$ percent of free-market land income (since free-market land returns are by assumption one-fourth of free-market revenues: $K_a = 0.25$). While it costs a dollar in deadweight losses for every dollar transferred to landowners, and the amount that can be redistributed is not large, it is nonetheless incorrect to say

Table 8.1   Redistribution under Alternative Parameter Values

Value by Parameters

η	σ	e_a	e_b	K_a	Ea/EPa*	$\hat{a}/a_0$	$\Delta R_a^\dagger$	$\Delta R_b^\ddagger$	$\Delta BS^\S$	$\Delta W^\parallel$	MST#
-0.4	0.5	0.2	1.2	0.25	-0.47	0.85	6.4	0.4	-8.3	-1.5	-0.70
-0.4	0.5	0.2	1.2	0.25	-0.47	0.70	11.2	0.8	-16.7	-4.7	-0.56
-1.5	0.5	0.2	1.2	0.25	-0.67	0.85	4.2	-1.8	-3.8	-1.4	-0.59
-0.4	0.2	0.2	1.2	0.25	-0.24	0.85	13.6	-2.0	-13.8	-2.2	-0.82
-0.4	1.0	0.2	1.2	0.25	-0.81	0.85	3.3	1.4	-6.0	-1.4	-0.52
-6.0	1.0	0.5	2.0	0.25	-1.56	0.85	-1.7	-1.3	-1.1	-0.7	-0.50

*Computed from Eq. (4.15).
†From Eq. (8.36), integrating over $\hat{a}/a_0$ from 1.00 to 0.85.
‡From Eq. (8.37).
§From Eq. (8.38).
∥$\Delta R_a + \Delta R_b + \Delta BS$.
#MST-marginal rate of surplus transfer from Eq. (8.40).

that acreage controls are counterproductive to landowners even in this extreme case. However, in this case, much of the losses are borne by suppliers of non-land agricultural inputs. If these are farm-supplied inputs (rather than purchased inputs) the gains to farmers are reduced. If these inputs are purchased inputs, then we would expect their producers, for example, fertilizer and chemical manufacturers, to emerge as political opponents of the program.

Equation (8.39) is sufficient to establish that the deadweight loss from an acreage control program is fully measured by the standard triangular area in the land market, given that the demand function for land is a ''total'' function which permits other prices to adjust to maintain equilibrium in all input and the output markets. This follows from the definition of A as determined by elasticities of demand and supply for a as developed above. This is the same result as obtained by Wisecarver (1974) and Just et al. (1982) in slightly different contexts.

Optimal Acreage Controls?

Despite the deadweight losses, redistribution is optimal given $\Theta > 1$ for producers in the SWF. But it makes an important difference whether the interest group with high Θ is farmers or landowners. Suppose it is still farmers, as in Chap. 7. Then we are interested in measuring the sum of R_a and R_b, assuming farmers own both inputs. The SWF (at least locally) is

$$W = \Theta (R_a + R_b) + BS \qquad (8.41)$$

For a socially optimal acreage-control program, we differentiate with respect to a and set $dW/da = 0$:

$$\Theta \left(\frac{dRa}{da} + \frac{dRb}{da} \right) + \frac{dBS}{da} = 0$$

Using Eqs. (8.36) to (8.38),

$$\Theta \left[\frac{K_a (e_b + K_a \sigma - K_b \eta)}{D} + 1 - \hat{\alpha}^A + \frac{K_a K_b (\sigma + \eta)}{D} \right] \qquad (8.42)$$
$$- \frac{K_a (\sigma + e_b)}{D} = 0$$

where $\hat{\alpha}$ is $\hat{a}/a_0$, the percent of base acres cropped. Solving for the optimal $\hat{\alpha}$

$$\hat{\alpha}^* = \frac{(\Theta [1 + K_a (e_b + \sigma) /D] - K_a (\sigma + e_b) /D)^{1/A}}{\Theta} \qquad (8.43)$$

If $\Theta = 1$, then $\hat{\alpha}^* = 1$, i.e., no intervention is optimal.

The marginal rate of surplus transformation between producers and consumers is obtained by dividing Eq. (8.36) plus Eq. (8.37) by Eq. (8.38):

$$MST = \frac{ER_a + ER_b}{EBS_c} = \frac{K_a(e_b + \sigma) + 1 - \hat{\alpha}^A}{K_a(e_b + \sigma)}$$

$$= 1 + \frac{1 - \hat{\alpha}^A}{K_a(e_b + \sigma)} \tag{8.44}$$

From Eq. (7.18) we have the corresponding trade-off for a production control. As $\hat{a}$ decreases, we trace out an STC that lies inside the corresponding one (ϵ_x consistent with e_a, e_b, and σ) in Fig. 7.2. In this sense, an acreage-control program is less efficient than a production-control program, although in the limiting case in which $\sigma = 0$, they are equally efficient (controlling acreage is tantamount to controlling production).

Figure 8.4 may help show the economic intuition behind these facts. Pro-

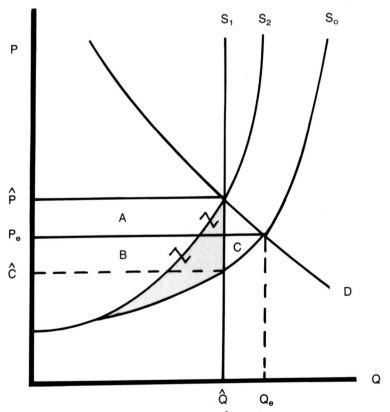

Figure 8.4 Acreage control versus production control.

duction controls that fix supply at $\hat{Q}$ generate producer gains $A - C$. Acreage controls can be set up to shift supply to S_2 and give the same output, and so the same consumer costs and producer benefits $A - C$. But in addition, the higher marginal costs, owing to using more nonland inputs per acre, create added producer costs of the shaded area. Therefore, the acreage control STC must be below the production control STC for any $\hat{Q}$ and consumer loss selected.

Income distribution with production controls must take into account the rents created for owners of rights to produce ("quota"). As analyzed in Chap. 4, the rental value of quota is a factor price that can be analyzed in the same way as P_a and P_b have been. In Chap. 6, Eq. (6.15), the effect of changing the production quota level was found, in elasticity terms, to be

$$\frac{ER_x}{Ex} = T_x\left(1 + \frac{1}{\eta}\right) - \left(1 + \frac{1}{\epsilon}\right)$$

where T_x is the ratio P_x / C_x. Quota rents are maximized by equating this expression to zero, which yields

$$T_x^* = \frac{1 + 1/\epsilon}{1 + 1/\eta} \tag{8.45}$$

The economic meaning of this result can be examined readily assuming ϵ and η are constant parameters. Then we have the constant elasticity demand and supply curves as given by Eqs. (7.34) and (7.35), which using Eq. (7.36) implies that the optimal cutback is given by

$$\frac{X^*}{X_0} = \frac{1 + 1/\epsilon}{1 + 1/\eta} \exp \frac{1}{1/\epsilon - 1/\eta} \tag{8.46}$$

where X^*/X_0 is the controlled output level as a fraction of no-program output. From Eq. (7.34), multiplying by Q and differentiating with respect to Q yields marginal revenue as $(1/\eta + 1) P_d$. The same operations on Eq. (7.35) yield marginal input cost as $(1/\epsilon + 1) P_s$. The profit maximization condition for a monopolist which is also a monopsonist is to equate marginal revenue and marginal cost, i.e., $P_d / P_s = (1/\epsilon + 1)/(1/\eta + 1)$. But this is just Eq. (8.45). Therefore maximizing quota rents duplicates the market solution for a joint monopolist/monopsonist.

COMPARISON OF INPUT AND OUTPUT SUBSIDIES

Referring back to Table 4.2, the effects of input subsidies are similar to those of acreage controls. They, too, are inefficient relative to a general production subsidy in transferring income to producers because they also distort input as well as output decisions. However, it was also shown in Chap. 4 that an equal rate of subsidy paid to all inputs is equivalent to a general production subsidy. They trace out the same STC and are therefore equally efficient.

Considering the possibility of subsidies on several inputs simultaneously, a possibility neglected in the preceding discussion of acreage controls, raises further issues. It turns out that we can, in general, find a combination of input subsidies that will be more efficient than equal subsidization of all inputs, and therefore more efficient than output subsidization, whatever the objective of policy is. This is shown by Chambers (1985) in a quite general model where the objective of policy is to ensure the survival of a subset of (marginal) farms. The proposition also holds in our simpler case of $\Theta > 1$ for producers, in which we want to transfer income to farmers as a group at least cost to consumers and taxpayers.

Consider the objective of aiding producers as owners of factors a and b. Their gains can be represented graphically as in Fig. 8.3 with reference to a subsidy V_a sufficient to drive the market price of the down to $\check{P}_a$ and the factor-owners' receipts up to $\hat{P}_a$. The gains to a owners are analogous to producers' gains from a deficiency payment program. Therefore, the optimum subsidy coefficient, defined as V_a, where $S(a) = V_a P_a$ (i.e., $V_a = 1 +$ subsidy rate), are given by Eqs. (8.14) and (8.16):

$$V_a^* = \frac{1}{1 - (1/\epsilon_a)(\Theta - 1)} \tag{8.47}$$

$$V_b^* = \frac{1}{1 - (1/\epsilon_b)(\Theta - 1)}$$

The rates are not equal unless $\epsilon_a = \epsilon_b$, and the input least elastic in supply gets the highest rate of subsidy.

To study the redistribution caused by alternative values for V_a and V_b, we use the relationships of Table 4.2 when T_a and T_b are both nonzero. The price and quantity changes can be used to calculate gains or losses to producers $(R_a + R_b)$, consumers, and taxpayers using formulas like Eqs. (8.8) to (8.11). An example may help clarify issues of inputs and output subsidies. Use the parameter values of the top line of Table 8.1, adding $\Theta = 1.05$. From Eqs. (8.47), the optimal subsidy rates are $V_a^* = 1.33$ and $V_b^* = 1.04$, a much higher subsidy rate for the inelastic input. This point can be plotted as in Fig. 8.2 for a commodity subsidy. In Fig. 8.5 we consider the quantitative consequences of setting the "wrong" subsidies. Using $\Delta w = \Delta G_c - \Delta T + 1.05 \, (\Delta R_a + \Delta R_b)$, we have an index that is zero when $V_a = V_b = 1.0$, i.e., no intervention, and has positive values for all subsidies that yield a social gain. (If Θ were 1.0 instead of 1.05, Δw would be negative for all $V_a, V_b \neq 1$, and so would be

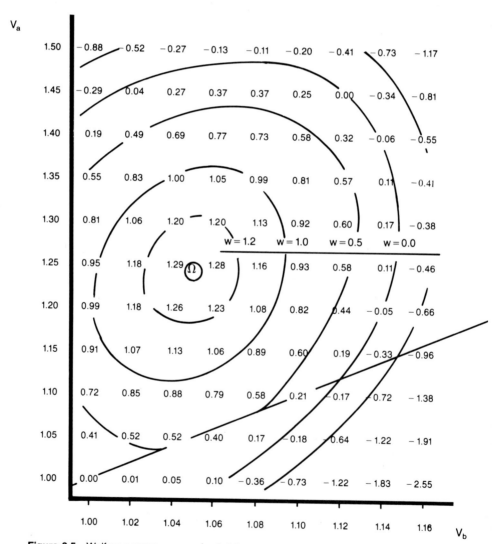

Figure 8.5 Welfare consequences of subsidies.

maximized at the origin). The numbers in Fig. 8.5 are the altitude of the welfare hill as given by the Δw index. The ray from the origin denoting equal subsidies for the two inputs is not a 45° line because the diagram is scaled to include much higher subsidy rates for V_a. The supply of a is so inelastic that the optimal point (Ω) requires a to receive a much higher subsidy rate than b. Some contour lines (SICs) of equal altitude are sketched in. Note that the optimum is different from the calculated values of Eq. (8.47), showing the approximation errors caused by omitting the higher order terms from the Taylor series approximation that underlies the Δw calculation using Eqs. (8.10) to (8.12).

If the subsidies are large enough to be outside of the $\Delta w = 0$ contour, despite favoring producers, we are worse off than with no intervention. Producers are better off, but not enough to offset the losses of consumers and taxpayers. If Θ were larger than 1.05, the $\Delta w = 0$ contour would be pushed further to the northeast. The same effect would result from lower input supply elasticities or a higher product-demand elasticity, since the rate of increase of deadweight losses (which are what prevent subsidization, once begun, from increasing indefinitely) would be less. The slope of the path or steepest ascent from the origin to Ω measures the marginal efficiency of surplus transformation.

GAINS AND LOSSES WITH A RETAIL SECTOR AND MIDDLEMEN

Difficulties in identifying areas under demand curves as consumers' gains have been discussed, but a possibly more important problem has been ignored: the people who buy farm products are typically not consumers. They are processors, cooperatives, or middlemen who use agricultural products as raw material. Instead of consumers' surplus we really have "buyers' surplus" when we calculate the gains in the X market in the preceding models. If changes in P_x were passed through dollar for dollar to final consumers of food products, the problem would dissolve. But, as shown in Chap. 5, this will not in general occur. The prices of marketing services will change when P_x changes, and thus the markup between farm and retail will change. So we need to deal explicitly with the relationship between areas under demand curves at different stages of a "vertical" market chain. We begin by spelling out such such relationships for input and output demand functions.

Economic Meaning of Some Quasi-Surpluses

Consider the surplus area under the derived demand function for a. This is defined analogously to consumers' surplus, i.e.,

$$CS_a = \int_0^{\hat{a}} D(a)\, da - aP_a$$

$$\frac{dCS_a}{da} = D(a) - a\frac{dP_a}{da} - P_a \qquad\qquad (8.48)$$

$$\frac{ECS_a}{Ea} = \frac{dCS_a}{aP_a}\frac{a}{da} = -\frac{EP_a}{Ea}$$

since $D(a) = P_a$. Normalizing on XP_x, as above, yields Eqs. (8.48) times K_a.

Our first result is that the surplus area under the demand function for input a is the sum of the surplus area under the demand function for product X and the rents of other inputs b. This is a particular result of the kind derived in Just et al. (1982, Appendix D). It is more restricted in that Just et al. permit many commodities and factors, but more general in that, in their model, resources are either fixed in quantity or else have given prices (perfectly elastic supply).

To demonstrate the result, we need to show that

$$\frac{ECS_a}{Ea} = \frac{EBS}{Ea} + \frac{ER_b}{Ea}$$

Substituting from Eqs. (8.48), (8.32), and (8.28):

$$-K_a\frac{EP_a}{Ea} = -\frac{EP_x}{Ea} + K_b\frac{EP_b}{Ea}$$

Using Eqs. (8.33), (8.37), and (8.38):[4]

$$-K_a\frac{e_b + K_a\sigma - K_b\eta}{D} = -\frac{K_a(\sigma + e_b)}{D} + \frac{K_a K_b(\sigma + \eta)}{D}$$

$$\frac{e_b + K_b\sigma - K_b\eta}{D} = \frac{\sigma + e_b - K_b\sigma - K_b\eta}{D} = \frac{e_b + K_a\sigma - K_b\eta}{D}$$

With this result, we are in a better position to understand the economic meaning of EBS, the percentage change (buyers surplus as a percentage of XP_x) in the surplus area under the farm-product demand function. For this purpose, we expand the model of Eqs. (4.1) to (4.5) to add the final demand function for food products, y, the supply function of marketing inputs, c, used to transform farm output into food, and an industry production function for the marketing process. The marketing sector is assumed competitive. The added equations are

Final demand:	$P_y = D(y)$	$D' < 0$	(8.49)
Supply of C:	$P_c = S(c)$	$S' > 0$	(8.50)
Production function, c.r.s.	$Y = g(x,c)$		(8.51)
Equilibrium condition	$P_c = g_c P_y$		(8.52)
and	$P_x = g_x P_y$		(8.53)

Equation (8.53) replaces the product-demand equation (4.6), giving a system of 10 equations in 10 variables [prices and quantities of 1 final (food) good, one intermediate (farm) good, and three inputs including one marketing input and two farm-level inputs].

The demand for the farm product X is now a derived demand. EBS/Ea can now be expanded just as ECS_a was in Eq. (8.48). This shows that farm-level "consumers'" surplus, called buyers' surplus, BS here, is equal to the sum of true consumers' surplus [using Eq. (8.49)] plus rents to marketing inputs, R_c. Figure 8.6 shows this result graphically for the special case in which $\sigma = 0$ in Eq. (8.51) — fixed proportions between c and x in marketing.

The determinants of changes in farm-level buyers' surplus can be analyzed from the expansion:

$$\frac{EBS}{Ea} = \frac{K_x (K_c \eta_y - K_x \sigma_y - e_c)}{\eta_y \sigma_y + e_c (K_x \eta_y - K_c \sigma_y)} \qquad (8.54)$$

where K_y is the share of farm product revenues in consumer food expenditures, $K_x + K_c = 1$, and η_y refers now to consumers' elasticity of demand for food.

Two special cases are of interest. First, when $\sigma_y = 0$, we have the fixed-proportions case shown in Fig. 8.6. Equation (8.54) becomes much simpler,

$$\frac{EBS}{Ea} = \frac{K_c \eta_y - e_c}{e_c \eta_y} \qquad (8.55)$$

Second, when in addition $e_c \to \infty$, we have

$$\frac{EBS}{Ea} = -\frac{1}{\eta_y} \qquad (8.56)$$

i.e., when marketing inputs are available at given prices (earn no rents), farm-level buyers' surplus changes equal final consumer surplus changes.

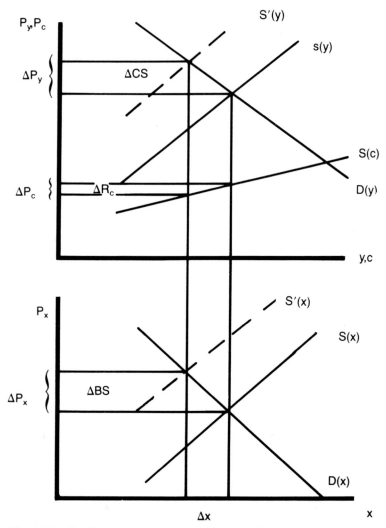

Figure 8.6 Retail consumers' surplus and farm-level buyers' surplus.

[1]With fixed proportions the units of measurement for c and x can be chosen such that c = 1 and x = 1 are quantities required to produce y = 1, and P_x and P_c are the input costs per unit so defined. The derived demand function for x is the vertical difference between D(y) and S(c). Therefore when a shift in S(x) generates Δx, the resulting distances add up as $\Delta P_x = \Delta P_y + \Delta P_c$, and since the quantity changes are equal, we have that the areas $\Delta BS = \Delta CS + \Delta R_c$.

Surplus Transformation in the Extended Model

The five-market system of Eqs. (4.1) to (4.5) and (8.49) to (8.53) is the basis for an analysis of surplus transfers that isolates the gains of middlemen (suppliers of marketing services) and final consumers' surplus. To analyze farm-level gains from acreage controls, we now replace η in Eqs. (8.36) and (8.37) by the derived demand elasticity:

$$\eta_x = \frac{\eta_y \sigma_y - e_c (K_x \eta_y - K_c \sigma_y)}{e_c + K_x \sigma_y + K_c \eta_y}$$

To normalize the changes on YP_y, both equations are also multiplied by K_x. Rents to middlemen are

$$\frac{ER_c}{Ea} = \frac{K_x K_c (\sigma_y + \eta_y)}{\eta_y \sigma_y + e_c (K_x \eta_y - K_c \sigma_y)} \tag{8.57}$$

Final consumers' surplus is

$$\frac{ECS}{Ea} = \frac{- K_x (\sigma_y + e_c)}{\eta_y \sigma_y + e_c (K_x \eta_y - \sigma_y)} \tag{8.58}$$

Derivations are by the same method as for Eqs. (8.37) and (8.38) in the simpler model.

Under the acreage control program, there is no independent surplus in the X (farm product) market. "Consumers' surplus" there (BS as defined earlier) is the sum of R_c and CS, from Eqs. (8.57) and (8.58). Producers' surplus at the farm level is the sum of R_a and R_b. However, rents could be created in the X market by means of production controls achieved by issuance of licenses or quotas as discussed earlier.

Grain-Livestock Interests

Conflicts of interest between grain and livestock producers were prominent in the U.S. PIK program of 1983, under which feed supplies were substantially reduced. The vertically extended model can be readily applied to analyze the surplus trade-offs between these groups. Let y be livestock output, x feed grains, c cattle feeders' nonfeed inputs, with a cropland and b nonland inputs in producing feed crops. Now, the change in R_c from Eq. (8.57) measures the gains of the cattle feeders from a production control program (assuming nonfeed inputs are owned by cattle feeders). The sign of Eq. (8.57) is negative whenever $\sigma_y > -\eta_y$. That is, if the elasticity of substitution between feed and nonfeed inputs in cattle feeding is greater than the elasticity of demand for fed cattle, then a reduction in feed output will increase rents to feedlot owners. The opposition of cattle feeders to feed grain output controls suggests that, in fact, $\sigma_y < -\eta_y$. Using USDA cattle feeding budgets with $K_x = 0.4$ and $K_c = 0.6$, and values of $\sigma_y = 0.1$ (feed and feedlot services are almost but not quite used in fixed proportions), $\eta_y = -0.8$ and $e_c = 1$, we obtain

$$\frac{ER_c}{EX} = \frac{(0.4)\,(0.6)\,(0.1-0.8)}{-0.8\,(0.1) + 1\,[0.4\,(-0.8) - 0.6\,(0.1)]} = 0.37$$

That is, a 10-percent feed grain cutback reduces the rents of cattle feeders by 3.7 percent. This moderate loss would disturb cattle feeders, undoubtedly, but more serious adverse consequences would occur if feedlot services were less elastic in supply. Suppose that in the very short run (a 2- to 3-month period), the number of cattle on feed is difficult to change, so that $e_c = 0.1$. In this case the 10-percent feed supply reduction causes the rents of cattle feeders to fall by 14.2 percent (as compared to 3.7 percent when $e_c = 1.0$).

Nonfarm Suppliers of Farm Inputs

In Chap. 6, we examined some implications of outside investment in agriculture which is induced by tax preferences. In general, there is a problem that commodity price supports create rents for both farm and nonfarm suppliers of inputs. Often it is presumed that farmers supply the more inelastic (low ϵ) ones and, thus, earn most of the rents. But this need not be the case, and in any event is not so relevant when we consider input subsidies or acreage restraints.

A straightforward way to analyze farm and off-farm owners of agricultural inputs as separate interest groups is by means of the two-input model where a is farm-owned inputs and b is inputs supplied by nonfarmers (workers, bankers, seed, fertilizer, and equipment sellers) We are not dealing here with off-farm ownership of traditionally farm-owned inputs (notably land).

The specification does not change the structure of the model used to simulate program effects. The major change is in the objective function. In contrast to Eq. (8.41), we express a SWF favoring farmers by multiplying only R_a and not R_b by $\Theta > 1$. To analyze how this changes the optimal input-quantity control, suppose we limit the quantity of farm-supplied inputs. This is analytically the same as acreage controls as analyzed in Eqs. (8.41) to (8.44), except that a now stands for a different collection of inputs. With the change in objective function, Eq. (8.44) becomes

$$\frac{ER_a}{ER_b + EBS_c} = -\eta_a(1 - \hat{\alpha})^A - 1 \qquad (8.59)$$

where η_a is the elasticity of demand for a [$= \eta\sigma + e_b(K_a\eta - K_b\sigma)/(e_b + K_a\sigma - K_b\eta)$] and the percentage changes in surpluses are now normalized on aP_a instead of XP_x. That is, Eq. (8.59) tells how much R_a rises as a percentage of a's gross receipts, when $R_b + BS$ fall by 1 percent of these same receipts.

The optimal percentage reduction in a, $\hat{\alpha}^*$, is now [modifying Eqs. (8.41) and (8.42) to eliminate as a Θ factor of R_b):

$$\alpha^* = \left(1 + \frac{1}{\eta_a} - \frac{1}{\Theta\eta_a}\right)^{1/A} \qquad (8.60)$$

If $\Theta = 1$, the $\eta\hat{\alpha}^* = 1$, i.e., no intervention is optimal. If $\Theta \to \infty$, i.e., farmers get all the weight and input suppliers and consumers get none, then $\hat{\alpha}^* = 1 + 1/\eta_a)^{1/A}$. This is the equilibrium condition for monopoly in a, paralleling the Chap. 7 outcome for producers under supply control.

If policy favors the a suppliers, then the optimal intervention is control of a; control of x is less efficient. This is the analog of the earlier conclusion (see Fig. 8.4) that a control is less efficient than x control when policy is intended to aid x suppliers. But there is a complication. Following from the results for optimal input subsidies, *all* of the options mentioned can be improved upon by supplementing controls on x or a with controls on b.

Continuing with the welfare function in which $\Theta > 1$ for R_a only, Eq. (8.42) as modified to analyze a change in b is:

$$\frac{EW}{Eb} = \frac{K_b(e_a + K_b\sigma + K_a\eta)}{D} + 1 - \beta^B \qquad (8.61)$$
$$+ \frac{\Theta K_a K_b(\sigma + \eta)}{D} - \frac{K_b\sigma - K_b e_a}{D}$$

where $B = 1/e_b - 1/\eta_b$ and $\hat{\beta}$ is b/b_0, the ratio of controlled to no-program usage of b. Simplifying, normalizing on aP_a, dividing by K_a, and equating to zero to find the optimal intervention $\hat{\beta}^*$:

$$\hat{\beta}^* = \left[1 + \frac{K_b(\sigma + \eta)}{D}(\Theta - 1)\right]^{1/B} \qquad (8.62)$$

If $\Theta = 1$, then $\hat{\beta}* = 1$, i.e., no controls on b, as for $\hat{\alpha}*$. The new result here is that $\beta* \neq 1$ even if $\Theta > 1$ (assuming $\sigma \neq -\eta$). Moreover, whether $\hat{\beta}* \gtrless$ 1 depends on whether $\sigma \gtrless -\eta$. The economic reason is that if $\sigma > -\eta$ reducing the quantity of b will increase the demand for a, hence increasing R_a. But if $\sigma < -\eta$ reducing b will reduce the demand for a. We would like therefore to increase the quantity of b, which means $\hat{\beta}* > 1$. Presumably this would require subsidy of b. We will analyze optimal policy *given* a subsidy of b, with b standing for off-farm capital in agriculture.

The preceding discussion suggests that even when $\Theta > 1$ for a owners, we still might want to subsidize b owners. For a concrete case of this the ΔW hill of Fig. 8.5 is recalculated for the R_a-favoring ΔW function. The new altitude map, with all elasticities the same as in Fig. 8.5, is shown in Fig. 8.7. We find V_a^* essentially unchanged, while V_b^* is greatly reduced (from a 4.8- to a 1.0-percent subsidy). But the rate of subsidy is not zero.

CONSUMERS VERSUS TAXPAYERS, AND OTHER WELFARE WEIGHTINGS

Consumers and taxpayers have been assigned the same Θ, by convention, $\Theta = 1$, throughout the preceding discussion. This can be justified because for many policies consumers and taxpayers are essentially the same group of people. However, in some commodity programs, the losses to consumers who would lose under production controls are quite differently distributed from the losses of taxpayers under deficiency payments. This is particularly the case when a price support applies to a commodity consumed heavily by the poor while the system of taxation is progressive. For example, suppose canned beans are consumed entirely by people with incomes less than \$20,000, but that if bean producers are subsidized, the payments are tied to a tax on BMW automobiles paid only by people with incomes greater than \$20,000. Then consumers and taxpayers are distinct sets of people, and if poor people are favored in the SWF, i.e., Θ is higher for them, this can readily change the optimal policy choice.

More generally, Θ's could be different over income classes; or it could vary continuously with income, for example, decreasing as income increases. In comparing production controls with subsidy payments, this situation again would lead to a tendency favoring payments over production controls (although deadweight losses determined by ϵ and η are still important). But more fundamentally, Θ's varying with income suggests a system of taxes and transfers geared to an income tax system rather than commodity market intervention. Optimal income tax structure for such circumstances (economy wide) have been

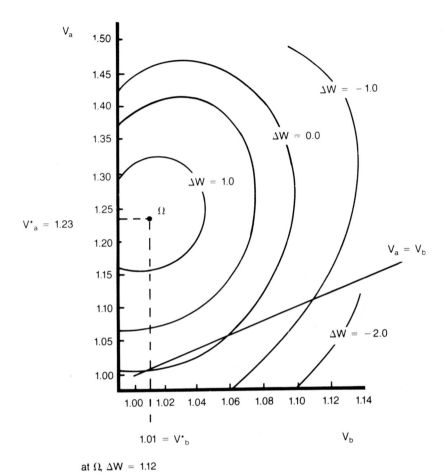

Figure 8.7 Welfare effects of subsidies, $\Theta > 1$ for *a* owners.

rigorously developed in recent public finance literature (summarized concisely in Atkinson and Stiglitz, 1980, Lecture 13). An analogous approach to a market in which different consumers have different Θ's leads to optimal nonlinear pricing—consumer prices which vary with quantities purchased—which has been thoroughly developed for pricing public utilities (see Brown and Sibley, 1986). Chambers (1987) has applied a similar approach to commodity market intervention where producers vary by their possession of an efficiency parameter, and Θ in the SWF depends on this parameter. This approach when fully developed may provide a means of unifying the welfare analysis of intergroup redistribution and structural redistribution within a group.

ENDNOTES

1. Note also that $EP_x/EV_x > -1$, because the numerator is smaller than the denominator in absolute value.
2. Note that as Θ becomes larger a point is reached (in this example, when $\Theta = \hat{\epsilon}_x + 1 = 1.307$) where the optimal V_x^* increases indefinitely. Allowing Θ to decrease as producers became richer relative to consumers, as a convex social indifference curve would do, can eliminate this possibility.
3. EV_x is approximated by $\ln 1.48 = 0.392$ and EV_y by $\ln 1.18 = 0.166$.
4. It similarly can be shown that the change in producers' surplus calculated from the derived supply curve of X is the sum of the change in rents $(R_a + R_b)$. The proof expands EP_x/EX using Eq. (4.12).

Chapter 9

Second-Best Policies

A point made in the quotation from Brandow (1977) in Chap. 7 and emphasized in many evaluations of farm policy is that agricultural markets are imperfect. This may seem an uncontroversial point since undoubtedly nothing is perfect in human affairs, but in fact all the models and calculations to this point
assume that, in the absence of intervention, the commodity markets would be
at a competitive equilibrium. Moreover, it has been assumed that, at this competitive equilibrium, the supply price (marginal cost) measures the full social
costs of the commodity and that the market price measures the full value of the
commodity to every consumer, that is, that no externalities or distortions exist
elsewhere in the economy.

Arguments are rife on the significance of monopoly power, externalities,
and other imperfections of agricultural markets, and whatever the outcome of
these arguments, we know that thousands of distortions exist in nonagricultural
markets. The existence of these imperfections opens the door for "second-
best" agricultural policies, defined as interventions that are Pareto improving
given the other imperfections. This chapter considers how to discover such policies and set policy instruments appropriately. It considers first economists'

conceptions of a ''farm problem'' of general market failure in agriculture. Then we discuss issues of monopoly and monopsony power, external costs, and incomplete markets. Finally, there is a treatment of second-best programs when distortions exist elsewhere in the economy.

ECONOMISTS' CONCEPTIONS OF THE FARM PROBLEM

The symptom of the ''farm problem'' that has received most attention from U.S. agricultural economists is a chronic tendency for low commodity prices and farm incomes, with a consequent decline in the number of farmers and problems in both rural and urban areas because of it. What needs to be explained is the nature of the problem (what do we mean by ''low'' prices and incomes), the causes of the problem, how the various manifestations of it fit together, and how remedies can be found. In particular, what needs to be explained is how the problem can be understood in terms of an elaborated supply–demand model.

In basic economic theory, the supply–demand equilibrium of a market is derived assuming perfectly competitive producers and full knowledge of prices and other relevant facts by all market participants. Perhaps the farm problem is attributable to failure of these assumptions. Consider the following critique of a proposal by the Eisenhower administration to reduce farm price support levels:

> Perfect competition is not an adequate model for agriculture, and it is not an appropriate norm for either agriculture or nonagriculture, the Administration's apparent views to the contrary notwithstanding.
>
> Reviewing the perfectly competitive model briefly in terms of its large numbers of firms, homogenous products, and easy mobility of factors suggests something that could be mistaken for agriculture. If the mistake is not realized, it is easy for a person's thinking to leave the real world and to endow agriculture with all the conduct and performance characteristics of perfect competition. These would include market prices that are equal to cost including normal profit, production adjustment within and among firms through exit so that supply and demand are equal at satisfactory prices. Any displacement from equilibrium brings about automatic, swift, and precise restoration of equilibrium again at prices covering the costs, including normal profits, or producers.
>
> From this point the Administration easily makes another mistaken shift to the welfare norms of the model. The equilibria are presumed to be consistent with an optimum allocation of resoruces, most efficient production, and payments to factors in accordance ''with what they are worth.''
>
> Both of these mistakes lead to policy proposals that presume to be good for farmers whether they know it or not and also good for society. This is the best of everything. Its consequence is that the Administration favors going from high supports to lower supports, to even lower support based on recent market prices, to freeing agriculture so lower prices will increase consumption, simultaneously re-

duce output, and the production machinery will be back in gear. It leads to a conviction that getting the government out of agriculture is an end to be sought as perfection itself.

These proposals are mistakes because the competitive model is inappropriate for the problem. Consideration of the market structure of agriculture should be convincing on this score.

Exit is not easy from agriculture. Because of the lack of realistic alternatives farm labor resources are not sufficiently mobile. Knowledge is not perfect. The arts are not static, as the technological revolution eloquently testifies. Yet easy exit, substitutability and perfect resource mobility, perfect knowledge and the static state are the factors that bring about the elegance and beauty of the equilibria in perfect competition where supply is geared to demand at prices including normal profits. In spite of this the Administration and its supporters cling to perfect competition as the model of what agriculture is and ought to be (Clodius, 1960, pp. 420–21).

A more recent critique of ''market-oriented'' farm policy uses second-best arguments to support the view that

Competitive sectors in an oligopolistic economy are made better off either by making the noncompetitive sector more competitive or giving the competitive sector more market power. The answer is *not* to make the competitive sector more competitive. . . . There is no *a priori* presumption in favor of a market-oriented approach'' (McCalla and Carter, 1976, p. 59).

The approach to policy analysis fostered by these views about the characteristics of the agricultural economy is well stated by Brandow (1977), who begins his comprehensive survey of agricultural policy studies by stating:

Farm price and income policy is about an actual world, not an abstraction in which simple, homogeneous resources are frictionlessly allocated to production of want-satisfying goods. . . . (p. 20)

He concludes that

The most fruitful appraisals are likely to come from addressing directly the real-world situations in which problems and programs are embedded, not from substituting unverified assumptions and static models for the dynamic world that actually exists (p. 280).

During the 1940s, 1950s, and 1960s, many agricultural economists were attempting to provide a framework appropriate for understanding the farm problem. Brandow's exemplars of realistic modeling derive from Schultz (1945) and subsequent refinements, such as in Johnson and Quance (1972). The models turn out to be refinements of rather than replacements for the simple supply–

demand model. There gradually emerged a consensus on the essential features of agriculture, stated as five characteristics by Hathaway (1964) and expressed by Rausser and Hochman (1979, p. 3) as

> The five characteristics of aggregate food systems, namely, (1) highly inelastic demand, (2) slow growth of total demand, (3) competitive structure, (4) rapid technological change, and (5) the tendency of resources to become fixed within the industry.

A remarkable feature of some of the farm policy literature is that it is seen to have policy implications, without venturing any normative judgments. It does not follow the recent pattern of welfare economics, which considers income redistribution and market interventions in an explicitly normative framework. Instead we again have the idea, familiar from macroeconomics, of the economist as a sort of doctor prescribing remedies for economics ills. The main exception is the set of arguments, examples of which are in the Clodius and McCalla–Carter quotations, that elaborate on characteristic number 3 of Rausser and Hochman's list, the contrast between competition in agriculture and the imperfectly competitive industrial organization of manufacturing and agribusiness. The general view, however, is that imperfect competition elsewhere is not agriculture's main problem, and that the other farm characteristics would lead to difficulties even without item 3.

In turning to the economic implication of these characteristics, it should be noted first that, although the development of agricultural economists' models of agriculture stems from disenchantment with the static model of competitive equilibrium, some of the characteristics that focus that disenchantment are not obviously incompatible with the static equilibrium model. Indeed, one may ask whether the static model might be generalized sufficiently to incorporate these characteristics without losing its essential equilibrium nature.

It is important to remember that what led agricultural economists to look for alternative models was the search for an explanation of a chronic tendency for low prices and incomes in agriculture. The five characteristics became accepted as a group because they were seen as capable of generating such a farm problem. Thus, the model is realistic in the sense that it generates a result consistent with the underlying observation. Still, items 1, 2, 4, and 5 are quite consistent with a competitive model of agriculture, and indeed are best grasped as empirical statements about the supply and demand functions. Rapid technical progress (4) means the supply function is shifting to the right over time. We could add another variable, T, to Eq. (2.1), with a positive coefficient, or add T with a negative coefficient in Eq. (2.3). Slow growth of demand (2) means that demand shifts to the right only slightly over time, even if income is growing. These two facts alone, assuming they imply that supply increases faster than demand (at given prices) imply that commodity prices must fall. The low price elasticity explains why price might fall a lot even if the relative differences in supply and demand shifts are small. Asset fixity (5) provides the same analytical service on the supply side, and adds the point that returns to farmers' investments in fixed capital equipment will decline. Labor immobility, an aspect of item 5, completes the picture of the commodity price decline translating through to lower farm incomes.

The preceding sketch is too informal; the model should be specified more precisely. Also, the nature of the "farm problem" in the model is still not clear, and is not established as the correct representation of what we observe in the farm economy.

The most elementary prediction of the model is that farm commodity prices will fall over time. This prediction is borne out in long-term trend declines in the United States and on a worldwide basis for the major agricultural commodities. Indeed, given the observation of these trends in prices along with increasing quantities, the decision to depict the facts in supply–demand terms implies that supply must be increasing faster than demand. But of course this occurs for manufactured goods, too, especially for high-technology products such as electronics, computers, or drugs. Why don't we have a "hi-tech problem?" The issue is whether the price declines just reflect cost or efficiency improvements. Inelastic demand then indicates that revenues will fall as supply shifts, but not that profits or returns to farmer-owned resources will fall, as discussed in Chaps. 2 and 6.

Such considerations lead, on the conceptual modeling front, to more detail in specifying supply–demand models for agricultural factors of production and their relationship to commodity markets. On the empirical front, these considerations lead to the examination of farm input price and farm income statistics. Statistics on U.S. farm wage rates and land prices (until the 1980s) do not show the chronic declines that we might expect from the declining commodity prices under the farm problem scenario.

Table 6.1 in Chap. 6 reviewed income and wealth data for U.S. farm families. It is apparent that farmers are in fact not a low-income group any more, and indeed may fairly be described as a relatively wealthy class of small businesses. Together with evidence that rates of return to investment in agriculture are not lower than in nonagriculture (see Tweeten, 1985), these data reduce the demand for models that explain the farm problem.

Note that in the preceding discussion, farm wage rates and rates of return to investment were judged with reference to returns in nonfarm employment. The model of the farm problem, as presented thus far, treats agriculture as a sector with no regard for interactions with the rest of the economy. This is unsatisfactory, and many economists have attempted to place the farm problem explicitly in a general equilibrium setting. In such a setting the farm problem can be generated as follows:

> We can divide the economy of any country into two sectors: the farm sector and the nonfarm sector. Let us first consider a stationary situation, in which there is no economic growth or decline in the economy as a whole. In such a situation

there will be equilibrium if the supply of farm products is just equal to the demand for them, and similarly for nonfarm products. The conditions of supply and demand in each sector will be determined by technology and by the preferences of consumers. In equilibrium the prices in each sector will be just high enough to clear each market. If a stationary state persists long enough, the income earned by comparable types of labor and capital will be the same in the two sectors, since in the long run labor and capital will be used in the market where they earn the highest return. It is possible that even in such a situation per capita incomes in the farm sector will be lower than elsewhere, for example, if farming requires less skill than is needed in the nonfarm sector. But apart from this there will be no farm income problem.

Let us consider economic growth, normally brought about by a general increase in productivity. Aggregate national income goes up, and consequently the demand for farm and nonfarm products goes up. But here we come to the heart of the matter: the demand for farm products will not increase in the same proportion as the demand for nonfarm products. . . . To equate supply and demand, farm prices will have to fall and nonfarm prices will have to rise. A necessary consequence of this fall in farm prices is a decline in per capita farm income as compared to per capital nonfarm income. This change in the income parity will induce movement of labor and capital from the farm to the nonfarm sector, which in due course will bring the distribution of resources between the two sectors in closer agreement with the distribution of demand. If labor and other resources could flow easily from one sector to another a relative fall in farm incomes could be eliminated altogether, but in fact the flow is far from easy. Consequently in an economy where productivity and income grow all the time, farm incomes are likely to be permanently below nonfarm incomes unless special steps are taken to speed up the necessary redistribution of labor.

The greater the increase in farm productivity, the greater the imbalance between supply and demand of farm products which has to be corrected by an outflow of labor or by lower farm prices. Unless the outflow of labor from farming is fast enough, an increase in farm productivity leads only to lower farm prices and lower farm incomes (Houthakker, 1967, pp. 5–7).

By making a few assumptions, Houthakker's model can be presented more formally. These assumptions are not realistic, but they do not rule out the special characteristics of agriculture listed. Thus the model does not assume away the problem. Our objective is to explore the farm problem in the context of the simplest possible economy in which it may appear, and to assess more fully the connection between the earlier five characteristics of agriculture and the farm problem. (Apart from this objective, the model is the one that underlies the UPF as discussed in Chap. 7.)

Let there be two sectors in the economy, the farm, or agricultural sector and nonfarm sector which comprises all other industries. Corresponding to the two sectors are two products: agricultural output (A) and nonagricultural output (N). Let there be only two inputs: owner-supplied resources of labor and land (L) and purchased material inputs (K). Production in each sector is represented in Fig. 9.1 by isoquants of a twice continuously differentiable production func-

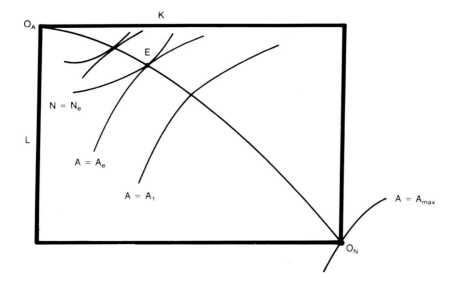

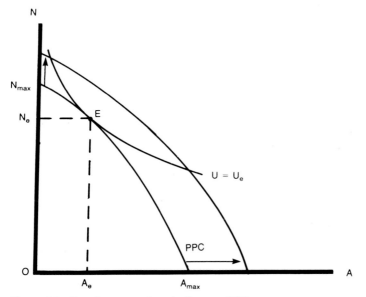

Figure 9.1 Box diagram and production possibilities.

tion in L and K with positive marginal products which diminish with added inputs, and with nonincreasing returns to scale.[1] This box diagram assumes further that the economy's L and K are in fixed supply and that all production is consumed in the economy in the same period produced (a stationary, closed economy). Equilibrium in the factor markets occurs when the prices (more precisely, rental returns) of L and K are the same in both sectors, possible equilibria lying on the contact curve $O_A O_N$. Each point on the contract curve determines an output pair (A,N), ranging from (O,N_{max}) to $(A_{max};O)$. These are plotted in the lower panel of Fig. 9.1 to generate the production possibilities curve (PPC). Each point on the PPC corresponds to a point on the contract curve. Thus, each point is a possible equilibrium point. The PPC function is concave [any point on a line segment between any two points (A_0,N_0) and (A_1,N_1) is below the PPC] because of nonincreasing returns (a sufficient condition for equilibrium to exist).

Demand is represented by a set of aggregate indifference curves assumed to have the usual properties of individuals' indifference curves (a big assumption), which implies equilibrium in the product market at E, where product supply equals demand for both A and N. This determines equilibrium quantities A_e and N_e, which in turn determines equilibrium point E in the box diagram, with common factor prices in the A and N sectors.

The exogenous factors triggering events in the farm-problem model are the growth of national income, particularly through technical progress. Both events are represented in Fig. 9.1 by an outward shift in the PPC, with a larger percentage shift toward increasing A (at least locally in the neighborhood of E, but shown globally in Fig. 9.1 as a longer arrow along the A axis). The consequences are:

1. Demand shifts: The lower income elasticity of demand for A implies that with economic growth, the economy demands less A relative to N at a given relative price P_A/P_N. But there will be no reduction in A unless A is not only an inferior good, but also is inferior enough that the income effect in demand offsets the changed relative supply price represented by the curvature of the PPC. This point is illustrated in Fig. 9.2. The vertically parallel indifference curves U_0 and U_1 imply zero income elasticity of demand for A but could generate a new equilibrium at F only if the PPC were linear. A concave PPC, with an equal rate of outward shift in the A and N direction implies P_A/P_N too low for equilibrium at F, and implies equilibrium at a point where $A > A_e$, such as G.

2. More rapid technical change in A: If the PPC shifts at a greater rate in the A direction, then at a point at which equilibrium would have been attained under and equi-proportional shift, such as G, has P_A/P_N too low. Therefore equilibrium must be at a point to the right of G, such as H.

3. The relationship between points F, G, and H: This depends not only on the income elasticity of demand for A (η_{AY}), the curvature of the PPC, and the relative rate of technical progress in A and N, but also on the curvature of the indifference curves. This is why the price elasticity of demand for A, more specifically the Hicksian (utility-constant) elasticity, is a key feature of the "farm-problem" model. For example, if the price elasticity were zero, then a negative income elasticity would be not only necessary but sufficient for equilibrium to lie to the left of point F. But if the price elasticity is nonzero, even if it is only -0.2 or so, as demand studies suggest for food as an aggregate,

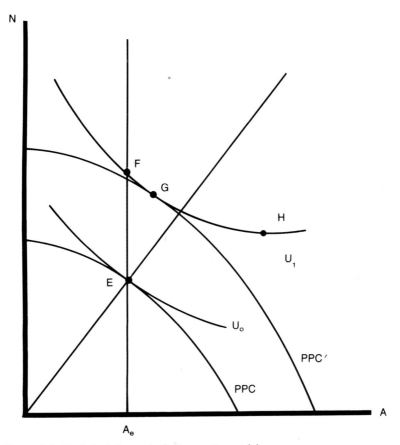

Figure 9.2 Technical change in the two-sector model.

it will be difficult for any plausible outward PPC shift to result in a decline in A below A_e. And, of course, it remains necessary that $\eta_{AY} < 0$.

In summary, it is implausible to expect that economic growth and technical progress will lead to a decline in A; and the five characteristics of the "farm-problem" model are not sufficient conditions for a decline in A/N (equilibrium on PPC' to the left of the ray in Fig. 9.2, e.g., point G.) However, we have in fact observed a decline over time in A in the United States and other developer countries. Therefore, we suspect that the parameter values are such that the increase in demand for A caused by a declining P_A/P_N due to more rapid technical progress in A has been insufficient to offset the demand effect of the lower income elasticity of demand for A as compared to N.

In terms of the box diagram, we have a shift toward O_A. Since technical change has occurred, the isoquants are relocated, and the shift toward O_A is consistent with more A being produced. The contract curve will have also been relocated. Nonetheless, if the equilibrium conditions hold after the change, we will be on the new contract curve. This means that wages and returns to wealth will be the same in both the A and N sectors, although it could be that the rate of return to capital will have changed relative to wage rates.

A movement to a position on the new (post-technical-change) contract curve, and correspondingly on the new PPC, is not in the spirit of farm-problem models. We need to model disequilibria in the sense that the ratio of marginal costs between the sectors does not equal the ratio of market clearing prices. How can this occur? Disequilibrium in a partial equilibrium context is shown in Fig. 9.3. The demand and supply for A have both shifted to the right from an earlier equilibrium position E (which may never have been fully attained) such that equilibrium exists at a lower price at E'. This requires movement along the supply curve S. But in the short run, this does not occur because of asset fixity. We observe a short-run market clearing equilibrium at G, where price is "too low" and output "too high" compared to the equilibrium point.

The corresponding point of disequilibrium in the two-sector model is a point like J or J' in Fig. 9.3. The point J is a special case in which relative factor prices are the same in A and N, so that we are on the contract curve and on the PPC. But the relative price of A (given by the slope of the indifference curve passing through J) is lower than at equilibrium E'. More generally we would expect some inputs to be more fixed than others, so that the difference between S and S_{sr} (sr meaning short-run) would be greater for L in A than for K in A. Then we find outselves off the contract curve inside the PPC, as at point J'.

The general equilibrium model is not well suited for the study of the dynamics of disequilibria, but it does indicate that in a policy perspective, the key feature of agriculture in generating the farm problem is the slowness of the factor markets to adjust to changing demand conditions. We may have too large a quantity of farmer-owned relative to purchased inputs in the A sector. The economic mechanism yielding this result could be that technical change reduced the demand for L more than K, or it could be that demand is reduced by the same percentage for L and K but L is more nearly fixed in supply (S_{sr} is less elastic). The two-sector diagrams cannot distinguish between these alternatives, although partial equilibrium supply–demand diagrams of the L and K market could.

An interpretation of a trend decline in P_A/P_N with periods of both rising and falling returns in agriculture that is consistent with the two-sector depiction of the farm problem is the following. Episodes of declining returns to farm-owned inputs occur when technical change reduces the demand for farmer-owned inputs rapidly or when demand for A is reduced rapidly, as after the first and second World Wars. These shocks led to movements to points like G in Fig. 9.3 for both agricultural ouput and for farm-owned inputs. But in the periods following these shocks, such as 1950–1970, the data are dominated by fac-

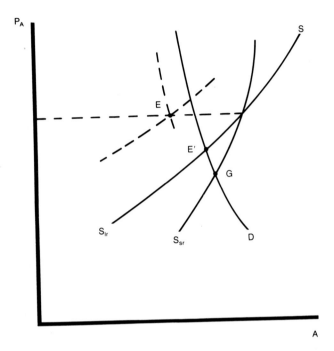

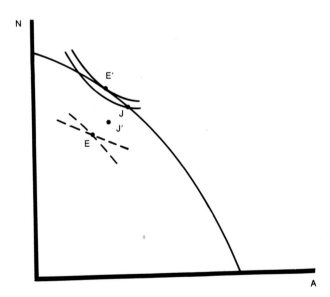

Figure 9.3 Disequilibrium.

tor market adjustment as from G toward E'. In these periods we see movement of excess resources out of agriculture accompanied by increasing factor incomes in farming.

Characteristic 3 of our earlier list, emphasized in the quotations, has been neglected so far. The consequences of perfect competition in A and imperfect competition in N can be examined readily in the two-sector model. The general equilibrium is at a point like J on the PPC in Fig. 9.3. The difference between relative prices now reflects not disequilibrium but monopoly power. The imperfectly competitive sector produces less than the competitive equilibrium quantity of N, which increases P_N, and remains on the PPC because the N sector allocates resources efficiently to produce the restricted output. The difference between the slopes of PPC and the indifference curve at J measures monopoly profit at the margin. The key point is that in the two-sector model a rise in P_N is equivalent to a fall in P_A. Indeed, there is really only one real (relative) commodity price in this model, P_A/P_N. Thus, monopoly power in N is equivalent to chronic overproduction of A in this model. In order to obtain factor-return differences between L and K in the two sectors, we need factor immobility along with monopoly in N.

Other oft-cited imperfections in N are monopsony power of buyers of farm products and monopoly power in selling material inputs to farmers. These do not lend themselves so readily to analysis within the two-product, two-input framework, because they involve "vertical" relationships among markets. We will not go further here than the partial equilibrium model of Chap. 5.

Let us turn now to the effects of farm commodity market intervention in the context of the two-sector model. Intervention can take two basic forms: (a) a guarantee of P_A higher than the market price, paying producers the difference between the guaranteed price and the market price; (b) achieving a higher P_A through mandated production cutbacks. If we begin at a competitive equilibrium position such as E in Fig. 9.4, policy (a) moves the economy along the PPC toward S, increasing the marginal cost of A relative to N. The increase in relative marginal costs is measured by the increasing steepness of the PPC slope. At the same time, P_A/P_N as paid by consumers falls to clear the markets. The new equilibrium is at point S, the difference between the PPC and indifference curve slopes measuring the government payment per unit A. In a box diagram (not shown) we would see movement along the contract curve away from O_A, with an increase in the relative price of the factor in which A production is relatively intensive (empirically, A is L-intensive, implying P_L/P_K rises). cally, A is L-intensive, implying P_L/P_K rises).

Policy (b), production control, moves the economy along the PPC, decreasing the marginal cost of A relative to N, but increasing P_A/P_N paid by consumers. This is the converse of the monopoly-in-N equilibrium. At production-control equilibrium point T, the difference between the slope of PPC and the indifference curve measures the rents generated for A producers (more specifically, holders of rights to produce A). These rents are analogous to monopoly

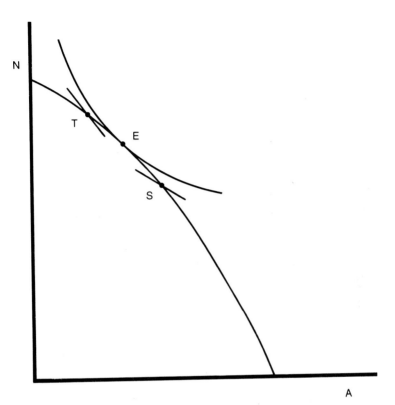

Figure 9.4 Price-support policies.

rents. In the box diagram, we would see a movement along the contract curve toward O_A with factor price changes in the opposite direction of policy (a).(If production control worked by limiting quantities of one factor, but not the other, we would move off the contract curve and inside the PPC. This means that for any given rise in P_A/P_N, as at T, the acreage control would put the economy on a lower indifference curve than a production control program. This is the two-sector analog of the Fig. 8.4 result on the relative inefficiency of an acreage control program.)

At either point T or S, the economy is on a lower indifference curve than at E. In this sense, which is of course not necessarily decisive in a normative context where $\theta > 1$ for some interests, we can say that either program (a) or (b) makes the economy as a whole worse off.

SECOND-BEST POLICY

Consider a situation in which the economy was already at point S because of monopoly power in N. Now policy (b) can in principle be implemented to move the economy back to point E. Thus, the original market imperfection is offset by the commodity program. Policy (a), however, is even less desirable than before, in that it moves the economy from point S to a new equilibrium even further to the right of E and hence on a still lower indifference curve.

[Some people call distortions like (b) that exactly offset other imperfections, and thus place the economy at the same Pareto optimum as with no imperfections, first-best policies. The earlier definition in this chapter of second-best policies as Pareto-improving, given imperfections, counts policies like (b) as second best even if they do achieve first-best results. This point is purely definitional and has no bearing on policy choice.]

If factor-market rigidities or imperfections cause chronic disequilibria, as discussed earlier, it will be more difficult for either policies (a) or (b) to improve this situation. Some sort of intervention in the L or K markets may be helpful, but as Houthakker argues, the most attractive option is to attempt to remedy the immobility that caused the chronic disequilibrium.

LIMITATIONS OF THE MODEL

Many features of the agricultural economy are omitted from the two-sector model: uncertainty, dynamics of adjustment, non–profit-maximizing behavior, the marketing sector, the international market. Even in its own comparative-static terms the model omits the commodity detail within agriculture (for example, crops versus livestock) that one needs for addressing many policy issues. For drawing implications about second-best intervention in agriculture, the aggregation of nonagriculture into one sector is particularly bad because in reality monopoly and other imperfections vary a lot from one nonagricultural commodity to another. If, for example, monopoly power is high in manufacturing but nonexistent in services, we know nothing, from the two-sector model, about proper policy in agriculture. Also severely limiting is the aggregation into two factors of production. Some policy issues turn on substitution between and distribution of income among farmer-owned inputs (land, capital equipment, and labor). Moreover, we sometimes need to analyze quality differences in labor or land and the fact that some labor is hired while some is provided by the farm family, and similarly for land tenure.

From the Chap. 4 models of input markets, the Chap. 5 analysis of multimarket equilibrium, and the models incorporating trade of Chap. 2 and 3, it should be clear that some of these limitations can be remedied. In recent years, "computable" general equilibrium models have been developed that can stimulate and provide a basis for evaluating combination of policies under a wide variety of complicated assumptions about the economy. Their application will be discussed in Chap. 11.

An inherent limitation of this whole family of models is its assumption of equilibrium at all times in all markets. This makes the approach well suited for comparative statics of long-term tendencies, and for short-term comparative statics also, where appropriate short-run behavioral functions are known. But these models provide no help in analyzing what goes on between the short-run and the long-run—the dynamics of adjustment to shocks (temporary or permanent). Although the key aspects of risks and risk aversion can be incorporated in equilibrium models insofar as risk influences equilibrium states, the models do not provide analysis of instability (cycles or random fluctuations) or of the role of expectations and lags in adjustment to policy changes. This is an important lack because many economists, especially in the 1970s, ceased to see the farm problem as one of chronically low prices and income, but instead as a problem of chronically unstable prices and incomes. A reasonable attempt at analyzing these issues requires us to go back to first principles and construct models especially suited to the purpose. This task is undertaken in Chap. 10.

QUANTIFYING SECOND-BEST WELFARE RESULTS

The empirical significance of imperfect competition in nonfarm markets and of disequilibrium are debatable, and some have questioned whether these market failures have any real chance empirically of justifying farm price support programs (e.g., Houthakker, 1967; D. G. Johnson, 1973). But it is widely believed that environmental externalities and public goods in agriculture justify policies such as regulating pesticides which run into streams and poison fish or the neighbors, or public investment in agricultural research and information dissemination. Moreover, we know that taxes, tariffs, and other intervention exist in nonagricultural markets, and that taking this intervention as given can change the picture considerably for intervention in agricultural commodity markets. How can we proceed to provide empirical assessments of policy alternatives in such second-best situations?

Calculation formulas for gains and losses from a single distortion are given in Eq. (8.8) to (8.12). The key new element with multiple distortions is that, whereas in Chap. 8, the gains and losses cancel out in all markets other than the once in which intervention takes place, now there are net gains and losses in the other markets, too. For example, the corn target price caused gains and losses in the soybean market, but the gains of soybean sellers equalled the losses of soybean buyers. If soybeans had already had an acreage control program, however, the corn program would change the deadweight losses in soybeans. Figure 9.5 shows an example. If corn output is reduced via production controls, from $\hat{X}$ to $\hat{X}'$ the additional deadweight loss is the hatched area (S and D being appropriate multimarket Hicksian demand curves.) If Y (soybeans) already has production control at $\hat{Y}$ with deadweight loss given by the shaded triangle, the corn output reduction increases the demand for soybeans from D to D', increasing price from P_y to P'_y. For a given soybean control level, this means that the wedge between the consumer price and producers' opportunity costs has increased, and therefore, the deadweight loss from the soybean program has increased. The increase is the hatched area in the right-hand panel.

Harberger (1974, p. 10) provides the following formula for calculating net

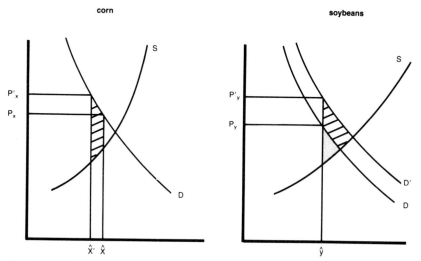

Figure 9.5 Corn program with pre-existing production controls in soybeans.

social gains from a change in a policy variable (tax, subsidy, acreage control, or whatever):

$$\Delta w = \int_0^{\hat{Z}} \sum_i D_i(Z) \frac{\partial X_i}{\partial Z} \, dZ \tag{9.1}$$

where D_i refers to the difference between consumers' prices and producers' prices in each good's market, or $P_d - P_s$ in the earlier single-product notation. If Z is a subsidy on the jth good, then a change in X_j will occur (unless supply or demand is perfectly inelastic). If *either* (a) $\partial X_i/\partial Z = 0$ for all $i \neq j$, or (b) $D_i = 0$ for all $i \neq j$, then Eq. (9.1) just obtains the usual deadweight loss triangle by adding up vertical slices of it. (Δw is negative because, if $\partial X_j/\partial Z < 0$, then $D_j > 0$; but if $\partial X/\partial Z_j > 0$, as for an input subsidy, then $D_j < 0$.) But if we have effects of D_j on X_i, $i \neq j$, and the markets are related, then we have to add terms for all the commodities for which this is the case. Now Δw may well be positive. For example, a subsidy on X_j could result in less output of X_k, and if D_k were large, this could make Δw positive.

In many practical applications, the effects of policy instruments on other markets are ignored on the ground that the relevant $\partial X_i/\partial Z$ are negligible. For example, a subsidy on corn is assumed not to change the quantity of automobiles. A subsidy redistributes income from one group to another and this can change product demands, but recall that the relevant effects for Δw calculations contain only substituion effects. These are assumed quite small between goods that serve different needs, so that we seriously consider cross-elasticities between different agricultural commodities but not between food and nonfood (except where clear substitution possibilities exist on the supply side, e.g., between soybeans and cotton.) This separability is a maintained hypothesis in almost all empirical studies of food-demand systems.

An example where distortions outside agriculture can be important is imperfect competition in the nonfarm economy generally, as has already been discussed in terms of the two-sector model. In terms of Eq. (9.1), $D_i > 0$ for all X_i in monopolized markets, since $P_d > P_s$ there. Thus, if $\partial X_i / \partial Z > 0$ (that is, if the policy increases the X_i) it increases Δw.

Accordingly, a production control policy in agriculture, because it increases nonagricultural X_i, can increase welfare, even when all groups have $\Theta = 1$. This is the same result as discussed with reference to the two sector model in Fig. 9.4. Using Eq. (9.1) makes it clearer how to obtain estimates of the magnitude of gains from optimal second-best intervention.

Note that the general equilibrium context implies using $\partial X_i / \partial Z$ which are pure substitution effects in a different sense than the Hicksian demand elasticities. They are general equilibrium responses, incorporating both demand and supply interactions, keeping the economy on its PPC. (For discussion of the conceptual basis, see Bailey, 1954). Algebraically, the $\partial X_i / \partial Z$ are related to the structure of a multimarket economy in just the way that total elasticities such as Eb/EP_a of Chap. 4 are related to the structural model of that chapter, but for many markets they are too cumbersome to make an algebraic expression useful. In practice, numerical simulation can be used with information for key structural parameters estimated econometrically. But these simulations often do not spell out the role of particular structural parameters in the way that our elasticity formulas do. Consequently, we will continue dealing with simple two- or three-market models. We consider the welfare effects of D_1 when distortions D_2 or D_3 already exist.

Equation (8.12) is a linearized version of Eq. (9.1) in which the $D_i(Z)$ are subsidy rates in a two-good model. When $\Theta > 1$ the optimal subsidies were found in Chap. 8. This would be a second-best problem if we took one of the subsidies as given at a nonoptimal level and then maximized w. We would then in general find it welfare-increasing to intervene in the other market even if $\Theta = 1$ for all interests. In terms of Fig. 8.2, the problem is choosing V_x to achieve the highest W level for a given V_y. One result that is clear from the earlier discussion is that a commonly asserted proposition about second-best intervention is not true; namely, a 10-percent subsidy of say, manufactured goods does not imply that a 10-percent subsidy of agricultural goods would be welfare increasing. Still, it is also unlikely that no intervention in agriculture is the optimal policy either. The remainder of this chapter considers some particular problems of choosing second-best agricultural intervention.

SUBSIDIZED CAPITAL IN AGRICULTURE

Conflict between farm commodity policies and input policies receives a lot of attention because of seeming absurdities: subsidizing irrigation projects and then paying farmers to hold irrigated land idle, or storing up surplus grain produced with subsidized water. In 1986, the federal government was paying dairy farmers to slaughter their herds while a Georgia county was offering subsidies for an Irish company to set up a large dairy operation. Given an aim to redistribute income to producers ($\Theta > 1$), however, some of these policies might make sense.

Suppose the income tax code has provisions that result in a subsidy on all material inputs used in agriculture. Such tax policies have to be taken as given when devising agricultural programs. The positive economics of a subsidy of purchased inputs was analyzed in Chap. 6. The normative question here is what might be promising second-best policies—commodity price supports, subsidizing other inputs?

Let the subsidy rate V_b on purchased inputs be 15 percent, and let the parameter values be $\eta = -0.4$, $\sigma = 1.0$, $K_a = K_b = 0.5$, $e_a = 0.5$, and $e_b = 2$. This is a rough two-factor representation of purchased inputs, and farm labor and land aggregated. Using the equations of Table 4.2, the subsidy increases the use of purchased inputs by 12.8 percent, decreases farm land and labor use by 1.4 percent, and increases output by 2.9 percent. The resulting decline in the product price is 7 percent. Nonetheless, the rents received by producers (including subsidy payments) rise by 2 percent.

Consider a second-best policy through intervention in the a market. Can intervention increase welfare even when $\Theta = 1$? To assess the options, we need data on Δw for alternative policies such as are plotted in Fig. 8.5. But here our interest is only in one column of these numbers, the one corresponding to $V_b = 0.15$. This restriction makes it feasible to plot the welfare alternatives in two dimensions. Figure 9.6 shows the height of the welfare hill in a vertical cross section. (However, the Δw values are different in Fig. 9.6 than in Fig. 8.5 because the parameter values are different.)

Consider first the case where $\Theta = 1$, where producers are not favored in the SWF. In this case, intervention can only reduce welfare (all the numbers in Fig. 8.5 would be negative except $\Delta w = 0$ at the origin). We find that, nonetheless, there is indeed a second-best policy: $V_a = 0.1$ generates Δw less negative than $V_a = 0$. The policy is a subsidy on a. One might have expected a tax on a to be optimal: since the subsidy in b causes too much output, we need to intervene in a in such a way as to reduce output, i.e., to tax a; but this would not remedy the distortion of the input markets. With $\sigma > -\eta$ in this example, it is more important to reduce the disparity between input prices then to get output right. If σ is low enough, then a tax on a is the second-best optimum.

Even if an input tax was otpimal for $\Theta = 1$, this would not be consistent with the idea of using policy to aid producers. If we let $\Theta = 1.1$, Fig. 9.6 shows second-best optimum as being a subsidy of 25 percent. If $\Theta = 1.2$, the optimal V_a rises to 40 percent. Thus, as Θ increases the subsidy rate increases. The reason is that for $\Theta > 1$, as we increase producers' rents we generate

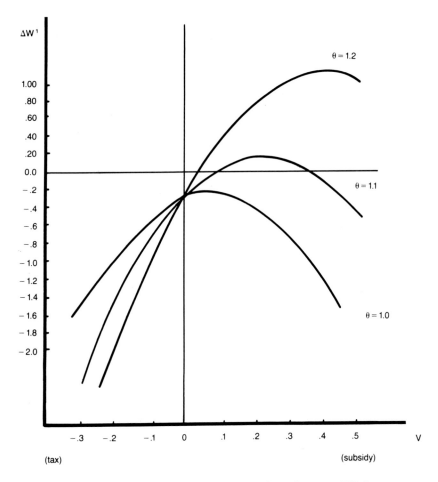

[1]Units are percentages of the no-intervention value of output (XPx).

Figure 9.6 Welfare effects of subsidy for input *a*, given a subsidy of input *b*.

higher and higher deadweight losses (as seen by the rate at which Δw declines when $\Theta = 1.0$, since Δw in this case *is* the deadweight loss); thus, it takes a higher Θ to offset these losses with the producers' gains.

Figure 9.6 provides us with good news and bad news about our capability to prescribe second-best subsidies. The good news is that for given market parameters and a given subsidy rate for one input, we can calculate the optimal subsidy for the other input, as long as we know Θ. The bad news is that we do not know Θ, and within the range of plausible Θ's and σ's subsidy rates ranging from -20 percent to 40 percent can be justified.

The notion of taking one tax or subsidy as given and then intervening in other ways to achieve a second-best optimum can be extended to the relationships between input and output markets. Newbery (1986) shows that a combination of output and input taxes can be used to attain a second-best optimum given an initial set of policy constraints in either output or input markets. In our example, by taxing output at 15 percent and subsidizing input a at 15 percent, we would exactly offset the given V_b of 0.15. This would just be a roundabout way of achieving the no-program state of affairs. We have already shown in the two-sector model how farm-level adjustments can be made in response to retail-level distortions. Lichtenberg and Zilberman (1986) present an interesting case study how the benefits and costs of a pesticide ban are changed by the prior existence of price supports for corn, cotton, and rice.

Distortions in input markets not caused by governmental policies can also be the given constraints under which the search for a second-best optimum takes place. Barker and Hayami (1976), in a case study of fertilizer subsidies in the Philippines, find an appropriately chosen subsidy rate to be welfare increasing as compared to an output price support, and as compared to no intervention, even with $\Theta = 1$. The reason is that they estimate fertilizer to be underutilized in the free-market situation, so the optimal subsidy eliminates a preexisting deadweight loss rather than creating such losses.

DEADWEIGHT LOSSES FROM REVENUE RAISING

Another type of second-best problem arises with subsidies. Consider the simple case of a commodity market when a deficiency payment scheme is put in place. The revenue to pay them must be raised by taxes. Since tax rates already are nonzero, we have $D_i > 0$ in Eq. (9.1), and imposing these taxes will itself cause additional deadweight losses elsewhere in the economy. This loss is external to the regulated commodity market. It might be approximated by marginal deadweight losses per dollar of additional federal income tax levied. If this loss were negligible, then D_i could be taken as zero. However, this loss is not negligible. Stuart (1984) estimates the marginal cost at 24 cents per dollar raised, in the United States. The review of Browning (1986) places the cost between 20 and 50 cents. Even if the deadweight loss per dollar of additional taxes is low, the cost per dollar transferred to producers is likely to be substantially greater. The reason is that part of the tax revenue is distributed back to consumers through lower prices.

In terms of Eq. (9.1), Δw reduces to a sum over two terms but is expanded because changes in two policy instruments (Z's) are involved.

$$\Delta w = \int_0^{\hat{v}_a} \left(D_a \frac{\partial X_a}{\partial V_a} + D_t \frac{\partial X_t}{\partial V_a} \right) dV_a + \int_{t_0}^{t_1} \left(D_a \frac{\partial X}{\partial t} + D_t \frac{\partial X_t}{\partial t} \right) dt \qquad (9.2)$$

where $\hat{V}_a$ is the payment rate on agricultural commodities and $t_1 - t_0$ is the corresponding taxes. Assume that cross-effects are negligible, $\partial X_t / \partial V_a \doteq 0$ and $\partial X_a / \partial t \doteq 0$, that is, payments to farmers have negligible effects on nonfarm output and the resulting taxes, spread over the whole economy, have negligible feedback effects on farm output. $D_t \cdot \partial X_t / \partial t$ is, using Stuart's estimate, the 24 cents per dollar of taxes raised.

Carrying out the integrations requires us to know or assume a functional form relating V_a and X_a or use an approximation formula. For the tax-burden part, assume linearity in the relevant range (raising another \$1 billion or so added to \$600 billion already collected doesn't change the overall marginal deadweight loss of taxes appreciably). So the second part of the deadweight loss is simply $0.24 \, \Delta T$, where ΔT is taxes required to raise deficiency payments. The first part has already been calculated assuming log-linear supply and demand function in Eq. (7.57).

The amount of taxes that must be raised to pay the subsidy is

$$T = [P_s (\hat{Q}) - P_d (\hat{Q})]\hat{Q}$$

When the subsidy is increased, the amount that is recycled to consumers is

$$\frac{dCS/dQ}{dT/dQ} = \frac{- nA\hat{Q}^n}{- (n+1) A\hat{Q}^n + (e+1) B\hat{Q}^e}$$

Using the same algebraic tricks as in Chap. 7, and converting to Q-dependent elasticities via $\eta = 1/n$ and $\epsilon = 1/e$,

$$\frac{dCS}{dT} = \frac{1}{1 + \eta \left[1 - (1 + 1/\epsilon) (Q_0 / \hat{Q})^{1/\eta - 1/\epsilon} \right]} \tag{9.3}$$

The change in external deadweight loss (dD) per dollar transferred, $dM = d(CS - T)$, is

$$\tau = \frac{dD}{dM} = \frac{dD}{dT} \frac{dT}{dM} = D_t \frac{dT}{dM}$$

Since the change in transfers is the change in taxes minus the amount recycled to consumers in the form of lower prices, we have

$$\frac{dM}{dT} = \frac{dCS}{dT} - 1$$

Therefore,

$$\tau = D_t \left(\frac{1}{dCS / dT - 1} \right) \tag{9.4}$$

where dCS/dT is from Eq. (9.3).

The quantitative significance of τ, which must be subtracted from Eq. (7.57) to obtain the full deadweight loss from a deficiency payment program, can be judged by looking at selected parameter values for ϵ and $-\eta$. If $\epsilon = -\eta$, and intervention is small so that $Q_0/\hat{Q} \doteq 1$, then $dCS/dT = 1/2$ and $\tau = -2D_t$. That is, of a dollar in subsidies paid by taxpayers, half a dollar is recycled back to consumers (the other half going to producers). Therefore, the deadweight loss from increasing P_T at the margin is not just the value of Eq. (7.57) plus 0.24, but Eq. (7.57) plus 0.48. As η becomes closer to zero, and ϵ larger, this factor increases. If $Q_0/\hat{Q} = 0.8$, i.e., we have a subsidy that increases output 25 percent, and $\epsilon = -\eta = 0.5$, then $\tau = 0.32$. From Table 7.2, $dPS/dM = -0.77$, making a subsidy more efficient than the production-control approach. But taking into account the external deadweight losses, $dPS/dM = -0.77 + 0.32 = -0.45$, making the production control preferable.

Change the assumptions to let $\epsilon = 1.0$ and $\eta = -0.2$. Then $\tau = -0.42$. From Table 7.2, we already had $dPS/dM = -0.57$, with production controls much preferred. Now $dPS/dM = -0.15$, so the choice still more strongly favors production controls.

Change the assumptions again to let $\epsilon = 0.2$ and $\eta = -1.0$. Then $\tau = 0.25$. From Table 7.2, dPS/dM was -0.87. Now it is -0.62. But the subsidy approach is still more efficient than production controls.

The external deadweight losses should be taken into account in all the entries of Table 7.2, and will generally reduce the optimal intervention in the form of subsidies. By the same token, the fact that import tariffs reduce the need for other tax revenues means there is an external gain from their use. Import tariffs can therefore be welfare increasing even if $\Theta = 1$ for all parties.

SECOND-BEST BORDER MEASURES?

Domestic producers sometimes complain that they would be able to compete successfully in a fair market, but that trade restrictions by other countries are spoiling their markets. Can countermeasures by the domestic country achieve second-best results in such cases? A related issued not discussed here is intervention by a large trading country to exploit its world market power. This is not really a second-best issue, and raises complications that are postponed to Chap. 11. Here we deal only with small-country situations, where the domestic country faces a given world price for its commodities.

Distortions elsewhere in the world, by a single large country or an independent collection of small ones, change the given world price. But once changed, the price is given at the new level. The country could set its internal price at its estimate of what the world price would have been under free trade. The analysis of gains and losses is the same as in Chap. 2. There is a net loss even though the "second-best" policy has just re-established the free-trade situation. To see why, consider Fig. 9.7. The free-trade world price is P_W^*, at which price the country is an exporter. Now suppose that many countries around the world intervene in the market, importers restricting imports and competing exporters subsidizing exports. This drives the world price down to P_W'. The country shown, because of these policies of others, experiences a loss $A + B$ of producers and a consumer gain of A for a net loss of area B. An attempt to recapture the loss by means of guaranteeing price P_W^* to producers via deficiency payments would gain back $A + B$ for producers, and would permit con-

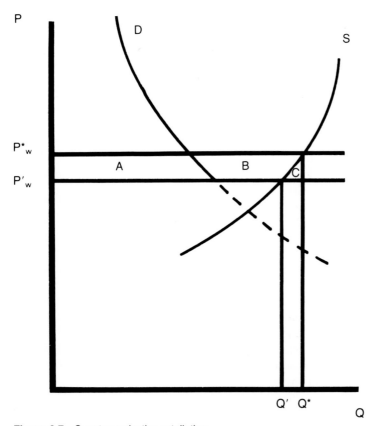

Figure 9.7 Counterproductive retaliation.

sumers to keep the gains A. But it would cost taxpayers $A + B + C$ and so generate a net loss of C. Thus, as compared to the original free-trade situation, other countries' policies causes a net loss of B and the offsetting response causes a further loss of C. Instead of second-best we have even-worse.

By similar methods it can be shown that export subsidies, production controls, or a legislated minimum price to achieve P_w^* in Fig. 9.7, yield results even worse than the deficiency payment policy. Any of these policies could of course be welfare increasing if $\Theta > 1$ for producers, but that would be the case whether imposed starting from price P_w' or P_w^*. It makes no difference whether P_w was caused by other countries' policies or other countries' increased efficiency.

Consider the response in agricultural policy to a distortion in trade in the nonagricultural sector. For example, suppose that manufacturing is protected by means of an import tariff. This draws resources into manufacturing and, at least in a two sector model, out of agriculture. This may or may not reduce the incomes of farmers. It will increase the prices of inputs that are intensively used in manufacturing. If farmers own these inputs, they will gain. It seems more likely, however, that farmers get a relatively large share of their income from inputs like farmland whose relative price can be expected to fall when manufacturing is protected. Farmers also lose as consumers of manufactured goods. Generalizing the model to include produced inputs like tractors gives a third way in which manufacturing protection can harm farmers, by increasing their input costs.

Farmers in these circumstances would be expected to join with consumers in opposing protection of manufacturing. In the United States, this has indeed been the position of Southern agrarians, and later, populists, from Jefferson to the present. The second-best issue is the following. Assuming protection of manufacturing cannot be avoided, is there an intervention in agriculture that will improve matters? Of course, there are policies that will improve the farmers' position—price supports, input subsidies, and so forth—but the question is whether such policies can increase overall (equally weighted) welfare?

The answer is that there are such policies, and we assess them just as was done earlier for the input subsidy, by using Eq. (9.1). The appropriate type of policy and optimal level of intervention depends on the particular nonagricultural policy maintained and supply–demand parameter values in both agriculture and nonagriculture. The interesting general result is the one established in the international trade literature (H. G. Johnson, 1966; Dixit and Norman, 1980, Chap. 6); namely, that second-best responses to any given distortion involve other domestic distortions and, except in some special cases, not other border distortions. This is a generalization of the results obtained in Fig. 9.7, and to be expanded upon in Chap. 11, that optimal policy for a small country either to aid farmers or as a second-best policy for the country as a whole is obtained more efficiently by domestic taxes or subsidies than by tariffs or export subsidies. Moreover, for a large country, intervention in trade is optimal only for the purpose of exercising market power vis-à-vis foreigners; any further redistribution is more efficiently accomplished using domestic taxes and transfers (Dixit and Norman, pp. 175, 190).

COMBINATION OF INSTRUMENTS

In Chap. 8, we discussed the optimal levels of two or more subsidy rates simultaneously. The optimization problem there is like the second-best optimization in this chapter, except we did not take one intervention as given when optimizing in Chap. 8. Related problems arise when we take the *existence* of two policy instruments as given, but find the optimal levels for both of them jointly. An example is deficiency payments, which induce overproduction, accompanied by acreage controls to hold output down. Both of them together, optimally set, could be more efficient than either one alone. The prospects depend, however, on a low elasticity of substitution in production between land and nonland inputs.

Figure 9.8 shows a target-price guarantee of P_1 which yields producer gains of the area left of S between P_0 and P_1, with deadweight loss of the vertically hatched triangle. To reduce output, acreage controls are imposed to shift supply to $\overline{S}$, re-establishing the no-program output, X_2. This would be a clear second-best optimum, eliminating the losses, except that $\overline{S}$ involves higher costs as farmers substitute nonland for land inputs. Producers only gain $X_2 \times (P_1 - P_0)$ minus the horizontally hatched area. This area is the deadweight loss of the "second-best" policy, which may be greater or less than the vertically hatched triangle, depending principally on σ and η. If σ is zero, the horizontally hatched triangle disappears. The decision of the USDA in 1986 to freeze the yield bases on which deficiency payments are made is an attempt to reduce this substitution. Current programs, however, add to deadweight losses by requiring that some diverted land be held idle. This is a producer loss for which there is no corresponding gain to consumers or taxpayers.

ADMINISTRATIVE ISSUES

Problems in enforcing price ceilings, determining eligibility for payments, and collecting taxes have been discussed, but only peripherally. Costs of administration of policies are always present and sometimes are decisive in policy choice. A subset of these costs, not even mentioned to this point, are costs of implementation, of deciding which policy to follow and setting it in place. A recent Australian debate on agricultural subsidies as a second-best policy given protection of manufacturing seems to have turned more than anything else on the great difficulty of ever figuring out what rate of subsidy is in fact optimal (see Edwards, 1987).

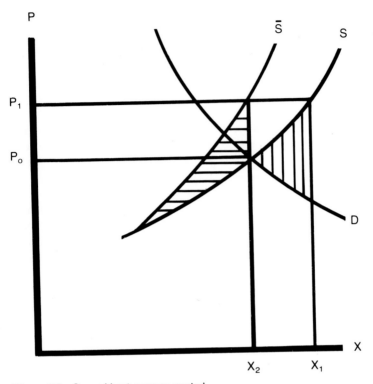

Figure 9.8 Second-best acreage control.

Administrative costs are just as central to comparison of policies as the deadweight losses which have been emphasized so much in this book.[2] They could be incorporated into the surplus transformation curves as additions to deadweight costs. Assuming that establishing a policy involves fixed costs, though, these costs per dollar transferred may decrease as the amount transferred increases. Because these costs are substantial even for the smallest intervention, the STC loses its property of tangency to the efficient redistribution line (slope -1) at the market equilibrium allocation of surpluses. This reflects the reality that it takes a substantial initial push to get intervention started; and once started it is never observed to be very small—like a 1-percent output cutback. Indeed, decreasing average administrative costs can give the STC a convex (to the origin) range for small interventions.

SUMMARY

Chapters 7, 8, and 9 have laid out a set of closely related models and calculating formulas that permit cost–benefit analyses of redistributive commodity policies under a variety of circumstances. Any such calculations require assumptions and simplifications, but developments in theoretical welfare economics permit applications to be carried out without assuming as much as is typically done with simple graphic analysis, as in Chap. 2. We know how to measure supply and demand elasticities appropriately, for a single market as well as several related commodity markets. We can measure consistently the vertically related gains and loses at the input-market level, and in the marketing sector as compared to the farm level. We have methods for handling market imperfections and for considering changes in some policy instruments while others, including nonagricultural market interventions and foreign countries' policies, are held constant. We have at least in principle the tools to correct the problems that Brandow, Clodius, and other critics have found with simple deadweight-cost judgments about policies.

Serious problem areas remain, notably the whole area of policy analysis under dynamics and uncertainty, on which an attempt at analytically useful methods is made in Chap. 10. Chapter 11 expands on another area of incompleteness, policy analysis in an international context. Finally, Chap. 12 tries to go further in the areas of the single biggest gap in applying normative optimization methods; namely, where do we find the SWF?

ENDNOTES

1. By assuming constant returns to scale, the relationship among the contract curve, the production possibilities curve, and factor shares could be specified more precisely than in the following. See, for example, H. G. Johnson, *The Two Sector Model of General Equilibrium*, Aldine, Chicago, 1971. For present purposes we can permit either decreasing or constant returns to scale, including local variation in the scale parameter.
2. These costs are emphasized in a general trade policy context by Corden (1974, Chap. 3) and have been developed in an agricultural context by Monke (1983).

Part Four

Special Topics

Chapter 10

Instability and Risk

In discussing the rationale for governmental intervention in agriculture, Hathaway (1964, p. 53) states a key point:

> When we understand that the market price theory developed for static economic systems has different effects in dynamic situations, we have taken a long step toward recognizing one of the basic factors underlying the need for conscious economic policy in an economy such as ours.

The argument is similar to that of Boulding at the beginning of Chapter 1. It has a normative thrust but positive content; the policy prescription is of the problem-solving or disease curing type, promising Pareto improvement. This possibility implies market failure. The purpose of this chapter is to provide an analysis of the economics of "dynamic situations" in agriculture and of intervention in commodity markets in such situations.

The economics of policy as treated in Chaps. 1 to 9 involves analyzing equilibrium states of models as we move from one policy regime to another. Dynamics is the study of the economy's movements from one state to another, often described as disequilibrium. Since key economic problems of agriculture are matters of disequilibrium, the question arises about usefulness of the comparative statics we have been developing. The notion of equilibrium is still important because the dynamics of prices and quantities between static equilibria are not chaos, but result from the same kind of economic behavior that characterizes static equilibrium situations—achieving objectives as well as possible given the constraints. In commodity markets, prices are set to equate supply and demand each day, even each minute in commodity exchanges. The paths between long-run equilibria, which may never be observed, are composed of a series of short-run equilibria which can be analyzed by just the types of models we have been using. Thus, in Chap. 9 we were able to incorporate about as much as economists have been able to say about disequilibrium in agricultural labor markets without bringing in explicitly dynamic models.

Nonetheless, there are important aspects of commodity markets and policy that have not yet been expressed in our supply–demand models. Indeed, so many complications involving dynamics and uncertainty exist that there is no hope of doing justice to them all. This chapter focuses on six features of agricultural commodity markets, particularly the first three listed:

1. Market developments occur randomly, i.e., unpredictably, in both farm production and demand.
2. Production requires sufficient time that neither output nor product price can be known when input decisions are made.
3. Some poeple are risk averse in that they are willing to accept a lower income stream if it is guaranteed to be more stable.
4. Investing in information makes it possible to learn about some random events sooner.
5. Even when such information is available, changing plans is costly.
6. Information is a public good.

We also consider one feature of the dynamics of policy: that policies also have a random component.

These elements explain why farm prices and incomes are variable, why the variability creates opportunities as well as costs, and why markets have developed for commodity storage, forward contracting, futures, options, crop insurance, weather forecasters, price statistics, and perhaps economists. But what is the connection with policy? One argument is that some of these markets are underdeveloped, for reasons that are discussed later. This market failure can be remedied by second-best policies: government storage of commodities, provision of insurance, weather reports, and price forecasts. Or, as emphasized by Arnott and Stiglitz (1986), taxes and subsidies could be used to encourage goods and services complementary with risk reduction (e.g., commodity storage, pesticides) and to discourage goods complementary with risk-taking (fertilizer, cash rental contracts).

Before going into normative economics of policy under risk, however, it is necessary to consider how the uncertainty and instability change the positive economics of policy. How must we modify or augment the supply–demand models of the preceding chapters? First, since farmers do not know the price they will receive, we need to model their best use of the information available. This we do using a rational expectations model. Second, since even the best information available will usually be wrong, we need to model responses to uncertainty. This we do in two stages, first considering effects of variable prices on expected returns, and second the complications introduced by inherent dislike of uncertainty (risk aversion). For all the topics the treatment is introductory and selective in coverage. We pay particular attention to the economics of price-support policies under these conditions.

RATIONAL EXPECTATIONS

The modification of supply–demand models goes right back to Eq. (2.1) explaining output as a function of price. In modeling supply behavior under conditions (1) and (2), we assume that the producer decides how much to produce based on the best information available about future market conditions at the time that production decisions are made (usually identified, for crops, as the planting season). The producer's (subjective) expectation of price is a good candidate as a sufficient statistic for this information (although it will be found ultimately unsatisfactory later). So we simply replace P in Eq. (2.1) by P^*, the (market's) expected price at planting time.[1] Unfortunately, P^* is unobservable. able.

We can proceed by identifying the statistical expectation of P and P^*. Consider a linear model:

Supply: $\quad Q_t = a_0 + a_1 P_t^* + U_t$ $\qquad\qquad$ (10.1)

Demand: $\quad Q_t = b_0 + b_1 P_t + V_t$ $\qquad\qquad$ (10.2)

Error terms, assumed to have means equal to zero, are added since if there were no uncertainty there would be no reason for expected values to differ from actual values. To find equilibrium, we define it as the situation when (statistically) expected supply and demand are equal, implying expected Q, denoted $\overline{Q}$, and $\overline{P}$ are equal in Eqs. (10.1) and (10.2). Equating (10.1) and (10.2),

$$a_0 + a_1 \overline{P} = b_0 + b_1 \overline{P} \qquad\qquad (10.3)$$

$$\overline{P} = \frac{a_0 - b_0}{b_1 - a_1}$$

which is the same equilibrium as for the usual supply–demand model. Thus, if $\overline{P}$ becomes a policy instrument, it is analyzed just as $\hat{P}$ was analyzed earlier.

The new wrinkle occurs when an *unanticipated* policy change occurs in $\hat{P}$. For example, if we have a target price change announced after producers have made their production decisions, there will be no effect on intended output and thus no effect on the expected market price. If the market price is itself a proximate target, as in USDA purchases of dairy products, then purchases made after production is determined will affect market price as government buying forces others back along the demand curve.

Equations (10.1) to (10.3) present a simple problem because the policy variable is the price. Most policy instruments are not the product price, but affect it. So producers need to judge the effects. Consider a policy of restricting use of an input, say the use of subsidized water on an irrigated crop. Following Fisher (1982), this can be modeled as follows. Let intended supply be a linear function of expected prices and a measure of acre-feet of water allocated, W. We add a random error term to determine actual output, Q_t.

$$Q_t = a_0 + a_1 P^* + a_2 W_t + U_{1t} \tag{10.4}$$

Demand is a linear function of actual price and consumers' incomes, Z, (to represent demand shifters). It is written in price-dependent form to simplify manipulations.

$$P_t = b_0 + b_1 Q_t + b_2 Z_t + U_{2t} \tag{10.5}$$

In expected value, denoted by overbars, we have zero error, and substitution of Eq. (10.5) into Eq. (10.4) yields

$$\begin{aligned}
\overline{Q} &= a_0 + a_1 (b_0 + b_1 \overline{Q} + b_2 Z) + a_2 W \\
&= a_0 + a_1 b_0 + a_1 b_1 \overline{Q} + a_1 b_2 Z + a_2 W \\
&= \frac{a_0 + a_1 b_0}{1 - a_1 b_1} + \frac{a_1 b_2}{1 - a_1 b_1} \overline{Z} + \frac{a_2}{1 - a_1 b_1} \overline{W}
\end{aligned} \tag{10.6}$$

$$\begin{aligned}
\overline{P} &= b_0 + b_1 (a_0 + a_1 \overline{P} + a_2 \overline{W}) + b_2 \overline{Z} \\
&= b_0 + b_1 a_0 + b_1 a_1 \overline{P} + b_1 a_2 \overline{W} + b_2 \overline{Z} \\
&= \frac{b_0 + a_0 b_1}{1 - a_1 b_1} + \frac{a_2 b_1}{1 - a_1 b_1} \overline{W} + \frac{b_2}{1 - a_1 b_1} \overline{Z}
\end{aligned} \tag{10.7}$$

Now substituting Eq. (10.7) into Eq. (10.4) to work with observed values,

$$Q_t = a_0 + \frac{a_1 (b_0 - a_0 b_1)}{1 - a_1 b_1} + \frac{a_1 a_2 b_1}{1 - a_1 b_1} \overline{W} + \frac{a_1 b_2}{1 - a_1 b_1} \overline{Z} + a_2 W_t + U_{1t} \tag{10.8}$$

(This is the key step.)

Equation (10.8) is the reduced-form equation for Q_t, since P_t does not appear. The reduced form equation for P_t is obtained by substitution Eq. (10.8) into Eq. (10.5).

$$P_t = b_0 + b_1 a_0 + \frac{b_1 a_1 (b_0 + a_0 b_1)}{1 - a_1 b_1} + \frac{b_1^2 a_1 a_2}{1 - a_1 b_1} \overline{W} \qquad (10.9)$$

$$+ \frac{b_1 a_1 b_2}{1 - a_1 b_1} \overline{Z} + b_1 a_2 W_t + b_2 Z_t + b_1 U_{1t} + U_{2t}$$

From Eqs. (10.8) and (10.9), we can analyze the effects of a change in the input subsidy, whether forecast or not. Suppose the permitted water use changes by ΔW. If the change is announced when farmers can still adjust plantings, fertilizer use, and so forth, we have $\Delta \overline{W} = \Delta W_t$, and

$$\frac{\Delta Q_t}{\Delta W_t} = \frac{a_1 a_2 b_1}{1 - a_1 b_1} + a_2$$

$$= \frac{a_1 a_2 b_1 + a_2 - a_2 a_1 b_1}{1 - a_1 b_1} \qquad (10.10)$$

$$= \frac{a_2}{1 - a_1 b_1}$$

which is the reduced form effect in a standard supply–demand model when a supply function shifts [i.e., coefficient of $\overline{W}$ in Eq. (10.6)].

If the change in W is announced too late for farmers to adjust, we have $\Delta \overline{W} = 0$ and the effect of the change is

$$\frac{\Delta Q_t}{\Delta W_t} = a_2 \quad \text{and} \quad \frac{\Delta P_t}{\Delta W_t} = b_1 a_2 \qquad (10.11)$$

This case simply gives the horizontal shift in the supply curve from having more or less water available as the quantity effect, and this quantity times $\Delta P / \Delta Q$ from the demand curve slope as the price effect. Equation (10.11) is larger than Eq. (10.10) because $- a_1 b_1 > 0$, so that $(1 - a_1 b_1) > 1$.

The distinction between W and $\overline{W}$ is not applicable to some types of policy, for example, if W represented subsidy payments on fertilizer. The full effect of Eq. (10.10) occurs when producers adjust their production plans to account for the product price change that the subsidy will cause. The effect of Eq. (10.11) occurs when the producers adjust their own production but do not consider the output price effect, i.e., do not consider the production adjustments of others. This is not plausible in the case of policy instruments like input subsidies, because the producers should each expect others to make adjustments at the same time that they do. If a policy change is announced too late for the producers to make adjustments, then there is no supply effect at all, i.e., $\Delta Q_t / \Delta W_t = 0$.

The model is most helpful in analyzing policies that require an instrument to be set repeatedly, year after year, but producers do not know the level of the instrument until some production decisions have been made. For example, wheat program provisions may be (and in the United States have been) changed in the spring, long after winter wheat has been planted. Then the production decisions will be made in the fall based on the anticipated policy. These anticipations would be based on prior years' policies, or on a preannounced policy adjustment rule if one exists. In Eqs. (10.8) and (10.9), $\overline{W}$ is then the anticipated policy and W_t is the actual policy announced after production decisions are made. The model thus provides a means to identify both types of policy change, and by specifying anticipated policies as weighted averages of past policies, the model can be used to estimate policy effects econometrically (see Wallis, 1980).

It is sometimes said that the rational expectations model assumes too much expertise among farmers. Even it if does, it is more promising than the alternatives. If we are going to take uncertainty seriously, yet still carry out quantitative assessment of policy alternatives, some modeling of expectations is required. Available models other than rational expectations (decisions based on inertia, random choice, last year's price) all have undesirable properties, even the ones that seem most plausible at first glance such as adaptive expectations (see Muth, 1961, and Wallis, 1980).

Moreover, the rational expectations approach focuses on the events and behavior that farmers appear to be focusing on. We do see a great deal of effort devoted to forecasting market conditions and policies. For example, with respect to CCC stocks, market participants are constantly trying to assess the "overhang," the prospects for future dampening of price appreciation if these stocks should be released. This enters naturally as an expectational variable in a rational-expectations model, but has no role in adaptive expectations or similar "chartist" models based on past prices. Similarly, U.S. dairy farmers during the implementation of production control programs in 1984 and 1986 were basing decisions on their expectations of what policies would follow these programs in future years. Cotton and grain growers in deciding on planted acreage must try to determine how their current acreage planted will affect acreage bases for future programs, even though the program may be changed.

Consider the simple price-support program mentioned in Chap. 2 in which a law requires all purchasers to pay a minimum price above the expected no-program price. Producers would profit by expanded output at this price but the demand will contract. Supposing black-market and home use of the product are foreclosed, how do producers decide the quantity to produce? In practice, some nonprice rationing scheme would evolve, and producers' surplus gains would be capitalized into the value of whatever gave access to the rationed market or dissipate in trying to sell the commodity in the limited market at the minimum price established. Producers would have to solve much more difficult informational and decision problems under more dimensions of uncertainty than is required for a rational expectations model of supply response in an unregulated market. In this light the model of Eqs. (10.1) to (10.3) is perhaps not just the best available of a bad set of modeling options, but not unreasonable at all in the demands it places on farmers.

MARKET CONSEQUENCES OF PRICE SUPPORTS UNDER UNCERTAINTY

Since all things change, it is necessary to narrow the discussion down to the changes that matter most. Among the phenomena that have been identified as problems in U.S. agriculture, the following involve instability:

- sharp short-term commodity price fluctuations
- long periods of low farm prices and farm income
- random production due to biological and meteorological events
- unpredicted macroeconomic policies
- "disorderly marketing" of farm products

These phenomena are relevant to policy because they impose losses on people which may be moderated by governmental intervention.

But these phenomena do not encompass all changes that cause losses. For example, the closing of an export market for U.S. soybeans can impose losses on soybean producers without there being an instability problem; or the meat packing industry may become monopolized and impose losses on cattlemen without there being an instability problem. This is perhaps too obvious even to mention. But it is not easy to state precisely what makes a problem an instability problem.

Trends in prices do not imply instability. This is important in the measurement of instability of, say, a price series. It means we should consider deviations around trend in calculating price instability. But what if a price series deviates from trend only gradually and predictably, as exponential or quadratic functions may do over a range of data? Should instability be defined as deviation from such a function? Going a step further, what if a price series followed a perfectly predictable cyclical pattern, with known period and amplitude? At least some such price series would be judged unstable by most observers. My suggested measurement would be based on deviations around the best-fitting monotonic (no turning points), continuously differentiable (no corners or gaps) function through the time series data, perhaps the mean squared logarithmic deviation.

Instability fosters unpredictability. But unpredictability is not necessary for instability, as the sine-wave cycle example shows. Unpredictability creates additional problems for economic agents. It is more costly to cope with a change of given magnitude when it comes without warning, even though change that is foreseen generates costs also. Predictable changes will be referred to as the simple dynamics of the market. Two types of unpredictable instability can be distinguished: "variability," which is unanticipated change to which economic agents can adjust; and "uncertainty," which refers to a situation in which choices must be made without knowing what will occur, with no opportunity to adjust the decision later.

The three terms—simple (nonrandom) dynamics, variability, uncertainty—may be made clearer with reference to a producers's supply response to a commodity's price. If a controlled price is changed from year to year according to a pre-established pattern (as in a 4-year farm bill), then the time path of changes in acreage planted in response to the price changes constitutes simple dynamics. If the price is changed unpredictably (with a random component, so that the controlled price is a random variable) from year to year, but the price is announced before the planting season, then we have variability. If the price is not announced until all production decisions have been made, then we have uncertainty. In both of the latter two cases, the controlled price is a random variable (although it may have a predictable component, such as a trend). It is tricky to distinguish between variability and uncertainty in an algebraic model, but sometimes it is important to do so.

This is what is accomplished with the $\overline{W}$ and W effects in Eqs. (10.8) and (10.9). For concreteness, let us characterize instability as randomness in price received by producers caused by (unpredicted) variability in demand, e.g., export demand for grains. The introduction of a price-support program can be analyzed at the following levels: (1) effects on (the frequency distribution of) prices facing a farmer, (2) effects on a farmer's profits or returns, (3) effects on a farmer's utility, and (4) effects on market equilibrium. Effects (1) to (3) pertain to an individual farmer taking market conditions as given, while (4) analyzes the consequences of action by all farmers. In existing literature effects (1) to (3) are well known in general although practical procedures for calculating effects of price supports are not well developed. Effects 4 have hardly been investigated but are the most important effects.

Effects on the Frequency Distribution of Producer Prices

The first step in analyzing price supports under uncertainty is to replace the concept of equilibrium or expected price by a frequency distribution of producer prices. Certainty is then a special case in which the frequency distribution degenerates to a spike at the mean price with zero frequency for all other prices. In this special case, a support price has no effect if the support price level P_s is below the market equilibrium level P_e. In the uncertainty case, the support price truncates the frequency distribution at P_s, and so has an effect even if $P_s < P_e$.

How can we quantify the effect? If we consider the frequency distribution of price, we want to know, first, the difference between the mean of the underlying distribution, P_e, and the mean of the distribution when the tail with $P < P_s$ is eliminated. This expected gain, $E(\Delta P)$, is

$$E(\Delta P) = \int_{P_s}^{\infty} Pr\,(P)\,PdP \int_0^{\infty} Pr\,(P)\,PdP \qquad (10.12)$$

We rule out negative prices and assume that $Pr\,(P)$, the probability that price is at level P, is the same for all $P \geq P_s$ whether the lower tail is truncated or not. This implies that the integrals from P_s to infinity cancel out and the expected price change is

$$E(\Delta P) = P_s\,G(P_s) - \int_0^{P_s} Pr\,(P)\,PdP \qquad (10.13)$$

where $G\,(P_s) = \int_0^{P_s} Pr\,(P)\,dP$, i.e., the cumulative probability of prices below P_s in the absence of price supports. The additive terms in Eq. (10.13) can be collected to yield

$$E\,(\Delta P) = \int_0^{P_s} Pr\,(P)\,(P_s - P)\,dP \qquad (10.14)$$

This is the value of an option to sell at P_s, i.e., a put option with strike price of P_s. This value can be readily approximated if we know the frequency distribution of prices below P_s.

Even more simply, if we are willing to assume that the commodity price is normally distributed, we have

$$E\,(\Delta P) = \int_0^{P_s} \left(\sigma\sqrt{2\pi}\right)^{-1} e^{-[(p-\bar{p})/2\sigma]2}\,(P_s - P)\,dP \qquad (10.15)$$

The integral is taken from 0 since negative prices do not occur; but since a normal distribution of P can generate negative prices, the log-normal distribution is preferable. For practical purposes, however, the assumption of normality may not make much difference and it makes the algebra a little simpler. Results for log-normal prices are given by a logarithmic version of Eq. (10.15), which is the same as the formula of Black (1976) for the market value of a put option one period from expiration.

Equation (10.15) can be simplified for calculating purposes by the trick of expanding $(P_s - P)$ to $(P_s - \overline{P} - P + \overline{P})$, dividing the integral into two parts, and converting to a standard normal form by setting $Z = (P - \overline{P})/\sigma$. This implies that $dp = \sigma dZ$. These manipulations yield

$$E(\Delta P) = (P_s - \overline{P}) \int_0^{Z_s} \frac{1}{\sqrt{2\pi}} e^{-\frac{1}{2}z^2} \, dZ - \int_0^{Z_s} \frac{Z}{\sqrt{2\pi}} e^{-\frac{1}{2}z^2} \, \sigma dZ \quad (10.16)$$

$$= (P_s - \overline{P}) F(Z_s) + \frac{\sigma}{\sqrt{2\pi}} e^{-\frac{1}{2}z^2}$$

Where F is the cumulative normal density function and Z_s is the normalized support price, $(P_s - \overline{P})\sigma$.

For example, suppose that for soybeans $\overline{P}$ = \$6.00 per bushel, the standard deviation of price is 80 cents, and the support price is \$5.60. This means that $Z_s = (5.60 - 6.00)/0.80 = 0.5$. Since the cumulative normal probability to -0.5 is 0.309, we have

$$E(\Delta P) = -0.4 \, (0.309) + \frac{0.8}{2.507} e^{-0.25/2}$$

$$= 16 \text{ cents}$$

Thus, we can estimate the expected price gain from a support price below the mean price. Note that as $\sigma \to 0$, $E(\Delta P) = P_s - \overline{P}$ for $P_s > \overline{P}$ and zero for $P_s \le \overline{P}$. Also, if $P_s = \overline{P}$, then $E(\Delta P) = 0 + \sigma/\sqrt{2\pi}$, which in this example is $0.8/2.505 = 0.32$.

Effects on Farmers' Profits or Returns

The effects on a farmer's expected profits are, to a first approximation, straightforward. Profits rise by the amount of the expected revenue gain. However, we need to consider a producer's supply response to an increased expected price. The increased costs associated with output expansion must be subtracted from the expected revenue increase. The net increase is the increase in producers' surplus.

Following Oi (1961), there have been many studies of the effects on profits of variability in price when the mean price is unchanged. The findings generally are that price variability makes producers better off, assuming that producers can respond to random price changes after they occur. For example, if export demand increases, and hence output price rises, producers can increase production to take advantage of the enhanced profit opportunities. In such models, the stabilization element of a support price makes producers worse off, so that a static analysis overstates their gains.

If variability takes the form of uncertainty, in which producers must choose a desired production level before the random price is known, the effect of price variability on profits is ambiguous. If a producer's output is uncorrelated with price, then a change in variability leaves expected revenue unchanged, and since costs are the same for all outcomes, expected profits are unchanged. If price and output are correlated, then expected profits may increase or decrease depending on the functional form of the demand function, the form of disturbances, and the correlation coefficient between the farm's output and market price (see Just et al., 1982, Chap. 11).

Effects on Farmer's Utility

The effects on a farmer's utility are the same as the effects on profits if utility is a linear function of profits, i.e., if the marginal utility of profits is constant. This condition is equivalent to the farmer's being risk neutral. If the farmer is risk averse, i.e., the marginal utility of profits declines as profits increase, the stabilization element of the price support program can make producers better off even if their expected profits were to decline. Helms (1985) illustrates this point with examples for consumers. The usual result for producer support prices would be that risk aversion implies producer gains even greater than the expected profit gains would indicate. Moreover, if consumers are highly risk averse and the commodity supported is large enough in consumers' budget shares, it is possible that consumers as well as producers can be made better off by a price-support program. This is, however, unlikely to be an important point in practice, as suggested by the results of Helms' simulations. The most extreme risk aversion he considers is an Arrow-Pratt relative risk aversion coefficient of 6, which implies that consumers would give up about 12 percent of their (mean) income in exchange for stabilizing an income stream that, unstabilized, would have a coefficient of variation of 0.2 (i.e., expected deviation from mean income is 20 percent of mean income). Helms finds that even in this case consumers are worse off when price is stabilized at 5 percent above its mean value.

Effects on Market Equilibrium

The preceding are partial results because they do not consider change in market equilibrium caused by price supports. Analyzing the consequences of price supports in this context is a problem in comparative stochastic statics; stochastic because randomness is incorporated in the model, but static in that we look at stationary mean values rather than adjustment paths over time. Some complications in such analysis are apparent in even the simplest models. Consider a two-state model with linear supply and demand as specified in Eqs. (10.1) and (10.2) where the error term in demand is zero, and in supply takes on constant values $\pm u$, each with probability 0.5. The market equilibrium is defined in expectational terms as equality of producers' anticipated price P^* with the (statistical) expectation of price $\overline{P}$, yielding Eq. (10.3), which is the intersection of demand and mean supply. For present purposes, it is convenient to express demand in price-dependent form, so that we have

$$\overline{P} = \beta_0 - \beta_1 (a_0 + a_1 \overline{P}) \tag{10.17}$$

where $\beta_0 = -b_0/b_1$ and $\beta_1 = -1/b_1$.

Introduce a price support level P_s, at which the government buys all that the market will not take at P_s. This means that the demand function becomes perfectly elastic at P_s. Now P will be P_s when u is positive and at the market clearing price when u is negative. The average of prices at the two outcomes is

$$\overline{P}_s = \frac{1}{2} [\beta_0 - \beta_1 (a_0 + a_1 \overline{P}_s - u)] + \frac{1}{2} P_s$$

Solving for $\overline{P}_s$,

$$\overline{P}_s = \frac{[\beta_0 - \beta_1 (a_0 - u) + P_s]}{(2 + \beta_1 a_1)} \qquad P_L < P_s < P_H \tag{10.18}$$

where P_L is P when $u > 0$ and P_H when $u < 0$. $P_s < P_L$ has no effect. For $P_s > P_H$, $\overline{P}_s = P_s$. Equation (10.18) enables us to calculate the mean price associated with any price-support level. Consider the particular price-support level where P_s equals the mean price with no intervention, so that in a static framework the program would have no effect. Solving for this level of P_s from Eq. (10.17) and substituting into Eq. (10.18),

$$\overline{P}_s = P_s + \frac{\beta_1 u}{2 + \beta_1 a_1} \tag{10.19}$$

In order to see what this amounts to, Fig. 10.1 shows a special case in which $\beta_0 = 13$, $\beta_1 = 0.1$, $a_0 = 70$, $a_1 = 10$, and $u = 10$. This implies a mean supply–demand intersection at $\overline{P} = 3$ and $Q = 100$. The price support at $P_s = 3$ implies $\overline{P}_s = 3.33$ and $\overline{Q}_s = 103.3$, plotted as point R. From Eq. (10.19), we see how the expected price differs from the support level, and how this difference depends on u. In particular, defining $\Delta P = \overline{P} - P_s$, we have

$$\frac{d(\Delta P)}{du} = \frac{\beta_1}{2 + \beta_1 a_1} \tag{10.20}$$

which is positive for normal-sloped demand and supply. Thus, point R rises along the mean supply curve as u increases.

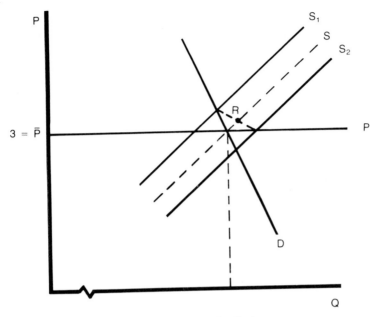

Figure 10.1   Stochastic supply (first approximation).

But there are complications. This first approximation does not generate full competitive equilibrium. Consider the example. We have the following price-quantity pairs under the support program: if $u = -10$, then P, Q is (3.67, 93.3), and if $u = +10$, P, Q is (3.00, 113.3). This implies that revenue is 342.4 if $u = -10$ and 339.9 if $u = 10$, for a mean of 341.15. If this is to be represented as competitive equilibrium at point R, then $P \cdot Q$ on the mean supply curve should have the same value. But $3.33 \times 103.3 = 344.0$. Therefore, R is not the equilibrium. What went wrong? Retracing our steps through the underlying model, we find deeper trouble: $P = 3$ and $Q = 100$ is not the equilibrium with no program!

With no program, the P, Q pairs are (3.50, 95) if $u = -10$ and (2.50, 105) if $u = +10$. Mean revenue is $0.5\ (332.5) + 0.5\ (262.5) = 297.5$, which is less than 3×100 as shown in Figure 10.1. Equation (10.18) reflects a situation in which current output responds to $\bar{P}$, not P_t, so the no-program P, Q pairs are (4.00, 90) and (2.00, 110), and mean revenue is 290. In either case, cost is 300 so $\bar{P} = 3.00$ cannot be the long-run equilibrium. An industry-wide expectation of loss is not consistent with long-run competitive equilibrium.

The root cause of the problem is the specification of the "rational expectations" equilibrium as $\bar{P} = P^*$. For (risk-neutral) models like this one (the same as in Turnovsky, 1974), we need a zero-profit condition for equilibrium. In expected value, this is

$$E(PQ) = E(P^*Q) \tag{10.21}$$

or expected revenue equals expected economic cost. Expected economic cost is an opportunity cost concept, the receipts necessary to induce producers to provide the quantity of expected output that consumers will purchase.

The implication of this equilibrium condition for the linear two-state model is that we cannot simply set $\overline{P} = P^*$. Instead, we have, where $\overline{Q}$ is expected output,

$$E(R) = E(PQ) = \frac{1}{2} [\beta_0 - \beta_1 (\overline{Q} + u)] (\overline{Q} + u) \qquad (10.22)$$
$$+ \frac{1}{2} [\beta_0 - \beta_1 (\overline{Q} - u)] (\overline{Q} - u)$$

and

$$E(P^*Q) = - \frac{a_0}{a_1} \overline{Q} + \frac{1}{a_1} \overline{Q}^2 \qquad (10.23)$$

Equation (10.23) is obtained by solving Eq. (10.1) for P^*, expressing it in terms of intended output (omitting u), and multiplying by $\overline{Q}$. Intended output is assumed equal to (statistically) expected output—a condition for equilibrium. This specification implies that producers cannot adjust their intended output in response to the price effects of the random shock, u, as in the specification of Eq. (10.1). If P_t replaced P_t^* in Eq. (10.1), we would have a model of variability.

Equating (10.22) and (10.23), obtains the quadratic

$$\left(\frac{1}{a_1} + \beta_1 \right) \overline{Q}^2 - \left(\frac{a_0}{a_1} + \beta_0 \right) \overline{Q} + \beta_1 u^2 = 0 \qquad (10.24)$$

For parameter values above, Eq. (10.24) is

$$0.2Q^2 - 20 Q + 10 = 0$$
$$Q = 99.5$$

The resulting equilibrium is shown in Fig. 10.2 most straightforwardly as the intersection of total cost and expected revenue. From the upper panel, this is not the quantity at which intended supply and demand intersect. The appropriate depiction of competitive equilibrium in P, Q space is the intersection of the expected average revenue (EAR) function with the intended supply function. The EAR function specifies, for every intended quantity Q^*, the expected

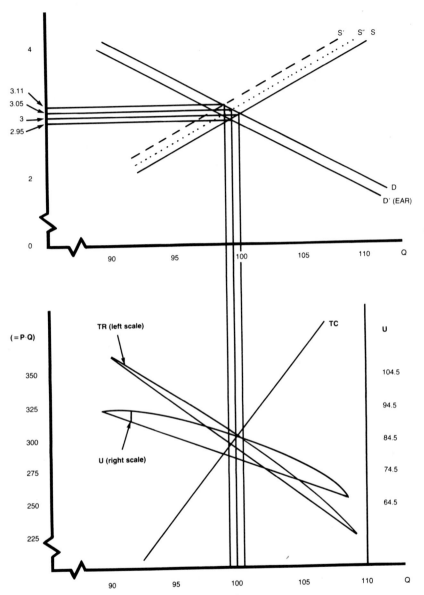

Figure 10.2 Stochastic supply (full equilibrium).

revenue per bushel. (This would be a point on the demand curve only if the total revenue function were linear, which would occur only if the inverse demand function were of the form, $P = b_0 + b_1 Q^{-1}$.)

Because EAR is less than the demand price at each quantity for a linear demand curve (quadratic total revenue function), competitive equilibrium is characterized by less output than at the supply–demand intersection. This implies that mean price will be above the price at supply–demand intersection. In Fig. 10.2, the price under uncertainty is $3.05 per bushel and EAR is $2.95 at the competitive equilibrium Q of 99.5, while stationary supply equals demand at $P = 3.00$ and $Q = 100$.

RISK AVERSION

For risk-averse consumers and/or producers, the analysis of full equilibrium is more complex. We need to know how revenue translates to income, and then how income translates to utility. Following on the preceding example, suppose that half of the costs of intended output are purchased inputs and the other half are returns to producer-owned inputs. Suppose, further, that these returns constitute half of producers' income, the other half being nonstochastic income from some other source. This means that in the two-state example with equilibrium as shown in Fig. 10.2, we have: when $u = -10$, $Q = 89.5$, $P = 4.05$, $PQ = 362.48$; and when $u = 10$, $Q = 109.5$, $P = 2.05$, $PQ = 224.48$; which implies that mean net returns are $293.48/2 = 146.74$. Under the assumptions, there is an equal amount of nonstochastic income, so total income y is 293.48. Since all the variation in revenue is residual income to the farmers, when $u = -10$, $y = 362.48$, and when $u = 10$, $y = 224.48$. The coefficient of variation of y is 0.236.

Continuing the example with utility in the two states, suppose all the farmers are identical and have equal shares of market income, and all have the same utility function, of the constant risk-aversion form.

$$U(Y) = C + (1-R)^{-1} Y^{1-R} \tag{10.25}$$

where C is a constant and R is the relative risk-aversion coefficient $U''(Y)/U'(Y)$ $\cdot Y$. Let $R = 1.5$, so that $U(Y) = C - 2/\sqrt{Y}$. This degree of risk aversion implies that producers would exchange the example's income stream for a stable income stream that was 4 percent smaller.

To find competitive equilibrium under risk aversion, we equate the expected utility of the uncertain income from producing the crop to the (certain) utility loss of opportunity returns (costs) required to generate the income. The utility loss is simply the utility of the cost as given by Eq. (10.23) which in our example is

$$U(P^*\overline{Q}) = C - 2 \left(\frac{a_0}{a_1} \overline{Q} - \frac{1}{a_1} \overline{Q}^2 \right)^{-1/2}$$

Similarly, the expected utility gain is obtained from Eq. (10.22), and we find the market equilibrium by equating (10.22) and (10.23), as modified, solving for $\overline{Q}$

$$
\begin{aligned}
C - 2\left(\frac{a_0}{a_1}\overline{Q} - \frac{1}{a_1}\overline{Q}^2\right)^{-\frac{1}{2}} \\
= \frac{1}{2}\left(C - \frac{2}{[\beta_0 + \beta_1(\overline{Q} + u)](\overline{Q} + u)]^{1/2}}\right) \\
+ \frac{1}{2}\left(C - \frac{2}{[\beta_0 + \beta_1(\overline{Q} - u)](\overline{Q} - u)]^{1/2}}\right)
\end{aligned}
\tag{10.26}
$$

Note that C cancels out, so that R is the only parameter of the utility function that affects the solution for $\overline{Q}$. Using the parameters of the Fig. 10.2 example, Eq. (10.26) reduces to

$$
\begin{aligned}
-2(0.1\overline{Q}^2 - 7\overline{Q})^{-0.5} + (-0.1\overline{Q}^2 + 11\overline{Q} + 120)^{-0.5} \\
+ (-0.1\overline{Q}^2 + 15\overline{Q} - 140)^{-0.5} = 0
\end{aligned}
$$

which (using numerical methods) solves for $\overline{Q} = 98.9$. This implies a mean price of \$3.11. As shown in Fig. 10.2, risk aversion approximately doubles the output decline and price rise that occurred under risk neutrality, as compared to the supply–demand intersection (certainty case).

In the way risk analysis is typically applied, the entire difference between certainty outcomes and results under uncertainty is attributed to risk aversion. For example, one could draw a supply curve through the point where $P = 3.11$ and $Q = 98.9$, as shown by the curve, S', in Fig. 10.2. The shift from the certainty case is then interpreted as an indicator of risk aversion. But this sort of "shift" occurs even without risk aversion; in the example only about half the output reduction occurs because of risk aversion. It might be less open to misinterpretation to represent equilibrium uncertainty by using the EAR function to show the (risk-neutral) revenue effect and a shift in S to represent the risk-aversion effect, as in the dotted curve S''. The intersection of D' and S'' then shows full equilibrium under uncertainty.

What is the empirical significance of the four types of complications? Consider the corn program in the 1985 farm bill. Several members of Congress proposed freezing the 1986 target price at the 1985 level of \$3.03 per bushel. Others, including the Reagan administration, wanted to reduce the target price by making it a declining function of past prices, e.g., 100 percent of the past 5-year average in 1986, 95 percent in 1987, etc. The farm prices of corn for the past 5 years are: \$3.11, 2.50, 2.68, 3.25, and 2.68 per bushel. The 5-year average is \$2.84. The practical question for policy analysis is the same as in static analysis: what difference will it make if the target price for corn is $3.03 or $2.84?

Supposing that $2.84 is the appropriate mean price, we can calculate from Eq. (10.15) the increase in expected price caused by increasing the target price to $3.03 if we know the parameter σ (assuming normality). The sample standard deviation of price for the past 5 years is 16 cents per bushel. Using these values in Eq. (10.15), the expected producer price gain is 20 cents, as compared to the 19 cents that a deterministic approach would assume. The accuracy of estimates of both $\overline{P}$ and σ is questionable, but the difference between the stochastic and the crude deterministic estimates is too small to cause excitement. (But of course for support prices below mean price, the stochastic estimate of price effect can be substantially greater than the zero effect that a deterministic model gives.)

Bringing in expected profits or producers' surplus gains requires knowledge of the supply function, and cost components of farmer-owned and purchased inputs. Our information here is weak, but this difficulty applies as much to policy analysis in a deterministic as in a stochastic framework.

Bringing in risk aversion for farmers and consumers is important if: (a) they are significantly risk averse, *and* (b) the commodity in question accounts for a significant fraction of farm income or consumers' budgets, *and* (c) market participants do not manage risk by nonprogram means, e.g., hedging, diversification, insurance. We really do not know enough about any of these factors to assert that policy analysis that ignores risk aversion and just adds up monetary gains and losses is misguided.

Specifying market equilibrium has occupied most of the discussion in this chapter. It becomes a factor in applied policy analysis only when we have already dealt with the preceding microlevel complications 1 and 2, and with additional serious problems, not discussed here, with aggregating over diverse individuals. Given the difficulties of undertaking these preliminary steps, the full stochastic competitive equilibrium methods discussed are not in the cards for analyzing policy alternatives. Nonetheless, it is good to be aware of what is being ignored when we ignore uncertainty doing comparative statistics of the usual kind. The main practical lesson is that even "low" price supports can have substantial effects. For policy research, the bottom line is the difficulty of separating out the consequences of risk aversion from the (risk neutral) effects of variability on expected profits, a subject on which the authors of estimates of farmers' risk aversion coefficients or supply shifts due to risk aversion have been unduly optimistic about their capabilities.

WELFARE ECONOMICS OF RISK

The standard results in quantitative welfare economics that were so helpful in providing formulas for Chap. 8 and 9 do not provide useful methods for assessing policies under risk. The attitude of the "higher" theorists may be represented as a philosophical throwing in of the towel. For example, Nath (1969) recognizes the importance of uncertainty of the type that confronts agriculture, and concludes:

> This kind of uncertainty makes it impossible to be sure that any pattern of allocation which is at present considered desirable will still be considered desirable by the time it has been achieved. This is a kind of uncertainty conditioning human existence which simply has to be lived with (p. 60).

Ng (1983), Rowley and Peacock (1975), and Brown and Jackson (1978) are recent examples of texts that say nothing about the topic without even an apology. Dasgupta and Heal (1979) and Newbery and Stiglitz (1981) emphasize the absence of forward markets and contingent (option) markets as a market failure, but not in a practically usable way. Cost–benefit analysis has taken risk more seriously as a practical matter, particularly in choosing the appropriate discount rate, but this isn't the issue in the agricultural policy area.

Agricultural economists have argued that stabilization through price supports can make (risk-neutral) consumers as well as producers better off because producers are risk averse, and therefore they will produce more when revenues fluctuate less. Thus we have a downward shift in the supply function and, hence, a lower consumer price. How do we measure the gains? In fact, are we sure that net social gains will be generated? If so, we don't have to be able to measure the gains quantitatively to make the policy recommendation that some stabilization program is a reasonable social investment. But there remains the problem of devising an operational risk-reduction program.

In this section three aspects of this issue are discussed, as they relate to recent work on the economics of risk. This discussion is divided into three parts: first, measuring the social benefits of risk reduction; second, provision of the public goods which will achieve risk reduction; and third, market substitutes for these public goods.

Measuring the Social Benefits of Risk Reduction

The most straight-forward method of measuring producer gains is provided by Just et al. (1982, pp. 255–262). Their measure of gains for a single, competitive producer is shown in Fig. 10.3; s_1 is the producer's supply function given an uncertain price, which is determined by a random process after production decisions are determined so that the producer responds to expected price. In order to focus on price uncertainty, assume that output is nonstochastic. (Price variability is generated by random changes in demand, or foreign producer's output). If the variability of price were reduced to zero, but its expected value remained at $\overline{P}$, supply would shift to s_0, the producer would increase output, and the net gain to the producer would be measured by the area between S, and

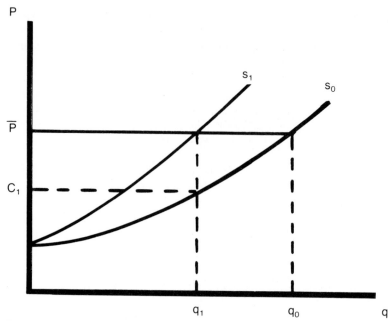

Figure 10.3 Risk-averse firm.

S_0 below $\overline{P}$. Note that this is a gain in utility, not profits or economic rents as money returns. Indeed, when uncertainty is present, profits exist equal to $(\overline{P} - C_1)q_1$. But money profit is in this case a risk premium just sufficient at the margin to cover the disutility caused by uncertain prices.

The industry equilibrium is found by horizontal summation of all the producers' s_0 and s_1 curves, yielding S_0 and S_1 in Fig. 10.4. At the industry level, the market demand function must be incorporated. Mean price falls from P_2 to the equilibrium certain price P_0. Producers' gains if the market price had not fallen (if market demand were perfectly elastic) would have been $A + B + C$. But with the price decline to P_0, producers' surplus of $E + B + C$ is lost. Thus, the net gain to producers is $A - E$. This can easily be negative. The less elastic the demand function, the more likely that risk-averse producers will lose from stabilization.

The industry equilibrium change in Fig. 10.4 is identical to the supply–demand analysis of a technical change which shifts supply from S_1 to S_0. In that analysis, it would be said that consumers gain area $E + B$, and that the social gain (the sum of producers' and consumers' gains) is $A - E + E + B = A + B$.

Area $A + B$ is also the social loss from a production control program which shifts supply from S_0 to S_1. Thus, this simple supply–demand analysis of gains and losses places the welfare analysis of risk reduction on the same basis as the analysis of policies under certainty. The key difference is that

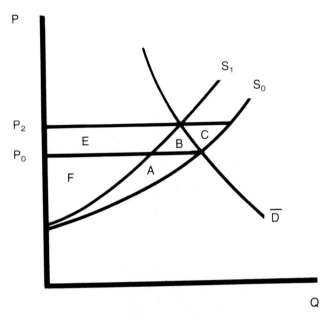

Figure 10.4 Industry of risk-averse firms.

where the standard analysis gives $A + B$ as a deadweight loss from production controls under certainty, Fig. 10.4 gives $A + B$ as the social gain from stabilizing price. This helps give an intuitive grasp of some policy issues. For example, it shows that if a supply-control program has the same effect on the supply function as an increase in risk, then if farmers gain (lose) from supply control, they must lose (gain) from price stabilization, i.e., if one of these programs is good for farmers, the other cannot be.

Having attained a conceptually simple and quantitatively tractable measure of gains from price stabilization when producers are risk averse, let us turn to things that are wrong with it.

First, note that even if the model is appropriate, the measure of social gain to price stabilization is gross (as opposed to net). It is gross because the costs of the stabilization program must be subtracted, just as the costs of generating new knowledge must be subtracted to get the social gain from technical change. There will be costs to the stabilization program. The only way not to have costs would be for the government to operate a buffer stock at a profit or at least to break even. But the unregulated market equilibrium characterized by S_1 already incorporates the extent of stabilization created by private speculative storage. Equilibrium in private speculative storage occurs where expected profits are approximately zero.[2] Therefore, added stocks in a stabilization program must drive expected (average) profit negative. So there will be some amount to subtract from $A + B$ to measure the net social gain.

More fundamental problems with $A + B$ as the social gain involve the model itself. Consider the gains to consumers, which were simply taken by analogy to technical change as equal to $E + B$. One problem is that consumers might be risk averse, too, so that stabilization makes them better off. This would show up as a rightward shift in the demand function when price is stabilized, hence, generating more producer gains, perhaps more consumer gains, and more social gains.

Even if consumers are risk neutral, Fig. 10.4 does not tell the full story of consumers' gains. The curve D contains all the information about price at S_0, where price is stabilized, but the intersection of D and S_1 is not actually observed since it is random-demand shocks that cause the uncertainty. In calculating producers' profits, the distribution of price can be replaced by mean price $\overline{P}_1$, because producers do not respond to the random component it output is nonstochastic. But consumers can respond to short-term price fluctuations (unless our model introduces uncertainty by a mechanism such as a random-number generator in supermarket cash registers, with customers not permitted to alter their purchases after seeing the bill). This brings in issues of consumers' gains to variability as shown to exist by Waugh (1944). However, because the uncertainty here is generated by shifts in demand, given quantity available, the ability to adjust consumption is created by the stabilization program, so that consumers will gain from stabilization (even if mean price stays constant). This means we have to add something to $E + B$ to get the consumers' gain (and the full social gain).

Just et al. (1982, pp. 260–61) provide an instructive example in which price is stabilized by means of a buffer stock. This permits consumers to buy all they wish at P_1 when demand is randomly high, but requires them also to pay P_1 when demand is low. The net gain to consumers from such a policy, with no risk response by producers, is shown in Fig. 10.5. There are two states of demand, D_H and D_L, each with probability 0.5. Q_1 is always available, produced in response to $\overline{P}$. Without stabilization, price is at P_H in state D_H. With stabilization via a buffer stock, Q_H is available to consumers at P_1. The gain in D_H is, therefore, the upper hatched trapezoid. In state D_L with no stabilization, price falls to P_L. With stabilization, price P_1 is maintained, and consumers lose the lower hatched trapezoid. The expected consumer gain from stabilization is one-half the difference between the upper and lower hatched areas. Because D_H, D_L, and D_1 are parallel, the difference in the hatched areas is equal to the parallelogram with area $A + B$, with $\frac{1}{2}(A + B) = B$. Thus, area B measures the net gain from pure stabilization via a buffer stock. This has to be added to $E + B$ from Fig. 10.4 in order to measure the total consumer gain and to $A + B$ in order to measure the gross social gains from stabilization with risk-averse producers. In the Just et al. example, $E + B$ is \$5 billion, $A + B$ is \$4.5 billion, and area B is \$0.25 billion.

Note that if stabilization had been achieved by a policy other than a buffer

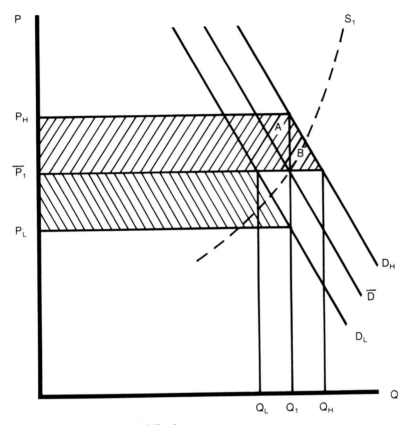

Figure 10.5 Gains from stabilization.

stock the area B gains would not have occurred. For example, if D_H and D_L were generated by real-income fluctuations and stability was achieved by social income insurance, then we would observe P_1 and Q_1 each year in Fig. 10.5 (ignoring producers' risk aversion) and there would be no area B gains. This shows that the mechanism used in stabilization is important.

Another issue, referring back to Fig. 10.3 is the intramarginal behavior of s_0 and s_1, particularly the depiction of s_0 and s_1 as having a common origin on the vertical axis. Why wouldn't risk aversion shift s throughout its length, as in the Just et al. example, rather than rotating s around a point on the vertical axis? An economic rationale for the rotation approach could be that when no output is produced, risk aversion is irrelevant. However, the intercept has economic meaning as the minimum price necessary to induce suppliers to produce any of the product. It seems reasonable that risk aversion should increase this minimum price. But perhaps the amount of income at risk is trivially small for small output? This raises the issue of how risk aversion changes with income, and also, apart from risk considerations, what is going on at small quantities supplied for an individual producer.

Two alternative ways of conceptualizing the supplier's situation are given by Just, Hueth, and Schmitz (JHS) and by Newbery and Stiglitz (NS). JHS depict the supplier as a firm, with utility a function of profit, profit being defined as revenue minus variable costs, that is, the returns to fixed factors. This means that the supply curve which is defined for fixed price (no risk) is the firm's short-run marginal cost function. This means, for typical U-shaped average cost functions, that there will be a shutdown price, equal to average (variable) cost at its minimum. As price falls enough that q approaches the shutdown output, quasi-rents disappear, so by the same argument as above, the firm's supply curve rotates around the shutdown point. This makes it less likely that producers will gain from price stabilization as the area $A + B$ is reduced.

However, it is necessary to consider the issue of whether quasi-rents (plus profits) is the proper argument for a farmer's utility function. What is usually considered the proper argument in an individual's utility function is (income useable for) consumption, or in an intemporal formulation, wealth. But some returns to fixed factors pay off past investments in equipment or land, and do not enter the consumption stream. Moreover, some variable inputs are the source of income for consumption, notably returns to the farmers' own labor. Labor is a variable input if the farmer can shift labor to other employment (another farm commodity or off-farm work or even leisure) in response to changes in the return to labor in the commodity being analyzed. So some part of variable costs, which is excluded from the surplus calculations, seems relevant to the farmer's risk position. On the other hand, it is true that if commodity price falls, the farmer must still pay the mortgage payments, so that the variability of returns to fixed factors, even if not owned by the farmers, affects the variability of income. The issue for income risk is not whether a factor is fixed or not, but whether a factor is contractually paid or is a residual claimant. Land rented may be technically a fixed factor but the issue for risk analysis is whether it is rented for cash or shares. There is no room for this distinction in the JHS approach and the approach is therefore suspect.

What we need for risk analysis of farm policy is the variability of net returns of all farm resources that are not prepaid, and the risk premia required by their owners. With this information we can estimate the shift in supply caused by a risk-reducing policy. Then to compute the market-level incidence of the policy, we need the rents generated for all factors that are fixed or have upward-sloping supply curves to the industry, whether prepaid or not. Thus, for example, the hybrid seed corn distributors supply a specific factor to corn producers and so earn rents that are included in the producer surplus areas above the market supply curves of Fig. 10.4 and 10.6. Yet because they are prepaid, their risk is not (directly) reduced by a corn price-stabilization program. Consequently they do not share in the firm-level supply shift. This shows up as an aggregation problem: horizontal summation of the firms' supply curves (for which seed prices are fixed) overstates the supply slope at the industry level.

Returning to farmers' returns in the JHS model, what is excluded in their quasi-rent formulation is returns to farmer-owned inputs, which are upward sloping in supply but neither perfectly elastic (variable) nor perfectly inelastic (fixed), like the farmer's labor in the NS model. In this situation, the firm's supply function may shift through its length when risk is reduced. Shown in Fig. 10.6 is a special case of a vertically parallel shift in supply when risk is reduced. This outcome requires constant absolute risk aversion (CARA) if income is linear in P and the supply curve is linear (or else the right degree of increasing or decreasing absolute risk aversion to offset nonlinearities in the relationships between P, Q and income).

The case of vertically parallel supply curves is interesting in that producers necessarily gain from price stabilization. To prove this proposition, consider the surplus areas of Fig. 10.6. Producers' surpluses are the boat-shaped areas below P_1 and P_0 for the risky and stabilized situations, and above S_1 and S_0, respectively. To show that the area below P_0 is larger, note that the constant distance between S_1 and S_0 means that $C_1 - C_0$ is the distance between S_1 and S_0 at Q_1. But the price decline $P_1 - P_0$ is less than the distance between S_1 and S_0 at Q_1 (the "cost" decline is greater than the price decline). This implies that

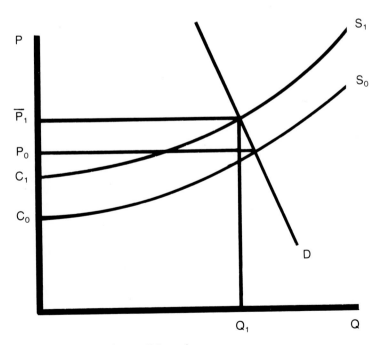

Figure 10.6 Vertically parallel supply curves.

$P_0 - C_0 > P_1 - C_1$. So if we integrate the surplus area for S_1 and S_0 up to Q_1, we find

$$\int_0^{Q_1} \left[P_0 - S_0(Q) \right] dQ > \int_0^{Q_1} \left[P_1 - S_1(Q) \right] dQ$$

because $P_0 - S_0 > P_1 - S_1$ at all Q. Moreover, producers' surplus for S_0 also includes the small shaded triangle to the right of Q_1. Thus, the producer gains $A - E$ from Fig. 10.4 are always positive for vertically parallel supply curves.

Another aggregation problem arises because of the heterogeneity of farms. They have different shutdown prices, different contractual arrangements, and require different risk premia. They require different premia not only because they have different utility functions but also because they differ in diversification, such as other commodities, off-farm work, income of family members, and investments in nonfarm assets. Moreover, farmers differ in access to credit markets which can smooth the consumption stream while income remains variable; indeed, with perfect credit markets there might be no risk premium at all. Such heterogeneity raises issues of measurement at the market level and of the economic meaning of what is measured. The measurement problem is that it is not reasonable to expect market-level gains and losses from policy to be deducible from individual-firm considerations, as discussed earlier with reference to Fig. 10.5.

The natural willingness-to-pay measure for risk is the risk premium. The risk premium, ρ, measured as the return necessary for a producer to accept a risky prospect with mean return $\overline{Y}$ is approximately

$$\rho \cong \frac{1}{2} A \text{ Var } (Y) \tag{10.27}$$

where A is the coefficient of absolute risk aversion $[U''(Y)/U'(Y)]$ for any twice continuously differentiable utility function $U(Y)$ (for details, see Newbery and Stiglitz, 1981, Chap. 6). In order to have a unit-free measure, the expression for relative risk aversion is

$$\frac{\rho}{Y} \cong \frac{1}{2} R \cdot CV(Y)^2 \tag{10.28}$$

where R is the relative risk aversion coefficient, $\overline{Y}A$, and $CV(Y)^2$ is the squared coefficient of variation of Y, Var $(Y)/\overline{Y}^2$. The equations are exact if Y is normally distributed.

With uncertainty in Y arising only from price, the risk premium is $\frac{1}{2} AQ^2$

Var(P) and the firm's supply curve is shifted vertically by the marginal risk premium,[3]

$$\frac{dP}{dQ} = AQ \, \text{Var}(P) \tag{10.29}$$

Dividing (10.29) by P gives the marginal relative risk premium. This is a conceptually handy indicator in that it tells directly by what percentage price has to be increased to offset risk aversion. Alternatively, it permits the forecasting of supply effects of a stabilization program from information on the risk premium, which in turn can in principle be estimated econometrically from farmers' responses to past changes in risk. Problems arise however in that Eq. (10.29) is defined for an individual and, again, there are problems of interpreting it in market data with heterogeneous firms. An industry may contain both high-cost firms with low risk premia, and lower-cost firms with high risk premia.

As an example of empirical work on risk in policy analysis, consider Thraen and Hammond (1983) on the U.S. dairy program. They estimate an econometric model of milk production in which investment in dairy herds and facilities responds not only to expected milk price but also to price risk. Price risk is measured for milk relative to crop prices by constructing a moving average of deviations of observed annual price from the trend price for both milk and crops (Thraen and Hammond, pp. 18–20). This variable has a significantly positive effect on investment in dairy production capacity, which as specified implies risk aversion—more uncertain milk prices shift the supply function upward as expected. The magnitude of the shift is so large that after adjustment to deregulation, the price of manufacturing milk is simulated to be 23 to 36 percent *higher* without dairy price supports than with price supports at the actual levels. Therefore, the policy conclusion is that consumers have gained substantially—roughly $3 per hundredweight times 1.2 billion hundredweight, or between $3 and 4 billion per year—from the existence of the price support program for milk.

Are the results believable? Since the support price holds the market price up in most years, the vertical shift in supply must have been even greater than 23 to 36 percent. Suppose it is 40 percent, which is the marginal relative risk premium and is equal to

$$\frac{d(\rho/P)}{dQ} = R \cdot CV(P) \tag{10.30}$$

substituting P for Y on the assumption that output is nonstochastic, which is the assumption in Thraen and Hammond. The risk aversion necessary to yield a value of 0.4 on the left-hand side of Eq. (10.30) depends on the coefficient of variation in price that confronts producers. In the dairy simulations, price supports almost eliminate price variability around trend; with no price supports, the coefficient of variation of price around trend is about 0.1 (derived from a standard deviation of 85 cents per hundredweight and an average price of $8.90 during 1970–1978). Thus, according to these results dairy producers have to receive a bonus of 40 percent of gross receipts (or roughly $4 billion) to induce them to undertake a risk characterized by a standard deviation of gross receipts that is 10 percent of mean gross receipts. This seems high.

Econometric estimation of any interesting parameters usually raises as many questions as it answers, and this is particularly true with risk aversion parameters. It is particularly important not to confuse supply response to risk with supply response to expected profit, as discussed earlier. Apart from this problem, the dependence of mean revenue on price and output variability creates big problems for welfare analysis. The problem is that the mean price and output point will not be at the intersection of mean demand $(\overline{D})$ and supply curves; and when we change price variability this will change the location of mean price and quantity relative to this intersection. Strictly speaking, this rules out any simple graphic surplus areas in P, Q space. One can argue that the magnitudes of displacement, related to the curvature of total revenue and cost functions, will be second-order magnitudes relative to surplus areas, especially for comparative (stochastic) statics involving small policy changes. But these effects can be easily be of the same order of magnitude as area B in Fig. 10.5. Unfortunately, as has been apparent since the equations of Chap. 8 using the second-order terms of Taylor series expansions were presented, many key welfare-economics magnitudes are similar second-order magnitudes.

Second Best Policies: Stabilization, Storage, and Insurance as Public Goods

The preceding discussion follows the usual approach of analyzing price stabilization without much attention to the mechanism used to achieve it. Although the farmer's price could be supported by production controls, direct payments, or just passing a law that everyone must pay a minimum price, the mechanism typically invoked for stabilization is government acquistion of commodities at the support price. To analyze this activity fully, however, we have to consider the disposition of the commodities. To a first approximation, the sale of government stocks has a downward effect on price equal to the upward effect of the purchase of the stocks. Therefore, if every bushel purchased is subsequently sold, there is approximately no effect on the average price. Since almost all issues in stabilization turn on second-order effects, this is not a sufficient analysis. Wright and Williams (1984) provide results showing how the effects of price supports on mean price depend on the curvature of demand and supply curves. There is a large prior literature on gainers and losers from stabilization. These studies will not be discussed here because, unlike Wright and Williams, they do not model the storage regime but just assume that variability is eliminated, mentioning storage as the mechanism. But every stockpiling regime will run out of stocks under some circumstances so that complete stabilization is impossible. Optimal stabilization cannot be specified without paying attention to the stochastic dynamic maximization problem involved, which this literature omits completely. This issue is treated in the following section.

Market stabilization may in any case not be the first-best solution to the problems arising from uncertainty that we have been discussing. The producers' aversion is to variability in returns, so that shifting money from periods of plenty to periods of scarcity would be just as effective in reducing risk, and cheaper, than commodity storage. But then the question arises of why producers do not buy insurance policies, hedge on futures or option markets, and stabilize consumption via credit. If the appropriate insurance policies or option contracts do not exist, then it seems more straightforward for the government to establish and supply the appropriate risk transfer contracts. This approach to policy suggests a corresponding approach to economic analysis of producers' risk aversion, namely to measure the surplus area as the area under the demand function for insurance. Unfortunately, applicable supply–demand models of insurance have not been developed. A problem that arises immediately is specifying the appropriate quantity of insurance. One could adapt Fig. 10.3 to 10.6 by identifying the quantity of insurance with the amount of expected revenue covered. But this leaves unspecified the coverage level; for example, one could specify the expected dollar value of a farmer's corn crop as $100,000, but this would not determine the "quantity of insurance" the farmer bought; for this we need to specify the hazards insured against, the amount of loss that triggers an indemnity, and perhaps such details as deductibles.

Consider a specific insurance contract, such as price insurance which pays an indemnity equal to the difference between the actual (Chicago Board of Trade) market price and the (preplanting) expected CBOT price whenever the harvest season market price falls 5 percent or more below the prior expected price. This is a straightforward contract to consider in that it is equivalent to a put option on futures purchased in the preplanting season which expires in the harvest season and has a strike price 5 percent below the planting season futures price. The analogy permits a clear conceptualization of the price of the insurance policy as equivalent to the premium on the put option. On March 13, 1985, CBOT corn futures for December 1985 were priced at $2.62 per bushel, and put options with a strike price 5 percent less, at $2.50, were priced at 4.5 cents per bushel. The right to sell at $2.50 in December is equivalent to an indemnity payment equal to the difference between $2.50 and the actual December price. Since $100,000 of corn is about 40,000 bushels (eight contracts of 5000 bushels each), the farmer's price paid for the insurance policy on the crop is $1,800. (The equivalent contract for $100,000 of soybeans was selling on March 13, 1985 for about $2,500, presumably because of the greater volatility of soybean as compared to corn prices, hence the greater probability of indemnity payments being made on soybeans.)

The price paid for the price-insurance policy determines a supply–demand equilibrating point, but how to analyze other points on the demand and supply functions for insurance, and how to construct surplus measures is not so clear. The most disaggregated approach is to consider the supply and demand for a particular contract by a particular person. In a competitive insurance market, the policy would cost the actuarial value of the expected indemnity payments plus the insurer's administrative costs, assuming the insurer has a diversified portfolio of policies or reinsures such that the insurer requires no risk premium. This is what the farmer would actually pay. The farmer's willingness to pay is measured by a point on an all-or-none demand curve—the lowest price of the insurance contract at which the farmer chooses not to buy insurance. The vertical distance between the all-or-none demand curve and the market price, times market quantity (one contract) is the farmer's surplus from having the contract available. This links the surplus concept for insurance with standard consumer surplus concepts (Patinkin, 1963).

Market Substitutes for Stabilization Policy

Several market means of risk reduction have been mentioned: insurance policies, forward contracting, futures and commodity options, credit markets, private storage, enterprise diversification, and off-farm income. A problem with public stabilization programs is that they reduce the supply of these services. This is well documented for the effect of public grain stocks on private storage, and is apparent in the market for put options in price-supported commodities (why buy price insurance when the government gives it away). A general issue along the same line is that public stabilization blunts the incentive to invest in information and flexibility that are necessary to respond to emerging changes in economic conditions.

The policy relevance of instability is not just a matter of providing public-good stabilization services needed because of random crop yield or demand. Cyclical and longer-term shifts in markets are also important in agriculture, as elsewhere. Much of the entrepreneurship in modern farm management, especially financial management, involves detecting and adjusting to these events as they are revealed. The problem for policy is to avoid spoiling the market for these skills.

COMMODITY MARKET STABILIZATION VIA BUFFER STOCKS

Whatever the pros, cons, and pitfalls of policies aimed at dealing with dynamics and instability, these policies continue high on the agenda of many countries. The moral authorities in most countries distrust profit-seeking speculation, reflecting the view that "He who withholds his grain is cursed by the people, but he who sells it is blessed" *(Proverbs 11:26)*. Nonetheless, market activity persists along with public stabilization policies. The paradigm of such a policy is a buffer stock. When prices are unusually low, commodities are held off the market, to be sold when prices are unusually high. Since such policies depend on the policy instrument's ability to influence market price, buffer stocks are not feasible for small countries in internationally traded goods. Stabilization policies for them are discussed in Chap. 11. However, buffer stocks are the key component of stabilization policies proposed by the United Nations Conference on Trade and Development (UNCTAD) for countries acting jointly under its Integrated Program for Commodities (IPC). In the past 50 years, about 40 international commodity agreements have been established, many relying on a buffer-stock authority to stabilize world prices (see Gordon-Ashworth, 1984). They have been tried for wheat, sugar, cocoa, coffee, and rubber, among others. The United States has operated its own stockpiling programs for various farm commodities since the Federal Farm Board of 1929; currently the Commodity Credit Corporation holds substantial stocks of several commodities.

The lure of these policies is ancient. An early Chinese emperor, Wang An-Shih, declared: "We propose . . . to sell when grain is dear and buy when it is cheap, in order to increase the accumulation in government storage and to stabilize the prices of commodities" (quoted in R. Gilmore, *A Poor Harvest* Longmans, New York, 1982, p. 232). In the past 10 years, however, disenchantment with this approach has dominated the trend of opinion. The IPC is moribund. None of the international commodity agreements, with the possible exceptions of coffee and rubber, has proved even sustainable, much less a provider of big social benefits. In the United States, the CCC's chief concern is how to unload the stocks acquired when its ostensible stabilization function was usurped by farm income support objectives. The analytical issue may be stated as follows: "Buy low and sell high" is a paradigm of emptiness when given as advice on how to make money in the stock market. How is it that this empty advice is transformed to wisdom when recommended as the basis for governmental policy in the grain markets?

Optimal Stock Management

Since the idea of stockpiling policy is that market participants can jointly benefit from stabilization, consider the optimal policy assuming a SWF with $\Theta = 1$ for everyone. In contrast to Chaps. 7 to 9, it is necessary here to take variation over time into account. The simplest SWF to do this is

$$W = \sum_{t=1}^{\infty} (B_t + R_t - T_t) \frac{1}{(1+r)^t} \qquad (10.31)$$

where B, R, and T are buyers' surplus, producers' rents, and taxpayers' costs, r is the annual discount rate, and t is time in years.

The constraints are that B_t is limited to surpluses generated through the commodity market, that R_t is rents from producing the commodity, and that T_t is the cost of storing it. B_t is a function of quantity consumed in each year, Q_t; R_t is a function of quantity produced, X_t; and T_t is a function of inventories carried from t to $t+1$, I_t.

I_t is the policy instrument whose optimal value is to be chosen. Let the demand function and cost function of storage be the same for all t and the supply function stable also, but with an additive error term (reflecting random weather). The issue then is to decide how much to store when random production is high, and when to release these stocks onto the market.

The problem is to maximize Eq. (10.31), subject to these constraints by choice of I_1^*, inventories carried out of the first year. We could specify a series of expected I_t for subsequent years, but this is irrelevant because next year we will observe a new production error and then choose I_2 accordingly. The future enters the calculations only to the extent that it influences choices made in the current year.

The solution to the constrained maximization problem can be found by the dynamic programming methods, using methods developed by Gustafson (1958). The first-order conditions for a maximum are:

$$B'(Q_t) = C'(X_t^*) \qquad (10.32)$$

i.e., the marginal benefit of more output equals the marginal cost of producing the intended output, X_t^*; and the complementary inequalities

$$\frac{E[B'(Q_{t+1})]}{1+r} = B'(Q_t) + T'(I_t) \qquad I_t > 0 \qquad (10.33)$$

$$\frac{E[B'(Q_{t+1})]}{1+r} < B'(Q_t) + T'(0) \qquad I_t = 0$$

i.e., if stocks are held, then discounted expected marginal benefit next year equals the marginal benefit this year plus storage costs. $T'(0)$ is the marginal cost of holding stocks when stocks are zero. Subtracting the convenience value of having stocks available can make $T'(0)$ negative, but this is not pursued here.

In a market context, we measure the marginal benefit $B'(Q)$ by price on the demand curve, $D(Q)$. Thus, Eq. (10.32) is the market-clearing condition that expected marginal cost equal price in the current period, and Eq. (10.33) states that expected price next year is current price plus storage costs (including interest charges).

Gustafson (1958) showed that Eq. (10.33) is the equilibrium condition for profit-maximizing stocks held in a competitive storage industry. The economics of this result is simply that if the expected price next year exceeds the current price plus storage costs, expected profit exists from holding stocks. Therefore, in a competitive storage industry, stocks will be increased. This will increase the current price and decrease the expected future price, until equilibrium I_t is reached with expected price equal to current price plus storage costs. On the other hand, if expected price is less than current price plus storage costs, there will be no speculative stocks. (There may be "pipeline" stocks or other stocks held for nonspeculative purposes, year-in and year-out. These are not included in I_t because they do not contribute to price stabilization.)

The market model is conceptually as simple as those presented in Chap. 2, but expanded to include equilibrium in two periods, t and $t+1$, one of which is currently observed. Equilibrium for $t+1$ must be stated in terms of values expected at t. The equations determining equilibrium are as follows. First, the supply of grain available in year t consists of production and carryover stocks from the preceding year:

$$S_t = X_t + I_{t-1} \qquad (10.34)$$

Planned output is a function of the price that had been expected at planting time and other variables which are already determined when output is observed at t. Actual output is this predetermined quantity plus a random error term,

$$X_t = g(P_t^*) + U_t \qquad (10.35)$$

On the demand side, there are two main categories of grain usage: current-period disappearance and storage for future use. Disappearance may take many forms, the most important of which are food production, animal feed, and exports. The demand for each use is a function of price and several demand-shifting variables. The most important of these are typically consumer income, population, livestock prices and quantities, and prices of substitute commodities (for U.S. domestic demand), and foreign market conditions, exchange rates, and policy variables such as trade barriers and farm policies of foreign countries (for export demand). Collecting these variables in the vector Z_t, disappearance is represented as

$$Q_t = h(P_t, Z_t) \qquad (10.36)$$

The demand for stocks, the second main category of grain use, is more difficult to conceptualize. Although the quantity of stocks held by the private trade can be expressed as a function of current price, it is not an ordinary demand curve like Eq. (10.36). The expected gains from stockholding depend not only on current price, but on expected price next period, $P^*(t+1)$. And we cannot arbitrarily hold $P^*(t+1)$ constant while observing the response of $I(t)$ to

$P(t)$, because a change of $I(t)$ necessarily increases supply available in period $t+1$ and, therefore, necessarily decreases $P^*(t+1)$. Therefore, it is dubious to refer to the effect of $P(t)$ on $I(t)$, holding $P^*(t+1)$ constant, as a "demand" curve though it is tempting to interpret a plot of $I(t)$ against $P(t)$ in this way.

Consequently, the demand for stocks is best specified not analogously to Eq.(10.36), but in terms of the market equilibrium conditions. Private stocks will be increased if the present value of expected future returns at the margin exceeds the marginal cost of stocks. The basic component of expected returns to storage of $I(t)$ is the expected price for which grain can be sold in the next year, $P^*(t+1)$. The marginal cost is the price paid in the current year, $P(t)$, plus the marginal costs of storage, $T'(I_t)$.

Analogously to Eq. (10.33), equilibrium is represented by the complementary inequalities, assuming competition and profit maximization:

$$P^*_{t+1} = P_t(1+r) + T'(I_t) \qquad I_t > 0 \qquad (10.37)$$
$$P^*_{t+1} < P_t(1+r) + T'(0) \qquad I_t = 0 \qquad (10.37a)$$

where P^*_{t+1} is the (statistically and psychologically) expected price. [Note the slight change in economic assumptions between Eqs. (10.33) and (10.37) required for dividing the left-hand side by $(1+r)$ in Eq. (10.33) but not multiplying the whole right-hand side by $(1+r)$ in Eq. (10.37), namely whether storage costs are paid at the beginning or end of the year.] If Eq. (10.37a) holds, then $X_t = Q_t$ and Eqs. (10.35) and (10.36) determine price and quantity as usual. But if Eq. (10.37) holds, we have two uses that exhaust supply:

$$S_t = I_t + Q_t \qquad (10.38)$$

Now, Eqs. (10.36) to (10.38) constitute a system of three equations in four mutually determined variables $(P_t, P^*_{t+1}, Q_t, I_t)$. Equations (10.34) and (10.35) do not help to solve the system because neither contains any of the four endogenous variables.

To close the system, we need to consider equations determining expected values for $t+1$. Expected output, from (10.35), is

$$X^*_{t+1} = g(P^*_{t+1}) \qquad (10.39)$$

Expected consumption is

$$X^*_{t+1} = h(P^*_{t+1}, Z_{t+1}) \qquad (10.40)$$

If all supplies available are expected to be consumed in $t+1$, we would have $I^*_{t+1} = 0$ and

$$Q_{t+1}^* = X_{t+1}^* + I_t \qquad (10.41)$$

Now we have six equations [(10.36) to (10.41)] in six unknowns, $(P_t, P_{t+1}^*, Q_t, I_t, X_{t+1}^*,$ and $Q_{t+1}^*)$, and an analytical solution is possible.

But in general $I_{t+1}^* \neq 0$, and we cannot close the system, even by adding further years in the future indefinitely. Still there must be a solution because if we go far enough into the future, the effect on current demand for stocks must be negligible. The dynamic programming approach begins with an ultimate time when I_{t+n} is zero, and works backward by reducing n. This makes it possible to find equilibrium for P_t, Q_t, and I_t, given values for the exogenous variables, but algebraic comparative statics are no longer possible. One can only learn by calculating.

Consider the following example. Suppose that grain demand is $P_t = 13 - 0.1Q_t$, and supply is perfectly inelastic, with production either 90 or 110 $(x_t = 100 + \epsilon_t, \epsilon_t = \pm 10)$. The problem is to determine how much grain to put in storage in the years when $\epsilon_t = 10$, assuming storage costs are 0.2 per bushel per year, and the probability of each state of ϵ_t is 0.5. The solution to this problem that maximizes the expected future and current values of buyers' and sellers' surpluses is spelled out in Gardner (1979, Chap. 2), yielding a storage rule giving I_t^* for each plausible value of $I_{t-1} + X_t$.

The resulting storage rule (top panel of Fig. 10.7) can be equivalently specified as a demand function for stocks (middle panel). Note that the demand carryover stocks at each supply level is the quantity given by the storage rule for that supply level. Expressing the optimal storage rule in terms of a reservation demand for stocks clarifies several aspects of the economics of grain markets with optimal storage.

Nonlinearity of Supply–Price Relationship. Nonlinearity in a closed economy's (or world aggregate) grain demand has been widely observed and incorporated in econometric work. Figure 10.7 establishes an economic basis for this nonlinearity. It is the result of total demand being the sum of two components, one of which, the (reservation) demand for stocks, is zero at prices above P^*. Indeed the nonlinearity is sharp enough to yield a "kink" in the supply-price relationship. In the constant-elasticity case, the elasticity of total demand is constant at prices above P^*, while a substantially higher elasticity is observed for all lower prices (in the example shown, the jump is from -0.1 to about -0.4).

Optimal Price Stability. Assuming that the storage rule in Fig. 10.7 is socially optimal, a stochastic time series of harvests generates a time series of prices whose variability is socially optimal. However, if the expected marginal social benefits exceed the marginal costs of storage, carryover stocks should be

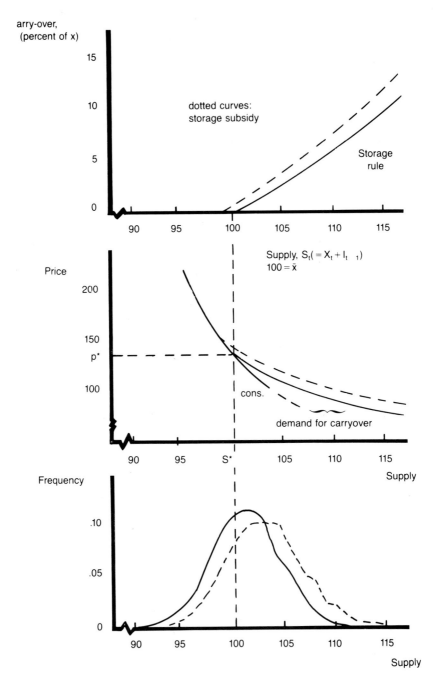

Figure 10.7   Storage rule and demand for stocks.

managed as if future grain were more valuable than the expected price indicates (or as if the "true" costs of storage are less than private costs). Since privately optimal storage results in grain being held to the point that expected price gains equal storage costs, additional stockpiling results in pecuniary losses to the stockpiling activity. An appropriate policy measure is a subsidy to private grain storage to achieve the socially optimal storage rule (and the consequent socially optimal degree of price instability).

An example of a storage rule to reduce price instability from that attained by privately optimal storage is shown by the dashed-line curves in Fig. 10.7. Privately optimal storage generates a year-to-year coefficient of variation of grain price of 0.24, i.e., in a typical year, price is 24 percent above or below the mean price. The socially optimal policy reduces the coefficient of variation of grain prices to 0.19 by holding an average of 1.8 percent more of mean production in carryover stocks at an average additional cost of 1/4 of 1 percent of crop value per year. The change in the frequency distribution of supply due to the storage subsidy is shown in the bottom panel of Fig. 10.7.

The supply-price relationship makes clear that optimal additions to stocks do *not* provide a price floor. When supply increases by a million bushels, it never pays to add the *entire* increase to carryover stocks. Similarly, the optimal policy does not hold stocks until a fixed ceiling price is reached, and then dump them; instead stocks are reduced gradually as prices rise. In this sense the price support, price ceiling, or buffer stock programs typically proposed are suboptimal.

Public Stocks. The reservation demand approach provides a convenient means of introducing the effects of a buffer stock operated by a government or international agency. While buffer stocks operated via a price band—a floor price defended by stock acquisition and a ceiling defended by sales—are suboptimal, for grains they are a natural possibility to consider because of long-standing legislation which establishes a price floor for political reasons. The floor price, even if below mean price, increases the expected price of grain and, therefore, tends to draw resources into production. Both the higher average price and the increased output create problems, which may be prevented by introducing a ceiling price, and using a buffer stock rather than production controls to defend the floor price.

In contrast to the reservation demand for private carryover stocks shown in Fig. 10.7, the "demand" for public stocks under a price-band regime is as follows. Demand is zero at prices above the ceiling price. Between the ceiling and floor price, demand may be anywhere between zero and the maximum size of stocks that can be acquired to support the floor price. (Even if the buffer stock rules do not specify a maximum stock, one will be imposed implicitly by means of limitations in financing.) Below the floor price, demand will be at the maximum stock.

Determinants of the Effect of Public on Private Stocks. An *optimal* stock policy operated by the government would remove the incentive for private speculative stockpiling, since the expected returns would be zero or negative. However, a suboptimal government storage policy could leave room for private stocks. For example, a wide price band under a buffer stock policy could allow profitable speculative storage for sale at prices below the ceiling price.

It is insufficient to discuss the relationship between public and private stocks in terms of a trade-off between the quantity of grain in a public buffer stock and the quantity of grain that the private trade will hold. There are two basic effects to be considered: the effects of a public buffer stock rule on the private trade's storage rule, and the effect of a given buffer stock level *under that rule* on private stocks. Trying to conflate these two effects can produce misleading results. For example, a substantial public stock may have little effect on private storage if the public stock is only to be released at exceptionally high prices; while very small or even zero existing public stocks can inhibit private storage significantly if the buffer stock rules specify a narrow price band with floor price not far below current price.

An illustration of simultaneous public and private stockpiling is shown in Fig. 10.8. Total demand, including private demand for stocks in the absence of any governmental intervention, is shown as a dashed curve. The kink in the total demand curve is the point at which speculative stockholding (above working stocks) begins to be profitable. The buffer stock has a floor price, P_L, and a ceiling price of P_H, which are equidistant from mean price P and a maximum level of G_{max} equal to the distance, *ab*.

Consider first the behavior of private stock demand when the buffer stock is empty at the beginning of crop year t $(G_{t-1} = 0)$. At supply levels that clear the consumption market at prices above $\overline{P}$, ending stocks are zero. As supply increases, such that prices fall below $\overline{P}$, it becomes profitable to carry small quantities of speculative stocks. Indeed, the demand for private stocks is slightly higher than demand in the absence of the buffer-stock regime (the dotted curve). The reason is that the floor price P_L reduces the probability of a substantial price decline in the following year, while no public stocks exist to dampen price gains the following year. Therefore, more private stocks are required to satisfy equilibrium condition (10.37). However, if large supplies reduce current price down to the floor level, the buffer-stock authority begins to acquire stocks, and these trade off with private stocks. If supply is large enough to reduce price to point c, then the buffer stock reaches its maximum level (distance *ab*) and privately held stocks are zero. If supply is still larger, then the buffer-stock regime is unable to support the current price at the floor level, and private stocks may again begin to be accumulated. In this case, there is another kink in the total demand curve at or below point c.

Consider now the behavior of private stockholding when a crop year begins with the maximum public stock $(G_{t-1} = G_{max})$. Private carryover stocks

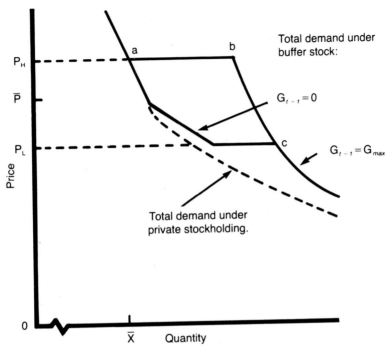

Figure 10.8 Public and private stockpiling.

will now frequently be zero, even at prices that would have resulted in substantial private stockholding in the absence of a buffer-stock regime. Once acquired, public stocks are held until price reaches the ceiling level P_H. At prices between $\bar{P}$ and P_H, there is no trade-off between public and private speculative stocks since no private stocks would have been held at these prices.

The interaction between public and private stocks has important implications for the optimal conduct of price stabilization policy. The main effect is to increase substantially the costs of attaining even slight reductions in price variability. But this does not imply that public stockpiling or stabilization policy involves a net social loss. There may be externalities of several kinds which justify public stocks. However, there may be serious political difficulties in putting a socially optimal storage regime into practice. It is often necessary to consider second-best approaches to public storage which are not optimal but are not far suboptimal even if based on incorrect information. Certain buffer-stocks regimes are attractive in this respect.

The discussion with reference to Fig. 10.8 indicates that private stockholding is zero at current prices above mean price. Yet, buffer stocks typically involve holding stocks until prices are substantially above mean price. A public buffer stock would provide a much better approximation to privately optimal stockholding if it had a price range centered well below mean price, with a ceiling price in the neighborhood of mean price. Thus, if a buffer stock is adopted purely for political expediency and not to offset social costs of externalities due to insufficient private stocks, then the costs can be minimized by choice of a low price range. On the other hand, if there are substantial externalities that should be countered by means of public stocks, then the optimal price range is centered well above mean price.

The case for public stocks generating any net social gains depends on lack of congruence between conditions (10.33) and(10.37). The social benefit of having grain available can exceed the private benefit because of the income effect of higher prices on poor people's demand in periods of extreme scarcity. Welfare accounting is based on Hicksian demand functions which exclude income effects. This does not mean, however, that "the use of standard theory to rationalize and determine the size of reserves is inadequate if not irrelevant" (Hathaway, 1976, pp. 2). It means we need to estimate the difference between social benefits and price, and subtract this from storage costs in Eq. (10.37). That is, we should continue adding to stocks even though expected losses occur up to the point that the expected loss equals the excess social benefit.

It will still be the case that public stocks will replace some private stocks. For evidence on this trade-off in recent U.S. grain storage programs, see Wright (1985).

SUMMARY

This chapter provided a tour through some quite complicated analytical territory, highlighting results that emphasize the limitations of our capabilities as much as providing methods of policy assessment. Concluding points are as follows:

1. Modification of commodity supply and demand functions for purposes of either positive or normative economic analysis of policy alternatives has not provided usable methods for evaluating the standard types of commodity programs under uncertainty. Policy analyses have not in practice been able to incorporate risk considerations quantitatively in any convincing way.

2. Instead of modifying commodity supply and demand functions, consideration of risk is more fruitfully introduced in terms of supply and demand for price insurance. Price support via deficiency payments under uncertainty is analytically identical to the provision of price insurance. The relevance of this point is further enhanced by the isomorphism of price insurance and commodity options traded on organized futures exchanges.

3. Policies directed specifically at market stabilization, notably buffer stock policies, can be usefully analyzed using models of the supply and demand for stocks of commodities carried from one harvest period to the next. The approaches used are conceptually continuous with the comparative statics methods used earlier—the criteria for optimization still involve equating marginal benefits and marginal costs—but the dynamic and random elements of time series of prices add complications. Much of the detail in the chapter involves the analysis and understanding of these complications.

4. The normative issue in price stabilization turn out to be more complex than simply improving the economy's functioning by having the government buy commodities when prices are low and sell when prices are high. There are good reasons for doubting that unregulated commodity markets can generate a Pareto optimum, but also good reasons for doubting that commodity market intervention can in practice remedy this situation.

END NOTES

1. The market's expectation is used because, with the existence of futures markets, all producers and consumers should act as if the expected price is the futures price in this model (see Black, 1976; Holthausen, 1979; or Feder et al., (1980).

2. "Approximately" because private stockholders may not be risk neutral. The risk premium, if one exists, may be positive or negative. It depends on whether speculators in stocks are risk averters or risk preferrers, and whether holders of stocks are speculators or hedgers (hedgers here are people for whom the addition of commodity stocks to their assets reduces the variance of returns to the whole set of assets, e.g., millers or livestock feeders).

3. See Just et al. (1982, Chap.11). They use a risk parameter α, which is related to the parameter A as $\alpha = 2A$. Anderson et al. (1977, Chap. 6) provide a more general analysis which shows that the parameter is the slope of the indifference curve between variance and return, and they use it in firm-level input demand relationships. Pope et al. (1983) extend these results to the market level, finding that surpluses in input price-quantity space are appropriate for measuring gains and losses from risk reduction when production is stochastic.

Chapter 11

International Trade and Commodity Policy

The basic economics of price supports for importing and exporting countries have been outlined in earlier chapters, and comprehensive treatments are available elsewhere, notably in Dixit and Norman (1980) on general trade policy issues and McCalla and Josling (1985) on agricultural trade. This chapter considers several topics in trade that bear on the models used in Chaps. 7 to 10. The conclusions derived from some closed economy models are substantially altered by international trade considerations. The topics are: (1) surplus redistribution due to market intervention by (a) small countries, and (b) large countries; (2) global aspects of trade policy; (3) trade and market stabilization, and (4) monetary-financial and macroeconomic issues in commodity policy.

SURPLUS TRANSFORMATION FOR TRADED COMMODITIES: SMALL-COUNTRY IMPORTERS

For a country that imports a commodity at a given world price (small-country case), the policy instruments available to raise farmers' incomes include border measures as presented in Chap. 2. In this section, we expand on the analysis using surplus transformation curves. STCs for a tariff, import quota, production subsidy, and production control used in a small importing country are shown in Fig. 11.1.

Tariff

Raising the domestic price to P^* by means of a tariff of t^* generates a gain of area A for producers at the cost of $A + B + D$ to consumers and taxpayers jointly. Plotting this redistribution as surplus transformation gives point R. Varying P^* ($>P_W$) generates the locus of points on the surplus transformation curve shown. This STC plots the gains (rents generated) to domestic producers, G_P, against the losses of consumers and taxpayers (who gain from tariff revenues) jointly. Since $A + B + D > A$, we know that the slope of the STC is less than the slope of the tangent to the STC at point E, which is -1; indeed it is apparent by construction that the deadweight loss $B + D$ is measured by the horizontal distance between point R and the tangent at E.

If a social indifference curve is tangent to the STC at point R, which corresponds to price P^*, then the tariff of t^* is optimal for the level of $\theta > 1$ for producers (as compared to $\theta = 1$ for consumer and taxpayers) that is implied by the SIC slope at R. The tariff t^* is optimal given that a tariff is the type of policy that will be chosen, but other types of intervention must be considered.

Import Quota

A quota allocated to exporting countries (without cost to them) yielding the same domestic price, P^*, has the same redistributional results except that area C now is lost to domestic taxpayers, so that the instigating country's total loss is $B + C + D$. Since the producers' gain is still A, the corresponding point on the STC for the quota is at R_q. Varying $\hat{Q}$, the upper limit on imports, generates the STC for the quota policy. It differs from the ones derived so far in being convex to the origin and in not having a slope of -1 at E. It does not have a slope of -1 at E because even the first dollar redistributed causes a net loss that is not negligible compared to the producers' gains. At any level of G_p, the horizontal distance between the STCs for the quota and tariff policies measures area C. It can be seen from the upper panel that as P^* rises, C first increases and then decreases until it goes to zero at the "choke" price where imports are completely squeezed out and the country becomes self-sufficient (as has happened for Japan in rice and the EEC in wheat and sugar). At the choke price, C disappears and $B + D$ becomes a maximum, measuring the whole of the country's (lost) gains from access to the world market in wheat. Thus, the two STCs coincide at point C, where redistribution is at the level corresponding to the choke price.

Production Subsidy

This policy achieves P^* by paying $P^* - P_w$ to producers, leaving the consumer price at P_w and replacing a relatively small quantity of imports by domestic out-

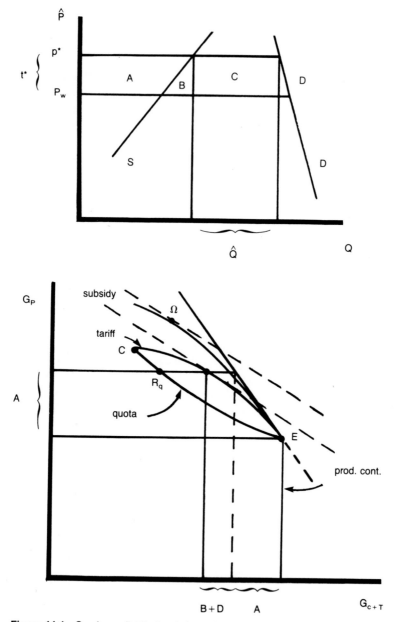

Figure 11.1 Surplus redistribution in importing country.

put. Since the subsidy is costly to taxpayers while the tariff raises revenue, it is tempting, especially for Ministers of Finance, to view tariffs as preferable. However, the opposite is the case. The additional deadweight loss of area D implies an STC (subsidy) that is to the right of STC (tariff) for any level of G_p.

The horizontal differences between the STC for the tariff and the STC for the subsidy measures area D. The absence of these deadweight losses under the subsidy means that for any G_p, the slope of STC (subsidy) is nearer -1, i.e., the marginal rate of transformation between consumer-taxpayer losses and producer gains is greater. This means that for a given $\theta > 1$ for producers, more is optimally redistributed when the more efficient policy is available—the economy is at position like Ω rather than R.

The label Ω encourages an analogy between the STC farthest from the origin and the UPF from the general welfare model. As mentioned in Chap. 7, it may be asked whether the tangent through E with slope -1 is not the more appropriate analog to the UPF. This tangent would be the STC for administratively costless lump-sum transfers between consumer-taxpayers and producers. If feasible, they should be chosen above any commodity program. But, as discussed in Chap. 7, it seems clear that they are not feasible. Therefore, Ω is plausible as a Pareto optimal point, and as a point on the UPF. There is no way to make both groups better off than at Ω, or any other point on STC (subsidy), and all points inside this STC are Pareto inferior to at least one point on it.

If the most efficient feasible redistribution involves a deadweight loss of area D in Fig. 11.1, it is questionable whether this should be referred to as a "social" cost or net loss to the country. If we accept the SWF with $\theta > 1$ for producers, then the economy is at its optimum at Ω and there is no loss to society in any meaningful sense. Instead, area D measures the cost of achieving a socially desired service—redistribution to producers. It is the price of redistribution in a sense analogous to resource costs being the price of an irrigation project. Of course, we can give the deadweight loss a normative meaning by asserting that the "proper" θ is 1 for everyone, and that area D is the social loss from society's failure to agree. But this is not something we can do as economists.

Production Controls

On an imported commodity, these just force consumers to replace domestic goods with more imports at P_w. Consumers are not made any worse off, but producers lose rents. Thus, the STC is a vertical line segment from E to the horizontal axis, and is Pareto inferior everywhere.

Policies for Exporters

Policy instruments reviewed in Chap. 2 yield STCs as shown in Fig. 11.2. The production subsidy is again most efficient. It has deadweight losses of area D,

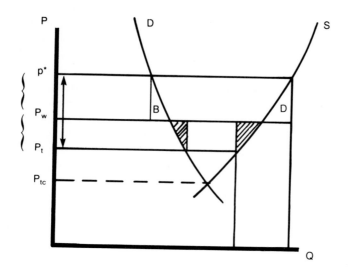

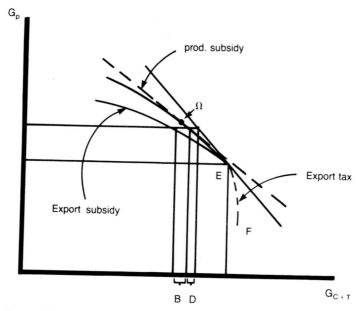

Figure 11.2 Surplus redistribution in exporting country.

and with $\theta > 1$ for producers would imply an optimum as at Ω, with producers' price of P^* achieved by payments at a rate of S^*. The marginal rate of surplus transfer is the same as specified earlier, with $\eta \rightarrow -\infty$.

An export subsidy policy charges domestic consumers P^* but leaves the export price at P_w, causing an additional deadweight loss of area B. This implies an STC to the left of STC (production subsidy) by amount B at each G_p.

A production control policy again accomplishes nothing for producers, although the possibility exists of raising domestic price after all exports are ended. (This depends on domestic consumers not being able to import at price P_w.)

An export tax is a popular policy in some developing countries. It reduces the domestic consumer price to the world price minus the tax rate (P_t in Fig. 11.2). The after-tax receipts of producers are also at P_t. The economics of this result are that producers can only receive P_w in the world market; the effective demand curve facing them is perfectly elastic at P_w. If domestic consumers were still to pay P_w, sellers could make profits by diverting goods from the export to the domestic market.

This they do until equilibrium is reached, with domestic use increasing to the point that the net price, after taxes, is the same whether the product is sold domestically or for export. The resulting deadweight loss is the two hatched triangles, with producers losing the area between P_w and P_t to the left of the supply curve, and consumers-taxpayers gaining the unhatched portion of this area.

The resulting STC is the dashed curve to the right of E in the lower panel of Fig. 11.2. It could not involve optimal redistribution unless $\theta < 1$ for producers. This STC ends at point F, where the export tax has been raised to the point that all exports are choked off, at price P_{tc}. Under the Fig. 11.2 conditions, producers have lost more than half their original rents by this point.

If the tax were imposed on all production rather than on exports only, consumers would still pay P_w, and producers would still receive P_t after taxes and produce the corresponding output on the supply curve S. But exports would be larger than under the export tax. Consumers would pay P_w instead of P_t, but this actually contributes to efficiency. The left-hand hatched triangle is not lost. Therefore, if $\theta < 1$ so that policies to redistribute income away from producers and toward consumers/taxpayers are optimal, it is more efficient to tax all production than exports only. The all-production tax generates an STC (not shown) which lies to the right of the dashed curve EF.

OPTIMAL INTERVENTION BY LARGE COUNTRIES

Export and Production Controls

Being large means having a share of a commodity market big enough, on either the buying or selling side, to influence the world price. Our previous discussion of imported and exported commodities has assumed a given world price, the actual position for most countries most of the time. The United States in grains, tobacco, soybeans, and cotton; Brazil in coffee; Ivory Coast in Cocoa; and Australia in wool are examples of exporters who can change world prices significantly by varying their exports. The Soviet Union, Japan, and the United States are among importers large enough to influence world prices through variations in their purchases.

What difference does this make for the assessment of policy alternatives? Consider the case of an exporter, say the United States in rice. The situation differs from Fig. 2.4 only in that foreign demand, D_f, is no longer perfectly elastic at P_w. The implication is that an export control or production control program can now increase the sum of gains to domestic consumers and producers. In Fig. 11.3, a production control reducing output from Q_0 to $\hat{Q}$ generates losses of area A to domestic consumers and gains of $A + B - D$ to producers. The net gain to both groups is thus $B - D$. Note that as sketched, the net gain is positive even though export demand is elastic (exports decline about 30 percent and price rises about 10 percent, i.e., $\eta = -3$). It has been argued that production controls are counterproductive if export demand is elastic, but this proposition is not true. Production controls can yield net gains so long as export demand is anything less than perfectly elastic. It is true though that only a quite small reduction in $\hat{Q}$ is profitable with an elastic demand function (because area D tends quickly to become larger than B, even though D always starts out smaller for small enough ΔQ).

To see exactly how the optimal production control is determined we need a mathematical representation of the model. Let welfare be the sum of gains to producers and to *domestic* consumers with foreigners getting no weight:

$$W = G_p + G_d \tag{11.1}$$

where G_p and G_d are producers' and consumers' surpluses. Optimization involves choosing Q^* to maximize W:

$$\frac{dW}{dQ} = \frac{dG_p}{dQ} + \frac{dG_d}{dQ} = 0 \tag{11.2}$$

Using the results from Eqs. (7.15) and (7.16), we obtain surpluses from the supply and *total* demand curves. To convert the latter to domestic demand, we have

$$\frac{dG_d}{dQ} = \frac{dG_d}{dQ_d} \frac{dQ_d}{dP_d} \frac{dP_d}{dQ} \tag{11.3}$$

Making these substitutions and dividing through by P_d, we obtain

$$\frac{1}{\eta_T} + \frac{P_d - P_s}{P_d} - \frac{1}{\eta_T} \frac{Q_d}{Q} = 0 \tag{11.4}$$

where η_T is the elasticity of total demand. Letting $(1 - Q_d)/Q = K_f$, the share of total demand accounted for by exports, we have

$$\frac{P_d - P_s}{P_d} = - K_f \frac{1}{\eta_T} \tag{11.5}$$

The optimal markup between marginal cost and price is the export share times the inverse total demand elasticity. If there is no export market, $K_f = 0$ and no intervention is optimal. Similarly if demand is perfectly elastic. If all output is exported, $K_f = 1$ and monopoly output is optimal.

To get results in terms of quantities, we need to know how price responds to quantity over the range of the production cutback. Assume constant elasticities over this range. Then we have the result (from Chap. 7) that $P_s/P_d = (Q*/Q_0) \exp(1/\epsilon - 1/\eta_T)$. This implies that the optimal output from Eq. (11.5) is

$$\frac{Q^*}{Q_0} = (1 + \frac{K_f}{\eta_T}) \epsilon \eta_T/(\eta^T - \epsilon) \tag{11.6}$$

This expression gives optimal output as a function of no-program output. Suppose that, for U.S. rice, we have $K_f = 0.5$, $\eta_T = -3.0$, and $\epsilon = 0.4$. Then $Q^*/Q_0 = 0.94$, that is, a 6-percent production cutback is optimal.

While consumers and producers jointly gain, this is not necessarily so because both groups gain but because producers gain more than consumers lose. In order to visualize both the trade-offs and the net gains, Fig. 11.4 shows the relevant surplus transformation curves. Superimposed are tangent lines with slope of -1, which are social indifference curves for the SWF: $\Delta W = \Delta G_{ct} + \Delta G_p$, where ΔG_{ct} is area A and $\Delta G_p = A + B - D$. The STC for production control is tangent to the SIC at point R, the point at which $B - D$ is a maximum.

The striking new fact about this situation is that the no-program equilibrium E is not the social optimum, whether $\theta = 1$, the case we have just worked out, or $\theta > 1$. If $\theta > 1$ for producers, the optimum is northwest of R, reaching a maximum at M as $\theta \to \infty$. All the producer-favoring optima lie between R and M. At point M the United States acts as a monopolist in its whole market (domestic and foreign).

The fact that a policy that cuts back exports does not necessarily favor farmers is apparent in the case of an export tax or embargo. Such policies differ from the preceding policies in that they involve a border distortion which drives up the price abroad relative to the domestic price.

Because such a policy necessarily reduces the domestic price by redirecting grain from abroad to the home market, consumers gain (in the case of an export tax, consumers plus taxpayers). Producers could gain, too, if export demand were inelastic and producers received the higher world price caused by the embargo or, in the case of the tax, had the revenue distributed to them. But as the controls tighten and the export market is choked off, these gains eventually disappear and are replaced by losses to producers.

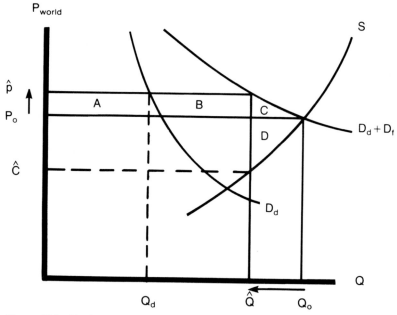

Figure 11.3 Production control by large-country exporter.

The conditions required for producer gains to exist are analyzed for the case of linear supply and demand curves in Carter et al. (1980). They also provide a case study of wheat exports by the major wheat exporting countries in 1980. The exporters in aggregate are taken to have the following supply and demand functions:

Domestic supply: $Q_s = 90 + 0.38P$
Domestic demand: $Q_D = 45 - 0.05P$
Excess supply, (supply of exports): $Q_E = 45 + 0.43P$
Import demand from ROW (demand for exports): $Q_M = 190 - 0.69P$

where the Q's are measured in millions of metric tons and P is dollars per metric ton. Carter et al. (1980) analyze export controls (export quotas or an export tax rebated to consumers). In the case of a single, large country, this would constitute an exercise of monopoly power in world markets. In the treatment of Carter et al. it is the action of an exporters' cartel.

The resulting surplus transformation curve is the one going southeast from point E in Fig. 11.4. It shows *both* producers and consumers in the exporting countries gaining from small interventions, but consumers soon gaining at the expense of producers. This later result is what is commonly assumed to have occurred as a result of the U.S. export embargos on grain and soybeans in the

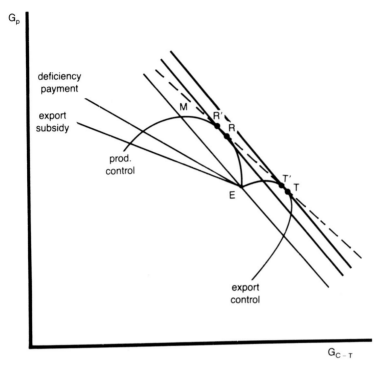

Figure 11.4 Surplus transformation curves for large-country exporter.

1970s, but this is certainly not an inevitable result of export controls. Indeed, there is an optimal intervention which maximizes the sum of producers' and consumers' surpluses in the exporting countries. It is shown as point T, where the STC has a slope of -1.

Note that the optimal intervention by means of production controls, at point R, yields a lower sum of surpluses. This result is contrary to the social-cost ordering of trade interventions as compared to domestic interventions under competition. Recall that in Chap. 2 we found that a domestic production subsidy or tax caused a smaller deadweight loss than an export subsidy or import tariff that yielded the same producer gains. It is still the case for a large country that a deficiency payment program is preferable to an export subsidy, as discussed below and shown in Fig. 11.4. But for quantity controls, the optimal export quota is more efficient in the sense of maximizing the sum of surpluses.

It remains the case, however, that if one's goal is aiding producers, more can be done with production controls, the maximum producers' benefit being at point M. The distinction between points M and T can be understood also in terms of different kinds of monopoly in the grain trade. If, say, Continental Grain were a pure monopolist in exports but competitive domestically, we would observe point T (with G_p now including Continental's as well as farmers' rents). But if the monopolist controlled all grains, point M would be observed.

Bringing in political preferences in terms of θ, if $\theta = 1$ then the optimal policy is the export control to place the economy at point T. As θ increases, there occurs a critical value of θ at which R' and T' give the same level of social welfare. This creates a possibility of unstable policies in that a small change in either the STC or social preferences can switch a country from producer-favoring to consumer-favoring policies. (This sort of thing occurred in the 1970s when U.S. grain policies shifted from acreage controls to export embargoes when export demand increased and apparently became quite inelastic.) Finally, if θ becomes large enough, we may find deficiency payments the preferred policy.

Deficiency Payments

Deficiency payments without production controls generate an STC as shown in Fig. 11.4 which is less efficient at generating producer gains. It is less efficient because it generates gains to foreign consumers, which in the SWF used in these examples is equivalent to a deadweight loss. Figure 11.5 shows the gains and losses from such a policy. Producers gain B, domestic consumers gain A, but the cost to taxpayers is $A + B + C + D$. Since D, the gains to foreign consumers from being able to buy at the lower price, P_c, is of the same order of magnitude as domestic consumer gains even for the smallest intervention, the slope of the STC is less than 1 even at point E in Fig. 11.4. However, the marginal rate of surplus transformation falls less rapidly than for production controls. The deadweight loss may grow just as rapidly, but the transfers to producers are limited only by the pocketbooks of the taxpayer under the payment regime. So if $\theta > 1$ is not much above 1, production controls will usually be preferred for a large country, but if θ is far above 1, deficiency payments may be. If they are, the optimum may actually move into negative G_{ct} space. All this means is that taxpayer costs minus consumer surplus gains exceed the initial consumer surplus. Still, the big change comparing the small-country case of Chap. 2 to the large-country case is that in the former export or production controls were useless but in the latter they may be the policies of choice.

Export Subsidies

Export subsidies have an advantage over deficiency payments in that the taxpayers' costs are less. However the consumer costs are larger and, as in the small-country case, deficiency payments have an STC that is always outside the STC for export subsidies. To see why, refer to Fig. 11.5. If the price $\hat{P}$ is achieved by an export subsidy, producers' gains are still B, but now domestic consumers will pay $\hat{P}$. This reduces total demand at all (export) prices below $\hat{P}$ by the horizontal difference between the domestic demand curve and $\hat{Q}_d$, yield-

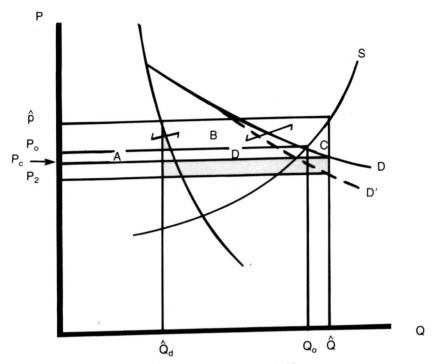

Figure 11.5 Production subsidy compared to export subsidy.

ing the dashed total demand curve, D'. Now it requires a larger subsidy per bushel, $\hat{P} - P_2$, to boost total demand to $\hat{Q}$. The deadweight loss is increased by the shaded areas, in the case shown almost doubled, so that deficiency payments are roughly twice as efficient as export subsidies as an income redistributional measure to favor producers (no matter what θ is).

Export subsidies might be efficient as a second-best policy in adjusting to past policy mistakes, where a "mistake" is not necessarily due to incompetence, but may be an unwanted consequence of a policy that was optimal given the information available when the policy decision was made but which new information makes suboptimal. For example, a commodity's support price may lead to an unanticipated buildup of stocks. The stocks may have sufficiently high storage costs that receiving even, say, half the support price for them would reduce taxpayers' costs. In these circumstances, an export subsidy may be efficient. However, domestic consumption subsidies and a move toward production controls also should occur, since these are more efficient adjustment mechanisms. In U.S. grains policy, all of these policy instruments were being used in the 1980s.

In 1985–1986, the United States implemented a program of export subsidies limited to fixed quantities targeted to particular countries, for example,

100,000 tons of wheat to Algeria. The supply–demand analysis of this type of program is quite different from the subsidy paid on all exports. Indeed, we would expect that typically such a program would not change either exports or imports at the margin for any country, and therefore would have no effect on world prices or any country's internal price. It simply constitutes an income transfer from the U.S. taxpayers to Algeria of the amount of the subsidy. A possible net effect would occur if the 100,000 tons to Algeria exceeded their normal annual imports from all sources, and re-exports to third countries were prevented.

Similar issues arise with respect to targeted export embargoes, like the U.S. limits on sales of grain to the Soviet Union in 1974, 1975, and 1980. They could only affect the U.S. market or the Soviet market significantly if they held down Soviet total imports, apart from modest transportation cost increases if the grain trading companies actually ship grain to the USSR from more distant than usual locations (instead of the company swapping a cargo of say, Australian for U.S. wheat, and then shipping ''Australian'' wheat that left a U.S. port). It does not appear that total Soviet imports were significantly affected by the U.S. actions, so it is difficult to see how there could have been significant world or U.S. price effects. A large-scale research effort by the USDA (1986) reached the conclusion that there were, in fact, no significant effects.

Special circumstances arise when a country's price support programs result in large surplus stocks that have low expected value in the market. In this case it may pay simply to dump stocks on the market. But it still remains true that domestic welfare is increased more (or reduced less) by dumping stocks in the domestic market than in foreign markets.

SURPLUS TRANSFORMATION FOR TRADED COMMODITIES: LARGE-COUNTRY IMPORTERS

For a large-country importer, the results of price supports are somewhat different. A deficiency-payment program, shown in Fig. 11.6, generates producer gains A, consumer gains $B + C$, and taxpayer costs $A + B + D$. Thus, the net gains are $C - D$, which can be positive if the supply curve of imports, which shifts to the right by the distance α (equal to the domestic production increase) is inelastic enough and the share of consumption accounted for by imports is large enough. Thus, the program can generate an STC similar to the net-gain area caused by production controls in Fig. 11.4.

A production control program to achieve $\hat{P}$ would involve less producer gains and greater deadweight losses. Shifting S_α to the left (in a diagram like Fig. 11.6) would increase excess demand in the instigating importer, thus increasing world price and domestic price (which are the same since this policy places no price wedge between domestic and world markets). And part of the revenue gain accrues to foreign producers, since the instigating country by

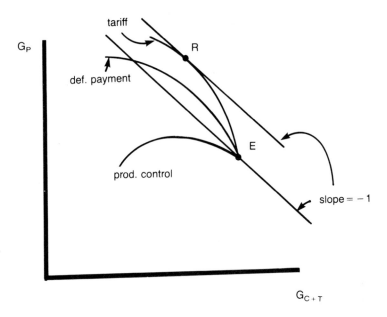

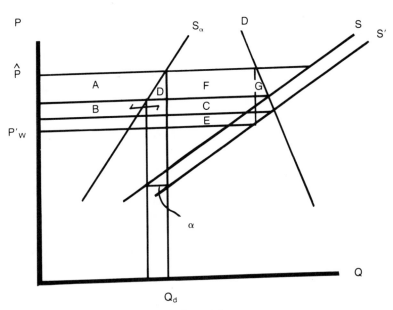

Figure 11.6 STCs for large-country importer.

definition consumes more than it produces. The resulting STC, as shown in the top panel of Fig. 11.6, starts out at a slope shallower than -1 at point E, just as deficiency payments did for an exporter. However, production controls are even worse in that the few benefits they can provide producers are quickly dissipated; the maximum of G_p on this STC is rarely much above G_p at point E.

An import tariff can cause the sum of producers' and domestic consumers' surpluses to increase. A tariff that achieves price $\hat{P}$ in Fig. 11.6 generates producer gains of A, consumer losses of $A + D + F + G$, and tariff revenues of $F + C + E$. Area $C + E$ results from the large country's reduced imports causing the world price to fall to P'_w. There is a net gain to the instigating country if $C + E > D + G$. Varying the tariff rate traces out the STC shown. As compared to deficiency payments, the tariff generates additional deadweight loss G but additional gains E. Since $E > G$ in Fig. 11.6, the STC for the tariff is drawn outside the one for a deficiency payment. Point R, maximizing the sum of domestic gains, is at the same P and Q as equilibrium for a monopsony importer.

The optimum at point R corresponds to $\theta = 1$ for producers and consumer-taxpayers in the SWF. If $\theta > 1$ for producers, the optimal tariff or deficiency payment is higher, but the ranking of policies according to efficiency is the same. Note the change in efficiency ranking between the small- and large-country cases. For a small country that wishes to aid its producers, domestic intervention is preferable to trade intervention; deficiency payments are preferred to import tariffs in small-country importers, and to export subsidies in small-country exporters. But for a large country that wishes to aid its producers, trade intervention is preferred to domestic intervention. Import tariffs are more efficient than deficiency payments if the country is an importer. If the country is an exporter, deficiency payments are preferred to export subsidies, as for a small country, but the large country finds export restraints preferable to either, at least at low levels of intervention.

The overall picture of a country's optimal intervention can be summarized as follows. Trade policies are introduced only because of large-country effects: to raise the world price of an exported commodity or lower the world price of an imported one. Domestic income redistribution calls for domestic market intervention. For a small country, domestic policies dominate trade intervention as a means of income redistribution. This section has developed these results for a restricted set of policies in a single commodity market. For a demonstration of the analogous results in a general equilibrium context, see Dixit and Norman (1980, pp. 168–175).

GLOBAL ASPECTS OF TRADE POLICY

Strategic Interaction in Trade Policies

Suppose a trade policy instigator imposes an import tariff. When a respondent country has a large enough share of trade in a commodity to influence prices in an instigator country, the impotence of second-best intervention (Ch. 9) may not apply. When the importer imposes a tariff, a respondent exporter may be able to increase its domestic surpluses by (further) export restraints. The clearest case involves retaliation by means of quotas. Suppose the United States is able to increase its sum of surpluses by an export quota on shipments of grain to the Soviets, allowing 5 million tons, and this makes the price $10 per ton higher in the Soviet Union than in the United States. The United States collects $50 million in rents (but recall from Fig. 11.3 that this overstates the U.S. net gain). The Soviets might respond to the U.S. quota by an import quota of their own, permitting, say, only 4 million tons of U.S. grain to be imported. This would cause a slightly bigger price wedge between the countries, and now the *Soviets* would collect the rents as U.S. exporting companies bid for access to the high-priced Soviet market. It might not be optimal for the Soviets to impose such a quota—they might not have as much monopsony power as the U.S. has monopoly power. (Given large third-country sources of grain, neither side is likely to have significant market power using bilateral restrictions, but imagine a two-country world if necessary.) If the Soviets did reduce their U.S. purchases, then the U.S. would have to rethink its own policy. Should it try to recapture the rents by cutting Soviet sales to 3 million tons? If so, further retaliation could soon reduce trade to zero.

An interesting prospect is that even if the Soviets did not gain from retaliation, they could well gain from the threat of retaliation. Neither side wants a trade war that drives grain sales to zero. On the other hand, if a threat is going to be credible, it has to be used sometimes. So we could well observe trade wars that leave both countries worse off.

The bilateral tariff retaliation possibilities are explored for two countries trading two commodities in Johnson (1954) and much subsequent work. Among other complications, tariffs and quotas lose more of their already strained isomorphism when retaliation is considered. A quota-war leads to an autarkic result more readily than a tariff war, but this might mean that quota-wars are less likely to be started. For a clear review of the analytical issues, see Copeland (1986). These strategic interactions lend themselves naturally to game theoretic analyses. The equilibrium reached by the parties in a situation such as the U.S. and Soviet grain-sales case described is the solution to a noncooperative game. The possibilities for disaster on both sides encourage negotiations, a cooperative solution in which each side emerges better off than with the noncooperative solution. This is the hope, on a bigger scale, in multinational trade negotiations.

Global Welfare

The welfare economics of these policies is considerably changed if we take a global perspective. With a global social welfare function, the trapezoids representing foreigners' gains or losses would not receive zero weight. From a global perspective with equal θ for all market participants everywhere, there would be no optimal interventions. All STCs would imply maximum welfare with no intervention anywhere. And as we saw in Chap. 9, if a small-country respondent intervenes in countervention to the instigator's policies, it will make itself (consumers and producers aggregated) worse off still. This situation has fostered coordinated international efforts to reduce trade barriers, notably in the General Agreement on Tariffs and Trade (GATT) negotiations, and at the policy analysis level to estimating the global gains from liberalized trade. For agricultural trade, GATT has not accomplished much, but analysis proceeds.

In order to simulate the counterfactual situation of liberalized trade, a natural approach is to specify and estimate supply and demand functions including trade and existing domestic policy variables, and then simulate the free-trade situation by dropping the policy variables and solving for market-clearing prices and quantities. This is the basic approach followed in all of the published simulation studies of agricultural trade liberalization. The essential features of these exercises in comparative statics can be seen in a simple one-commodity, two-country model, looking at how, say, a tariff in country 1 affects consumer and producer welfare in country 1, country 2, and both countries together. However, to fit the complexities of actual trade and policy situations, the model must be elaborated in: (a) country coverage, (b) commodity coverage, (c) specification of national policy behavior, (d) length of run in simulated effects, (e) inclusion of cross-price effects, (f) inclusion of nonprice variables that shift supply or demand, for example, technical change, (g) inclusion of exchange rates to permit aggregation over currencies. An example of this type of approach is work by Tyers and Anderson (1986) simulating trade and price-support liberalization by various countries and country groups. Their handling of the issues itemized is as follows:

    a.   There are 30 countries and country groups, including Bangladesh, Burma, China, India, Indonesia, Korea (Republic), Malaysia, Pakistan, Philippines, Singapore, Sri Lanka, Taiwan, Thailand, Australia, Canada, EEC, Japan, New Zealand, United States and European countries outside the EEC. Africa, Latin America, and the centrally planned economies are modeled in regional groups.

    b.   Seven commodities are covered: rice, wheat, coarse grain, beef, pork-and-poultry, sugar, and dairy products.

    c.   The reference (unliberalized) levels of protection are measured as the percentage difference between internal producer and consumer prices and the border prices for each commodity in 1980–1982. The border price used is the country's export or import unit value, as opposed to a central world market price, e.g., wheat at Rotterdam, adjusted for transport costs. A sample of these protection coefficients was shown earlier (Table 1.1). Internal price-setting policies are made endogenous by means of price transmission equations explaining domestic policy-determined prices.

    d.   The model is annual, but uses a Nerlovian lagged dependent variable specification of supply functions, so that "long-run" effects can be estimated.

e. Cross-elasticities of supply and demand are included, some estimated, some taken from other studies.

f. Trends are essentially extrapolations of the history of the dependent variable, with no attempt to model exogenous causes of these trends.

g. Exchange rates in the base period are used to convert all currencies to dollars, and the exchange rates are kept the same in all later years as simulated.

Some results of liberalization experiments in this model are shown in Table 11.1. When the industrial countries stop protecting their agricultural sectors, the world prices of the protected commodities go up! The reason is that these countries generally guarantee producer prices without offsetting production controls, and the resulting surpluses are in part dumped on world markets. When they stop dumping, world prices go up. This has important implications for the transition from protection to market orientation. It means the cost to farmers in a liberalizing country will be less if the liberalization is done by many countries simultaneously. Note, however, that for coarse grains the simulated price rise is less when all the OECD countries liberalize than when the EC only does. This occurs because in the current U.S. policy, as modeled, acreage controls result in less output and a higher world price. So U.S. liberalization reduces the world price.

The gains and losses shown are sums of producers' surplus, consumers' surplus (using a compensating variation measure) and government cost changes. Thus, all three interest groups are weighted equally and the worldwide sum is the overall deadweight loss caused by the countries' agricultural protection. At \$25.6 billion for OECD countries, this is more than many deadweight loss calculations. Since world prices fall, producers lose and consumers gain in

Table 11.1   Results of Agricultural Trade Liberalization

	Liberalization scenario*			
	EC	OECD	DC	Global
Percentage change in world price:				
Wheat	1	2	7	9
Coarse grains	3	1	3	4
Rice	1	5	− 12	− 8
Dairy products	12	27	36	67
Sugar	3	5	3	8
Change in net surpluses of (billions of 1980 dollars):				
OECD countries	—	48.5	− 10.2	45.9
Developing countries	—	− 11.8	28.2	18.3
Centrally planned countries	—	− 11.1	− 13.1	− 23.1
Worldwide		25.6	4.9	41.1

*The liberalization scenarios are: EC: the European Communities (excluding Spain and Portugal); OECD: 24 industrialized market economics; DC: developing countries; all countires in the model.
Source: Tyers and Anderson (1986).

food importing countries. The OECD countries gain but the developing countries lose because the latter, as a group, consume more than they produce. Within the OECD countries, the $48.5 billion net gain is composed of a $103 billion gain to consumers and taxpayers and a $54.5 billion loss to producers. Most of this redistribution occurs with the EC and Japan, which protect these commodities at rates that the United States approaches only for sugar. For further details and a stout denunciation of worldwide agricultural policies as practiced in both developed and developing countries in the 1980s, see World Bank (1986).

Customs Unions and Cartels

Partial liberalization does not in principle generate the global gains that worldwide freer trade generates. The ambiguity is apparent in the case of customs unions which eliminate trade barriers between countries but may even increase them between their members and other countries. An agricultural example in the 1980s is the EEC's inclusion of Spain and Portugal. When these countries were brought under the EEC's common agricultural policy (CAP), they ceased what had been substantial grain imports, causing greater price distortions between EEC and non-EEC market and retaliatory threats of the United States to increase tariffs on food products it imports from the EEC.

Joint action by a group of countries that even more clearly is the opposite of trade liberalization is an international commodity agreement to establish an export cartel. Countries that individually have insignificant market power when banded together can act as a large country to extract consumers' surplus from importers, as in the earlier wheat example. Two levels of policy-making are necessary to establish a cartel: first, each nation's exports must be controlled, requiring a system of export licenses or the equivalent; second, the cartel countries must agree on their aggregate export level and on each member's share of it. The difficulties in establishing and then maintaining these arrangements are analogous to those of a domestic producer's cartel, and they are formidable. Consider the following problems: (1) agreement on aggregate sales and market shares, and (2) cheating.

Agreement on Aggregate Sales and Market Shares. The underlying problem is that the gain-maximizing restraint of sales will be different for different countries.

Consider a hypothetical case using the earlier wheat imported demand, $Q_M = 190 - 0.69P$. Let there be three wheat exporting countries with three different excess supply functions of exportable wheat:

$$q_1 = -5 + 0.33P$$
$$q_2 = 25 + 0.10P$$
$$q_3 = 25$$

The sum of the three gives $Q_E = 45 + 0.43P$ as stated earlier. Solving for P gives the marginal cost function of exported grain. At the competitive market equilibrium $P = 129$ and $Q_E = 100.5$ with $q_1 = 37.6$, $q_2 = 37.9$, and $q_3 = 25$.

If a monopolist were to conduct world grain exports, the profit maximizing strategy would be to equate marginal export revenue (MR) to marginal cost (MC), and allocate output such that each country produces up to the point at which its marginal cost (MC_i) equals the common MC. In our example, we have:

$$MR = 275 - 2.9Q$$
$$MC = -105 + 2.33Q$$
$$MC_1 = 15.15 + 3.03\,q_1$$
$$MC_2 = -250 + 10.0\,q_2$$

and MC_3 is infinite (q_3 being fixed). Equating $MC = MR$ gives $Q = 72.6$, with $P = 170$, and $MC = 64.3$. Output is reduced 28 percent from the competitive quantity. Output is allocated such that $q_1 = 16.2$, $q_2 = 31.4$, and $q_3 = 25$. The producer's gain as compared to competition is $(170 - 129)(72.6) - .5(100.5 - 72.6)(129 - 64.3) = 2074$. (This calculation is analogous to the $A - C$ area of Fig. 2.1.)

Is this monopoly solution plausible as the result of a grain exporting cartel composed of these three countries? Probably not. Country 1 would have to reduce its output by more than half, while country 2 has a 27-percent cutback, and country 3 maintains its output. This makes sense from the viewpoint of efficient production because the low supply elasticities mean that in countries 2 and 3, grain-producing resources do not have alternative uses as attrctive as in country 1. (The elasticity of supply at competitive equilibrium is 1.1 in country 1; 0.3 in country 2; and 0.0 in country 3.) Still, it is unlikely that country 1 would acquiesce in carrying so much of the burden of output reduction.

A more likely outcome of cartel negotiations is that each country would maintain its share of the export market; all would reduce output by an equal percentage. Maintaining market shares of 3/8, 3/8, and 1/4, the overall 28-percent output cutback results in $q_1 = q_2 = 27.2$ and $q_3 = 18.2$. This generates aggregate gains for the cartel members of 1382. The considerable reduction from the multiplant monopolist's gains of 2074 occurs because this is not the low cost allocation of output among exporting countries. An even greater difficulty for the cartel is the distribution of these profits. As compared to competition, country 1 gains 954, country 2 gains 559, and country 3 *loses* 131. The reason for country 3's losses is that it has no alternative use for resources taken out of grain; its objective is to maximize revenue from grain sales. But the cartel has moved price up to the elastic range of the aggregate import demand curve, so revenue is falling as price rises.

Country 3 could be allocated a larger share of sales, or could receive monetary side-payments from countries 1 and 2 as bribes to go along with the cartel. The general point is that countries with different supply conditions will have quite different views about the best sales level for the cartel, and any simple rule for allocating market shares is likely to be unsatisfactory. The multiplant monopoly solution with side payments is optimal for the group, but there are no economic principles for determining the amount of the side payments, without which this solution cannot be attained.

With respect to the much studied OPEC cartel in oil, the problem has been stated as one of low-cost versus high-cost producers. For agricultural commodities, this notion provides little guidance; all we can work with are quantities produced at different prices, i.e., the supply functions as indicators of marginal cost. But, of course, price equals marginal cost for each country. The characteristic that divides exporting countries' interests is the elasticity of supply.

Cheating on Agreements Reached.   The low-elasticity producers especially want to produce more than their allocated share because of the availability of resources with few nongrain uses. But all exporters can gain handsomely by "free-riding" on other members' restraint. In the example, even country 1 can substantially increase its gains by selling above its agreed share. Since the world price is 170 under the cartel agreement, and marginal cost in country 1 is 98, a rate of return of $(170 - 98)/98 = 73$ percent is earned on each dollar spent producing more output. Such powerful incentives to cheat are difficult to resist. And of course if all or most members cheat, the cartel soon breaks down.

Even if these problems could be solved, others exist, depending on the dynamics of the market, the role of stockholding, the strategic behavior of cartel members in other respects, and possible retaliation by consuming countries. It is not surprising that despite many attempts at organizing agricultural export cartels—in coffee, sugar, cocoa, as well as grains—none seems to have been viable and none exists today. For empirical treatment of cartel issues in grain exports, see Schmitz et al. (1981), and for commodity agreements generally, Gordon-Ashworth (1984).

If potential cartel members cannot maintain cooperation, their activity becomes similar to oligopoly in a domestic market. The main difference is that there are few buyers as well as few sellers. Attempts by a subset of sellers to reduce sales and drive up prices can be blocked by a coalition between buyers and the remaining sellers. Karp and McCalla (1983) consider some possibilities for solution of dynamic games where strategies are border distortions imposed by buyers and sellers. The "dynamic" element refers to dependence of the economic environment in which the strategies are chosen in one period on previously chosen strategies by all countries. The key question of positive analysis of policies is whether a set of countries, set to trade and negotiate, will end up forming cartels on the one hand or free-trade agreements on the other; and what characteristics of domestic and world markets lead to one outcome or the other.

Theory does not seem to provide much guidance on this, except perhaps to say that the greater the number of producing countries the less likely we are to observe a sellers' cartel.

Food Aid

The industrialized countries have for many years been providing agricultural commodities to poorer countries on favorable terms, the paradigm case of such a policy being the U.S. Trade and Development Act of 1954, known as P.L. 480, or, in the 1960s, "Food for Peace." These policies have been controversial. They have involved help for the needy and as such have been applauded. But at the same time their motivation has been criticized as being primarily a commodity-surplus dumping policy which has hindered agricultural development in the receiving countries.

In terms of supply–demand analysis, food aid is essentially isomorphic with an export subsidy. The relevant domestic effects in the instigating donor country are two. First, the sum of producer, consumer, and taxpayer income falls, so the program is like charity by the donor in this respect. Second, demand is increased for the donor's commodities, so the donor country's producers gain. These are the same effects as an export subsidy has.

The second effect, however, is expected to be weaker for food aid than for an export subsidy. The reason is that with an export subsidy (by a large country) everyone in respondent countries buys at a lower price, so demand for the commodity increases, whereas food aid provides commodities only to certain consumers at reduced prices. It creates two prices for the same commodity in the receiving countries. Market forces tend to pull the two prices together, for example, because recipients of grain at low prices can resell it at higher prices. The U.S. legislation attempts to rule out such practices and requires that receiving countries increase their overall demand for grains and not just use food aid to replace commercial purchases. But is is difficult to ensure this result. The analysis of food aid is thus like that of targeted export subsidies as discussed earlier.

From the viewpoint of the receiving countries, food aid would be a pure income transfer with no direct relative price effects if the law of one price prevails and all recipients of subsidized commodities are free to resell at the market price. Even if some recipients consume distributed food, they would value it at the market price and presumably consume accordingly. If the recipients are poor people with a high income elasticity of demand for food, then food aid would increase the country's demand for food. But if the recipients are officials or others who resell at market prices, then the income effect may increase the consumption of nonfood relative to food items. On the other hand, if the food aid shipments are large enough to exceed commercial imports, or if the commodities are channeled to poor people and cannot be resold, then aggregate food demand will rise.

The problem in the receiving country is that increased imports will reduce the demand for their domestically produced food commodities. Increased consumption occurs only at a lower price, and it is almost inevitable that some aid will spill into commercial channels, reducing prices there and, hence, producers' incomes. So receiving countries' producers are losers.

Since an importing country consumes more than it produces, the food aid must increase the sum of consumers' and producers' incomes. The concern is that the aid might cease after domestic production has been reduced at lower prices. In general, this argument is no better than the one that any protection-seeking producer gives for keeping out foreign goods; it is dangerous to depend on foreign supplies. Whatever the truth to this, it is not regarded as a decisive argument for protection against commercial imports, so why should it be a good argument against accepting subsidized imports?

Donor countries may cut back on aid when commodities are scarce in them (as the United States did in the 1970s), but on the other hand, food aid has been increased despite donor scarcity when famines have occurred in receiving countries (as in the Sahel in the 1970s). Still, problems with delivering such emergency aid in time, and to the right places, raise legitimate questions. In general, are subsidized imports more variable in availability than domestic supplies? And if they are, does this outweigh the gain from having cheaper commodities available part of the time? The answers to those questions turns on attitudes toward risk and the receiving countries' capabilities in risk management.

TRADE AND STABILIZATION

For a small open economy, a buffer stock is not a feasible stabilization policy. If it holds commodities off the market, the domestic price remains at the world price level; and if, when world prices are temporarily high, stocks are released into the domestic market, they just replace imports (or are exported) at the given world price. Economic planners may engage in stockpiling, but if they do they are simply speculating on the world price level as an individual might do.

Border measures, however, can achieve domestic price stabilization quite readily. An importing country simply decides on a domestic price above the world price, introduces an import tariff just sufficient to establish the domestic price, and when world price fluctuate, weekly, monthly or annually, adjusts the tariff as necessary to maintain the domestic price. This is the general approach used in the variable levels of the EEC and other European countries in grain and sugar. (An exporter could accomplish the same result using a variable export subsidy.)

This type of policy insulates the domestic economy from external shocks. If internal demand and supply are stable, a variable levy maintains a constant level of imports, and thus is depicted in supply–demand terms as equivalent to a fixed import quota.

If supply or demand shocks occur in the domestic market of the insulated country, the country adjusts its imports enough to offset the shortfall or surplus, and in this respect acts as if it had a fixed tariff. Thus, the insulating country transmits its own supply or demand shocks to the rest of the world, but does not absorb any shock created elsewhere.

Insulating policies in several countries simultaneously, if they account for a substantial share of world consumption, create additional instability in world markets. When worldwide output declines, due to a drought in the USSR, for example, someone's consumption will be reduced. If some countries insulate their domestic economy so that their consumption is not reduced, other countries must reduce their consumption more. The market generates this result by causing prices to rise more than they otherwise would in the noninsulating countries and in world trade. Johnson (1975) identifies insulating policies as a major cause of world grain price instability in the 1970s. Empirical studies of insulation and its consequence have been reported in Bale and Lutz (1979) and Bredahl et al. (1979). The latter estimate how much less elastic the demand for U.S. grain is made by insulating policies of grain importers. They find quite low elasticities for some commodities, notably wheat. This result raises the question of whether the United States might not enjoy substantial monopoly power caused by such insulation, greatly improving the prospects for the success of a wheat exporters cartel, or lacking the ability to solve the cartel problems, for the United States to gain from unilateral production controls. But because the inelasticity of demand depends on importers' policies, which could be changed if the importers came to see them as too costly, this is a risky source of market power. Still, the combination of randomness in supply with inelastic demand for a storable commodity creates the potential for shirt-lived interruptions of exports as a strategy for large-country exporters. Loury and Lewis (1986) investigate the circumstances under which such a spolicy is profitable.

The notion of worldwide gains from trade takes on a quite different complexion when each country's output is random. The gains from trade in manufactured goods arise from different countries exploiting their comparative advantages—specializing in production of what they make at relatively low cost. Gains from trade in agricultural commodities, especially staples produced in many countries but which have variable yields, arise just as importantly from the capability of a country to import in a year of domestic shortfall rather than having to let price rise enough to retain domestic supplies. Thus, trade serves as a substitute for a buffer stock. Stocks are still necessary to moderate price fluctuations owing to worldwide supply variation, but these will be smaller for the world than for the sum of individual countries in the same years. Johnson and Sumner (1976) compared optimal storage of grain with free trade and autarky for a sample of 14 countries and regions. They found that on average eight times more stocks were required under autarky. The costs of holding these stocks, plus the fact that instability is greater under autarky even with the larger stocks, are a measure of the gains from trade over and above the static gains attributable to comparative advantage.

Strategic Stockpiling in an International Context

In Chap. 10, market stabilization through commodity stocks was analyzed for a closed economy. A full analysis of governmental stockholding by a large country, such as the United States, should take into account not only private speculative storage but also stocks held by other governments. If other governments have objectives the same as private stockpilers—they add to storage whenever the expected future price exceeds current price plus storage costs—these governmental stocks can be incorporated with private stockholding. However, if other governments hold their stocks abroad, then the U.S. export demand function becomes, in part, a demand function for foreign stocks. Therefore, a change in U.S. stockholding policy would shift the demand for exports as well as the demand for private domestic stocks.

Consider optimal stockpiling policy by a governmental agency in a world containing other stockholding entities, some of which hold stocks for broader policy purposes. It is not clear that the distinction between public and private stockholding dischotomizes stockpilers according to these purposes. The relevant analytical distinction is that the stockholding environment in which country A must develop an optimal policy contains two types of noncontrolled stockpiling agents: (1) competitive stockholders [whose actions force Eq. (10.37) to hold], and (2) stockholding entities which, for one reason or another, attempt to manipulate price, not taking current or expected price as exogenously given variables. The behavioral entities in this latter category must necessarily be larger, but it does not necessarily contain governmental agencies only. Moreover, the first category may contain governmental agencies or quasi-governmental business entities undertaking relatively small-scale stockholding for commercial purposes. The key element added in the second category is the potential for strategic interaction of stockpiling policies.

The analytical problems of optimal public stockholding in a strategic context are distinct from the issues raised by monopoly power in the grain trade. Monopoly power in storage space at a particular location, for example, a port, may be achieved by a large grain-exporting firm. The exercise of monopoly power in stockpiling involves storing smaller quantities than in a competitive market so that $E(P_{t+1}) > P_t + C_t$, and expectations of pure profit exist. While short-term monopoly profits in particular locations may be achieved by large stockholders, this is a less plausible outcome for economy-wide storage of carryover between crop years. For this broader purpose, stocks on farms or in other commercial positions must be almost perfect substitutes for stocks held by large corporations. Thus, anticipations of price gains in excess of storage costs become inconsistent with market equilibrium even in the presence of large stockholders.

Consider a two-country market in which neither isolates its domestic grain price from the joint (world) market. Each country may be described by a model, such as Eqs. (10.24) to (10.39), with the additional constraints that one country's grain exports are the other's imports and that current price in the importing country equals price in the exporting country plus the marginal cost of transportation.

If either country introduces a buffer-stock regime that adds to the total carryover, prices will be stabilized in both countries. One country can promote stability in its internal prices at no cost to itself by convincing the other country to increase its carryover stocks. These possibilities add a strategic element to grain stockpiling.

Suppose each country faces a comparable social aversion to price instability and has the same storage technology and that price variability has no known distributional consequences for welfare between the countries. Thus, both countries see the same quantity of stocks as optimal for given world market conditions. Consider the following circumstances: world supply (production plus initial stocks) is 125 percent of next year's expected production, both countries estimate that stockholding over and above privately optimal storage ("stabilization stocks") would not yield net social benefits, and the schedule of benefits in each country is:

Stocks (million tons)	Benefits (million dollars)
0	0
5	100
10	150
15	175
20	190
25	200
30	205

The technique of grain storage, costs of resources, and private storage response to the program mean that the least-cost means of generating stabilization stocks (above equilibrium private speculative stocks) is $6.00 per ton. This cost may be associated with governmental storage, a subsidy to private storage, or a combination of the two.

Regardless of the country which holds and finances them, the strategic possibilities arise because the benefits in each country are assumed to arise from the level of stocks (more precisely, the price-stabilization insurance provided by the stocks). Considering discrete intervals of 5 million tons of storage, the resulting payoff matrix for the two countries is as shown in Table 11.2. If this matrix were reduced to 2 × 2 by selecting the third row and column and either

Table 11.2   Expected Payoffs from Stockpiling

Country B stocks	Expected payoffs (million dollars)*			
	Country A stocks			
	0	5	10	15
0	0, 70	70, 100	90, 150	85, 175[a]
5	100, 70	120, 120	115, 145	100, 160
10	150, 90	115, 145	130, 130	110, 140
15	175, 85	150, 100	140, 110	115, 115

*The first number of each entry is the gain to country A, and the second is the gain to country B. The gain is calculated as benefits resulting from world (A + B) storage minus storage costs for the country. For example, in the 85, 175 entry, country B gains 175 because it has 175 of benefits (from the text table) but no storage costs. Country A also has 175 in benefits but incurs 15 × 6 = 90 storage costs for a net gain of 85.

the first or second row and column, we would have a "mixed motive" game in the terminology of Rapoport et al. (1976). Consider the 2 × 2 game consisting of the intersection of the first and third rows and columns of Table 11.2. Its Nash solution for a cooperative game is that each country stores 10. This may be thought an obvious result. Each country, ignoring storage by the other, would choose to store 10 to maximize its own expected gain (90). Moreover, this solution is a saddle point and so is the pure minimax-maximin strategy for both countries in the noncooperative game; by choosing to stockpile 10 million tons, neither country can do worse than a $90-million gain.

Nonetheless, it is not clear that this storage game will result in a Pareto-optimal equilibrium. If country A knows that country B will store 10, then country A can do better by storing nothing for a net gain of 150. Therefore, one cannot assume that the cooperative solution will be arrived at "as by an invisible hand." It requires negotiation and agreement to ensure the jointly optimal storage outcome.

The incentive to attempt a free ride on another country's storage leads to various strategic moves and countermoves. For example, the crop year for grains begins later in the calendar year in the Soviet Union than in the United States. Therefore, the Soviets may be able to gain an advantage by waiting for the United States to reveal its stock levels. On the other hand, the United States may be able to make an initial move, for example, a preliminary decision to impose set-asides that forces the Soviet Union to a position of disadvantage. A general strategy could be for a country never to reveal its stock level, a policy that has, in fact, been adopted by the Soviet Union.

Differentiated Products in Trade

The picture for stabilization as well as other commodity policies is complicated further if countries' goods are not perfect substitutes for one another. This means that the price of U.S. rice related to Thai rice, for example, can differ even at the same location. This makes each substantial exporter a monopolistic competitor and generally complicates the economic analysis of trade flows and border prices. Some such situation seems to exist for more agricultural commodities. It explains why the EEC both imports and exports wheat and the United States both imports and exports tobacco. Models of differentiated products are too complicated to pursue here. Grennes et al. (1978) provide an interesting application to the world wheat market.

Differentiated demand functions for a large country's exports, a related but distinct issue, also have policy implications. If the U.S. faces inelastic demand in some foreign markets as compared to others, it could restrict exports more to the least-elastic markets. This price discrimination can increase the exporter's gains above those found in Fig. 11.3, just as a milk marketing order domestically can increase revenues from any given quantity sold. It could be argued that the U.S. embargo on sales to the USSR might be attributable to exploitation of elasticity differences. However, even if the USSR has a less elastic import demand than other importers (there is no evidence that it does), there is not sufficient differentiation between the United States and other exporters' grain for the United States alone to gain, and the U.S. share of the aggregate market is not so large as to preclude other exporters, who don't restrict exports, from being the principal gainers.

MULTIMARKET, MACROECONOMIC, AND MONETARY-FINANCIAL ISSUES

Moving beyond single-commodity supply–demand analysis brings in some new issues in the international context as it did in the closed economy models of Chaps. 5, 8, and 9. Multicommodity models, as used for example in the Tyers and Anderson simulations of liberalized trade, typically do not involve departures from single-market models at the conceptual or qualitative level. It is possible, however, that in either a general equilibrium model or multimarket partial equilibrium model paradoxical results can arise, notably that an import tariff can reduce the domestic (relative) price of the supposedly protected product and the real income of its producers. Paarlberg and Thompson (1980) show how this result could arise in the wheat market with sufficiently large cross-elasticities of supply and demand between wheat and coarse grains. They make the point that even though it is unlikely to have cross-elasticities high enough to generate the qualitatively paradoxical result, quantitative estimates of tariff effects are significantly affected by cross-commodity tariff effects.

It is also helpful in analyzing some policies to consider trade in factors of production or intermediate products as well as final products. For instance, the United States imports tomatoes from Mexico and also labor for growing tomatoes. Restricting U.S. tomato imports increases the demand for Mexican workers in U.S. tomato production; conversely, restricting immigration of Mexican farm workers increases the supply of Mexican tomatoes (and other vegetables).

Thus, liberalizing trade in vegetables can serve as substitute for liberalizing immigration (a partial equilibrium analog of the general factor price equalization result in trade theory); and liberalizing immigration can serve as a substitute for liberal trade.

A detailed analysis of liberalized temporary immigration in the form of a "guest-worker" program is developed in Morgan and Gardner (1982) and applied to the *bracero* program in which Mexican agricultural workers were employed in the United States between 1942 and 1964. The approach is to combine a derived demand model such as is used in Chap. 4 with an excess supply–demand trade model. Both the United States and Mexico gain when all interest groups within each country have equal welfare weights, but some interest groups within each country lose.

The same kind of comparative-statics result can be used to analyze a tariff or quantitative restraint on U.S./Mexican trade in agricultural commodities. Restricting trade increases the derived demand for U.S. labor and hence increases immigration (in the absence of restrictions). Liberalizing commodity trade reduces the demand for immigrants; it also increases the demand for labor in Mexico. Thus, liberal trade in commodities serves as a substitute for liberalizing immigration and lessens the distortion created by a given set of immigration restrictions. Torok and Huffman (1986) develop this argument empirically for the case of Mexican vegetable with reference particularly to illegal immigration.

Policy issues have also arisen with trade in agricultural products as raw material as compared to trade in processed products: cotton versus textiles, wheat and sugar versus cookies. There seems to be a presumption (more common among textile and cookie manufacturers than among economists?) that exports of these "high-value" products is preferable to exports of raw material. The analytical situation is similar to the one for tomatoes as compared to labor. It seems clear that trade at one level will often be a good substitute for trade at the other, but there does not seem to be a reason why trade at one level is intrinsically better for the exporting country than at the other. It should depend on the comparative costs of the processing operation. If a country does not process the products it exports under free trade, there is a net loss (of unweighted surpluses) from intervention to boost processed exports just as there would be for any other commodity which the country did not export under free trade. Of course, intervention via production subsidies, say, may be chosen to aid processors just as it is to aid farmers.

Macroeconomic Issues

With respect to monetary aspects of trade, in many developing countries regulation of agricultural prices is as much a matter of overvaluing the exchange rate of the local currency as of determining farm prices relative to other prices. (For a useful review, see World Bank, 1986, Chap. 4). Farm goods are affected relative to nontraded goods (some farm goods, too, may be nontraded). The main problems arise from governmental fixing of exchange rates. Under flexible exchange rates, a currency can only be overvalued or undervalued in the same sense as, say, common stocks are said to be overvalued or undervalued. It means no more than that some short-term influences are holding the current market price above or below a price that must eventually be realized. However, since we never are certain of the long-run price, it becomes conjectural whether the current market prices of currencies are overvalued or undervalued.

What is the implication for commodity policy? Mainly that we can expect volatility from exchange-rate uncertainty to influence the supply, demand, and price of traded goods. If a regulated commodity price is established, the excess demand or supply at that price will be less predictable. Indeed, it is possible that unless border policies are adopted to insulate domestic market, domestic commodity market intervention will have its intended effects swamped by exchange rate fluctuations even for large countries. Schuh (1985) emphasizes the relevance of this situation for the 1980s.

Another macroeconomic issue is the consequences of agricultural policy for the general economy. The budgetary outlays necessary for urban food subsidies, for example, can be a significant fraction of the total budget in some developing countries. Timmer (1986, Chap. 6) and McCalla and Josling (1985) contain helpful discussions of the issue. In industrial countries, agriculture has a small enough share of GNP that such effects may be reckoned inconsequential. But even in the United States, deficiency payments of $10 billion, concentrated in a few months of the year, can have a noticeable effect on national income. It is widely believed that commodity price shocks in 1972–1975 were a cause of the high inflation of that period. Although they were not entirely a matter of agricultural policy, one of the main ingredients was the decision of the Soviet Union to import grain in 1972 and in 1975 rather than make do with less as had been done during previous production shortfalls. For developing countries, where the agricultural sector is a larger share of consumers' budgets and the GNP, the importance of macroeconomic consequences of farm policy is even clearer.

The analytical apparatus for dealing with these effects is a general equilibrium model. A simple version of such a model was used in Chap. 9, for a closed economy. In recent years there has been much effort in developing small-scale mathematical versions of such models for open economies. Such a "computable" general equilibrium (CGE) model could be constructed from a two-product model as used in Chap. 9, or in the seven-product model of Tyers and Anderson cited earlier. What is principally needed is another sector to represent the nonagricultural part of the economy, and closure of the model by making receipts of suppliers of all products the base for calculating income to be spent on all products. This permits a support price for one commodity to have effects on demand for others over and above the consequences of cross-price demand and supply elasticities.

Whalley (1985) reports a number of trade-liberalization experiments using a CGE model. The model generates consumer incomes through factor payments, and it incorporates financial flows and international investment. But there is no monetary sector and no exchange-rate effects exist; thus the model is an application of the pure relative-price general equilibrium models of trade theory. One generalization is the use of a model of product differentiation by country that permits specification of trade between pairs of countries, rather than assuming uniform commodities and trade flows based on transportation cost minimization.

The lack of exchange rates or a monetary sector means that CGE models do not address some of the issues of concern, particularly misvalued or unstable exchange rates. This omission can cause systematic problems for comparative static analysis of policies when the policies have significant effects on exchange rates or other economy-wide financial variables. This can be important when a country relies heavily on export of a particular commodity whose world market price is strongly influenced by another country's agricultural policies, for example, U.S. rice policy influencing the trade position of Thailand. Not enough is known about exchange-rate effects in such instances to include them in a simulated model, and in most economies at most times they are probably weak effects anyway. This is not to say that macroeconomic events are unimportant influences on agricultural commodity markets. It is just that in comparing two policy options, A and B, there is typically not much point in studying which policy will have the greatest effect on exchange rates and, hence, on farm prices and incomes. The existence of volatile exchange rates might have important effects on the success of both options, and might favor one over the other. But exchange rates are generally an exogenous influence, like weather, conditioning but not themselves determined by farm policy choices.

Chapter 12

Explaining Policy

Why do governments do what they do in agricultural commodity markets? The topic was not discussed in the normative section (Chaps. 7 to 9) because the theory of welfare economics, on which that section is based, already presumes a concise and complete answer in the specification of a social welfare function. Its arguments were people's utilities, transformed for sectoral policy purposes to real incomes from the sector, i.e., surpluses, of producer, consumer, and taxpayer groups. This SWF presumes that the purpose of sectoral policies is income redistribution among these groups, particularly between consumers-taxpayers and producers. Apart from brief mentions of landowners and foreigners as interest groups in Chaps. 8 and 11, the SWF has been represented simply by the parameter Θ to measure the weight given to producers' income as compared to consumer-taxpayer income in social benefit/cost calculation of redistributional programs. At the beginning of Chap. 7, broader notions of normative economics were mentioned, but following Mark Twain's advice about troublesome things generally, we looked them firmly in the face and then went on our way.

Here the broader issue reappears as a matter of explaining observed facts.

This chapter discusses briefly a few possibilities of other arguments in the SWF. The bulk of the chapter explores the more fundamental question of explaining why the revealed SWF has the properties it is observed to have. This topic, although it deals with normative issues, is most productively viewed as a problem in positive economics. We would like to explain the behavior of governments as much as possible in the same way that we explain farmers' and consumers' behavior—as a result of maximizing economic gains subject to constraints faced.

POLICY GOALS AND INTEREST GROUPS

Chapter 9 presented a number of possible market failures that agricultural policies could correct, economic problems of the farm sector that have been seen by economists as justifying governmental intervention. The most enduring of these problems relate to uncertainty and instability in agriculture. A widespread view, expressed in the quotation from Arthur Schlesinger at the beginning of Chap. 1, is that people just cannot operate efficiently in the chaotic world of unregulated markets. Chapter 10 discussed the chief analytical issues involving risk aversion and optimal public stockholding, suggesting great difficulties in actually carrying them out.

It is possible that many governments no longer believe they have sufficiently better information than the markets to make price stabilization a viable policy. The U.S. Federal Farm Board of 1929 attempted such a policy, but it died in 1931 and was never resurrected. Why not? Because it proved incapable of supporting farm incomes. The latest stabilization schemes, in the U.S. Farmer-Owned Reserve Program and several international commodity agreements, have not proved viable as stabilization schemes although they have provided short-term price support (see Wright, 1985). Politically, programs labeled "stabilization" appear to be useful only in periods when they are accumulating stocks. The potential for reducing prices when stocks are released is seen as a regrettable liability rather than half the purpose of the programs. Modest attempts at downward stabilization in the United States, notably meat price controls and export controls of the 1970s, earned their sponsors such political obloquy that both political parties have ever since been trying to outdo one another in promising never again to attempt such things.

Food security through self-sufficiency is a related goal especially emphasized in the importing industrial countries. Proponents of Japanese agricultural policies invoke the lessons of World War II food shortages in arguing for high price supports, with producer prices three times the world price for rice. This argument is difficult to credit in that a war scenario that under today's technology disrupted Japan's ability to import staple foods would have more serious consequences in other sectors; Japan could probably boost rice output, if necessary, more readily than replacing other physical and human capital resources.

Apart from market risks and market failures, the argument has been put forth in industrial countries that certain social goals that transcend economic efficiency call for agricultural price supports. Traditional or family farm structures are said to be promoted by such programs. This type of argument is congenial to conservative parties, and several in Europe have become strong supporters of agricultural interests. Still it is reasonable to question whether the social argument is the real mainspring of farm policy. Look for policies that distinguish farmers' economic interests from the maintenance of traditional farm structures. One such policy might be price ceilings on the grounds that if farm prices get too high, outside investors will be drawn into agriculture and traditional farmers will want to expand. Or farmers might be penalized if they enlarge their farms or employ hired workers or adopt certain production practices. Yet we typically observe only those policies which seek social goals by supporting farm incomes. The United States encourages farmers to conserve land, but does so by subsidizing conservation practices, not by taxing failure to conserve.

In short, the set of farm policies we observe, in the United States and the industrial countries generally, whatever the stated goals may be, appear to be observationally equivalent to policies intended to support the incomes of farmers as an interest group. At the same time, in many poor countries, farmers have been taxed and urban consumers subsidized. And in all kinds of countries, from land reform in Mexico, to the expropriation of the richer peasants in Russia and Poland, to the U.S.-enforced postwar land reform in Japan, the more wealthy farmers have come under political attack.

The point of these assertions is not to criticize the policies but to argue for the standard approach in welfare economics of including the well-being of interest groups in the social welfare function, while excluding other social goals. This does not mean that the national interest is unimportant, but that the national interest is to be measured in terms of the *economic* well-being of all groups taken together.

THEORY OF COLLECTIVE REDISTRIBUTIVE DECISIONS

Redistribution from one group to another does not require an elaborate explanation when the group helped has suffered undeserved losses or is at grave risk of not surviving. Thus, it has seemed to historians only natural that farmers were aided in the Great Depression when farm families were the poorest of the poor (and made up 25 percent of the population). What is harder to understand is why in the 1980s, when farmers account for 2.5 percent of the population and (despite the problems of some highly indebted farmers) are wealthier than the nonfarm population on average, governmental intervention to aid farmers is even greater than it was in the 1930s. In the 1980s, the U.S. government spent more on farm programs in real terms, idled a larger fraction of acreage, and held a greater percentage of output in surplus stocks. For this we need some-thing more in the way of explanation than immediate intuition provides.

A theory of governmental behavior in general terms might be had from political science. However, this field of study is too diffuse: it has no standard theory or model that we could simply apply to governmental action in agriculture. Two strategies of investigation are however suggested by the political science literature: (1) close attention to the institutions and processes, such as the committee structure of the U.S. Congress, in which governmental decisions are made, and (2) treatment of the government itself, or the "bureaucracy" composed of its nonelected staff, as an interest group with powers and objectives of its own. Consideration of these two strategies for investigation, as well as the interest-group perspective, leads to a desire for a theory of collective choice: decision-making by a group. While political scientists appear increasingly interested in such theories, their development has been the work primarily of economists, as an elaboration of the economic theory of individual choice. The issues and approaches as applied to agricultural policy are discussed here with reference to U.S. political institutions, although many of the ideas should be readily adaptable for application in other contexts.

Overall Perspectives

The government's choice on a particular point (e.g., to raise a support price) could be taken to depend on:

1. the will of the majority
2. the special interest group having greatest concern with the issue, or spending the most on lobbying, or being constituents of the most powerful senators and representatives in the relevant committee of Congress
3. the interests of bureaucrats

These alternatives are listed in roughly descending order of their congruence with high school civics-class conceptions of democracy. Generally, food and agricultural policy determined by the will of the majority would be least shocking, and dominance of the interests of bureaucrats furthest from the wishes of the citizens. (At least some citizens outside the government itself have a role in the second point.)

Can U.S. agricultural policy be plausibly interpreted as reflecting the will of the majority? What is most clear is that policy reflects congressional majorities, and presidential assent. Agricultural policy is not an area where Congress legislated general legal guidelines and then created a regulatory body like the Federal Trade Commission, the Food and Drug Administration, or the Securities and Exchange Commission to carry them out for an indefinite period of years. Instead, Congress has, since the 1930s, passed a series of commodity-specific, limited-duration interventions which have often contained detailed instructions concerning prices and price-control mechanisms. There have been across-the-board policy changes mandated in recent years (in 1970, 1973, 1977, 1978, 1981, and 1985), with significant programs for specific commodities in every year between.

Thus, if Congressional majorities indicate majority support in the electorate, we could be quite confident that our farm policies have majority support. Yet there is a large quantity of writing by political observers that puts forth the second view on the list, the dominance of special interests. The winning special interests here are the producers of particular commodities, or owners of farmland in general. Since even the largest coalition of these landowning interests must account for less than 5 percent of the electorate, either some version of the special interest view must be correct, or there are large spillovers or public good benefits to the nonfarm population from agricultural policy such that it makes the majority better off. Reviews of policies by the more disinterested observers, for example, World Bank (1986), tend to reject the public-interest view. The World Bank estimated that if all developing and industrial countires abandoned their agricultural price policies, the world as a whole would gain about $40 billion annually.

In the United States, evidence that special-interest politics dominate is available by looking at the regional support for policies such as the tobacco program, and by comparing congressional with executive branch positions, regional special interests tending to be more self-canceling in the latter. Just to take one bit of evidence, the last seven Presidents (Eisenhower, Kennedy, Johnson, Nixon, Ford, Carter, and Reagan) have recommended in their budgets that the Agricultural Conservation Program—really a set of subsidies for capital improvements—be eliminated or greatly cut back as a waste of taxpayers' money. Congress has restored cuts in this program every time.

The object of practical politics on economic issues, then, is to gain the support of a majority for policies to benefit a minority. This involves the arts of persuasion, bargaining, threatening, and promising, to encourage support and mitigate opposition. Often the desired result is achieved through the emergence of coalitions that result in legislation that benefits a collection of minorities that constitutes a majority. Let us consider in more detail how this happens in the U.S. context.

Agricultural Policy Institutions

Within the general framework of the legislative and executive branches of the U.S. government, policy-making for a particular sector, such as agriculture, must be undertaken by specialists within the government. There is simply too much detail for the principals to be able to make all decisions. In the executive branch, the USDA has primary responsibility not only for carrying out programs but for formulating and communicating to Congress the administration's views on agricultural policy. In the Congress, the House and Senate committees on agriculture are delegated the task of developing farm legislation.

In both branches, but especially the Congress, the requirements of detailed expertise about the industry are onerous enough that private interest-group representatives (lobbyists) play an important role not only in arguing the pros and cons of policy alternatives but also in providing the detailed data and analysis necessary to assess the benefits and costs of proposed policies. Thus, if a support price for corn is proposed to be cut, representatives of the corn producers will be a main source of information on potential effects on the corn industry.

These three sets of actors—executive branch administrators, legislative committee members, and industry lobbyists—have been said to form a "golden triangle." They constitute a minigovernment on agricultural commodity (and similarly for other economic interest group) legislation. Because farm-district legislators can best serve their constituents on such committees, the committee tends to attract people who weight the interests of producers higher than consumers or general taxpayers. Similarly, the executive branch wishes to maintain good relations with the producers and finds a natural home for its representatives in the USDA. Consequently, all three components of the triangle tend to be friends of the industry and this is what generates the "golden" aspect. What restrains the industry's clout through the triangle mechanism? If nothing, we expect policy to maximize producers' gains, i.e., $\Theta = 0$ for consumers and taxpayers.

Nonagricultural interests can make their interests felt through general "watchdog" agencies within the government designed to keep the budget and regulatory actions generally under control. In the executive branch we have the Council of Economic Advisers (CEA), whose role can be seen as one of recommending policies to maximize the national income, i.e., the sum (unweighted) of surpluses, and the Office of Management and Budget (OMB) whose role is to monitor, plan, and try to keep a lid on the federal budget. Congress has budget committees in both the House and Senate, as well as the Congressional Budget Office (CBO) and, on occasion, the General Accounting Office (GAO) and Congressional Research Service (CRS) as evaluators of farm legislation from a broader perspective than that of the Agriculture Committees. These may be viewed as elements of a "counter-triangle" that may tarnish or even turn to dross the gold of the original one. The third element, corresponding counter-influences to agricultural lobbyists, has been weakest. There is in fact no "anti-farm lobby." But at times particular interest groups see an economic threat sufficient to cause substantial pressure in opposition to farm legislation. For example, the PIK program of 1983 had a large enough adverse impact on certain businesses in the farm-supply industry and in livestock feeding that in the debate on 1985 legislation their spokesmen became effective opponents of crop production controls.

At the same time, the golden-triangle interests can counter opposition by forming coalitions with nonfarm interest groups. Through the 1970s, this was effectively accomplished, especially in the House of Representatives, which contains many purely urban districts, by incorporating food-stamp assistance programs for the poor in the major farm bills. Sometimes, though, this broadening can go so far as to dilute the gains to agricultural producers seriously. For example, a "cargo preference" requirement that foreign food aid be shipped on U.S. vessels, when extended to rather modest subsidized export schemes, can increase the costs of shipping enough to offset the subsidy.

On the whole, it must be concluded that farm interests have been quite successful in attaining their legislative goals. Why? To answer this question systematically is to have a theory of politics, or of collective choice in the U.S. system of government. What we would like is a theory of a country's demand for farm programs derived from political preferences analogous to the theory of an individual's demand for a commodity derived from individual preferences.

This is a topic much too large and difficult even to outline here, but two aspects of the field should be at least mentioned: the theory of voting in a democracy and the theory of voluntary collective decisions in small groups. The former considers issues such as whether voting can be expected to generate political preferences (a revealed SWF) that satisfy axioms of rational choice—roughly, consistent pursuit of well-defined goals. Work by Kenneth Arrow caused severe doubts about this prospect, although some later work has been generally more hopeful (for review, see Ordeshook, 1986). Another set of issues involve questions of participation, notably why people vote when the likelihood of any individual's choice influencing the outcome is so slight. Finally, the role of political parties, and the number of parties in relation to the distribution of opinion on issues has been explored. (For detailed discussion, see Mueller, 1979, or Hinich, 1984).

The theory of collective choice in small groups was developed fruitfully in attempts to understand the provision of public goods (Tullock, 1970; Buchanan, 1968). It has been shown to be relevant to the economics of externalities (Cornes and Sandler, 1986). It is particularly appropriate for present purposes because in addition to the interaction of interest groups on the larger policy stage as discussed above, the interest groups themselves are the outcome of collective decisions by members of those groups. The issues in the context of agricultural policy may be stated in terms of how it occurs, or fails to occur, that the producers of a commodity voluntarily contribute to hiring a lobbyist to foster an agreed-upon policy position in Washington, D.C. What determines the scale of this activity, its longevity, and its chances of success?

A MODEL OF INTEREST-GROUP PRESSURE

A simplified and more formal treatment of the issue can help clarify the preceding discussion and focus on key factors in determining a group's political success. Start with four basic presuppositions:

1. Members of each interest group would like the government to intervene in the market to further their interests.

2. Each group has a potential source of economic rents or surplus—specific factors for suppliers and consumers' surplus for buyers—which provides a source of potential economic gains through intervention.

3. Intervention is supplied by governments in response to political pressure, which consists of electoral, financial, and other support of groups receiving favorable intervention and opposition by groups bearing the costs.

4. Political pressure is costly to generate, and can be generated more effectively by organized groups, thus providing incentives for collective action within groups.

Item (1) specifies individuals' objectives, analogously to assuming utility maximization in typical economic models. Items (2) and (4) specify technical features of the economy, analogous to resource constraints in microeconomic models. Item (3) could result from individuals' objectives or technical constraints or institutional constraints. Its function is to abstract from intervention for the purpose of generating economic rents to government officials. It can be thought of as an assumption that government is competitive rather than monopolistic.

The key elements in explaining intervention in markets are derived from items (2) and (4), with (2) determining the economics of intervention and (3) and (4) the political economy. With sufficient structural detail about (2), we can estimate the gains and losses from any intervention; we can generate the appropriate cost-of-redistribution or surplus transformation curves. With sufficient structural detail about (4), we can estimate the political preferences generated for redistribution of rents in favor of or away from each group. Observed intervention will reflect the balance of political preferences for redistribution and the cost of redistribution via the intervention.

Generation of Political Pressure

No group is powerless. Just by virtue of its having voters, or potential demonstrators or other disruptors of order, a group's interests have some weight. But this weight can be greatly increased through organized activity by the group, including developing a unified position, making sure it is understood in political circles, garnering popular support, and providing financial support to friendly politicans. The resultant force of these activities is summarized by the term *political pressure*. The determination of power can be represented by specifying the political good will toward a group as a function of its numbers and the political pressure it can bring to bear:

$$\Theta_r = V(N_r, P_r; N_s, P_s, W) \qquad (12.1)$$

where Θ_r is the political willingness to redistribute income to group r, N_r is the number of people in the group, and P_r is the political pressure they generate. Θ is quantified as the group's weight in the revealed political preference function. Variables to the right of the semicolon are held constant for the present. N_s and P_s aggregate the political power of opposition groups. W represents inherent preferences of politicans, caused, for example, by constitutional requirements or a tendency, even without interest-group pressure, to provide aid to groups suffering hardship.

Political pressure is generated by expenditures on political activities:

$$P_r = P\ (E_r,\ \alpha_r) \tag{12.2}$$

Equation (12.2) is an output function generating political pressure, with E being expenditures on these activities and α an indicator of efficiency or effectiveness. Effectiveness is reduced if a group has divided interests or disagrees on tactics, or for other reasons requires a substantial investment to act jointly.

Explaining E_r brings in a fundamental issue in collective action: how does an interest group obtain financial support from its members when every individual has an incentive to withhold support on the selfish but rational grounds that one person's absence will not appreciably harm the overall political effort? This free-rider problem appears serious enough that on a priori grounds one might predict that few if any interest groups could become effective political fundraisers. But in fact, we observe that the free-rider problem is overcome to an extent sufficient that collective interest-group activities exist for many commodity producers. Still, groups vary in their effectivness at collective action. The reasons can be expressed as a function explaining group effort in terms of factors that assist in overcoming the free-rider problem and making individuals willing to contribute. Write this relationship as

$$E_r = E\ (N_r,\ \alpha'_r,\ y_r) \tag{12.3}$$

Effort, E_r, could be represented by expenditures of the group on political action, as long as we remember that the cost of contributions in kind, such as lobbying trips to the capital, are a part of the group's political effort.

The number of members of the group has been discussed by several authors, notably Olson (1965) and Peltzman (1976), as a key to dealing with the free-rider problem. The issue is tricky because increased numbers increase the free-rider problem but also increase the volume of funds that may potentially be collected. Also, the larger the group, the harder it is for the group to arrive at an agreed-upon political strategy, and once arrived at, it is more difficult to convince individuals to contribute and to enforce their living up to commitments once made. The problems are similar to those confronting a cartel or market-sharing agreement among producers. On the other hand, a small group will find it difficult to mobilize the funds to hire professional lobbyists even if all participate. Thus, as Peltzman (1976) finds in a formal model incorporating these points, there may exist an optimal interest-group size compared to which either smaller or larger groups will have less clout, ceteris paribus.

The variable α_r', is a subset of α_r, representing determinants of coalition costs such as discordance of interests that may reduce individuals' willingness to contribute. The variable y_r is the share of the average member's income that comes from the protected commodity, the hypothesis being that the greater this share, the greater the willingness to contribute.

The variable E_r could also be analyzed as $E_r = N_r^* I_r$, where N_r^* is the number of people who actively participate and I_r is the contribution per participant. The right-hand-side variables in Eq. (12.3) are likely to affect N_r^* and I_r differently. For example, N_r might have a bigger influence on N_r^*, and y_r a bigger influence on I_r. We might gain more understanding of the causes of political pressure by decomposing E_r in this way and substituting separate equations explaining N_r^* and I_r for Eq. (12.3). Data are typically lacking for either N_r^* or I_r, however.

Substituting Eq. (12.3) into Eq. (12.2), and then Eq. (12.2) into Eq. (12.1), expresses political willingness to redistribute as a function of all the variables that have been discussed.

The objective of the interest group is not a higher Θ in Eq. (12.1), but the economic gains that result. These are measured as the economic rents generated by the government's choice of the policy instrument, V_r (a subsidy of r's output for example) impelled by Θ_r:

$$R_r = T(V_r; Z) \tag{12.4}$$

where Z is a vector of conditioning variables that influence the rents generated by a given subsidy level. Under an assumpton of stationary, constant-elasticity supply and demand curves, only two parameters are needed to completely specify the Z vector, namely the elasticity of demand, η, and the elasticity of supply, ϵ. Following Chap. 7, both are Hicksian (utility-constant) and multimarket equilibrium elasticities. R_s in the two-group representation is buyers' surplus. R_s is a function of the same elasticity variables. Thus we can construct a surplus transformation curve that specifies attainable combination of R_r and R_s achieved by varying V_r, given Z. In the constant elasticity case,

$$\frac{dR_r}{dR_s} = \frac{1}{\epsilon V_r (1/\eta - 1) - (\epsilon + 1)} \tag{12.5}$$

The economic outcome of intervention through V_r can be represented as $\Delta R_r / \Delta R_s$, and redistribution at the margin as the slope of the surplus transformation curve, dR_r / dR_s from Eq. (12.5).

The producers' problem is to maximize R_r given the economic constraint imposed by the surplus transformation curve and the political constraint caused by the activities of the s group. The choice variable is E_r, as discussed with reference to Eq. (12.3) above. The maximization problem is

$$\text{Max} \, [R_r \, (V_r) - C \, (V_r)] \qquad\qquad (12.6)$$
$$E_r$$

with the constraints given by Eq. (12.4) and (12.1) to (12.3). Equation (12.4) constrains $R_r \, (V_r)$ and Eq. (12.1) to (12.3) constrain $C \, (V_r)$. Substituting Eq. (12.2) into Eq. (12.1) eliminates the variable P_r, the producers' political pressure, which is unobservable, yielding

$$V_r = V_r \, (E_r; \, \alpha_r, \, N_r, \, P_s, \, N_s) \qquad\qquad (12.7)$$

Variables to the right of the semicolon are outside the industry's control. Equation (12.7) is a political production function of subsidy levels, with E_r the only variable input. (E_r is a capital expenditure input and in a full treatment would generate political pressure in the future as well as the present but this aspect of such expenditures is ignored here.) Equation (12.3) is the production function for E_r. We assume that both Eqs. (12.7) and (12.3) have the usual neoclassical properties with $\partial V_r / \partial E_r > 0$ and $\partial^2 V_r / \partial E_r^2 < 0$. Dual to Eq. (12.3) is a cost function that determines the shadow price (i.e., cost) of E_r, which is denoted C_E. Dual to Eq. (12.7) is a cost function of V_r that has C_E along with exogenous variables as determinants of $C \, (V_r)$ in Eq. (12.6). The neoclassical restrictions imply rental-revenue and cost functions as shown in Fig. 12.1. The optimal intervention, V_r^*, is obtained by choice of E_r^*, which is found by simultaneously solving Eq. (12.7) for E_r given V_r^*, or from the cost function via Shephard's lemma. This gives a condition for choice of E_r^* analogous to optimal input use for the firms in a cartel. The interest group equates the marginal value generated by use of funds in political activity to the marginal cost of those funds. The free-rider problem, as in the cartel case, affects the cost of political effort, and is assumed captured by the coalition cost variables α_r and N_r.

The lower panel of Fig. 12.1 shows E_r^* as the point at which the marginal value of political product of political effort equals its marginal cost [derived from Eq. (12.3)].

The comparative statics of changes in the exogenous variables can be illustrated with reference to α_r. If an element of α_r increases, with variables defined such that a higher α_r increases the cost of political pressure, then we increase the cost of raising any given E_r and hence the cost of obtaining V_r, as shown in Fig. 12.1. Although it is not shown in the diagram, elements of α_r can also reduce $\partial R / \partial V_r$ via Eq. (12.2).

Typically, variables that increase coalition costs will also reduce effectiveness via Eq. (12.2), and hence amplify the effect via Eq. (12.3), as with the

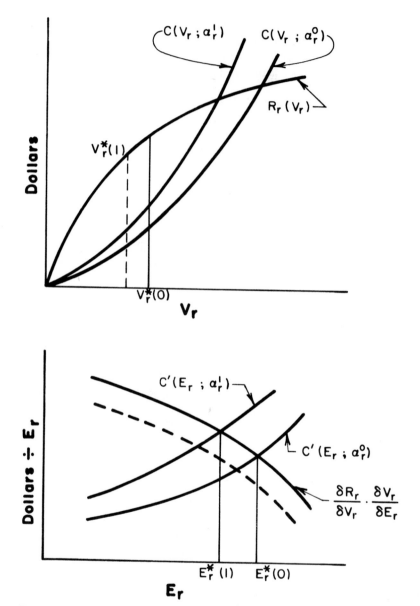

Figure 12.1 Optimal behavior of an interest group.

dashed curve in Fig. 12.1. But it is possible that some variables could have opposite effects. For example, compare an interest group scattered through many congressional districts (U.S. dairy) with one concentrated in a few (U.S. tobacco). Being dispersed raises the cost of organization, but could possibly increase the pressure generated for a given E_r, as Eq. (12.2) shows. In this case the overall effect on E_r^* and on C (V_r) is not predictable a priori.

The variable N_r is ambiguous in effect for the further reason that even if a bigger group contributes less per head, its aggregate E_r may be larger than for a smaller group; and even if a large group's aggregate spending is lower, the fact that it has more voters can influence V_r as Eq. (12.1) shows.

The nonlinearity of the marginal cost of redistribution means that redistribution will not be linearly related to shifts in the demand for redistribution. This is especially important for a commodity that uses production control. For example, suppose that the tobacco program, based on output restriction, was resulting in nearly the monopoly level of output. The marginal cost of increasing producers' surplus then approaches infinity, and even a substantial change in the demand for redistribution might not make much difference in the extent of intervention. Suppose that the demand for tobacco fell. Not only would there be little scope for increasing transfers because of high marginal cost, but since there is now less consumers' surplus to redistribute we might see less intervention even if the demand for redistribution increased with a fall in tobacco returns.

Interest-Group Equilibrium

Even after specifying the producer-optimal political activity, represented by E_r^*, we do not have the complete story of political determination of V_r because the interests and behavior of people other than the commodity producers have not yet been considered.

A full analysis of nonproducer interest groups would require a many-group general equilibrium model of income redistribution, perhaps along the basis of Becker (1983). For our pruposes, however, we will aggregate all nonproducer interest groups into one. The equation for the nonproducers analogous to Eq. (12.1) to (12.3) is:

$$V_s = V_s(N_s, \ \alpha_s, \ Y_s) \tag{12.8}$$

V_s does not consist of protection of nonproducers' commodities, but of failure to protect, and perhaps even taxation of (redistribution away from) producers. In any case, in a two-sector (agricultural and all other goods) model, there is only one relative commodity price, and increasing the price of nonagricultural goods is equivalent to reducing the price of agricultural goods. So we may as well consider the struggle of both groups as having at issue whether policy shall increase or decrease the price of agricultural goods, and by how much. This is why N_s and P_s appear as determinants of V_r in Eq. (12.1).

The distinction between r and s is that variables relating to r that increase political pressure will increase V_r, while variables relating to s that increase political pressure will reduce V_r. This means that the partial derivatives of V_r with respect to α, for example, will have opposite signs for α_r and α_s. However, we cannot draw this conclusion for N_r and N_s, because an increase in N may increase political pressure over one range of N but increase pressure over another range. Thus, if N_r is small and N_s is large, it is possible that $\partial V_r/N_r$ and $\partial V_r/N_s$ could both be positive; more producers reduces the cost of political pressure and hence increases V_r, while more nonproducers *increases* the cost of their political pressure and hence increases V_r also.

The analytically interesting complication raised by having two interest groups is that investment in political pressure by one group is likely to be responsive to investment by the other. For example, farmers might find it optimal to invest more when the nonfarmers spend more. This depends on the properties of Eqs. (12.1) to (12.4), in particular, what happens to $\partial R/\partial E_r$ when P_s increases.

The effect of E_r in influencing E_s is called the reaction function of the r group, and a similar reaction function exists for the s group. The question arises as to the nature of equilibrium reached with mutual reaction by the two groups to each other's political spending. Might we observe a mutually destructive "arms race" of ever-increasing spending? Figure 12.2 shows a reaction function for each group. The reaction function R for the r group says that when the s group spends nothing, the r group spends a_0. If α_s increases and the s group decides to become politically involved, and spends b_0 ($1 million), what will the r group do? It might do nothing. If so its reaction function would be a horizontal line at a_0. But if it does nothing, then, from Eq. (12.1), V_r will fall. So the r group might respond. But it seems impossible to preduct a priori how it will respond. Since the returns for investing in political pressure have fallen because of the new opposition to subsidizing rice, the r group might decide to invest less. On the other hand, the rate of return to further investment might be greater now, especially if it is directed at countering the s group's activity. Indeed, it could be that r's rational response to a $1 million expenditure by s is to increase its down spending by more than $1 million.

To determine equilibrium in political activity, we also have to consider the reaction function of the s group. In Fig. 12.2, r responds to s-group spending of b_0 by increasing its own spending to a_1. But the s group responds by spending b_1. Equilibrium is achieved where the reaction curves cross. Becker (1983) discusses sufficient conditions for such an equilibrium to exist, the condition being (in terms of Fig. 12.1) that the reaction curve of s be steeper than r. Plausible circumstances for this equilibrium to exist are that at least one group have positive spending when the other spends nothing, and that each group respond to an additional $1 of the other's spending by increasing its own spending less than $1. ($S$ and R in Fig. 12.2 meet these conditions.)

Application to U.S. Agriculture

Without formally extending the model to many competing interest groups, consider how the approach modeled here might help explain U.S. farm commodity

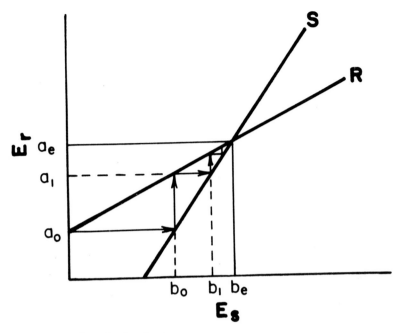

Figure 12.2 Reaction functions.

protection. Variables that may indicate the cost and effectiveness of organizing political pressure include the following indicators: (1) concentration of production, (2) variability of geographic production pattern, (3) the rate of growth of output, and (4) output per farm. The role of each variable will be discussed with reference to U.S. data. As Table 12.1 shows, protection varies a lot from commodity to commodity.

   1. Concentration of production among a few people or in a particular geographic area reduces costs of organization, may facilitate discouragement of free riders, and makes commonality of interests (e.g., more nearly similar production costs) more likely. Therefore, concentrated commodity producers should have better political results (higher producer gains), other things being equal. In addition, it has been argued that the Congressional representation system favors concentrated commodities because then a particular congressman or senator is more likely to have interest intense enough to press the appropriate committees for legislation favoring the commodity. Tobacco (concentrated in North Carolina, Kentucky, and a few neighboring states) and sugar are cited as examples. On the other hand, it can be argued that having some producers in many districts, i.e., geographically diffuse production, helps mitigate opposition to a commodity program. Milk can be cited as an example here. Few senators want to come out against dairy farmers.

   Concentration by geographic area can be measured as a Herfindahl index using shares of national acreage (for each crop) and animal numbers for live-

Table 12.1   Producers' Gains from U.S. Farm Commodity Policies

Commodity	Number of farms, 1974 (thousands)	Share of aggregate farm output value	"Typical" producer gains*
Beef cattle	1520	0.23	1
Corn	990	0.14	18
Hogs	500	0.10	—
Milk	410	0.10	26
Soybeans	540	0.08	—
Wheat	500	0.06	30
Broilers	40	0.03	—
Eggs	280	0.03	—
Cotton	90	0.03	34
Tobacco	200	0.02	30
Sorghum	120	0.02	24
Sugar crops	13	0.015	60
Potatoes	60	0.015	—
Oranges	—	0.01	—
Turkeys	—	0.01	—
Rice	9	0.01	12
Barley	90	0.01	10
Oats	360	0.01	3
Peanuts	30	0.006	18
Tomatoes	—	0.005	—
Apples	—	0.005	—
Wool	110	0.001	—
Others	—	0.06	—

*Percentage increase in producers' returns due to programs of 1950–1970 on average.
Source: U.S. Department of Agriculture; Author's estimate of producer gains

stock. The index is $H = \sum_i S_i^2$, where S_i is the share in aggregate output from area i. Equal shares of a commodity in each of 50 U.S. states would generate an index of 0.02 and complete concentration in one state, 1.0. As of the 1978 Census, the least concentrated commodity was beef cows (0.04) and the most concentrated was cotton (0.31). Generally, since 1910, U.S. commodity production has tended to become more concentrated, i.e., more regionally specialized. The Herfindahl indexes for poultry, hogs, dairy, cotton, and oats roughly doubled between 1910 and 1980. For rice, sugarcane and sugar beets, however, concentration declined.

    2. Variability of production by state might reduce protection because the higher it is, the greater the costs of organization and communication. In addition, for programs that base benefits on historical production, regional shifts create disagreements among the commodity producers. Political observers have attributed changes in the cotton and rice programs, in particular, to the opening up of new production areas. Variability can be measured in state data by changes in the percentage of a crop's U.S. acreage (or animal's population) that changed in rank between observations (in the United States, 10-year periods between agricultural censuses). The variability index has tended to be high for rice, broilers, soybeans, and sugar beets.

    3. The rate of growth of output should be considered because even when a commodity's geographic production pattern is stable, if output is rapidly growing, this may place obstacles in the way of political organizing. There are three U.S. commodities (soybeans, grain sorghum, and broilers) whose output has increased from insignificance to billions of dollars in the period since World War I.

    4. Higher output of a commodity per producer is hypothesized to increase the producer's expected return per unit time invested in political activity, and to promote redistribution. Two commodities are, and have traditionally had exceptionally large output per producer: rice and sugar crops. In recent years, average size of producers has also become large for eggs, broilers, cotton, and peanuts.

The empirical significance of these factors has been explored, but the issues are too complicated and the results too tentative to discuss in detail here. The factors discussed do appear to be significantly associated with the rate of protection. Most important of these appears to be the relative income of farmers. During the 1930s, U.S. farm prices were extremely depressed and farm incomes were well below the national average. People are often inclined to say that in these circumstances governmental intervention to aid agriculture is understandable. Analytically, this intuition implies convex political preferences (SICs convex to origin). The following section explores the rationale for and implications of such SICs.

CONVEXITY OF SOCIAL INDIFFERENCES CURVES (WHY Θ IS NOT CONSTANT)

The hypothesis of a declining marginal political preference for producers' and consumers' incomes as relative incomes change has the implication discussed by Peltzman (1976): intervention will tend to moderate market-generated gains or losses. Suppose that, with a given structure of the industry and supply and demand elasticities, market events make producers better off, e.g., an increase in foreign demand or a fall in costs specific to the industry occurs. This would not (necessarily) change the marginal cost of redistributing income. But it would change the relative income or surplus positions of producers and consumers from which the redistribution begins. If the political indifference curves are convex, this means that the demand for redistribution to producers will increase when producers' market-generated income decreases. With the opposite results for income increases, we have Peltzman's hypothesis that policy should tend to moderate the economic effects of market events.

An example: Suppose the SWF is the Cobb-Douglas political preference function:

$$W = R_p{}_\gamma R_c^{1-\gamma} \qquad (12.8)$$

where R_p is rents of producers and R_c rents of consumer. Let $\gamma = 0.6$. This parameter plays the role that Θ has had earlier. The higher is γ, the more producers will have redistributed to them. Let the STC for a production control program be derived from the linear supply–demand example of Chap. 7, Fig. 7.2, namely, using $a_0 = 120$, $a_1 = -2$, $b_0 = 30$, and $b_1 = 1$, we find from Eq. (7.14):

$$R_p = 90\sqrt{R_c} - 2.5\, R_c \qquad (12.9)$$

We are assuming that purchased inputs earn no rents, nor do middlemen, so $R_p = PS$ and $R_c = CS$.

The point of STC and SIC tangency for the social optimum is obtained by choice of $\hat{Q}$ to maximize Eq. (12.8) subject to Eq. (12.9). The slope of the SIC, from Eq. (12.8), is

$$0 = 0.6R_p^{-0.4} R_c^{0.4}\, dR_p + 0.4R_c^{-0.6} R_p^{0.6}\, dR_c \qquad (12.10)$$

$$\frac{dR_p}{dR_c} = -\frac{2}{3}\frac{R_p}{R_c} = \left(1 - \frac{1}{\gamma}\right)\frac{R_p}{R_c} \qquad \text{(SIC slope)}$$

As R_p rises or R_c falls, Θ (as defined earlier) declines, i.e., the political weight favoring producers declines. At an initial position in which $R_p = R_c$, we find $dR_p/dR_c = -2/3$. This implies that producers are weighted 1.5 times consumers in the revealed SWF, i.e., solving $dR_p/dR_c = -1/\Theta$ gives $\Theta = 1.5$ in the earlier terminology giving a weight of unity to consumers by convention. If some event, such as an export boom, causes R_p to rise or R_c to fall, so that, say $R_p/R_c = 3/2$, then the SWF now weights consumers and producers equally ($\Theta = 1$); so any intervention that was formerly called for politically now ceases.

Bringing in the surplus transfer aspects, from Eq. (12.9), the slope of the STC is

$$\frac{dR_p}{dR_c} = 45(R_c)^{-0.5} - 2.5. \qquad \text{(STC slope)} \qquad (12.11)$$

Equating the SIC and STC slopes yeilds

$$R_p = 67.5\, R_c^{0.5} + 3.75\, R_c$$

Expressing the surpluses in terms of the optimally controlled Q^*, substituting from Eqs. (7.7) and (7.8):

$$6.25 \, Q^{*2} - 157.5Q^* = 0$$
$$6.25Q^* = 157.5$$

which solves for $Q^* = 25.2$. This is 84 percent of competitive output ($Q_0 = 30$). It generates $R_c = 635$ and $R_p = 680$, for a common SIC and STC slope of -0.714. The maximized SWF, from Eq. (12.8), is $W^* = 661.6$.

The political equilibrium is at the point Ω in Fig. 12.3. For comparison, the figure also shows the competitive equilibrium distribution of surpluses, at point E, and the SIC that passes through E, with $W = 593.8$ at $R_c = 900$, $R_p = 450$. Whether we treat the social indifference curves as having normative significance (as in Chap. 7) or just as reflecting political behavior (as in this chapter), makes no analytical difference. There is, however, an important difference from the viewpoint of positive economics in that the nomative SWF interpretation of the SIC makes γ an exogenous parameter given by considerations of ethics or (if this is different) social justice, whereas the positive interpretation makes γ an endogenous variable determined in an economic model such as that of the preceding section.

COMPARATIVE STATICS OF INTERVENTION

In the example of agriculture in the 1930s, we have an exogenous shock caused by the Depression, alleged to have caused policy changes. The general form of comparative-static analysis of such events is to express the shock in terms of supply or demand changes, and trace through the effects to find how the SIC–STC tangency point changes and what are the associated changes in policy instruments. Expressing the SIC side in terms of Θ or the SIC slope, a possible source of confusion is that there are two senses in which Θ is now an endogenous variable. It is endogenous *for a given political preference function*, as the earlier example following Eq. (12.8) shows. It is also endogenous because, when economic conditions change, the determinants of the political preference function itself change as just mentioned. In this section, we will consider only the first source of endogeneity in Θ.

Pure Income Effects

Suppose that an exogenous event reduces farmers' incomes, but does not shift the STC. The political response depends on the curvature of the SICs. This is simple to analyze, but there is a complication that has not yet been considered. The idea that sentiment to aid producers increases when ΔR_p falls depends on

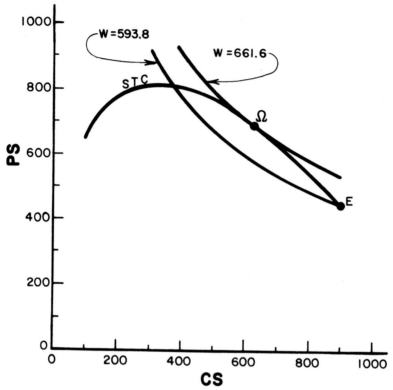

Figure 12.3 Political equilibrium.

changes in economic rents of producer-owned inputs being a proper indicator of change in well-being for producers. The main circumstances when this supposition fails are, first, when the observed $-\Delta R_p$ is only transitory and is expected to be offset by later $+\Delta R_p$, and, second, when much of the producers' incomes do not come from the commodity market. The former circumstance takes us back to the stabilization issues of Chap. 10, and is ignored here. The latter, however, is important because, in many countries, much farming is a part-time occupation, particularly for the smaller farms that make up the bulk the voters if not farm output. Rice policy in Japan is a particular instance in which part-timers appear to play a key political role (Egaitsu, 1982). In the United States, farms with $100,000 or less in sales, which account for 89 percent of all farms, get about 90 percent of their family income from off-farm sources. If their net returns from farming fall 10 percent, their family incomes fall only 1 percent.

Similarly, when consumers have to pay 10 percent more for food, and so lose consumers' surplus equal to about 10 percent of their food expenditures, their real incomes fall only by a much smaller percentage. If they spend 5 percent of their incomes on farm-level ingredients in food, then their loss is about 0.5 percent of income.

When we have real incomes rather than surpluses in the political preference function, what happens to the political equilibrium? Let $Y_p = N_p + R_p$ and $Y_c = N_c + R_c$, where Y is total real income and N is nonagricultural income. Then Eq. (12.8) becomes

$$W = (N_p + R_p)^\gamma (N_c + R_c)^{1-\gamma} \qquad (12.8')$$

The trade-offs between R_p and R_c on the STC are the same as before. To find the optimal production control level, Q^*, this time use a direct maximization method rather than equating STC and SIC slopes. To maximize W, find $dW/dQ^* = 0$. Following the earlier examples, Eq. (12.9) can be used to eliminate R_p, and we have

$$W = (N_p + 90\sqrt{R_c} - 2.5R_c)^\gamma (N_c + R_c)^{1-\gamma}$$

Since W is maximized when ln W is maximized, we can simplify the computations by taking logs.

$$\ln W = \gamma \ln (N_p + 90\sqrt{R_c} - 2.5R_c) + (1 - \gamma) \ln (N_c + R_c)$$

$$\frac{d(\ln W)}{dQ^*} = \frac{d(\ln W)}{dR_c}\frac{dR_c}{dQ^*} = \left[\frac{\gamma(45R_c^{-.5} - 2.5)}{N_p + 90\sqrt{R_c} - 2.5R_c} + \frac{1-\gamma}{N_c + R_c}\right]2Q^* = 0$$

This can be simplified, using $R_c = Q^{*2}$, to

$$\frac{45}{Q^*} - 2.5 = \left(1 - \frac{1}{\gamma}\right)\frac{N_p + 90Q^* - 2.5Q^{*2}}{N_c + Q^{*2}} \qquad (12.12)$$

The left-hand side of Eq. (12.12) is the STC slope from Eq. (12.11). The right-hand side is the SIC slope. It is the same as Eq. (12.10) except that Y_p (the numerator) and Y_c (the denominator) are used in Eq. (12.12) instead of R_p and R_c in Eq. (12.10). Solving Eq. (12.12) requires information about N_p and N_c. From the earlier example, we had $R_p = 450$ and $R_c = 900$ when there was no intervention. Consider a situation in which R_c is 5 percent of consumers' income and R_p is 50 percent of farmers' income including off-farm receipts. Then we have $N_c = 17,100$ and $N_p = 450$. Using these values in Eq. (12.12), we solve (numerically) for Q^* to obtain $Q^* = 18.35$.

The optimal intervention here is substantially greater than it was earlier at $Q^* = 25.2$. Indeed, output is cut back almost to the monopoly level of $Q = 18$ (where $dR_p/dQ = 0$). The reason for greater intervention is not only that the SIC slope now changes less rapidly as agricultural surpluses are redistributed, but also that we start out at the no-intervention point with a shallower slope of $dY_p/dY_c = (-2/3)$ $(900/18,000) = -0.033$, as compared to $(-2/3)$ $(450/900) = -0.333$ before nonagricultural incomes were brought in.

To isolate the effect of less sensitivity of the SIC slope, change γ so that the initial SIC slope is the same in the two cases. The appropriate γ gives $(1 - 1/\gamma)$ $(900/18,000) = -0.333$, which solves for $\gamma = 0.13$. Using this value with other parameters unchanged in Eq. (12.12) generates $Q^* = 22.1$. Thus, we can say that the more nearly linear SIC that results from large shares of income being of nonagricultural origin reduces the optimal production control from $Q^* = 25.2$ to $Q^* = 22.2$, or from 84 percent to 74 percent of no-program output.

The common slope of the SIC and STC at Q^* is -0.464, not much steeper than the -0.333 with no intervention. The earlier case with $N_c = N_p = 0$, we had the SIC slope changing from -0.333 to -0.714. The more nearly constant slope of the SIC when nonagricultural income is included means that the assumption of a fixed Θ used in earlier chapters may not be so bad after all.

In any case, the results obtained in Eqs. (12.8) to (12.12) enable us to determine how intervention changes when a group's income changes, and the resulting comparative statics of redistributional effects to buffer such change.

Supply–Demand Changes

For a given political preference function, what can be predicted about the changes in political equilibrium that result from underlying supply or demand changes? The answer depends on how shifts in supply and demand change the surplus transformation curve. This question involves difficulties that did not arise just now in considering the effects of pure income changes which did not affect the surplus transformation curve. We must also specify shifts in the market equilibrium point that is the basis from which redistribution takes place. In terms of Fig. 12.3, both the shape of the STC and its point of origin E may change.

Consider how the ratio of producers' to consumers' surpluses changes at market equilibrium when supply or demand shift. The endowments of consumers' and producers' surpluses depend on the whole length of the supply and demand functions, so that changes in PS/CS $(= R_p/R_c$ in the preceding example) are sensitive to changes in the functions at all points. An increase in demand or supply is taken to mean the same change in quantity at each price, or the same change in price at each quantity, that is, a horizontally or vertically parallel shift. This is most simply represented in the linear case, where the shift is a change in intercept, a_0 or b_0 in Eqs. (2.1) and (2.2). Since the ratio of consumers' to producers' surplus at market equilibrium is

$$\frac{PS}{CS} = \frac{1/2 \, b_1 Q_0^2}{-1/2 \, a_1 Q_0^2} = -\frac{b_1}{a_1} \qquad (12.13)$$

it follows immediately that a change in a_0 or b_0 leaves the ratio of surpluses unchanged. Therefore, with homothetic political preferences there is no intervention in a previously unregulated market when supply or demand shifts.

If intervention is already occurring, it is not immediately apparent how CS/PS changes with a shift in supply or demand. In the linear case, the ratio of surpluses when output is held at $\hat{Q}$ to benefit producers is

$$\frac{PS}{CS} = \frac{2(a_0 - b_0)/\hat{Q} + (2a_1 - b_1)}{-a_1} \tag{12.14}$$

$$= \frac{2(a_1 - b_1)}{a_1} \frac{Q_0}{\hat{Q}} - \frac{(2a_1 - b_1)}{a_1}$$

Consider an expansion of demand. With no change in $\hat{Q}$, the additional revenue generated goes to producers, so PS/CS rises. To investigate an equivalent degree of intervention after the demand increase, allow $\hat{Q}$ to increase such that it is the same fraction of α of Q_0 as before the shift; that is $\hat{Q} = \alpha Q_0$. Returning to Eq. (7.22) for the slope of the surplus transformation curve, we find that increasing a_0 while maintaining $\hat{Q} = \alpha Q_0$ leaves the slope unchanged. Since α is an arbitrary constant, $0 < \alpha < 1$, this establishes that changing a_0 generates a homothetic family of surplus transformation curves. The same is true for changes in b_0. Therefore, such shifts in demand or supply have no effect on the degree of intervention if political preferences are homothetic.

Nevertheless, the regulated price will not remain a constant percentage above the changed market equilibrium price, unless $\epsilon = |\eta|$, i.e., the elasticity of supply at Q_0 equals the elasticity of demand. Otherwise, even though $\hat{Q} = \alpha Q_0$, nonetheless, $\hat{P} \neq \alpha P_0$. The reason is that, while the difference between the regulated (demand) price $D(\hat{Q})$ and the supply price $S(\hat{Q})$ is proportional to P_0, the division between $[D(\hat{Q}) - P_0]$ and $[P_0 - S(\hat{Q})]$ depends on η and ϵ. If $|\eta| < \epsilon$, a demand increase will cause a larger change in $\hat{P}$ than in P_0. Thus regulation amplifies price changes resulting from demand shifts and buffers price changes resulting from supply shifts. This is the opposite of the result obtained in Peltzman (1976, p. 227). However, when $|\eta| > \epsilon$, price changes due to demand shifts are moderated by regulation, and supply shifts are amplified, which is Peltzman's result. (But in this case the subsidy approach is preferred to production control anyway.)

Moreover, although intervention is unchanged in that α remains constant along with PS/CS and ΔCS, it is true that the amount transferred does change— both PS and CS change, but in the same proportion. So if we are explaining the aggregate amounts redistributed rather than the rate of output reduction or subsidy per unit output, there is a straightforward size effect in that aggregate redistribution is proportional to total revenue in the market.

A crippling problem with the preceding analysis is that we have left out the earlier point about gains and losses from agricultural markets being more important to producers than consumers. Thus, if a 10-percent decrease in demand reduces both PS and CS by 15 percent, this would reduce farmers' real incomes by 7.5 percent and consumers' only 0.75 percent, according to the example in Eq. (12.12). So, even with homothetic preferences, the change will induce increased intervention to aid farmers.

If the slope of supply or demand changes along with the intercept, the analysis becomes more complicated. For example, if supply shifts to the right due to technical progress, and in so doing becomes more elastic, the producers' rents in the absence of intervention fall more drastically.

An example of the type of comparative static result that can summarize these considerations can be obtained by differentiating Eq. (7.37) with respect to n or e. This gives us the result that when supply becomes more elastic, the optimal production cutback is increased. But this does not tell us the change in redistribution, and it assumes that Θ is given.

For an example of comparative statics with endogenous Θ, let us return to the numerical example following Eq. (12.8). Suppose that the supply curve shifts to the right by rotating around the point $b_0 = 30$; specifically, let b_1 decrease from 1 to 0.5. Now the STC changes according to Eq. (7.14) so that Eq. (12.9) becomes

$$R_p = 90\sqrt{R_c} - 2.25R_c \qquad (12.9')$$

Now at the no-program market equilibrium, we have $P_0 = 48$, $Q_0 = 36$, and the surpluses $R_c^0 = 1296$ and $R_p^0 = 324$. Thus, the ratio R_p^0/R_c^0 is half what it was in the earlier example. Given the same political preference function, Eq. (12.8), this will lead to greater intervention than in the earlier case. But now the STC is also different. The new political equilibrium is found by equating SIC and STC slopes:

$$R_p = 67.5R_c^{0.5} + 3.37R_c \qquad (12.11')$$

or in terms of Q^*:

$$5.625 \, Q^{*2} - 157.5Q = 0$$
$$5.625Q^* = 157.5$$

which solves for $Q^* = 28.0$. Thus, as compared to $Q_0 = 36$, the restricted output is 78 percent of no-program output as compared to 84 percent before the supply shift.

Despite the larger production cutback, optimal production control generates more output when supply shifts to the right. Before, Q^* was equal to 25.2, and now $Q^* = 28.0$, so the political equilibrium gives us an 11 percent output increase. The free-market outcomes would have given us a percentage output increase of $36/30 - 1 = 20$ percent.

Policy Adjustment Rules

Writing the equilibrium condition in terms of parameters of linear supply and demand case, the STC and SIC slopes are:

$$\left(1 - \frac{1}{\gamma}\right) \frac{(a_0 - b_0)Q + (a_1 - b_1/2)Q^2}{-1/2\, a_1\, Q^2} \qquad \text{(SIC slope)}$$

$$\frac{1}{2} \frac{(a_0 - b_1)}{\sqrt{-1/2\, a_1}} \frac{1}{Q} + \frac{2a_1 - b_1}{-a_1} \qquad \text{(STC slope)}$$

Equating the slopes to find the optimal Q^* yields

$$-\frac{1}{\gamma}\left(a_1 - \frac{1}{2}b_1\right)Q^{*2} + \left[1 - \frac{1}{\gamma} - K(-a_1)^{0.5}\right](a_0 - b_0)Q^* = 0$$

where $K = 0.3536 = \left(\frac{1}{2}\right)^{1.5}$, a constant for all linear models with $a_0 > b_0 > 0$, $a_1 < 0$, and $b_1 > 0$. Solving by dividing through by Q^*,

$$Q^* = \left(\gamma - 1 - K\gamma\sqrt{-a_1}\right)\frac{a_0 - b_0}{a_1 - b_1/2} \qquad (12.15)$$

Equation (12.15) provides a policy adjustment rule for this model. Given the assumptions—linear supply and demand and Cobb-Douglas political preference function with fixed γ —we can calculate the Q^* consistent with political equilibrium for any changes in supply or demand parameter values. Note that an increase in a_0, the demand intercept, has the same effect on Q^* as a decrease in b_0, the supply intercept; and Q^* is a linear function of either a_0 or b_0. In particular, for our latest numerical example, $dQ^*/da_0 = 0.28$. This is a very simple adjustment rule. The effect of a change in supply or demand slope is not so simple.

For some purposes, it is convenient to express Q^* as a function of no-program output Q_0. Using the fact that $a_0 - b_0 = Q_0 (b_1 - a_1)$, Eq. (12.15) can be rewritten as

$$\frac{Q^*}{Q_0} = -\left(\gamma - 1 - K\gamma\sqrt{-a_1}\right)\frac{a_1 - b_1}{a_1 - b_1/2} \qquad (12.16)$$

The percentage cutback in output is thus unaffected by changes in a_0 or b_0. This result is the same as discussed earlier with reference to Eq. (12.14), i.e., the Cobb-Douglas assumption implies homothetic political preferences.

Further analysis of optimal adjustment in policy instruments for linear demand and supply is contained in Just (1985). He develops adjustment rules for given value of Θ (SIC slope), and incorporates uncertainty along with rules for adjusting policies before or after producers' adjustments to random events are made.

In none of the cases considered do we find adjustment rules of two kinds that have been important in U.S. farm commodity programs: changing support prices proportionally to (1) a parity index, or (2) a cost-of-production estimate. The parity index is a ratio of output price to purchased input prices. From the models used in Chaps. 4 and 8, it is apparent that the way in which output price changes with purchased input prices depends on the elasticity of substitution between purchased and farmer-owned inputs, the elasticities of supply of each type of input, and the source of change in exogenous variables. The most straightforward case occurs when a decline in demand for farm products is the exogenous event, the elasticity of substitution is zero, and purchased inputs are perfectly elastic in supply. Then, the whole loss of revenue per unit output is a loss of rents to farm-owned inputs, and the initial situation is restored by raising the support price to offset the demand decline. However, even in this case there are complications. First, the adjustment would not involve changing the output price by the same percentage as the parity index changes. Second, the adjustment should be of the subsidy rather than production-control type to restore the initial situation, but, third, the necessity of further intervention increases deadweight losses. For a given γ or Θ, it would not pay to restore all the producers' losses, i.e., to insulate them completely from weak markets, and the efficient form of insulation could be production controls or subsidies, the issue turning on costs of intervention as analyzed in Chap. 7.

If the source of product price decline is cost-reducing technical progress, then a parity adjustment is likely to be even less appropriate. The cost decline could increase producers' rents, so that not only should producers not be insulated from the price decline, but protection should actually be reduced for a given γ. Thus, a parity adjustment rule could indicate that when technical progress occurs in the dairy industry, the government should buy up a larger percentage of output, or impose strengthened production controls, whereas optimal adjustment, even with $\Theta > 1$, implies less intervention. (This assumes technical progress increases rents to farmer-owned inputs, which it may not do).

Indexing support prices to cost-of-production estimates is appealing in that it performs better than parity under conditions of technical progress. But while the idea that support prices should cover producers' costs of production has an immediate appeal, it does not survive second thoughts. The many difficulties that have been pointed out can be summarized as follows.

Cost of production may be thought of as the sum of technical coefficients specifying quantities of each input per unit output, each multiplied by the input's price (for durable inputs, rental rates). The technical coefficients vary from region to region and from farm to farm within a region. So do input prices. More fundamentally, though, some input prices are not determined until the product price is determined. This is most notably true of land but also applies to other inputs that are not perfectly elastic in supply to the product being considered.

The technical coefficients for different farms could be weighted by base-value input price weights and arrayed from "low-cost" to "high-cost" to attain a Marshallian "particular expenses curve." Such a curve would have some of the characteristics of, but would not be identical to an industry marginal cost curve. Of course this curve would not determine what support price to set. Based on Θ, a decision would be made about how much of producers' expenses to cover. Then a corresponding support price could be established. If one wished to cover all producers' expenses, the support price would be geared to the highest particular expenses of any producer.

A support price set at U.S. average cost of production does not make sense in terms of a particular expenses curve. Something like half of production would not be covered. The U.S. average cost is more meaningful if one supposes that each producers' costs include all the rents to land and other factor employed plus returns to managerial skills. Then, each farm should ideally have a measured average cost equal to price, by definition. Variations from farm to farm in cost per unit output would be the result of measurement error and the randomness of production, both of which can be considerable. In this case the U.S. average cost is a statistical estimate of industry marginal cost, but the estimate is dependent on product price.

In short, under either conception of what statistical cost data are measuring—particular expenses or industry average (and marginal) cost—cost data do not provide a meaningful guide for setting a support price.

PRICE TRANSMISSION EQUATIONS

Returning to the positive economics of intervention, attempts have been made to explain changes over time in levels of protection as market conditions change using price transmission equations. This approach gives up the idea of explaining why agriculture is protected at all, and simply presumes that there is a constant underlying desire to intervene (a given political preference function). The approach is most readily applicable to countries that do not attempt to influence world prices. Then, "market conditions" can be measured by world market prices, and empirical investigation of policy changes is undertaken by regressing a country's internal producer price on the world price. The resulting price transmission elasticity was used in Chap. 11 as an indicator of a country's insulation from short-term world-market fluctuations. Transmission of permanent world price changes reflects the kinds of adjustments discussed earlier in this chapter. Attempts to estimate internal producer prices as a function of world market variables are reported in Bredahl et al. (1979), Tyers (1984) and Roe et al. (1986). The results are sensitive to time period studied, functional form, and the choice of variables to include. It is clear that countries vary greatly in their policy responses to market conditions but it is not clear why.

CAPITALIZATION OF PROGRAM CHANGES

The idea that program benefits create wealth whose value is the present value of the expected future rental returns to rent-receiving assets was developed in Chap. 4. What happens when policies change, for reasons that have been discussed in this chapter, or simply because of random policy changes? The rational expectations model in Chap. 10 provided a way of modeling several alternative kinds of policy changes: a known, permanent change; a one-time transitory change; or a change about which producers have to make their own best judgments with limited information.

Given the expectations of future policy instruments after a policy change, we can estimate the change in capitalized value of program-created assets: the value of the right to market a cow's milk in Canada, the right to sell a pound of flue-cured tobacco in North Carolina, or the value of a acre of land with corn base on a farm in Illinois. A simple way of using observable data to indicate market expectations about policy change is available when marketing quotas can be both rented and sold, as in the case of tobacco. Market equilibrium in quota implies that the price of quota as an asset equals the discounted value of its expected future rental returns:

$$P = \sum_{t=1}^{T} \frac{R_t}{(1 + i)^t} \tag{12.17}$$

where P is the price of quota at the beginning of crop year 1, R_t is the rental return received at the end of each year t (but contracted for at the beginning of the year), T is the length of the program and i is the discount rate. The valuation formula is stated in discrete, annual terms on the assumption that one crop is harvested per year, and the shortest-term quota rental contract covers one crop year.

Two variables relating to commodity policy are unknown when P is determined: the future stream of R_t and T. (The future values of i are also unknown, but they are not determined by commodity policy, and i is assumed constant for convenience.) It is possible that producers have a particular set of values for future R_t in mind in $t = 1$, but more likely they have a general sense that the program will end at some point in the future, or that the program will go on indefinitely but that the R_t will either appreciate or depreciate. Consider this last possibility, with expected annual rate of depreciation d. Then, Eq. (12.17) can be rewritten:

$$P = \sum_{t=1}^{\infty} \frac{R(1 - d)^t}{(1 + i)^t} \tag{12.18}$$

where R is the initial rental value at the beginning of year t. Dividing P by R to obtain the ratio of sale to rental value, and letting $(1 - d)/(1 + i) = Z$, we have

$$\frac{P}{R} = Z + Z^2 + Z^3 + \cdots$$

With $Z < 1$, this series plus 1 converges to $1/(1 - Z)$, as can be seen by multiplying by $(1 - Z)$, expanding, and noting that $Z^t \to 0$ as $t \to \infty$ (see discussion of geometric series in any algebra text). Therefore, subtracting 1 from $1/(1 - Z)$ gives

$$\frac{P}{R} = \frac{1 - d}{i + d} \tag{12.19}$$

This expression can be used to estimate the unobservable expectations parameter d. For example, in the early 1980s, the ratio of sale price to rental value of tobacco quota in North Carolina was about 4 (Sumner and Alston). Assuming a discount rate of $i = 0.10$, Eq. (12.19) solves for $d = (1 - iP/R)/(1 + P/R) = 0.12$. Thus, the market data yield an estimate that the expected depreciation rate is such that R will fall 12 percent annually. If P/R is large enough, it implies that $d < 0$, i.e., that R_t will appreciate. In this case owning tobacco quota is like owning a "growth" stock. The limiting case is that if $-d = i$, then P/R is infinite—the denominator of Eq. (12.19) is zero. A rate of appreciation greater than i is also an anomaly economically since it implies market participants can increase their wealth indefinitely by borrowing funds and buying tobacco quota.

An expectation of any constant d is observationally equivalent to $d = 0$ but that the program ends and R becomes zero at some $T < \infty$. Equation (12.18) divided by R becomes

$$\frac{P}{R} = \sum_{t=1}^{T} \frac{1}{(1 + i)^t} \tag{12.20}$$

Using $P/R = 4$ and $i = 0.10$, we find T by summing until equality is reached:

$$4 = 0.909 + 0.826 + 0.751 + 0.683 + 0.621 + 0.210$$

After 5 years, we have a sum of 3.79, with a remaining 0.210 requiring $0.210/0.564 = 0.37$ of a year. Therefore, the implied T is an expected program life of 5.37 years.

Consider now the comparative statics of a policy change. Suppose in year 2, the policy is changed and R rises 10 percent. What happens to the capitalized value P? It depends on how the change is perceived, if it is expected to be permanent or transitory. If transitory, it would not affect P very much, just an increase of $\Delta P = 0.1R/(1 + i)$. If permanent, the effect would be larger. However, the preceding discussion indicates that we should be careful about defining "permanent." It should not be defined as a change lasting forever. In terms of our model, a natural definition is that a "permanent" increase in R is one that leaves d and T unchanged; the increase is expected to have the same characteristics as the preexisting R. This would result in P rising by the same percentage as R, and R/P being unchanged.

Considering the dynamics, the impact of changes that had been anticipated, complicates this story. From the earlier example, it was expected that R would fall by 12 percent between year 1 and year 2. Therefore, a rise of 10 percent in R is really a bigger change than it looked. Indeed, when policy is expected to depreciate or come to an end, if instead it just continues indefinitely this constitutes a change as compared to market expectations. The owners of quota would receive a windfall gain. They own an asset that pays a 25-percent current rate of return because its future returns are expected to depreciate; this return is extraordinarily high if the returns do not depreciate.

This discussion suggests another sort of policy adjustment rule, one to use in phasing out a program. If market expectations are for a 12-percent depreciation of program benefits (or a 5.37-year program life) then policy-makers can most painlessly end the program by, in fact, cutting benefits 12 percent per year (or ending it after 5.37 years).

EMPIRICAL WORK ON PROTECTION OF AGRICULTURE

The book by Anderson et al. (1986) contains papers attempting to explain nominal protection coefficients in several Asian countries. These papers, like the empirical work discussed earlier for U.S. policies, go beyond price-transmission equations by trying to explain why NPCs aren't all zero, and why all price transmission coefficients are not all equal to 1. Generally, the income of the interest group, and the income of the country as a whole, are found to be important explanatory variables. Analogs to the observation that U.S. farmers made political gains in the 1930s are found in other situations. An interesting case study is Russell (1983), which reviews how policies which were essentially price supports for U.S. oil producers were introduced in the 1930s and maintained until the 1970s, quite parallel to farm commodities. This highlights the problem of explaining why U.S. protection of agriculture in the 1980s is greater than it was even in the 1930s, while oil producers have received no financial support even though oil prices have fallen as much as grain prices since the mid-1970s.

Another set of empirical studies has taken the approach of assuming that a political equilibrium exists, and then inferring from estimates of policy effects (redistribution and deadweight losses) what the political weights (Θ) for producer groups must have been. Examples are in Josling (1974), Rausser and Freebairn (1974), Zusman and Amiad (1977), and Tyers (1986).

Also noteworthy are studies that go beyond the producer-consumer dichotomy and attempt to explain coalitions and redistribution between farmers and agribusiness, for example, Faminow and Benson (1986). Johnson (1985) contains an illuminating and thorough investigation of state regulation of retail milk pricing. Pashigian (1986) provides a similar approach in explaining farmers' support for regulation of futures markets.

SUMMARY

Reviewing the steps from grassroots opinion to ultimate policy choices, the policy process can be viewed as moving along two paths. The simpler path begins with individual voters. Each of them selects representatives, based on alternative candidates' positions, and the selected representatives then make political decisions reflecting the positions that got them elected. The more complex path follows collective action by interest groups. These groups have two main impacts: they influence voting in elections by mobilizing support for and mitigating opposition to their favored position; and they influence voting in elected bodies like the U.S. Congress. This chapter emphasized the nature of the political equilibrium that results. It discussed in detail some aspects of how that equilibrium is arrived at, particularly the determinants of interest-group formation and interaction. It did not discuss the determinants of interest-group success in the second area of their impact, influencing legislative outcomes. The U.S. farm policy institutions were briefly outlined, but not why they work as they do.

The analytical situation is similar to that of the analysis of market prices. We have a theory of market equilibrium as equating demand and supply, and the ideal efficiency properties of that equilibrium, but not of why people want the things they want, and not much on how prices actually get determined. The best we can do empirically is detect regularities in price and output determination.

With respect to policies, the STC–SIC tangency is a supply–demand equilibrium in a similar sense. Referring back to Fig. 7.4, the models developed in Chap. 12 give further details about the nature of the equilibrium and the determinants of the "demand curve" for intervention. Game theoretical analyses of voting and political negotiating as developed for example in Ordeshook (1986) can be criticized for not having more empirically usable and verifiable content, but the same might be said of theories of negotiation, contracting, and price-making in markets. The empirical work on explaining government policy in agriculture is similar to market demand studies in not getting at fundamental causes of behavior. Nonetheless, the explanation of governmental behavior in agricultural commodity markets, despite suggestive hypotheses, is admittedly at a scientifically primitive stage. It is more a field for future research than the topics discussed in the preceding chapters, and as such is an appropriate subject with which to end.

References

Adams, F. G. 1975. An interrelated modelling system for fats and oils, mimeo, University of Pennsylvania, Philadelphia, Penn.

Allen, R. G. D. 1938. *Mathematical Analysis for Economists,* Macmillan, London.

Anderson, J. R., J. L. Dillon, and B. Hardaker. 1977. *Agricultural Decision Analysis,* Iowa State University Press, Ames, Iowa.

Anderson, K., and Y. Hayami. 1986. *The Political Economy of Agricultural Protection: East Asia in International Perspective,* Allen and Unwin, Sydney.

Arnott, R., and J. E. Stiglitz. 1986. Moral hazard and optimal commodity taxation. *J. Public Econ.* **29**:1–24.

Atkinson, A. B., and J. E. Stiglitz. 1980. *Lectures on Public Economics,* McGraw-Hill, New York.

Auerbach, R. 1970. The effects of price supports on output and factor prices in agriculture, *J. Pol. Econ.* **80**:1355–1361.

Bailey, M. J. 1954. The Marshallian demand curve, *J. Pol. Econ.* **62**:255–261.

Bale, M. D., and E. Lutz. 1979. The effects of trade intervention on international price instability, *Am. J. Agric. Econ.* **61**:512–516.

Barker, R., and Y. Hayami. 1976. Price support versus input subsidy for food self-sufficiency in developing countries, *Am. J. Agric. Econ.* **58**:617–628.

Baumol, W. J., and D. F. Bradford. 1970. Optimal departures from marginal cost pricing, *Am. Econ. Rev.* **60**:265–283.

Becker, G. S. 1983. A theory of competition among pressure groups for political influence, *Quart. J. Econ.* **93**:371–400.

Black, F. 1976. The pricing of commodity contracts, *J. Financial Econ.* **3**:167–179.

Boadway, R., and N. Bruce. 1984. *Welfare Economics,* Basil Blackwell, New York.

Boulding, K. 1983. Review of P. Balogh, The irrelevance of conventional economics, *J. Econ. Lit.,* **21**:554–555.

Brandow, G. E. 1977. Policy for commercial agriculture, 1945–71, in: *A Survey of Agricultural Economics Literature,* vol. 1 (L. Martin, ed.), University of Minnesota Press, Minneapolis, Minn.

Braverman, A., J. S. Hammer, and A. Gross. 1987. Multimarket analysis of agricultural price policies in an operational context, *World Bank Econ. Rev.* **1**:337–356.

Bredahl, M., W. Meyers, and K. Collins. 1979. The elasticity of demand for U.S. agricultural products, *Am. J. Agric. Econ.* **58**:58–62.

Brown, C. V., and P. M. Jackson. 1978. *Public Sector Economics,* Martin Robertson, Oxford.

Brown, J. B., and D. S. Sibley, 1986. *The Theory of Public Utility Pricing,* Cambridge University Press, Cambridge.

Browning, E. K. 1986. The marginal cost of raising tax revenue, in: *Contemporary Economic Problems* (P. Cagan, ed.), American Enterprise Institute, Washington, D.C.

Buchanan, J. 1968. *The Demand and Supply of Public Goods,* Rand-McNally, Chicago.

Buse, R. C. 1958. Total Elasticities—A predictive device, *J. Farm Econ.* **40**:881–891.

Carter, C., N. Gallini, and A. Schmitz. 1980. Producer-consumer trade-off in export cartels, *Am. J. Agric. Econ.* **62**:812–818.

Chambers, R. 1985. Least-cost subsidization alternatives, *Am. J. Agric. Econ.* **67**:251–256.

———. 1987. Designing producer-financed farm programs, mimeo, University of Maryland, College Park, Maryland.

Clodius, R. L. 1960. Market Structure, Economic Power and Agricultural Policy: A Proposal for Forward Production Control, *J. Farm Econ.* **42**:413–425.

Cochrane, W., and M. Ryan. 1976. *American Farm Policy, 1948–1973,* University of Minnesota Press, Minneapolis, Minn.

Copeland, B. 1986. Tariffs and quotas: Retaliation and negotiation, Disc. paper no. 86–21, Dept. of Econ., University of British Columbia, Vancouver.

Corden, W. M. 1974. *Trade Policy and Economic Welfare,* Oxford University Press, Oxford.

Cornes, R., and T. Sandler. 1986. *The Theory of Externalities, Public Goods, and Clubs.* Cambridge University Press, Cambridge.

Dasgupta, P. S., and G. M. Heal. 1979. *Economic Theory and Exhaustible Resources,* Cambridge University Press, Cambridge.

Deaton, A. S., and J. Muellbauer. 1980. *Economics and Consumer Behavior,* Cambridge University Press, Cambridge.

Dixit, A., and V. Norman. 1980. *Theory of International Trade,* Cambridge University Press, Cambridge.

Dodgson, J. S. 1985. On the accuracy and appropriateness of alternative measures of excess burden, *Econ. J.* **95**:106–114.

Edwards, G. W. 1987. Agricultural policy debate: A survey, *Econ. Record* (in press).

Egaitsu, F. 1982. Japanese agricultural policy, in: *U.S.-Japanese Agricultural Trade Relations*, (E. Castle and K. Hemmi, eds.), Resources for the Future, Washington, D.C., pp. 148–181.

Faminow, M., and B. Benson. 1986. The incentives to organize and demand regulations, *Econ. Inquiry.* **24**:473–84.

Feder, G., R. E. Just, and A. Schmitz, 1980. Futures markets and the theory of the firm under price uncertainty, *Quar. J. Econ.* **94**:317–328.

Fisher, B. F. 1982. Rational expectations in agricultural economics research and policy analysis, *Am. J. Agric. Econ.* **64**:260–265.

Floyd, J. E. 1965. The effects of farm price supports on the return to land and labor in agriculture, *J. Political Econ.* **73**:148–158.

Gardner, B. L. 1979. *Optimal Stockpiling of Grain*, Lexington Books, Lexington, Massachusetts.

———, and D. M. Hoover. 1975. U.S. farm commodity programs and the inequality of farm household income. *Econ. Res. Rep. No. 35*, North Carolina State University, Raleigh, North Carolina.

———, and R. Kramer. 1985. Experience with crop insurance programs in the U.S., in: *Crops Insurance for Agricultural Development* (P. Hazell et al., eds.) Johns Hopkins University Press, Baltimore.

Gordon-Ashworth, F. 1984. *International Commodity Control*, Croom-Helm, London.

Grennes, T. J., P. R. Johnson, and M. Thursby. 1978. *The Economics of World Grain Trade*, Praeger Publishers, New York.

Gustafson, R. L. 1958. Carryover levels for grains, U.S. Department of Agriculture. *Tech. Bull. No. 1158.*

Harberger, A. C., 1974. *Taxation and Welfare*, Little, Brown and Co., Boston.

———. 1978. On the use of distributional weights in social cost-benefit analysis, *J. Pol. Econ.* **86**:s87–s121.

Hathaway, Dale E. 1964. *Problems of Progress in the Agricultural Economy*, Scott, Foresman and Company, Glenview, Illinois.

———. 1976. Grain Stocks and Economic Stability, in: *Analysis of Grain Reserves*, (S. Steele, ed.), U.S. Dept. of Agriculture, Econ. Res. Serv. Dept. No. 634, pp. 1–11.

Hause, J. C. 1975. The theory of welfare cost measurement, *J. Pol. Econ.* **83**:1145–1182.

Heady, E. O., and V. Y. Rao. 1967. Acreage response and production functions for soybeans. *Iowa Agric. Exp. Sta. Bu. 555.*

Helms, L. J. 1985. Errors in the numerical assessment of the benefits of price stabilization, *Am. J. Agric. Econ.* **67**:93–100.

Hicks, J. R. 1932. *The Theory of Wages*, MacMillan, London.

———. 1956. *A revision of Demand Theory*. Oxford University Press, London.

Hinich, M. 1984. *The Spatial Theory of Voting*. Cambridge University Press, Cambridge.

Holthausen, D. M. 1979. Hedging and the competitive firm under price uncertainty. *Am. Econ. Rev.* **69**:989–95.

Houthakker, H. S. 1967. *Economic policy for the farm sector*, American Enterprise Institute, Washington, D.C.

Huffman, W. 1974. Decision making: The role of education, *Am. J. Agric. Econ.* **56**:85–97.

Ippolito, R. A., and R. T. Masson. 1978. The social cost of government regulation of milk, *J. Law Econ.* **21**:33–65.

Johnson, D. G. 1973. *World Agriculture in Disarray.* Fontana/Collins, London.

————. 1975. World agriculture, commodity policy, and price variability, *Am. J. Agric. Econ.* **57**:823–828.

————, and D. Sumner. 1976. An optimization approach to grain reserves for developing countries. In: *Analyses of Grain Reserves,* U.S. Department of Agriculture, *ERS-634.*

Johnson, D. G., K. Hemmi, and P. Lardinois. 1985. *Agricultural Policy and Trade,* The Trilateral Commission, New York.

Johnson, G. L., and L. Quance. 1972. *The Overproduction Trap in U.S. Agriculture.* Resources for the Future, Washington, D.C.

Johnson, H. G. 1954. Optimum tariffs and retaliation. *Rev. Econ. Studs.* **21**:142–153.

————. 1966. Optimal trade intervention in the presence of domestic distortions, in: *Trade, Growth, and the Balance of Payments,* (R. Baldwin et al., eds.), Rand McNally, Chicago, pp. 3–34.

Johnson, R. N. 1985. Retail price controls in the dairy industry: A political coalition argument, *J. Law Econ.* **27**:55–76.

Johnson, S. R., A. W. Womack, W. H. Meyers, R. Young, and J. Brandt. 1985. Options for the 1985 Farm Bill, Food and Agricultural Policy Research Institute, *FAPRI #1–85.*

Jones, B. F., and R. L. Thompson. 1976. Interrelationships of domestic agricultural policies and trade policies, *Speaking of Trade,* pp. 27–58.

Josling, T. E. 1974. Agricultural policies in developed countries: A review, *J. Agric. Econ.* **25**:220–64.

Just, R. 1985. Automatic adjustment rules for agricultural policy controls, *American Enterprise Institute,* Washington, D.C., *Occasional Paper.*

————, and D. Hueth. 1979. Welfare measures in a multimarket framework, *Am. Econ. Rev.* **69**:947–954.

————, D. Hueth, and A. Schmitz. 1982. *Applied Welfare Economics,* Prentice-Hall Inc., Englewood Cliffs, N.J.

Karp, L., and A. McCalla. 1983. Dynamic games and international trade, *Am. J. Agric. Econ.* **65**:641–650.

Knutson, R. D., J. Richardson, and E. Smith. 1987. Policy alternatives for modifying the 1985 farm bill, Agricultural and Food Policy Center, Texas A&M University, College Station, Texas, *Pub. B-1561.*

Langley, S. 1984. U.S. rice model, presented at American Agricultural Economic Assoc. meetings, Ithaca, New York, August.

Layard, R. 1980, On the use of distributional weights in cost-benefit analysis, *J. Pol. Econ.* **88**:1041–47.

LeBlanc, M., and J. Hrubovcak. 1986. The effects of tax policy on aggregate agricultural investment, *Am. J. Agric. Econ.* **68**:767–777.

Lichtenberg, E. and D. Zilberman. 1986. The welfare economics of price supports in U.S. agriculture, *Am. Econ. Rev.* **76**:1135–1141.

Loury, G., and T. R. Lewis. 1986. On the profitability of interruptible supply, *Am. Econ. Rev.* **76**:827–832.

McCalla, A. F., and T. E. Josling. 1985. *Agricultural Policies and World Markets,* Macmillan, New York.

————, and H. O. Carter. 1976. Alternative agricultural and food policy directions for the U.S. with emphasis on a market-oriented approach, in: *Agricultural and Food Price and Income Policy*. (R. Spitze, ed.), Agric. Exp. Station, University of Illinois, *Special Pub. 43*, August.

McKenzie, G. 1985. A problem in measuring the cost of protection, *The Manchester School* (March): 45–54.

————, and I. F. Pearce, 1982. Welfare measurement: A synthesis, *Am. Econ. Rev.* **72**:669–682.

Monke, E. 1983. Tariffs, implementation costs, and optimal policy choices, *Weltwirtschaftliches Arch.* **119**:281–296.

Morey, E. R. 1984. Confuser surplus. *Am. Econ. Rev.* **74**:163–173.

Morgan, L. C., and B. L. Gardner. 1982. "Potential for a U.S. guest-worker program in agriculture: Lessons from the braceros," in: *The Gateway: U.S. Immigration Issues and Policies* (B. Chiswick, ed.), American Enterprise Institute, Washington, D.C., pp. 361–411.

Mueller, D. C. 1979. *Public Choice*, Cambridge University Press, Cambridge.

Muth, J. F. 1961. Rational expectations and the theory of price movements, *Econometrica* **29**:315–335.

Muth, R. F. 1965. The derived demand for a productive factor and the industry supply curve, *Oxford Econ. Papers* **16**:222–34.

Nath, S. K. 1969. *A Reappraisal of Welfare Economics*, Routledge and Kegan Paul, London.

Ng, Yew-Kwang. 1983. *Welfare Economics*, Macmillan, London.

Newbery, D. M. 1986. On the Desirability of Input Taxes, *Econ. Lett.* **20**:267–270.

————, and Stiglitz, J. E. 1981. *The Theory of Commodity Price Stabilization*, Oxford University Press, Oxford.

Oi, W. Y. 1961. The desirability of price instability under perfect competition, *Econometrica* **29**:58–65.

Olson, M. 1965. *The Logic of Collective Action*, Harvard University Press, Cambridge, Mass.

————. 1982. *The Rise and Decline of Nations*, Yale University Press, New Haven, Conn.

Ordeshook 1986. Game Theory and Political Theory, Cambridge University Press, Cambridge.

Paarlberg, P. L., and R. L. Thompson. 1980. Interrelated products and the impact of an import tariff, *Agric. Econ. Res.* **32**:21–32.

Parikh, K. S., G. Fischer, K. Froberg, and O. Gulbrandsen. 1985. Trade liberalization in agriculture, International Institute for Applied Systems Analysis, Laxenburg, Austria, mimeo, June.

Pashigian, P. 1986. Why have some farmers opposed future markets? Center for the Study of the Economy and State, University of Chicago, Chicago, Ill., *Working Paper No. 42*.

Pasinetti, L. 1980. Introductory note, in: *Essays in the Theory of Joint Production* (Pasinetti, ed.), Columbia University Press, New York.

Patinkin, D. 1963. Demand curves and consumer's surplus, in: *Measurement In Economics* (C. Christ, ed.), Stanford University Press, Stanford, Calif.

Peltzman, S. 1976. Toward a more general theory of regulation. *J. Law and Econ.* **18**:745–771.

Perrin, R. K. 1980. The impact of component pricing of soybeans and milk, *Am. J. Agric. Econ.* **62**:445–455.

Phipps, T. 1985. Farm Policies and the Rate of Return on Investment in Agriculture, American Enterprise Institute, Washington D.C. *AEI Occasional Paper*.

Pope, R., J. P. Chavas, and R. E. Just. 1983. Economic welfare evaluations for producers under uncertainty, *Am. J. Agric. Econ.* **65**:98–107.

Pope, R., and B. D. Gardner. 1978. The structure of agriculture and risk in: *Market Risks in Agriculture: Concepts, Methods, and Policy Issues* P. Barry, ed., *Texas Agr. Exp. Sta. DTR 78-1*.

———, and A. Hallam. 1986. A confusion of agricultural economists?, *Am. J. Agric. Econ.* **68**:572–593.

Randall, A. 1981. *Resource Economics*, Grid Publishing, Columbus.

Rapoport, A., M. J. Guyer, and D. G. Gordon. 1976. *The 2 × 2 Game*, University of Michigan Press, Ann Arbor.

Rausser, G. C. and J. W. Freebairn. 1974. Estimation of policy preference functions: An application to U.S. beef import quotas, *Rev. Econ. Statist.* **56**:437–449.

———, and E. Hochman. 1979. *Dynamic Agricultural Systems*, North Holland, New York.

——— and R. Just. 1981. Using models in policy formation, in: *Modeling Agriculture for Policy Analysis*, Federal Reserve Bank of Kansas City.

Roe, T., M. Shane, and D. H. Vo. 1986. Price responsiveness of world grain markets. *USDA—Econ. Res. Serv. Tech. Bull. No. 1720*, Washington, D.C.

Rosen, H. S. 1978. The measurement of excess burden with explicit utility functions, *J. Pol. Econ.* **86**:S121–S135.

Rosine, J., and P. Helmberger. 1974. A neoclassical analysis of the U.S. farm sector, 1948–1970. *Am. J. Agric. Econ.* **56**:717–729.

Rowley, C. K., and A. T. Peacock. 1975. *Welfare Economics: A Liberal Restatement*, Martin Robertson, London.

Russell, M. 1983. Energy politics in the years before the oil 'crisis', in: *Caught Unawares* (M. Greenberger, ed.), Ballinger, Cambridge, Mass.

Salathe, L. E., M. Price, and K. Gadsen. 1982. The food and agricultural policy simulator, *Agric. Econ. Res.* **34**:1–15.

Schmitz, A., C. Carter, A. McCalla, and D. Mitchell. 1981. *Grain Export Cartels*, Ballinger Publishing Co., Cambridge, Mass.

Schuh, G. E. 1981. U.S. agriculture in an interdependent world economy: Policy alternatives for the 1980's, in: *Food and Agricultural Policy for the 1980's*, American Enterprise Institute, Washington, D.C., pp. 157–182.

———. 1985. International agriculture and trade policies, in: *U.S. Agricultural Policy: The 1985 Legislation* (B. Gardner, ed.), American Enterprise Institute, Washington, D.C., pp. 56–78.

Schultz, T. W. 1945. *Agriculture in an Unstable Economy*, McGraw-Hill, New York.

———. 1975. The value of the ability to deal with disequilibria. *J. Econ. Lit.* **13**:827–846.

Stigler, G. J. 1975. *The Citizen and the State*, University of Chicago Press, Chicago.

Stuart, C. 1984. Welfare costs per dollar of additional revenue in the United States, *Am. Econ. Rev* 74 (June):352–62.

Sumner, D. A. 1985. The effects of commodity programs on farm size and structure, *AEI Occasional Paper*. American Enterprise Institute, Washington, D.C.

Sumner, D. A., and J. M. Alston. 1984. Effects of the tobacco program, *AEI Occasional Paper*. American Enterprise Institute, Washington, D.C.

Swanson, E. R., and C. R. Taylor. 1976. Potential impact of increased energy costs on the location of crop production in the corn belt, *J. Soil Water Conserv.* **31**:126–129.

Thraen, C., and J. W. Hammond. 1983. Price supports, risk aversion and U.S. dairy policy, Dept. of Agricultural and Applied Economics, University of Minnesota, Minneapolis, Minn., *Economic Report ER 83-9*, June.

Timmer, C. P. 1986. *Getting Prices Right*, Cornell University Press, Ithaca.

Tolley, G. S., V. Thomas, and C. M. Wong. 1982. *Agricultural Price Policies and the Developing Countries*, World Bank Publication, Washington, D.C.

Tullock, G. 1970. *Private Wants and Public Means*, Basic Books, New York.

Torok, S. J., and W. Huffman. 1986. Vegetable trade and illegal immigration, *Am. J. Agric. Econ.* **68**:246–260.

Turnovsky, S. J., 1974. Price expectations and the welfare gains from price stabilization, *Am. J. Agric. Econ.* **56**:706–716.

Tweeten, L. 1985. Diagnosing and treating farm problems, in: *U.S. Agricultural Policy: 1985 and Beyond* (J. Hillman, ed.), Department of Economics, University of Arizona, Tucson, Ariz., pp. 19–52.

———. 1971. *Foundations of Farm Policy*, University of Nebraska Press, Lincoln.

Tyers, R. 1984. Agricultural protection and market insulation, *Australia–Japan Research Centre, Pacific Economic Papers No. 111*, May.

———, and Anderson, K. 1986. *Distortions in World Food Markets: A Quantitative Assessment*, World Bank, Washington, D.C.

U.S. Department of Agriculture (USDA). 1986. Embargoes, surplus disposal, and U.S. agriculture, *Econ. Res. Serv., Staff Report No. AGES860910*, November.

———. 1984. Economic indicators of the farm sector: Costs of production, Econ. Res. Service, ECIFS 3-1.

———. 1987. Government intervention in agriculture: Measurement, evaluation, and implications for trade negotiations, *Econ. Res. Serv. Staff Report No. AGES861216*, January.

Varian, H. R. 1978. *Microeconomic Analysis*, W. W. Norton, New York.

Wallace, T. D. 1962. Measures of social costs of agricultural programs, *J. Farm Econ.* **44**:580–599.

Wallis, K. F. 1980. Econometric implications of the rational expectations hypothesis, *Econometrica* **48**:49–73.

Waugh, F. V. 1944. Does the consumer benefit from price instability?, *Quart. J. Econ.* **58**:602–614.

Welch, F. 1970a. Education in production, *J. Pol. Econ.* **78**:35–59.

———. 1970b. Returns to scale in U.S. agriculture, mimeo.

———. 1970c. Some aspects of structural change and the distributional effects of technical change and farm programs, in: *Benefits and Burdens of Rural Development*, Iowa State University Press, Ames. pp.161–182.

Whalley, John. 1985. *Trade Liberalization Among Major World Trading Areas*, MIT Press, Cambridge, Mass.

Wisecarver, D. 1974. The social costs of input-market distortions, *Am. Econ. Rev.* **64**:359–372.

World Bank. 1986. *World Development Report,* Oxford University Press for the World Bank, New York.

Wright, B. 1985. *An Assessment of the U.S. FOR and CCC Storage as Market Stabilization Policies,* American Enterprise Institute, Washington, D.C.

Wright, B., and J. Williams. 1984. The incidence of market stabilizing price support schemes, Yale University, Economic Growth Center, *Discussion Paper No. 466,* Dec.

Zusman, P., and A. Amiad. 1977. A quantitative investigation of political economy—The Israeli dairy program, *Am. J. Agric. Econ.* **59**:88–98.

Index